RAILS ACROSS THE ROCK

Kenneth G. Pieroway

A THEN & NOW CELEBRATION OF THE NEWFOUNDLAND RAILWAY

Canada Council for the Arts Conseil des Arts du Canada

Canada

Newfoundland Labrador

We gratefully acknowledge the financial support of the Canada Council for the Arts, the Government of Canada through the Canada Book Fund (CBF), and the Government of Newfoundland and Labrador through the Department of Tourism, Culture and Recreation for our publishing program.

Layout by Joanne Snook-Hann • Cover Design by Todd Manning
Printed on acid-free paper

Published by
CREATIVE PUBLISHERS
an imprint of CREATIVE BOOK PUBLISHING
a Transcontinental Inc. associated company
P.O. Box 8660, Stn. A
St. John's, Newfoundland and Labrador A1B 3T7

Printed in Canada

Library and Archives Canada Cataloguing in Publication

Pieroway, Ken, author, photographer
Rails across the rock : a now and then celebration of the Newfoundland Railway / Ken Pieroway.

Includes photos from some of the best railway photographers in Canada and the US.
Includes bibliographical references.
ISBN 978-1-77103-019-9 (bound)

1. Newfoundland Railway Company--History--Pictorial works.
2. Railroads--Newfoundland and Labrador--History--Pictorial works.
I. Title.

HE2809.N4P54 2013 385.06'5718 C2013-905074-4

MIX
Paper from responsible sources
FSC® C011825

RAILS ACROSS THE ROCK

Kenneth G. Pieroway

A THEN & NOW CELEBRATION OF THE NEWFOUNDLAND RAILWAY

CREATIVE PUBLISHERS

St. John's, Newfoundland and Labrador

2013

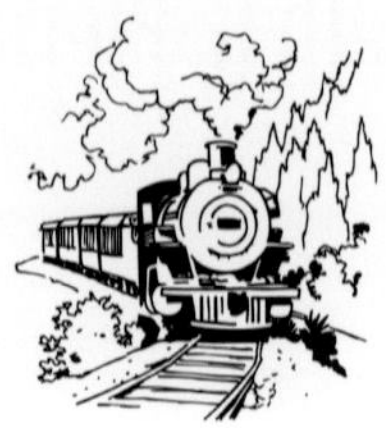

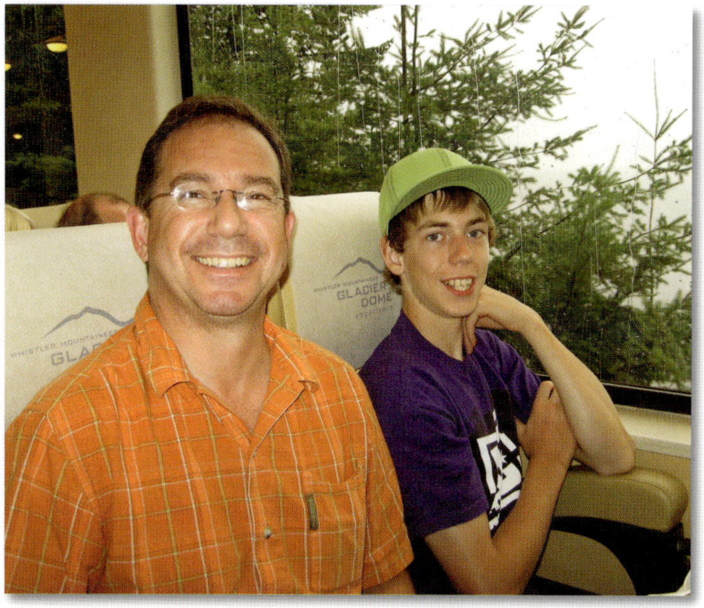

Dedicated to the memory of our eldest son William (1993-2010), who rode his first of many trains at the age of 9 months in Aviemore, Scotland and his last at age 15 in Whistler, British Columbia. Like the lights of the locomotive that reflect along the track, you will shine on in our hearts forever.

Love, Dad

TABLE OF CONTENTS

FOREWORD

The trains run no more, the roadbed stands denuded of all traces of the Newfoundland Railway. Each passing year brings more spruce, pine, and alders, which threaten the eroding roadbed. Those wonderful trains that once connected the interior of this bountiful province with St. John's and the sea now run only in our memory. Four-wheelers and snow machines have replaced the narrow gauge trains forever. Twenty-five years after the abandonment of the railway many of us still grieve.

Newfoundland lost the railway to politics and apathy in 1988 after a long and bitter struggle. People's lives were changing. They no longer had time to spend a full day on the train and the Trans-Canada Highway made it easy for Newfoundlanders to cross the Island in twelve hours. This change in lifestyle and infrastructure doomed the *Caribou* to its last run in 1969. All the tradition, pride, and accomplishment of running passenger trains through the wilderness faded away.

After the passenger train was discontinued, four mixed trains remained to serve areas isolated from conventional highway travel. Mixed trains 203 and 204 served communities from Bishop's Falls to Corner Brook. It was in 1986 that I made my first trip on these storied trains, and it was then that I fell in love with Newfoundland and the railway. This experience resulted in over fifty visits to the Island, and an everlasting fascination with the province.

Coincidently, Ken Pieroway was also riding mixed trains 203 and 204, discovering the railway, the railroaders, and the history of this unique and enduring mode of transportation. In July 1987, I took his picture as he enjoyed the view from "the break" (vestibule) of the coach at the tail-end of westbound mixed train 203 in Steady Brook, NL. An outstretched hand and beaming smile was forever burned in the Plus X black and white film loaded in my Canon F1. Twenty-four years later, I gave this picture to Ken as a reminder that things happen for a reason. Our meeting those years ago was a harbinger of things to come.

Rails Across the Rock celebrates the life of the Newfoundland Railway with dozens of previously unpublished photographs, detailing railway operations spanning the entire main line. Ken has worked tirelessly to compile the very best quality colour photos possible. He has researched the exact locations of the historic photographs, so a contemporary view of the scene could be cast in an image that contrasts the original, making this a guide for Newfoundlanders to once again connect with the railway.

The Newfoundland Railway has a worldwide fan club comprised of railway buffs devoted to preserving the history of this unique railway. The photographic journey in *Rails Across the Rock* provides another connection to the railway, images motivating a new generation to walk the track, study the photographs, and instill the memory of the railway in their hearts and minds. This new group will insure history will be remembered, cherished, and honored. The men and women who worked under the most challenging of conditions will be remembered as heroes, as people willing to serve fellow Newfoundlanders, and survive and prosper in a wild new land.

Rails Across the Rock reminds all of the sacrifice, dedication, and hard work that enabled this narrow gauge railway to serve this province for over a century. It is my sincere hope that this book will encourage more individuals to discover the Newfoundland Railway.

As we mark the 25th anniversary of the closing of the Newfoundland Railway, Ken's photographic celebration of this era reminds us all of what we lost when the rails came up in 1988. *Rails Across the Rock* offers young and old alike another chance to virtually ride the railway and to honour the men and women who kept the steam locomotives hot, and those wheels shiny. Thanks to historians like Ken Pieroway we can continue to discover new and interesting visual reminders of a railway that continues to live in the hearts and minds of thousands. Memories that will, hopefully, fan the flames of interest of a younger generation who were not yet born when the first rail was lifted at Mile 340, Bishop's Fall Subdivision on October, 12, 1988.

Mike Shufelt
May 5, 2013
Monroe, Michigan, USA

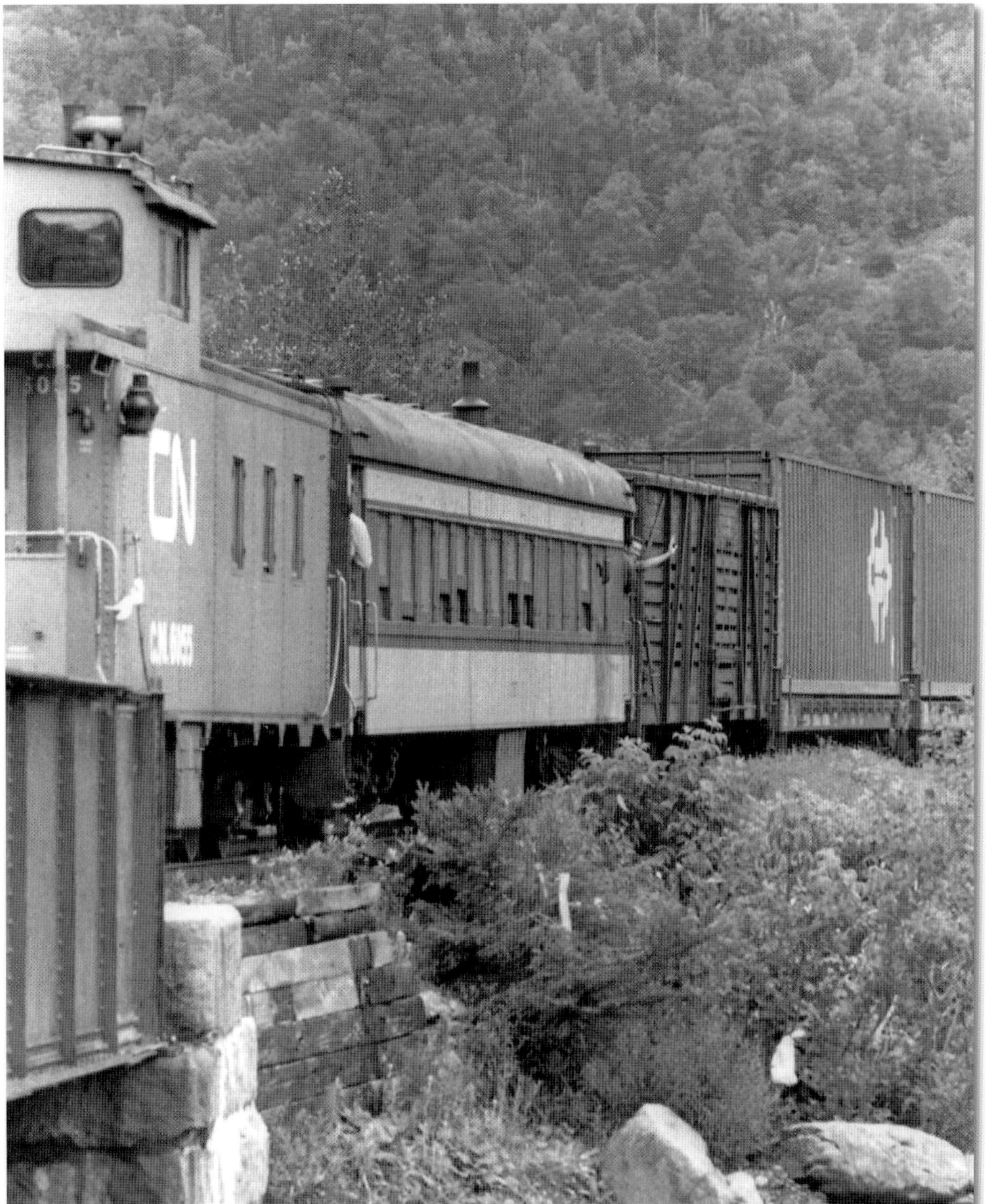
CN
CN 6065

PREFACE

Have you ever wondered what it would be like to travel by train across Newfoundland? Are you one of those who remember the mighty steam locomotives that hauled the Newfoundland Express? Have you ever felt the earth shake under your feet as a powerful trio of diesels rumbled by your backyard with dozens of loaded boxcars? If so, it's time to learn about the past and rekindle those pleasant memories when the railway was king. Sit back and take an all colour photographic journey by train across Newfoundland.

The unique narrow gauge Newfoundland Railway served the Island for over 107 years, from 1881 to 1988. Now on the 25th anniversary of the closure, it is amazing to look back at our trains in action and see how much has changed due to both economic development and nature reclaiming what was once rightfully hers.

With colour photographs from the 1950s to the 1980s by some of North America's top railroad photographers, travel along the entire 547 mile mainline from Port aux Basques to St. John's and virtually all stops in between. Then compare those to the same scene as photographed today and you will be surprised to see how much has changed. The rugged beauty of Newfoundland serves as a beautiful backdrop to some of the most colourful trains to ever grace this continent. Passing through the communities you will find 2-8-2-Mikado steam engines on the head end of the *Caribou* in the 1950s and with 1200 HP NF210 Diesels during the 1960s. The 1970s had lots of powerful freights and many mixed trains with G8's rumbling alongside the ocean. The 1980s, the final decade of operations, are filled with long container and mixed mainline trains.

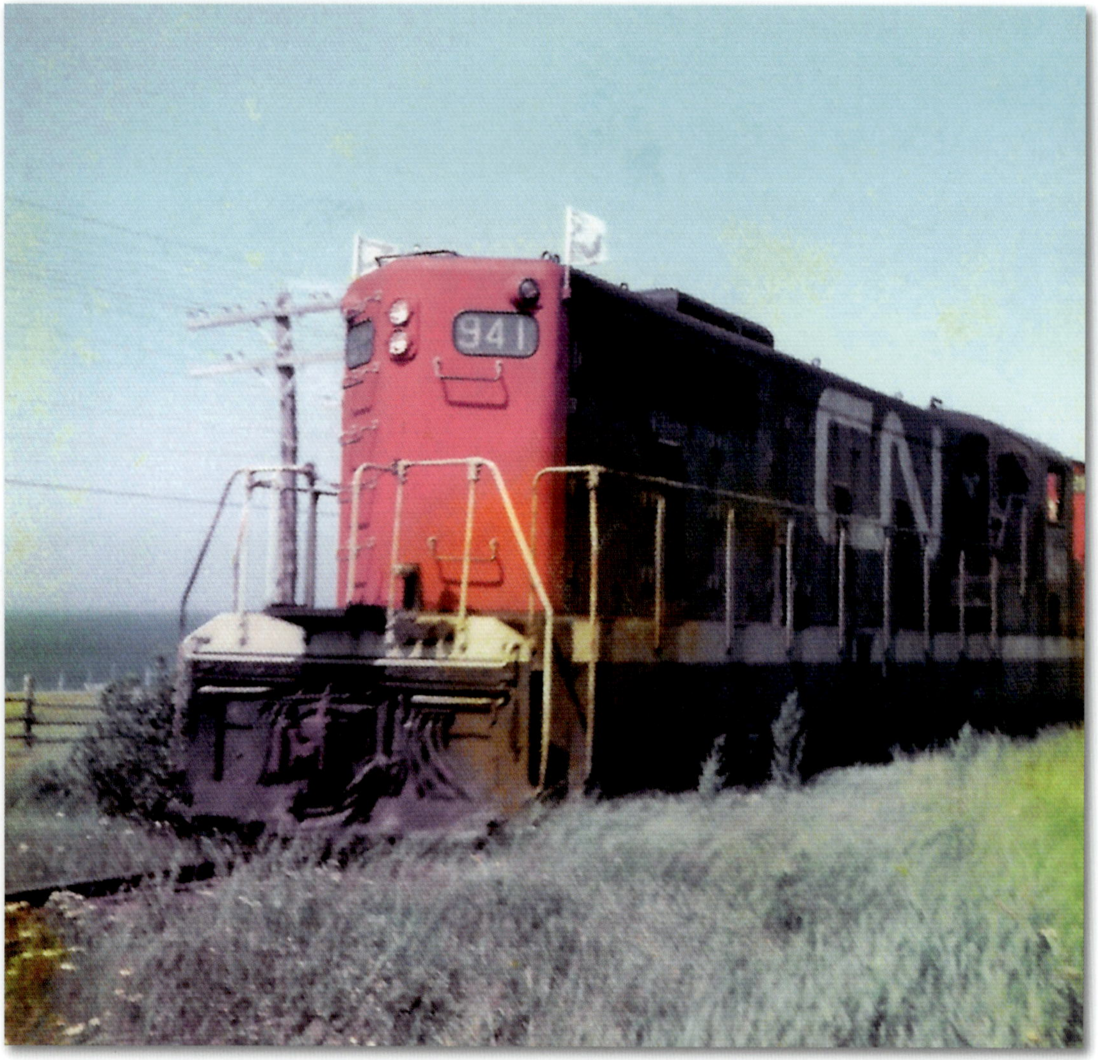

Your journey begins in the gateway town of Port aux Basques and you will travel eastward, as would a passenger after arriving from the gulf ferry heading to the capital city of St. John's. Eastward is also the superior direction for determining a train's right of way. On this journey you will see spectacular and amazingly detailed photos of our trains in action in geographical order based on the railway timetable from west to east.

My passion for the Newfoundland Railway and all things train-related goes way back to my early childhood in the 1960s. It was then that my late father would take me down to the station in Corner Brook to watch the arrival and departure of the *Caribou*, our trans-Island passenger train, adorned in the beautiful CNR green and gold colour scheme. Dad knew many of the engineers and often times he would hoist me aboard the cab of one the NF110 or 210 diesels, even allowing me to blow the whistle on occasion!

That early exposure was further augmented by annual vacations to my grandparents in St. George's, where the tracks ran just behind their backyard. Watching multiple diesel units pull the daily freights with loads of pulpwood, lumber, automobiles and countless boxcars; feeling the ground move and the window panes rattle as they rumbled by was always one of the highlights of those hot August days in the 1970s. It was also at St. George's that I took my first ever train photograph of Extra 941 West with Mom's old Brownie 127 camera in 1975 at the age of 12.

After moving to St. John's to attend Memorial University, watching and photographing the trains became a favourite pastime. Countless hours were spent at the pedestrian bridge in Bowring Park, waiting to watch 203 and 204 rumbling beneath and feeling the bridge shake under my feet. It was then I learned of the daily mixed freight running between Bishop's Falls and Corner Brook and took advantage of riding across the Gaff Topsails — five times before the closure in 1988. One can only imagine the joy of discovering that a passenger train service still existed long after the *Caribou* was discontinued in 1969.

It was also at Memorial that I happened upon a copy of Omer Lavallee's *Narrow Gauge Railways of Canada* at the Centre of Newfoundland Studies and discovered the works of James A. Brown and Robert J. Sandusky. These men travelled here in the 1950s and 1960s just to photograph and record our trains for posterity and their iconic images were nothing short of spectacular. In later years, this very book and its updated edition would become the basis for my work and I would make contact with the very same photographers. These men and many others shared my passion for the Newfoundland Railway and their kind and generous contributions can be found throughout the following pages. Some have even become close personal friends whom I have both visited and welcomed into my home.

I always wanted to celebrate what the railway was to Newfoundland and with the 25th anniversary of the last official train running fast approaching in September 2013 I was inspired to write this book. After years of collecting the images, I set out on the 547 mile road bed to search for and stand at the same location to recreate scenes that in some cases were over sixty years old. This book is the culmination of that three-year journey of discovery.

A BRIEF HISTORY OF THE NEWFOUNDLAND RAILWAY

CONSTRUCTION

In the late 1800s railway fever was gripping North America and the Island Colony of Newfoundland was no exception. The first proposal was by Canadian engineer Sir Sanford Fleming and in 1868 he sponsored a preliminary survey across the southern interior of the Island. Later, in 1875, the Newfoundland government commissioned a survey for a route that encompassed a more central route. In 1878, Sir William Whiteway was elected Prime Minister on a promise to build a railway and by 1880 the Newfoundland Legislature approved a narrow gauge line of 3 feet, 6 inches wide from St. John's to Halls Bay, a total of 340 miles.

Construction commenced on August 16, 1881 near what is the site of the present day Sheraton hotel in St. John's and worked progressively towards the waters of Conception Bay. By June of the following year, a passenger service was established between St. John's and Topsail and before summer's end, a daily except Sunday service was operating as far as Holyrood. Built by investor A.L. Blackman, the line reached as far as Whitbourne before the company went into receivership. Construction continued until the line reached Harbour Grace in October 1884. The Whiteway government then built a second branch southward to Placentia, completing it by 1888.

After winning a contract to complete the remainder to Halls Bay, the Scottish-Canadian Robert G. Reid commenced construction for $15,600 per mile, reaching the Exploits River by 1893. It was then decided to proceed westward towards Port aux Basques rather than end at Halls Bay and Reid was granted a ten year extension to complete the line. Work progressed steadily with the last rails being laid at Port aux Basques in June of 1898. The 547 mainline from St. John's to Port aux Basques was now complete and Newfoundland had caught up with the rest of North America. The first train arrived to meet the new Gulf steamship the *SS Bruce* after a 27-hour trip from St. John's on June 30, 1898.

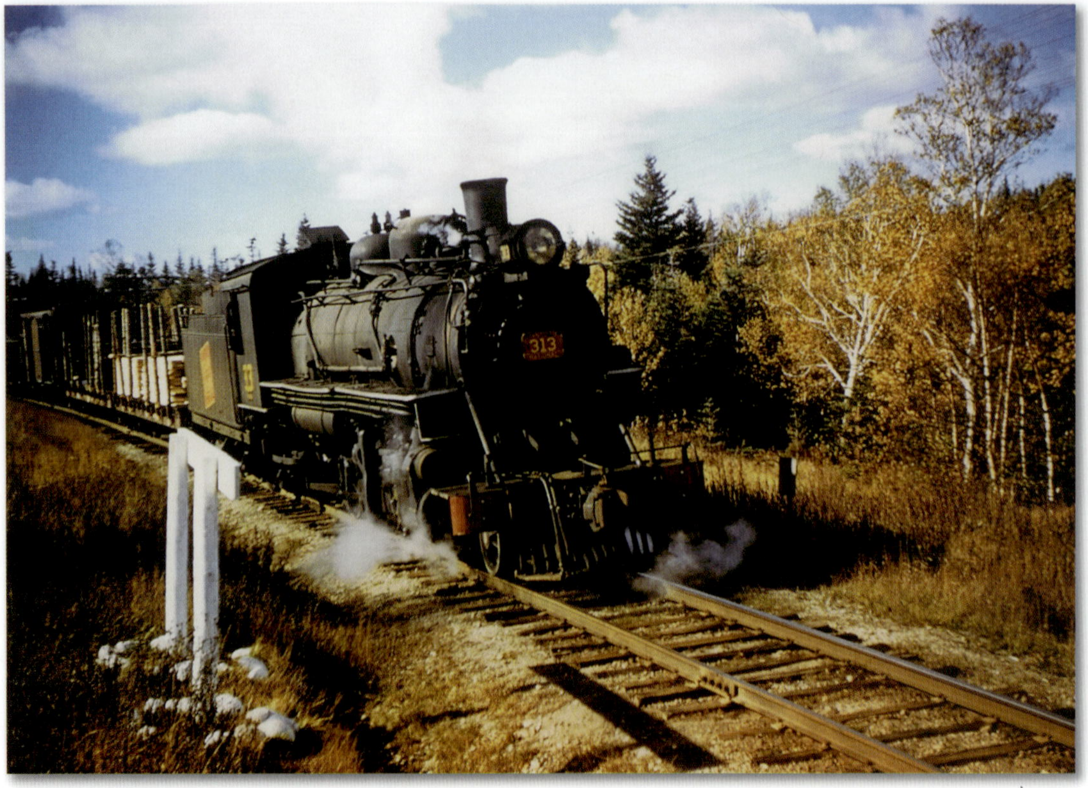

W. Robertson, Clayton D. Cook Collection

THE BRANCH LINES

The railway continued to operate under the Reid family and after the death of Robert G. Reid, it was carried on by his sons, William, Harry and Robert Jr. They had also assumed responsibility and operation of the dry dock, the telegraph system, and the coastal steamship system. In 1909, newly elected Prime Minister Edward P. Morris was swept to power on a commitment to build a series of branch lines. The Branch Line Contract, at $15,000 and 4000 acres of land per mile, was awarded to the Reids without tender in reward for their political support. It resulted in an additional 375 miles of track throughout the colony and created many employment opportunities.

The Trepassey Branch would run from The Waterford Valley in St. John's to Trepassey on the Southern Shore for a distance of 104 miles and was opened in January of 1914. The Bay de Verde Branch would run 48 miles from Carbonear to Bay de Verde and Grates Cove with service starting respectively in July and October 1915. The Heart's Content Branch would extend 42 miles north from Whitbourne and opened in July of that same year, while the Fortune Bay Branch would run 102 miles south from Goobies to Fortune on the Burin Peninsula. This line was also commenced in 1915 but the rails were only laid 42 miles to Terrenceville and never operated. The Bonavista Branch headed north from Shoal Harbour, near Clarenville, to Bonavista, a distance of 88 miles, and it commenced operation in November 1911. It even had its own 2 mile Branch from Port Union Junction to Port Union. Finally, the Bonne Bay Branch would run 35 miles north from Deer Lake to Bonne Bay on the Great Northern Peninsula but was only partially graded and no rails were laid.

These lines were very popular politically but never paid a profit for the Reids due to the light traffic they generated. That, coupled with the devastating effects of World War I and the Great Depression, would see many of these closed down with Trepassey, Bay de Verde and Grates Cove abandoned in 1934. By 1939, Heart's Content would also be abandoned and the unused Fortune Branch to Terrenceville dismantled.

WORLD WAR II

It's been said that during World War II the Newfoundland Railway saw its finest hour. With both Canada and Newfoundland declaring war on Germany in September 1939, the railway became a vital strategic asset. Prior to the declaration, in 1936, Canada, the U.S., Britain, Ireland and Newfoundland were setting up facilities to support trans-Atlantic aviation. With Newfoundland being the closest part of North America to Europe, construction commenced on the Newfoundland Airport at milepost 213 in what is present day Gander. All construction materials, heavy equipment, workers and supplies had to be brought in by rail as there were no roads leading into the area.

With the outbreak of the war, large military bases were being constructed throughout the Island as a result of the Lend Lease agreement with Britain exchanging colony land for warships.The USAF base at Stephenville, the RCAF bases at Gander and Botwood, and the US Naval Base at Argentia were among those constructed with the railway as a supply line. Traffic more than doubled both on a freight and passenger standpoint as thousands of troops and military equipment moved throughout the Island. Despite the heavy demands placed upon it, the Newfoundland Railway and its outstanding employees managed to keep up with it and actually turned a profit during those years.

Furthermore, the Lend Lease agreement brought with it a major upgrade in equipment as a result of $2.1 million from the War Department of the U.S. Government. A total of 13 Mikado 2-8-2 steam locomotives were delivered from 1941-44 by Montreal Locomotive Works, North British and ALCO. The railway also received 25 new steel passenger cars including coaches, diners, sleepers and observation cars from Canadian Car and Foundry in 1943, making it the newest on the continent.

CONFEDERATION AND CANADIAN NATIONAL RAILWAYS

On March 31, 1949, Newfoundland became Canada's tenth province and under terms 31-33 of the Terms of Union, the now 700 mile narrow gauge railway became part of the Canadian National Railway. This also included all connecting ferries and coastal boat services as well as communications. The rail system was badly run down following the war and the CNR set about with major capital investments in its newest acquisition for the next ten years.

One of the first major projects was the raising of the track bed in the Gaff Topsails by an additional 4-6 feet in order to deal with the massive snowfalls and clearing operations, a problem that plagued the railway ever since that route was chosen. The ties over the entire system were replaced with new creosote ones and the tracks re-railed and upgraded from 50 to 85 lbs.

Docking facilities in Port aux Basques were upgraded and expanded to handle the post-Confederation increase in traffic and a brand new gulf ferry was ordered. Arriving in 1955, this new vessel, the *MV William Carson*, an icebreaker with a roll on and roll off capacity, was the first of Canada's superferries. New passenger cars were ordered and before long shiny new steel coaches, diners and sleepers in olive green began entering service on the newly renamed *Caribou*, once the former Newfoundland Railway *Overland Limited.*

But perhaps the biggest initiative was the program of full dieselization and the elimination of steam locomotives which occurred from 1953-1957. In January of 1953, the first of a total of 47 1200 horsepower diesel electric locomotives, designated NF110s and 210s, arrived from General Motors Diesel of London, ON and the banishment of steam had begun. By 1956, the last 2-8-2 Mikados and 4-6-2 Pacifics operated on the mainline passenger trains and were later cut up for scrap, except for Pacific 593. Six new smaller and lighter 875 HP G-8s also arrived that year to service the branch lines. By 1960, the last remaining NF210's arrived at the St. John's dock.

END OF THE PASSENGER SERVICE

In 1965, the Trans Canada Highway was finally completed and Newfoundlanders took to the roads in droves, sounding a death knell for the *Caribou.* CN applied to the Canadian Transport Service in 1967 to eliminate the passenger train and substitute a trans-Island bus service, the Roadcruiser, in its place. The bus would take 14 hours versus the 22 hours by train to make the journey. Despite a huge public and political outcry, passengers chose the bus by a ratio of 5 to 1 when both services were offered and eventually permission was granted to abandon the train altogether. On the morning of July 2nd 1969, the very last *Caribou* with 3 diesels and 16 pieces of passenger equipment departed Port aux Basques at 10:00 a.m. and pulled into the St. John's station the next morning at 8:00 a.m., carrying a total of 350 passengers at various routes along the way.

THE SULLIVAN COMMISSION AND TERRA TRANSPORT

Throughout the 1970s the railway's share of freight traffic had dropped considerably. This was despite the use of dedicated railcar ferries such as *The Frederick Carter* and *Patrick Morris* and the transferring of standard gauge trucks to narrow gauge ones on boxcars arriving from the mainland at Port aux Basques, a practice that took only 15 minutes per car. Passenger service, except for the mixed trains on the Argentia, Carbonear and Bonavista branches which ran only a few times a week, was practically nonexistent.

With the situation somewhat dire and financial losses mounting, both the Federal and Provincial Governments set up a Commission of Inquiry into Newfoundland Transportation in 1977. Chaired by Arthur M. Sullivan, it recommended in 1978 that the railway be phased out over a ten year period, to be replaced by air, road and sea transportation. Again, the public and political outcry was unanimous that the railway not be abandoned and plans were made to reorganize and remarket the railway for a further 5 year period before revaluation.

As a result, CN in 1979 announced the formation of a Newfoundland Transportation Division to be known as Terra Transport whose purpose was to reduce the deficit to zero. With its own President, Ron Messenger, Terra Transport began to convert all rail shipments to containers from boxcars, thus eliminating the cumbersome truck to truck transfer in Port aux Basques and using trucks to deliver door to door to customers from divisional points in Corner Brook, Grand Falls and St. John's. By the mid- 1980s, Terra Transport had increased its market share from a low of 25% to 39% with this process. In order to reduce the deficit even further, nearly all stations along the main line were closed by 1984 and the branch lines closed. The Bonavista Branch mixed train would run for the last time on November 23, 1983 and Argentia and Carbonear would see the last mixed trains on September 19th and 20th of 1984 respectively.

THE END OF THE LINE AND RAIL REMOVAL PROGRAM

Due to rate increases by the CTC, Terra Transport continued to lose customers and money and CN wanted to rid itself of the entire operation once and for all. Newfoundland and Ottawa met secretly in December 1987 to close the railway in exchange for $800 million to be spent on improvements to the TCH. Rumours circulated for the next several months and the official announcement was made on June 20, 1988 at the Radisson Hotel in St. John's by Minister of Transport John Crosbie, Premier Brian Peckford and CN President Ron Lawless. The Newfoundland Transportation Initiative or Rails for Roads Deal would see all rail traffic cease by September 1988.

The very last scheduled train, Mixed Extra 917 West, departed Bishop's Falls for Corner Brook at 11:00 a.m. on September 30, 1988 with five diesels, two coaches, a baggage car and two cabooses and rolled into history. After 107 years of operation, the Newfoundland Railway was no more.

In less than two weeks, on Oct 12th, the Rail Removal Program began at Mileage 340 when the first piece of track was lifted from the ties, the quickest dismantling of any railway in North America and perhaps the world for that matter. For the next two years, railway employees would work tirelessly, removing the rails, ties and all traces of the operation until November 16, 1990.

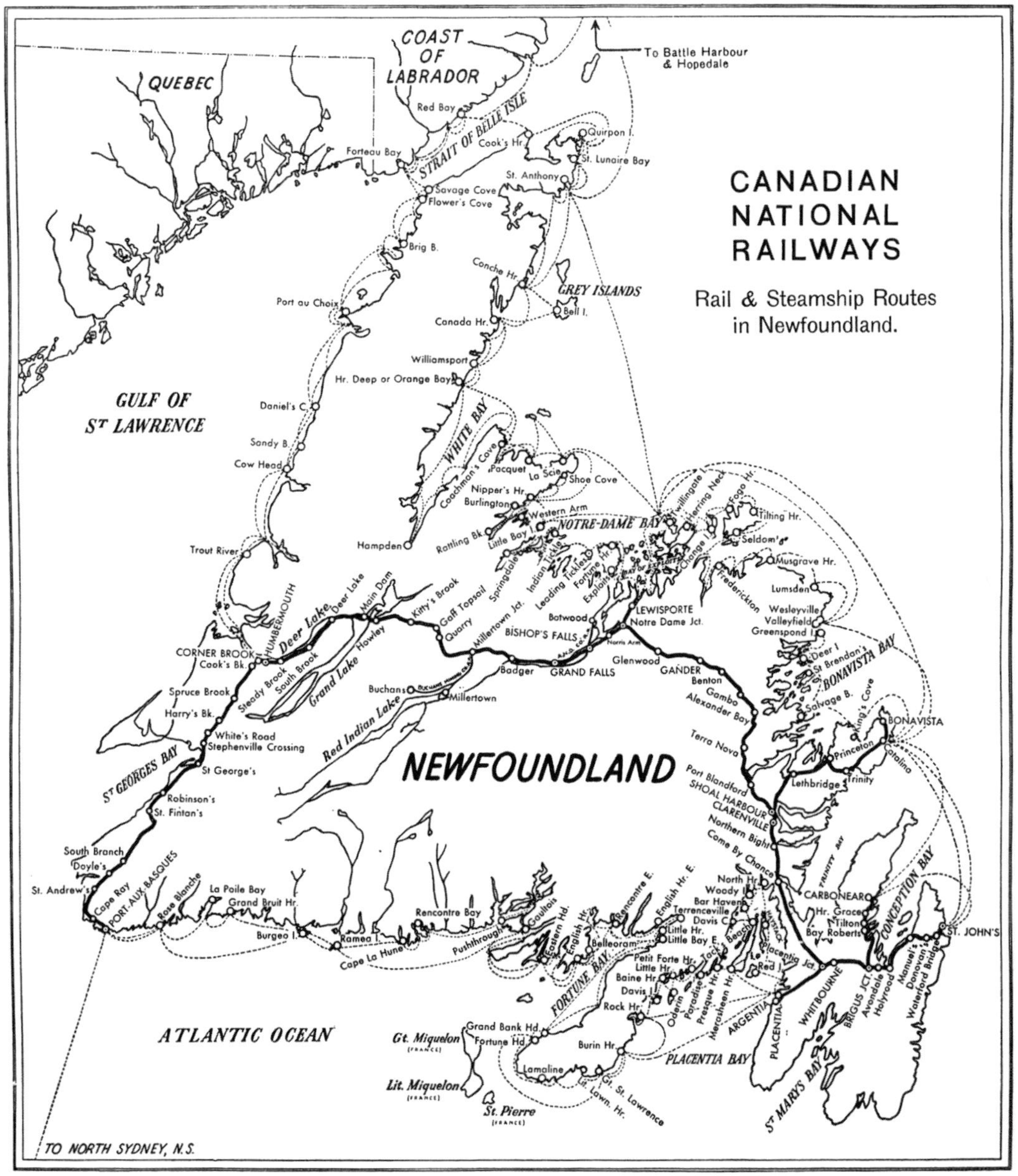

Library and Archives Canada, Copy Number E010788151

NEWFOUNDLAND

ST. JOHN'S — PORT AUX BASQUES — NORTH SYDNEY

Caribou ⊖101 Daily Quot.	M203 Sat. Sam.	Caribou ⊖101 Mon. Wed. Fri. Lun. Mer. Ven.	Miles Milles	7 Newfoundland DAYLIGHT Time Heure AVANCÉE de Terre-Neuve	Caribou ⊖102 Daily Quot.	Caribou ⊖102 Wed. Fri. Sun. Mer. Ven. Dim.	M204 Mon. Lun.
				(Hôtel Newfoundland Hotel)			
2330	1845	1201	0.0	Dp **St. John's, Nfld.** (9) Ar	0800	0930	2340
f0014	f1935	f1244	14.1	Kelligrews	f0706	f0840	f2225
f0040	f2004	f1310	30.1	Holyrood	f0639	f0814	f2158
f0055	f2024	f1325	36.2	Avondale	f0622	f0758	f2140
f0108	f2045	f1338	41.6	Brigus Jct. (8, 9)	f0611	f0746	f2125
0140	2130	1413	54.5	**Whitbourne**	0543	0718	2050
0153	f2148	1428	61.6	Placentia Jct. (9)	f0523	f0700	f1957
0208	f	f	65.9	Long Harbour	0510	f	f
f0230	f2230	f1505	80.0	Tickle Harbour	0441		f1917
0245	f	f	87.5	Rantem	0426	f	f
f0303	f2310	f1545	98.4	Arnold's Cove	f0358	f0537	f1832
0316	f	f	103.1	Come-By-Chance	0345	f	f
0335	2355	1614	110.2	Goobie's	0335	0510	1808
0420	0050	1700	131.1	Ar **Clarenville** (10) Dp	0250	0415	1705
0430	0140	1715		Dp Ar	0235	0400	1540
0513	0230	1758	150.9	Port Blandford	0140	0314	1444
f0542	0319	f1827	164.6	Terra Nova	f0110	f0246	1409
0615	0414	1900	181.1	Alexander Bay	0032	0208	1329
0633	0450	1923	190.1	**Gambo**	0012	0149	1250
f0701	f0520	f1951	204.2	Benton	f2340	f0117	f1205
0725	0620	2017	212.9	**Gander**	2325	0102	1148
f0759	0705	f2051	230.3	Glenwood	2240	f0020	1025
0832	0755	2126	244.5	Notre Dame Jct.	2213	f2353	0955
f0850	f0815	f2146	253.8	Norris Arm	f2148	f2328	f0910
0915	0845	2215	267.3	Ar **Bishop's Falls** Dp	2125	2305	0850
0935	1000	2240		Dp Ar	2100	2240	0720
1002	1050	2310	276.2	**Grand Falls**	2040	2219	0650
1038	1135	2346	294.2	Badger	1958	2139	0535
1110	1215	0021	310.0	**Millertown Jct.**	1926	2107	0450
	f		320.9	West Brook			f
f1159	f1325	f0104	332.9	Gaff Topsail	f1840	f2021	f0355
f1225	f1355	f0131	345.8	Kitty's Brook	f1810	f1951	f0310
1247	1425	0156	356.8	**Howley**	1750	1931	0245
1325	1515	0240	373.5	Deer Lake	1712	1855	0200
1348	f	f	387.2	Pasadena	1635	f	f
	f1545		395.3	South Brook			f0103
	f		398.7	Steady Brook			f
1435	1640	0350	405.3	Ar **Corner Brook** Dp	1550	1735	0025
1450	1820	0405		Dp Ar	1535	1720	2310
f1457	1835	f0414	408.0	Curling	f1527	f1710	f2253
	f		420.6	Tower Line			f
f1546	1925	f0501	429.9	Spruce Brook	f1434	f1624	2202
1550	f	f	434.9	Gallant's	1422	f	f
	f1952		438.2	Harry's Brook			f2137
	f2017		446.4	Black Duck			
1640	2055	0554	452.5	**Stephenville Crossing**	1348	1540	2055
	f		455.8	Western			f
f1700	2115	f0612	459.7	St. George's	1323	f1520	2027
1710	f	f	465.3	Flat Bay	1313	f	f
1720	f	f	469.0	St. Teresa	1256	f	f
f1727		f0639	473.1	Fischell	f1251	f1451	f1947
1740	f	f	477.2	Heatherton	1235	f	f
f1744	2208	f0656	480.3	Robinson's	f1230	f1430	1927
f1749	f2216	f0701	482.2	Cartyville	f1224	f1424	1917
1800	f	f	484.5	Jeffreys	1216	f	f
f1809	2240	f0716	487.8	St. Fintan's	f1208	f1408	1902
	f2310		498.5	Codroy Pond			f1832
f1907	f2350	f0810	512.9	**South Branch**	f1114	f1314	f1753
f1930	0016	f0832	522.7	Doyle's	f1054	f1254	1730
	f		525.5	Tompkins			f
f1941	0027	f0845	528.2	St. Andrew's	f1040	f1241	1710
1955	f	f	536.5	Red Rocks	1025	f	f
	f0050		539.0	Cape Ray			f1640
2030	0120	0930	547.8	Ar **Port aux Basques** ⊙ Dp	1000	1201	1620
	Mon. Lun.	Tue Thu. Sat. Mar. Jeu. Sam.				Tue. Thu. Sat. Mar. Jeu. Sam.	Sun. Dim.
Daily Quot.	Daily Quot.	Daily Quot.		**FERRY** (Daily Service) **TRAVERSIER** (serv. quot.)	Daily Quot.	Daily Quot.	Daily Quot.
A 2330	B 1100	C 1155		Dp **Pt. aux Basques, Nfld. NDT** Ar	0655	0655	1930
0630	1755	1755		Ar **North Sydney, N.S. ADT.** Dp (16)	A 2245	C 2355	A 1155

Caribou ⊖101 (Daily): Operates Mon. Wed. Fri., May 31-June 16, also Sept. 11-30 incl. / Circulera les lun. mer. et ven. du 31 mai au 16 juin, et du 11 sept. au 30 sept. incl.

M203: Until May 29 and after Sept. 30. / Jusqu'au 29 mai et après le 30 septembre.

Caribou ⊖101 (Mon. Wed. Fri.): Until May 29 and after Sept. 30. / Jusqu'au 29 mai et après le 30 septembre.

Caribou ⊖102 (Daily): Operates Sun. Wed. Fri., June 2-18, also Sept. 13-30 incl. / Circulera les dim. mer. et ven. du 2 juin au 18 juin, et du 13 au 30 sept. incl.

Caribou ⊖102 (Wed. Fri. Sun.): Until May 30 and after Sept. 30. / Jusqu'au 30 mai et après le 30 septembre.

M204: Until May 30 and after Sept. 30. / Jusqu'au 30 mai et après le 30 septembre.

Passengers may embark two hours prior to sailing time. Advance reservations required. Application for reservations between North Sydney and Port aux Basques may be secured through any Ticket Agent.

Les passagers peuvent s'embarquer deux heures avant le départ. Pour la traversée du détroit, la réservation est obligatoire et peut se faire par l'entremise de tout bureau de billets.

Library and Archives Canada, Copy Number E010788150

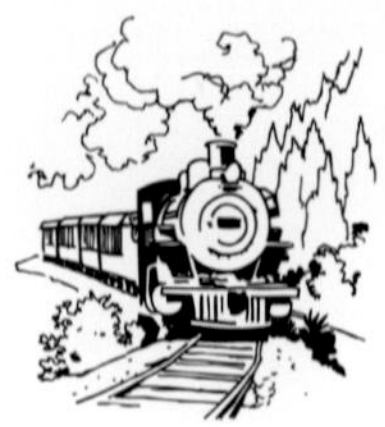

The railroading life was a wonderful life — a real treasure —
the best anyone could ask for.

Brendan D. Dicks, Engineer
34.5 years of service

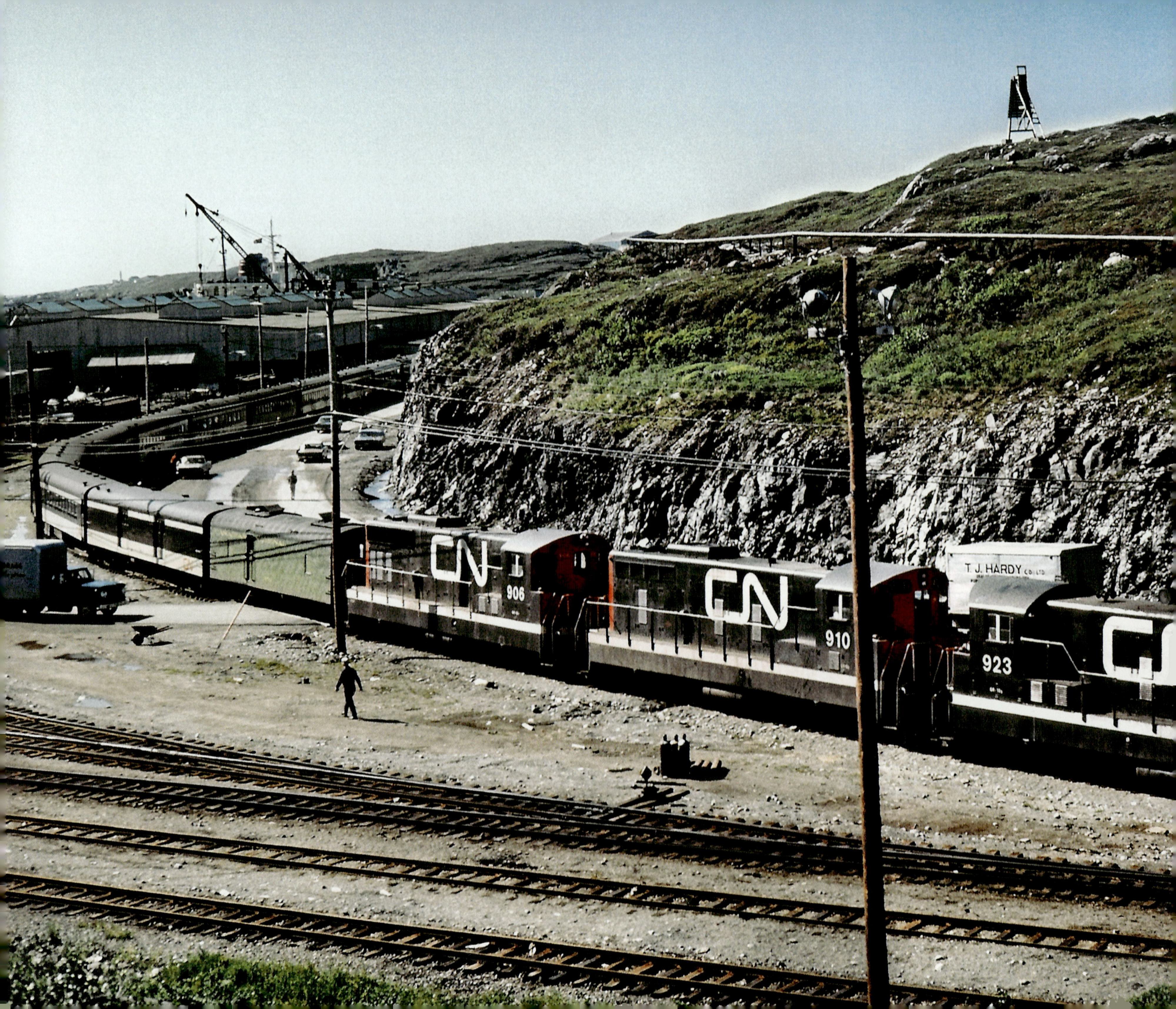
CN
906
CN
910
T. J. HARDY
923

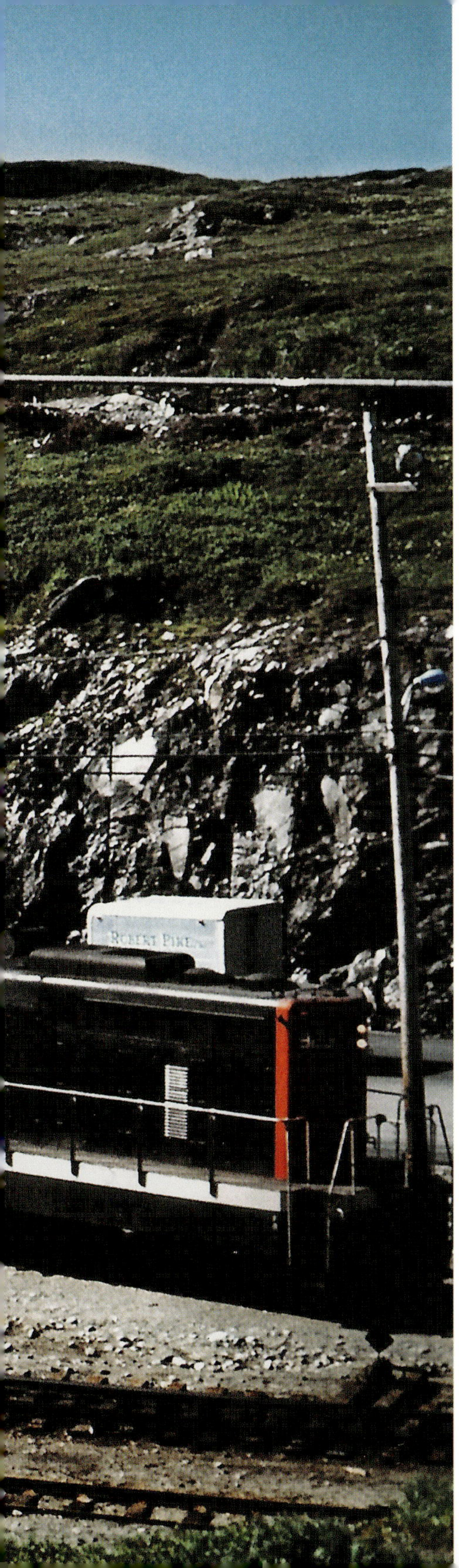

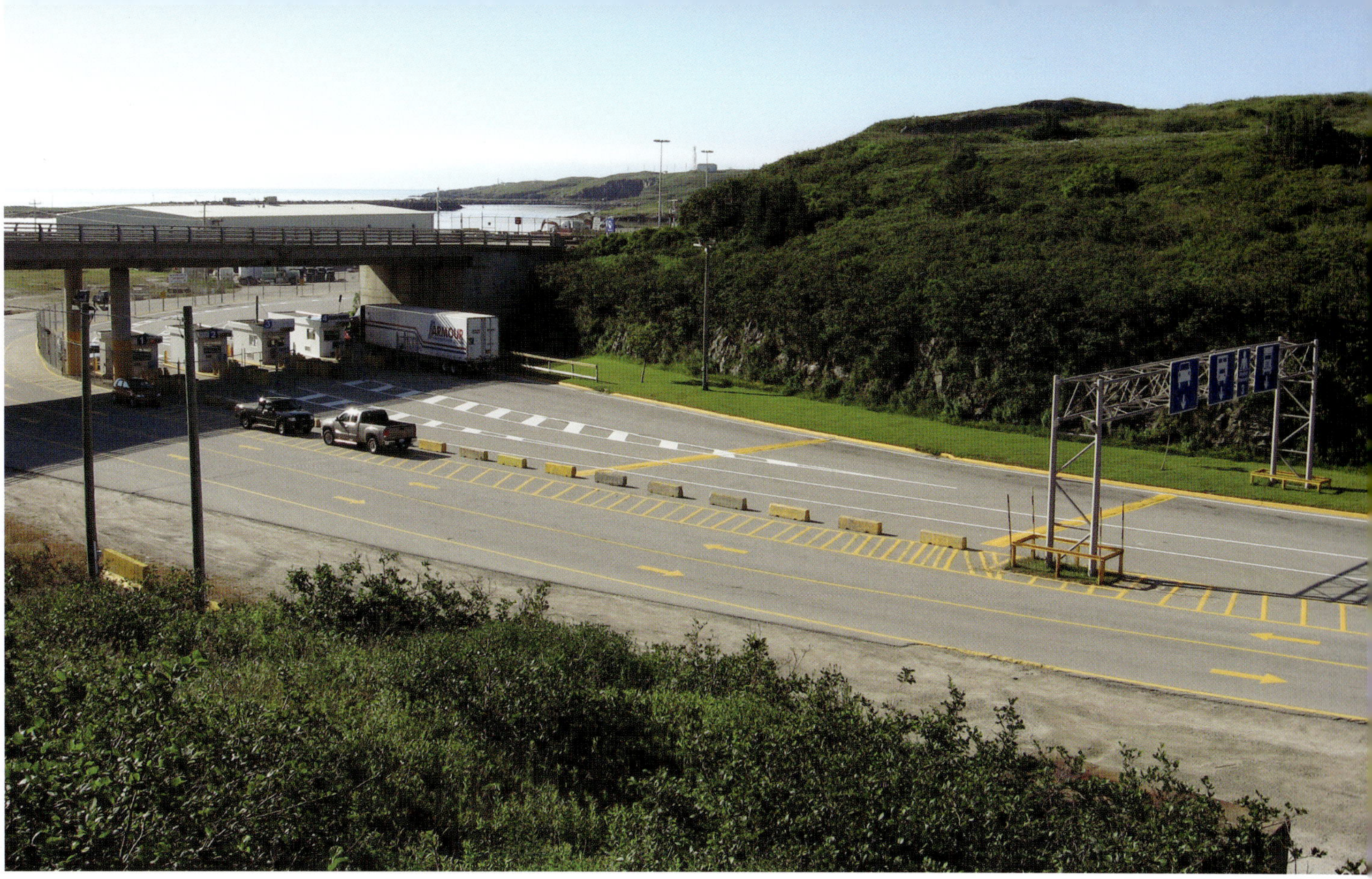

PORT AUX BASQUES 1969

CN Train 102, the *Caribou,* headed by NF210 923 with NF210 910 and NF110 906 prepares to commence its final 547-mile journey to St. John's on July 2, 1969. Its 10:00 a.m. departure would spell the end of rail passenger service from the gateway town of Port aux Basques. Photographer Robert J. Sandusky, on his second of four trips to record the Newfoundland railway, would soon join the 350 passengers carried that day as far as Stephenville Crossing. In the background, the *MV William Carson*, the first of the post-Confederation superferries can be seen, having arrived from North Sydney after an overnight crossing. *Robert J. Sandusky photo*

PORT AUX BASQUES TODAY

The last of the remaining vehicles hurry through the Marine Atlantic registration booths to make the 10:00 a.m. departure for North Sydney on the *MV Highlanders*, out of sight but docked on the other side of the hill. The town of Port aux Basques remains the official marine gateway to the island of Newfoundland and home to Marine Atlantic. It is now serviced by modern superferries such as the *MV Blue Puttees* and sister ship *MV Highlander*, each with a capacity of 1000 passengers and 2840 lane metres on the vehicle decks. *Author photo*

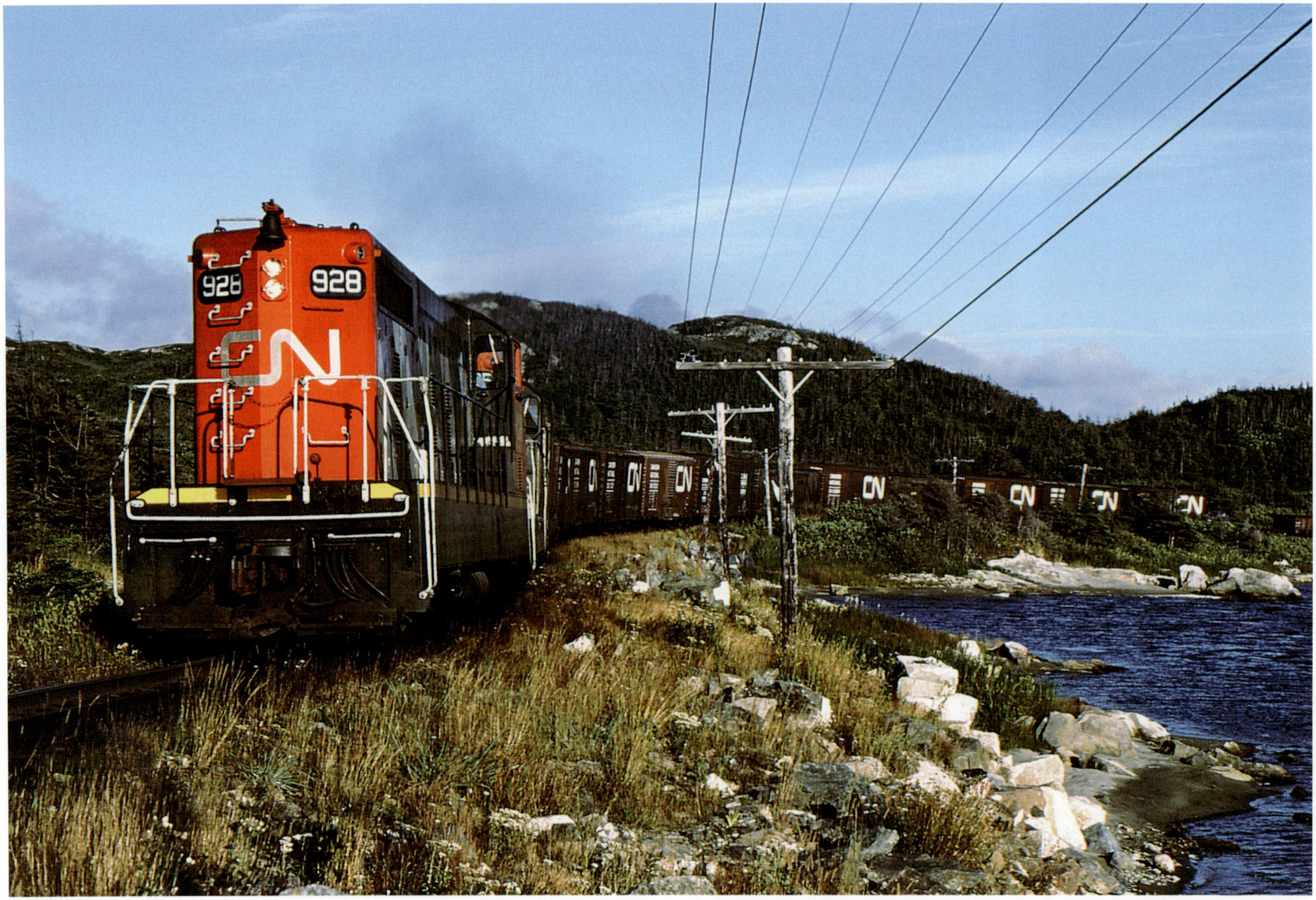

CAPE RAY 1978

Canadian National's eastbound freight #204, with NF210 928 in the 1970's zebra stripe paint scheme on the head end, turns inland at Cape Ray on a beautiful afternoon on August 30, 1978. This was among the last of the Newfoundland trains captured by Rich Taylor following a week of photography prior to his return to New Jersey. The loaded forty-foot steel boxcars will be dropped to customers at various points and sidings along the route. *Rich Taylor photo*

CAPE RAY TODAY

With the exception of the removal of the rails and ties, not much has changed since 204 ran past this spot. As for 928, it would find a second lease on life, after being sold to F.C. del Pacifico of Nicaragua in 1989. Cape Ray is famous for its 16 km white sandy beach and for being the site of the first submarine telegraph cable connecting Newfoundland to the North American continent in 1856. Brought to the Island by steamer from Cape Breton under the New York, Newfoundland and London Telegraph Company, it was in full operation by October of that year. *Author photo*

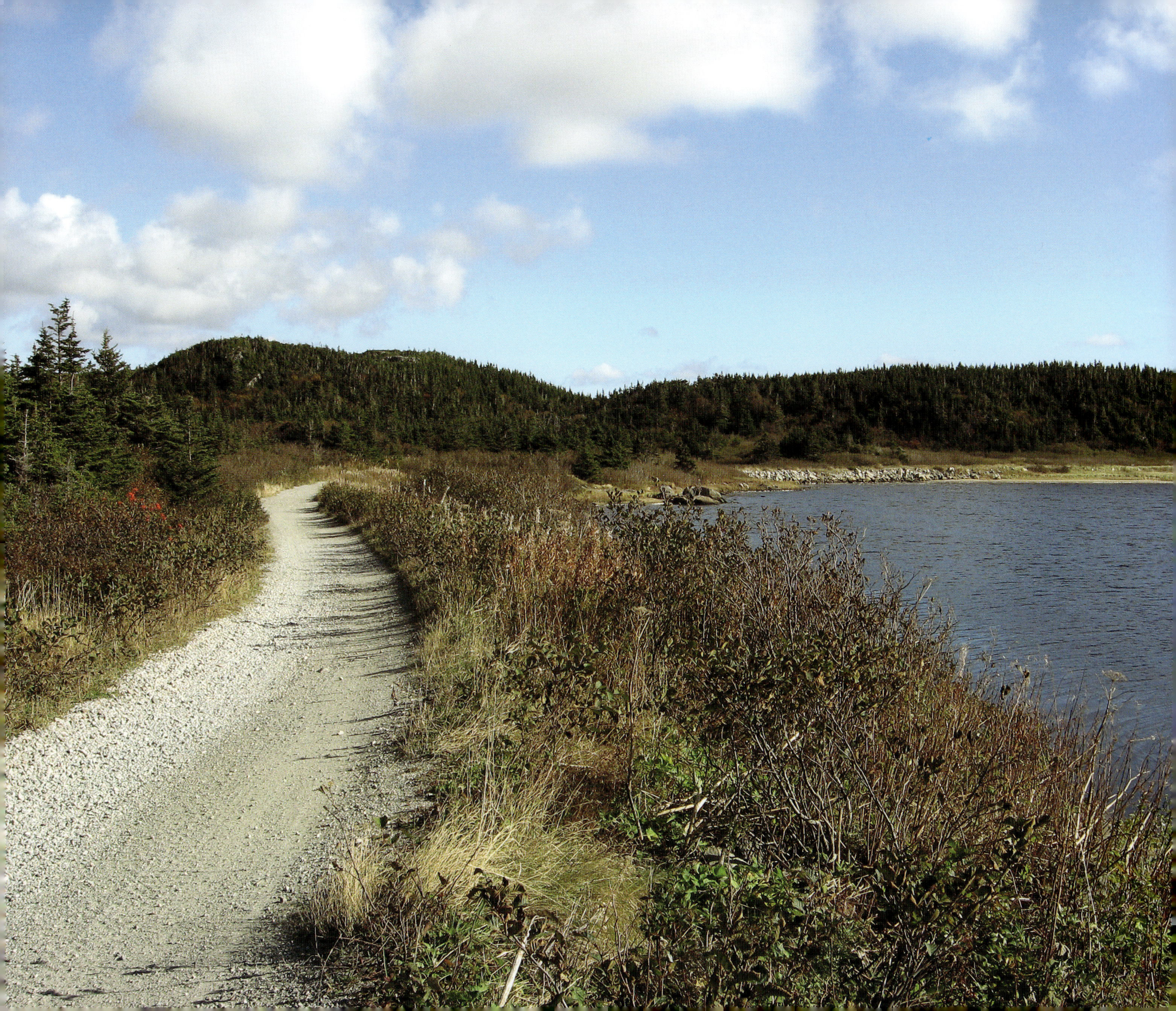

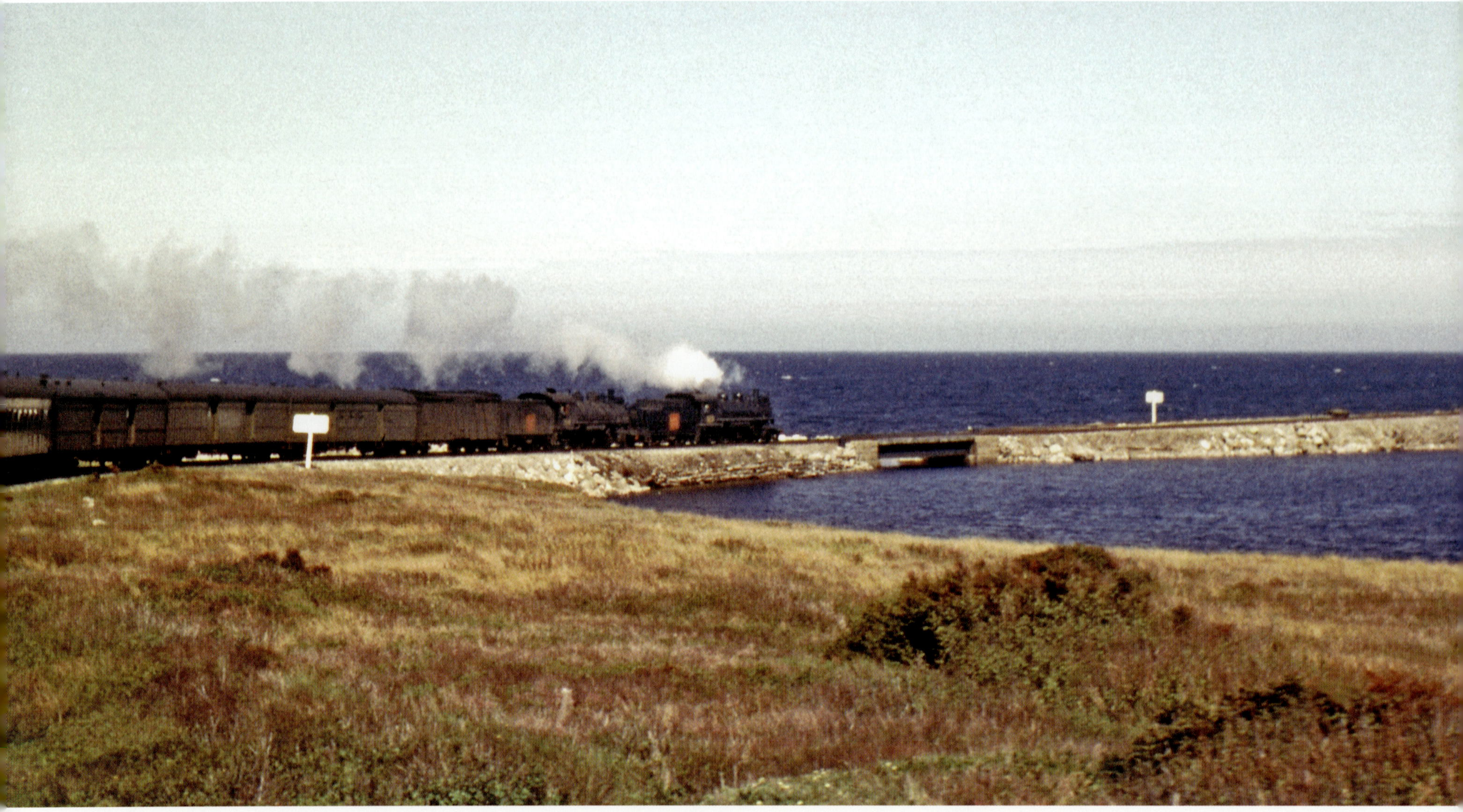

BEAR COVE 1956

CNR's Train #2, the eastbound *Caribou*, with double headed 2-8-2 Mikados, is about to cross the small bridge at Bear Cove during the last summer of steam operations on the Island. Bear Cove Bridge was only one of 130, with the railway averaging a bridge for every 4.2 miles of track. All passenger cars have been repainted in the olive green livery of the Canadian National Railways and at this point on the line, the train runs only several feet from the waters of the Gulf of St. Lawrence. *Photo from James A. Brown Collection*

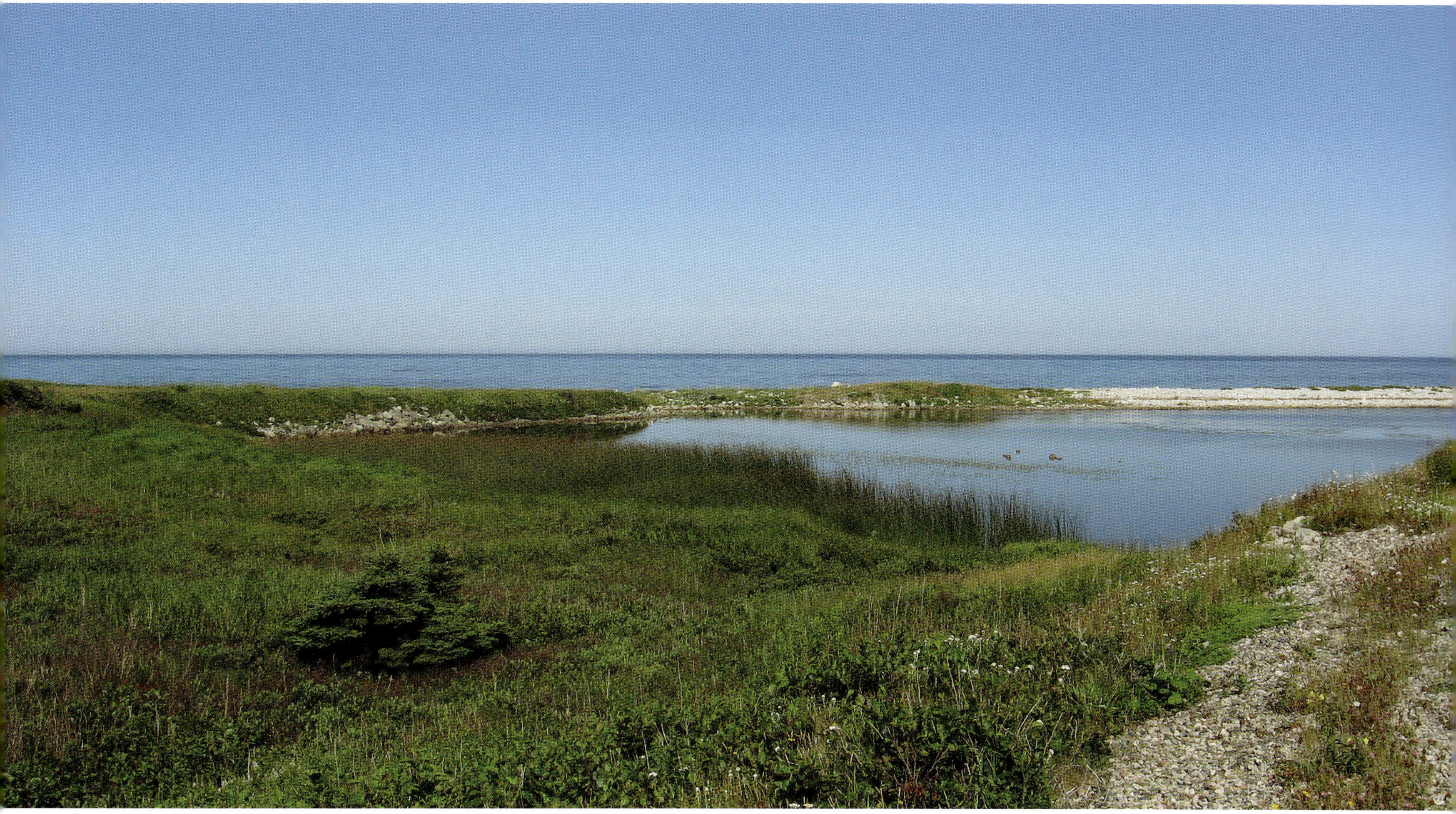

BEAR COVE TODAY

The Gulf of St. Lawrence is calm, unlike on October 20, 1974 when one of the worst storms to strike the South West Coast damaged the bridge and washed out several hundred feet of track near Cape Smokey, causing a derailment of two diesels. Work crews were forced to relocate the right of way much further inland to avoid any future storm damage and erosion. During World War II, all engines had to extinguish their headlights at this bridge due to the German U-Boats patrolling the area. It was so close to the ocean that a torpedo could easily strike the abutments, blowing up the bridge.

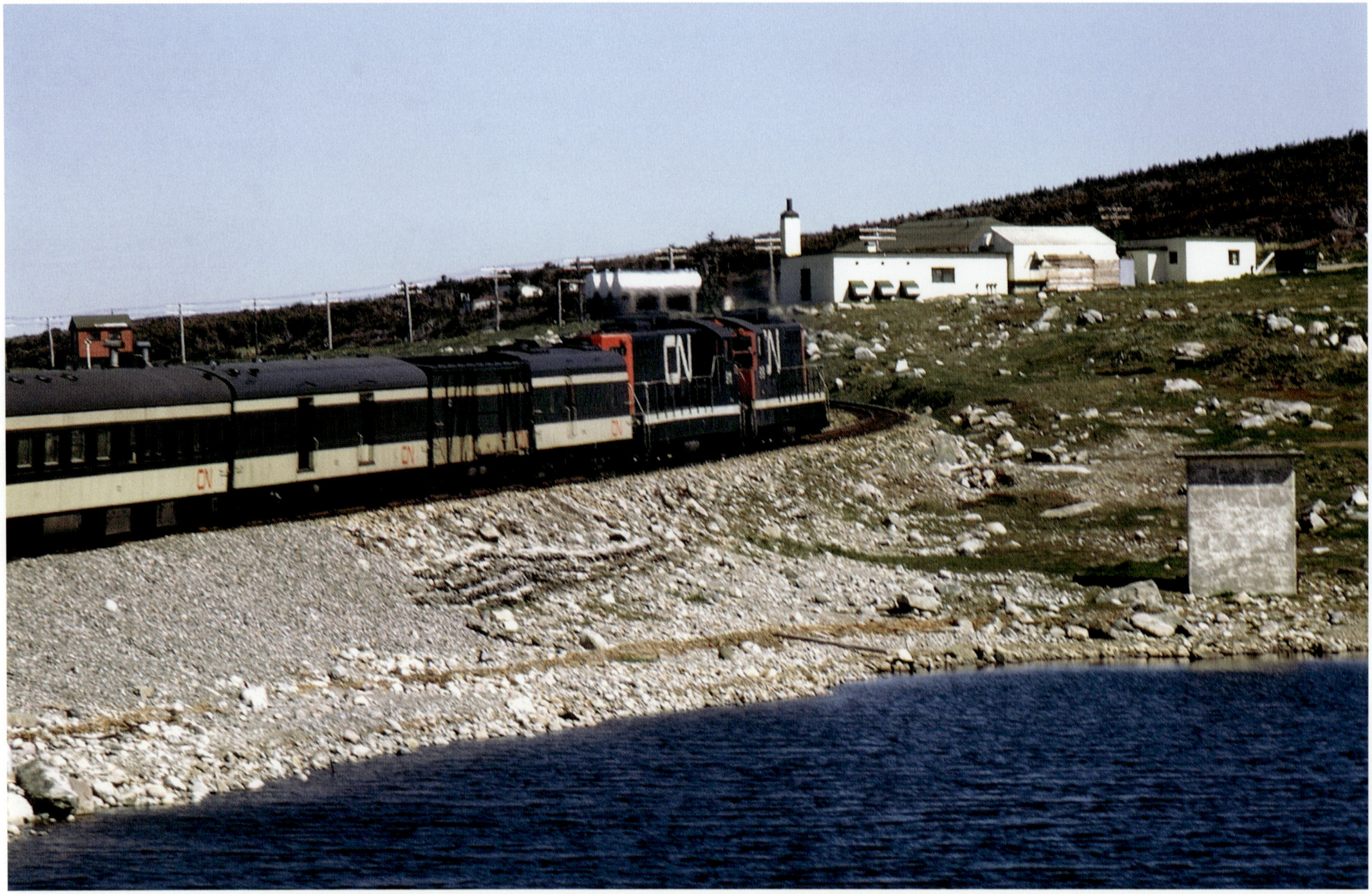

RED ROCKS
CN Train #102, the eastbound *Caribou*, turns in from the Gulf of St. Lawrence at Red Rocks on June 19, 1967. Salt water waves often washed across the steep grade, making it so slippery that trainmen would have to put small pebbles in front of the locomotive for traction. As part of a Centennial Year project, James A. Brown and several friends from the University of Toronto would ride this train until its final stop at the St. John's station the following morning. In just a few miles, the crews of NF210's 919 and 911 as well as their passengers will reach the infamous Wreckhouse area, the windiest in Newfoundland. *James A. Brown photo*

RED ROCKS TODAY
Forever exposed to the Gulf of St. Lawrence and hidden from sight by the Twin Hills for those travelling along the Trans Canada Highway, Red Rocks was once a mainline station flag stop and important ballast pit. It has been totally abandoned and depopulated since September, 1966. Only the remains of the concrete structures can be seen from the former right of way. *Author photo*

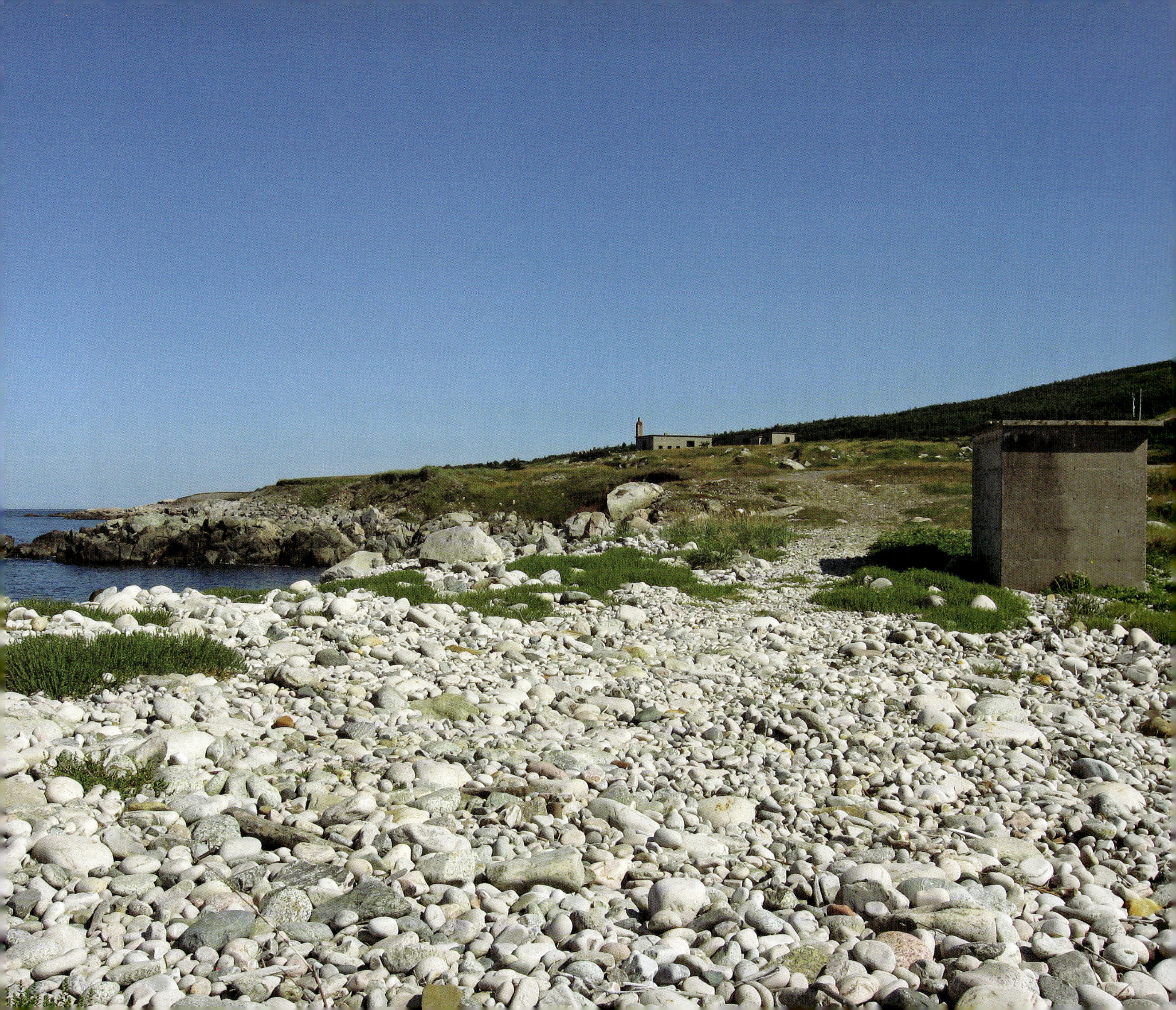

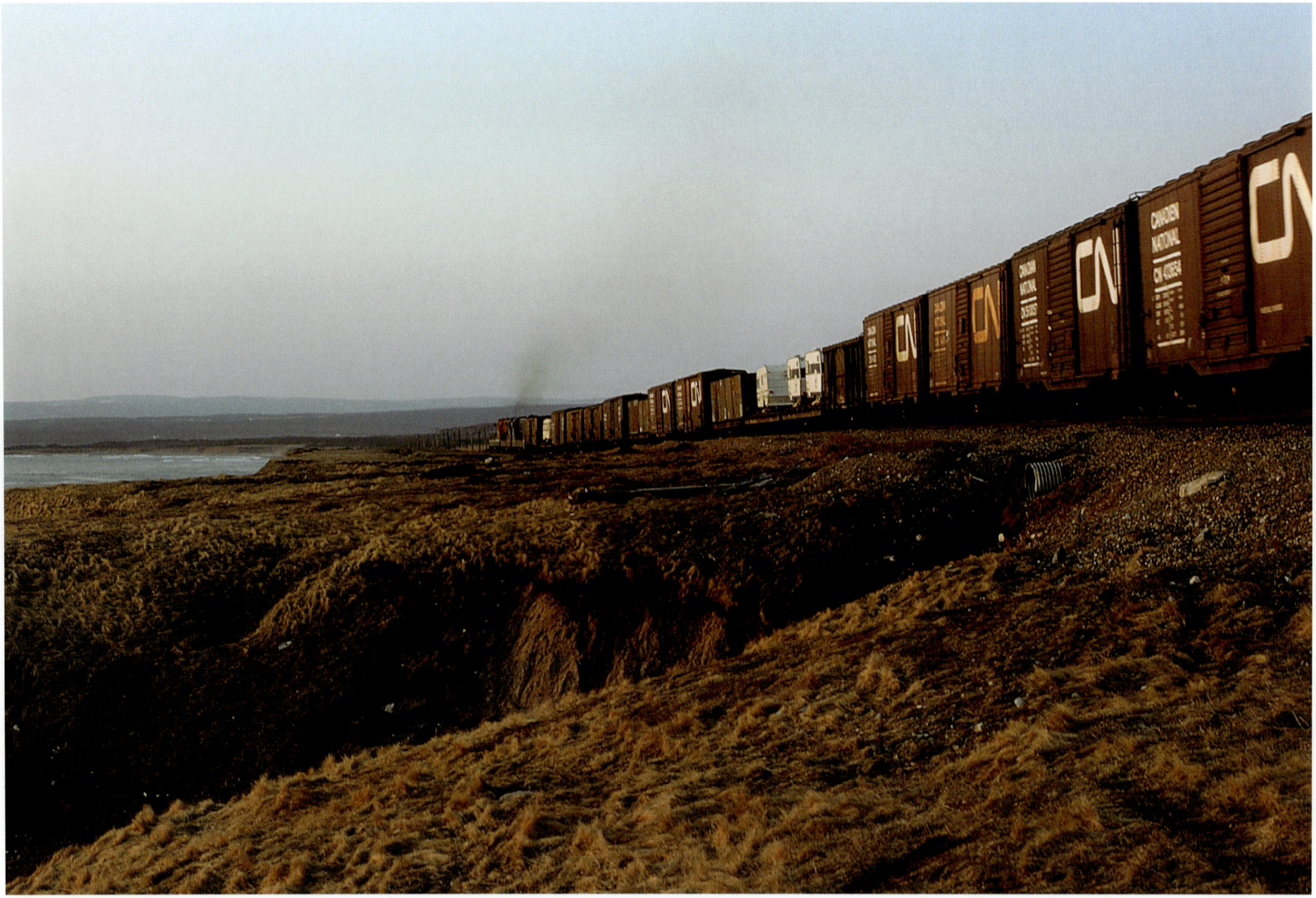

WRECKHOUSE 1975
While standing precariously close to the cliff's edge, Phil Mason wraps up a week of rail photography, capturing CN Train 204 passing by the infamous Wreckhouse area late in the evening of May 12, 1975. With 125/mph gales sweeping down from Table Mountain, the railway hired trapper Lauchie McDougall to "sniff the wind" in order to determine if it was safe for trains to pass. If not, they were chained to the tracks until the wind subsided. He continued this for thirty years until his death in 1965, after which his wife assumed the practice until 1972. *Phil Mason photo*

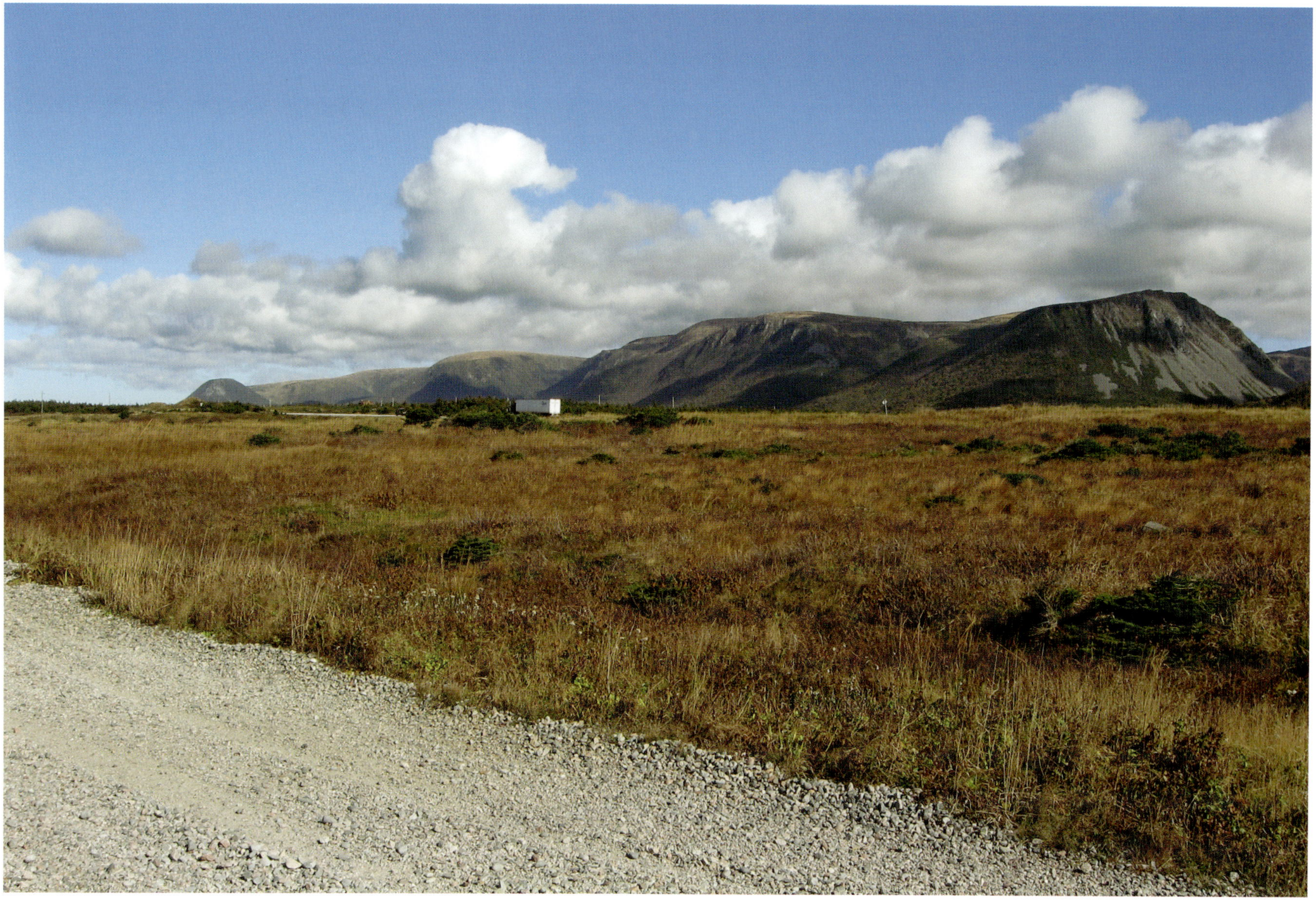

WRECKHOUSE TODAY
The Provincial Department of Transportation has two wind warning signs on both the eastern and western approaches to the Wreckhouse area. When wind gusts are in excess of 100/kph, the sign advises all traffic to pull over. Wreckhouse winds, now a metrological term, continue to wreak havoc on the parallel Trans Canada Highway at the base of Table Mountain. Here an eastbound tractor trailer passes by without delay on a calm October afternoon. *Author photo*

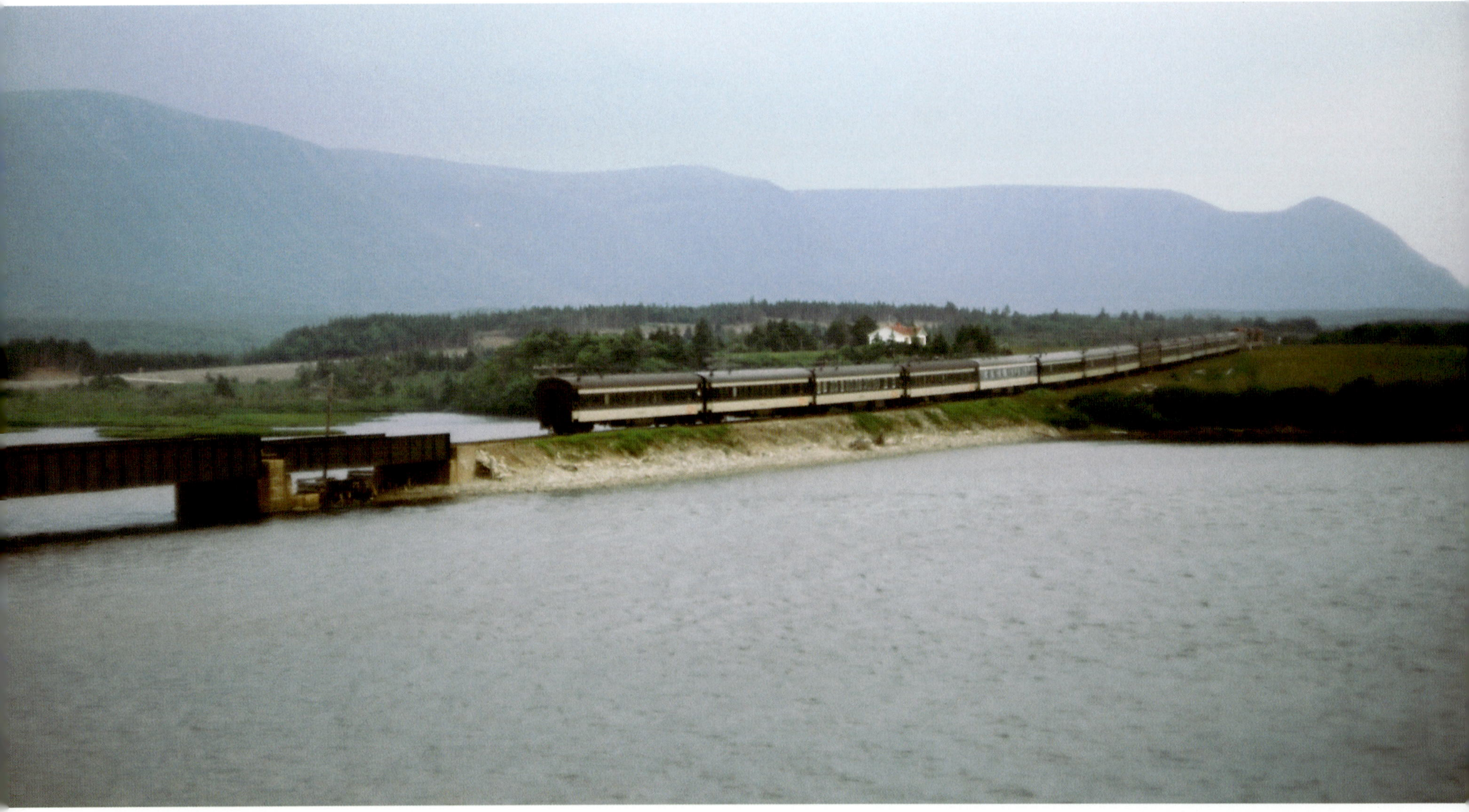

ST. ANDREWS 1969

The last westbound *Caribou*, CN Train 101 with locomotives 934, 910 and 906 leading 16 cars, including a steam generator car, crosses the trestle at the mouth of the Little Codroy River at St. Andrews on the hazy evening of July 1, 1969. The next and final stop will be at Port aux Basques, where this same consist will be turned around for the return trip to St. John's in the morning and 923 will replace 934. *Robert J. Sandusky photo*

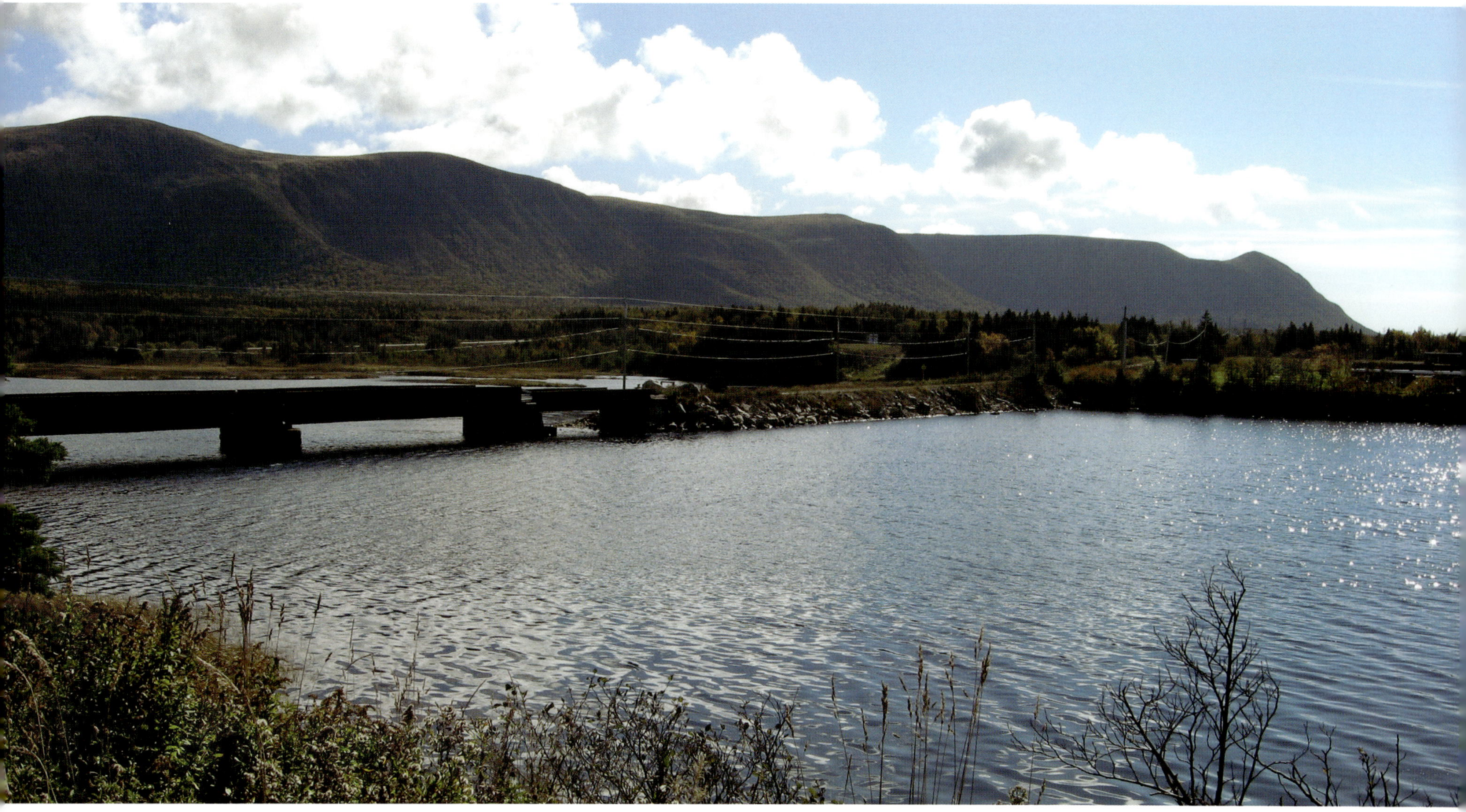

ST. ANDREWS TODAY
Sunlight shimmers on the waters of the Little Codroy River against the backdrop of the majestic Table Mountains. A testament to the railway's maintenance and engineering crews, the trestle has stood the test of time, still strong and secure on its abutments. St. Andrews was named for the patron saint of Scotland and the original route of the rail line was to be on the south side of the river. In 1897 Bishop Neil McNeil convinced the Reids to relocate it to the north side so his community could be closer to the tracks.

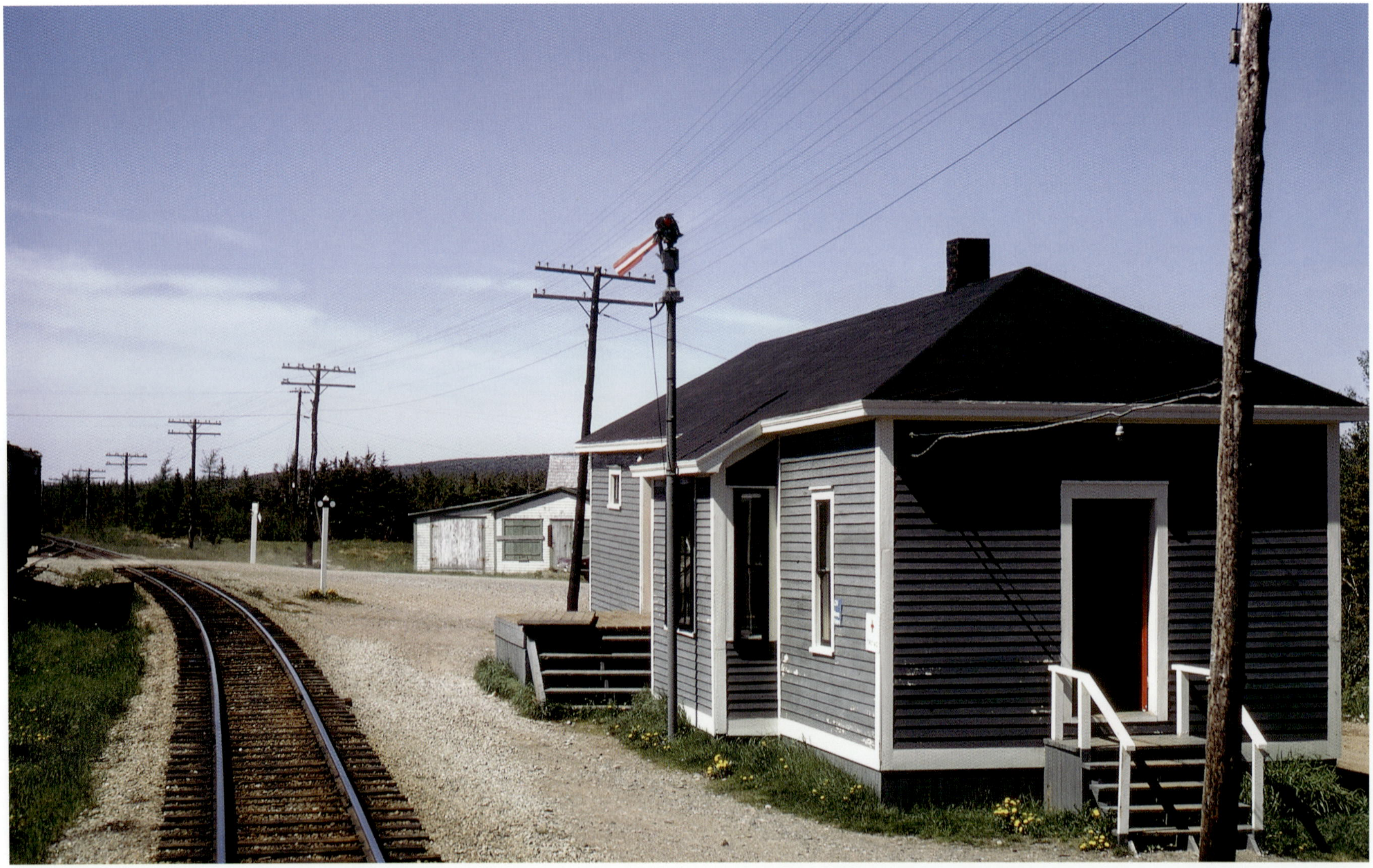

DOYLES 1967

The signal board is down and dandelions surround the tidy little station at Doyles in the Codroy Valley as viewed from the rear of the sleeper 'Clarenville'. Built in 1952 by the Canadian Car and Foundry Company of Montreal, this sleeper would remain in revenue service for another two years and the Doyles station would see passengers from the nearby communities of Upper Ferry, O'Regans, Great Codroy and Searstown. Train 102, the *Caribou* continues to proceed eastward on June 20, 1967. *James A. Brown photo*

DOYLES TODAY

The site where a station once proudly stood has become a veritable graveyard for used ambulances and other automobiles awaiting, somewhat ironically, a similar fate. Doyles was named after Mr. Jim Doyle, the first postmaster in the area. The post office he opened in 1898 was near the site of the former station. In later years, people cut ties for the railway from wood near Doyles and sold them for eighteen cents apiece. *Author photo*

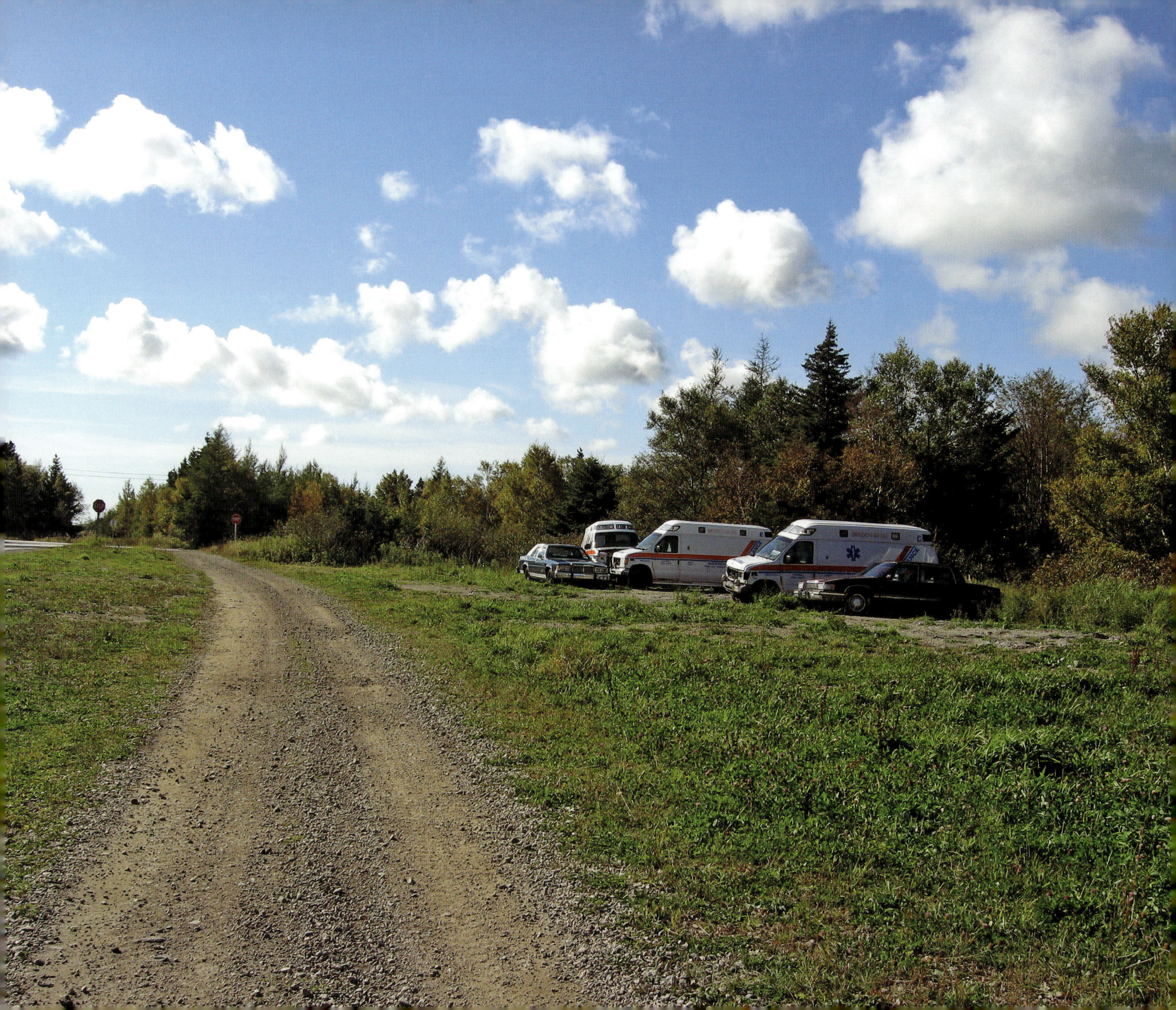

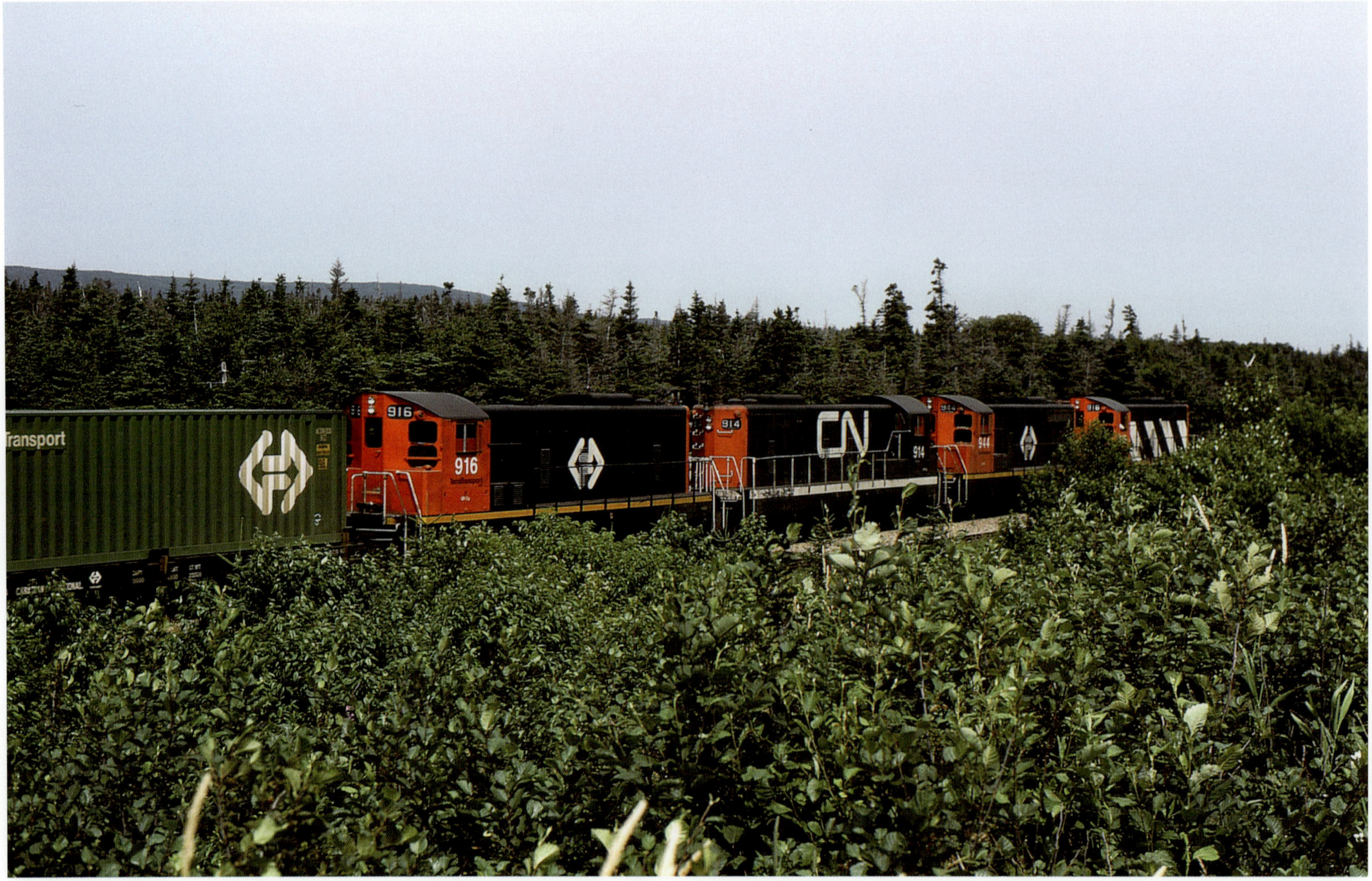

RIVERVIEW 1984
While rushing to catch the CN Marine Ferry at Port aux Basques, Gary Hadfield spies the headlights and stops to capture Terra Transport Train 204 with the distinctive 40-foot green containers at Riverview on August 5, 1984. The four NF210's, numbers 918, 944, 914 and 916 are all wearing three different paint schemes representing the 1960's, 1970's and 1980's on this daily scheduled eastbound freight. *Gary Hadfield photo*

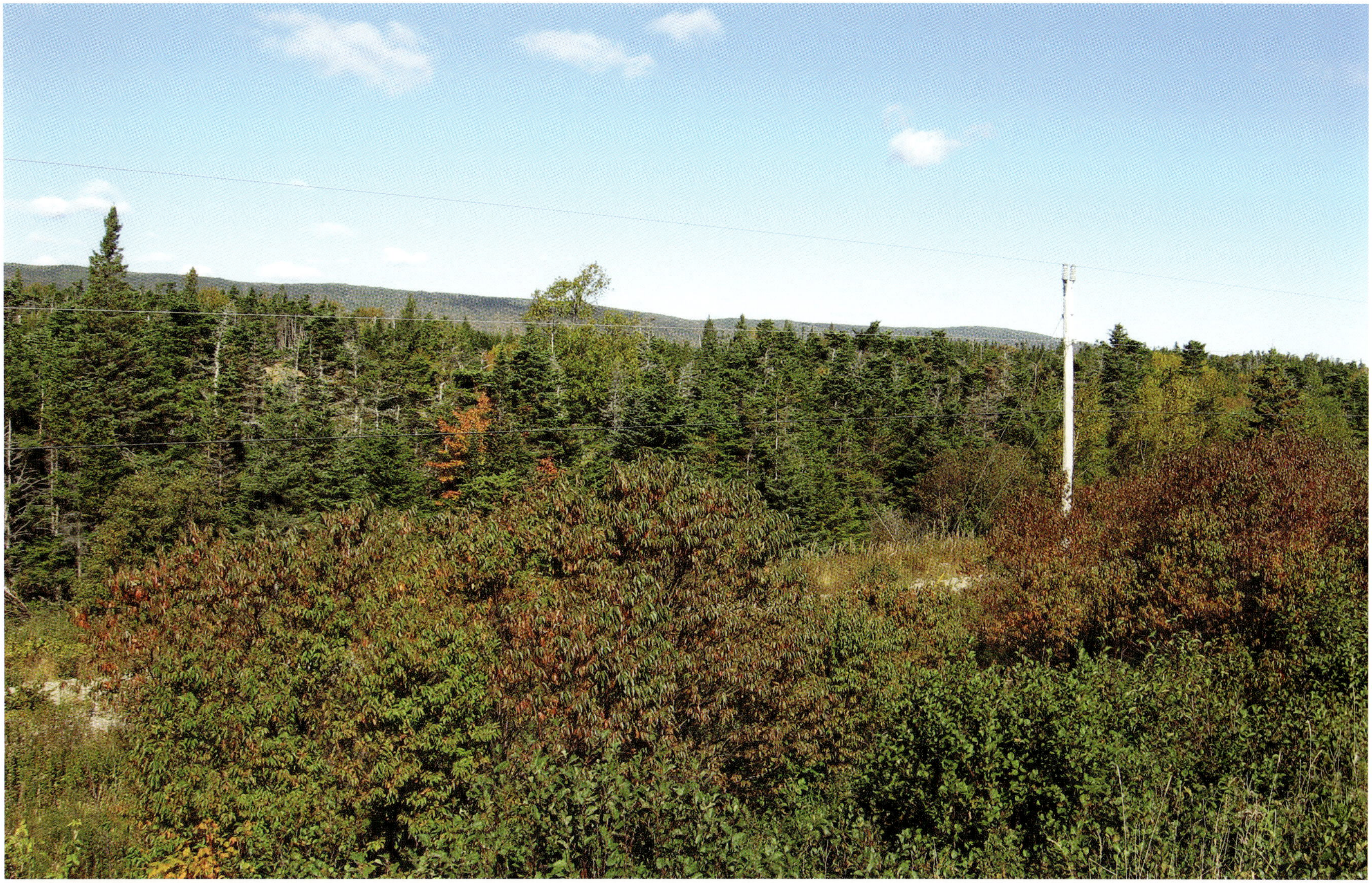

RIVERVIEW TODAY

The siding and former mainline is virtually hidden from view from the TCH due to overgrowth of vegetation. In its day, the siding at Riverview, named for its parallel view of the Grand Codroy River, had a capacity 5420 feet, making it the longest on the Island. It was also where westbound trains took shelter during Wreckhouse gales. Today however, the former right of way and once important pulp loading site does make for an easily accessible power transmission line. *Author photo*

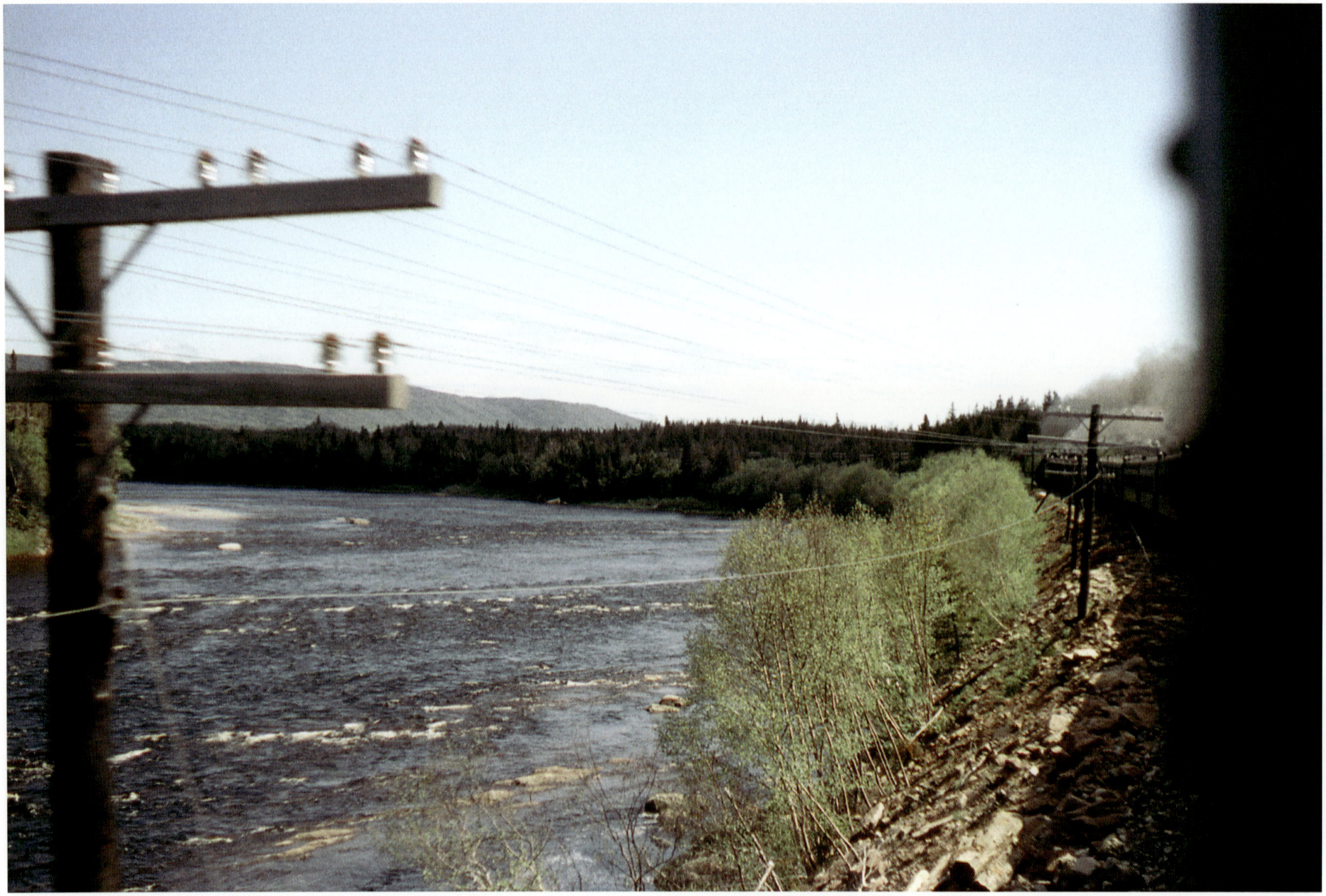

OVERFALLS 1956

The powerful 2-8-2 Mikados, each with a tractive effort of 27,540 pounds, spew plumes of smoke as CNR Train #2 follows the banks of the Grand Codroy River. On his second trip to the Island, Ronald Ritchie leans out the vestibule to record the *Caribou*, eastbound at Overfalls on June 19, 1956. A total of thirty of these sleek locomotives were delivered to the Newfoundland Railway between 1930 and 1949. *Ronald S. Ritchie photo*

OVERFALLS TODAY

The Anguille Mountains are a beautiful backdrop to the Grand Codroy River's perfect pools. With the recently upgraded trestle at Overfalls, this multi-use trail allows easy access for salmon fishermen and others. Renowned American angler Lee Wulff travelled here by train and a hand-pumped railcar in 1935 to both fish and later promote it to the rest of the world. *Author photo*

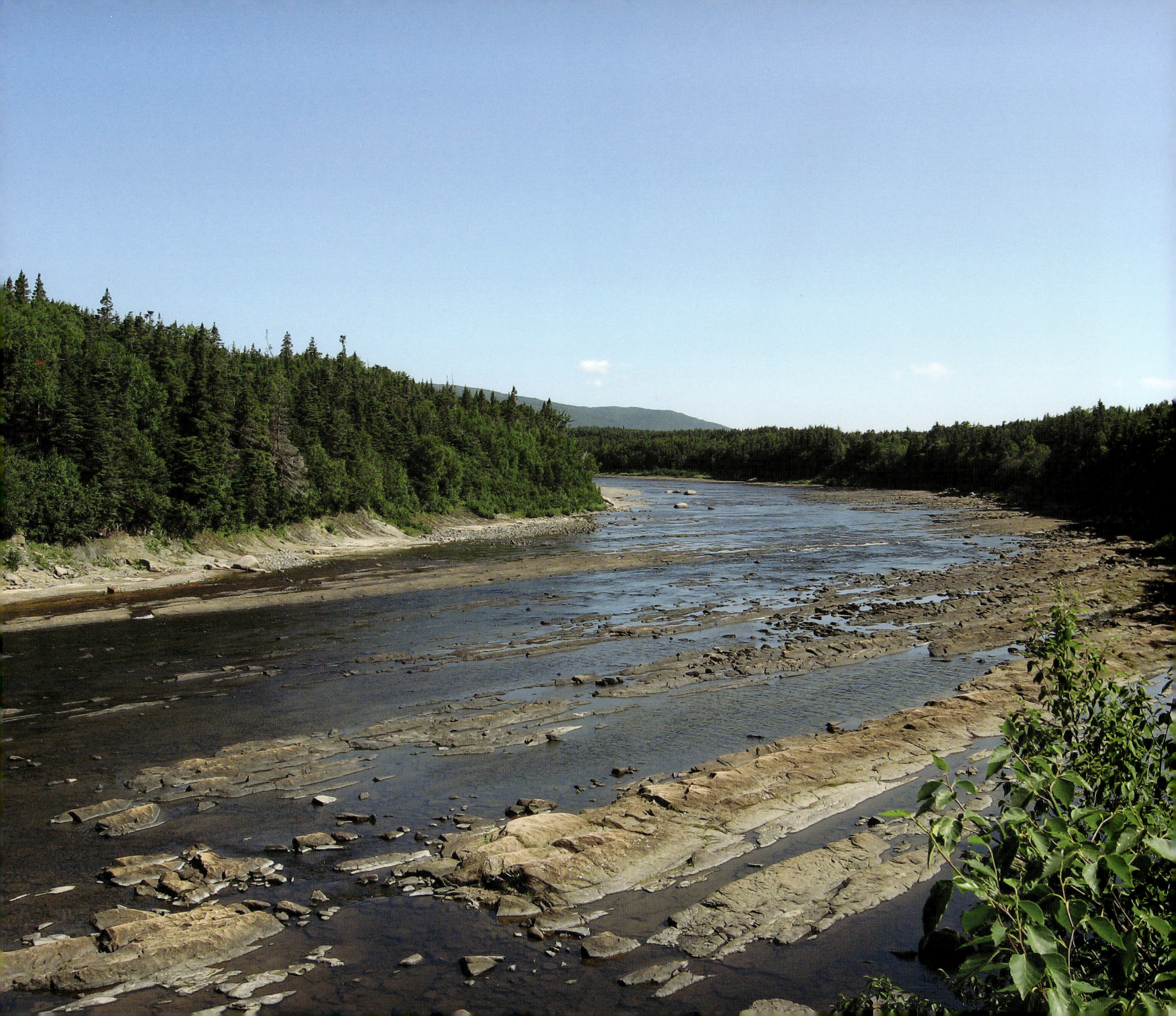

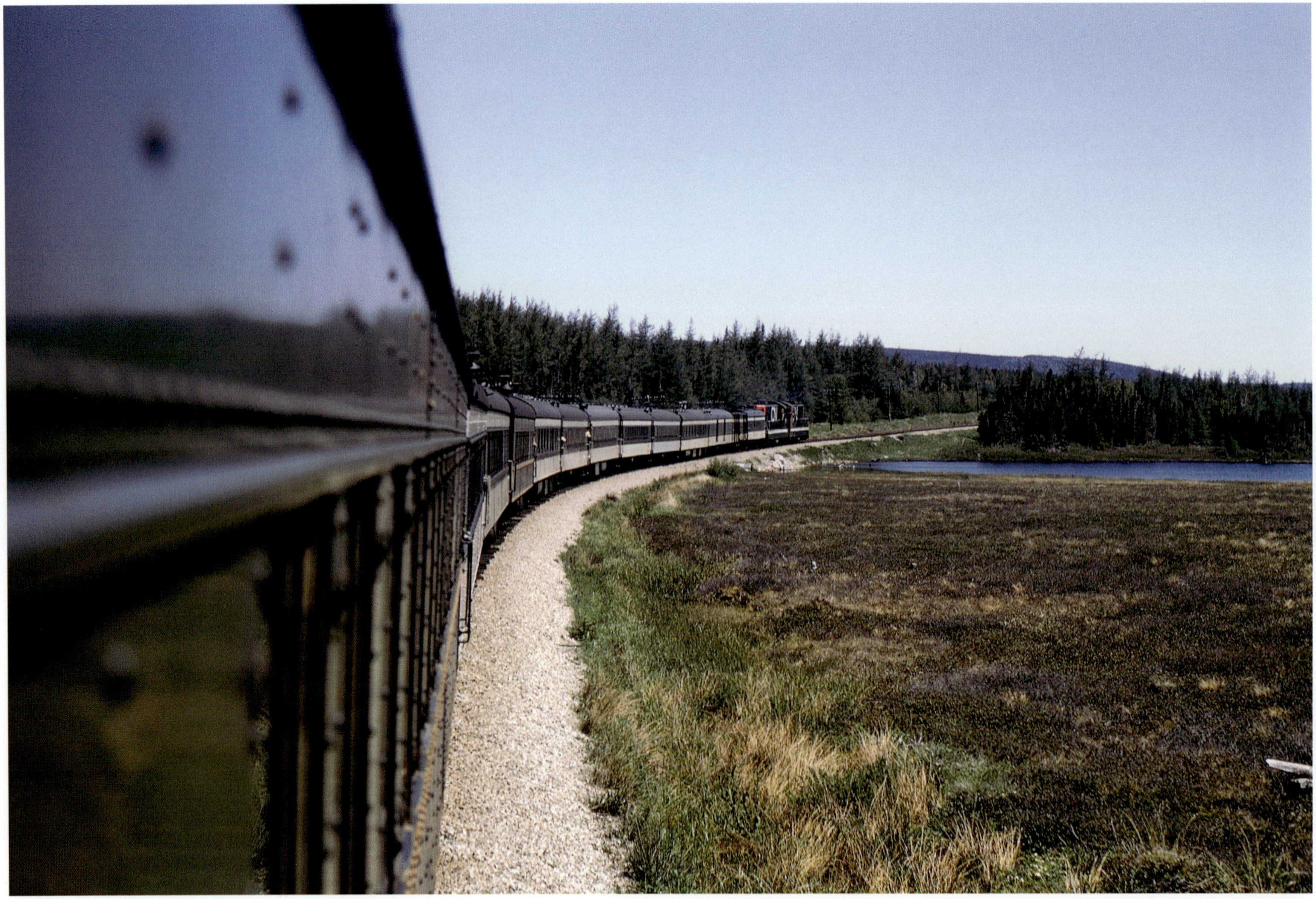

SOUTH BRANCH 1967
Viewed from the sleeper 'Clarenville', CN Train 102 is picking up speed just after crossing the trestle over the South Branch River on June 20, 1967. The two NF210's, trailing thirteen pieces of passenger equipment, will soon be exiting Newfoundland's scenic Codroy Valley. With a flag stop of 11:14 a.m. in the timetable, it won't be long before folks head to the diner for some of the best prepared meals anywhere. *James A. Brown photo*

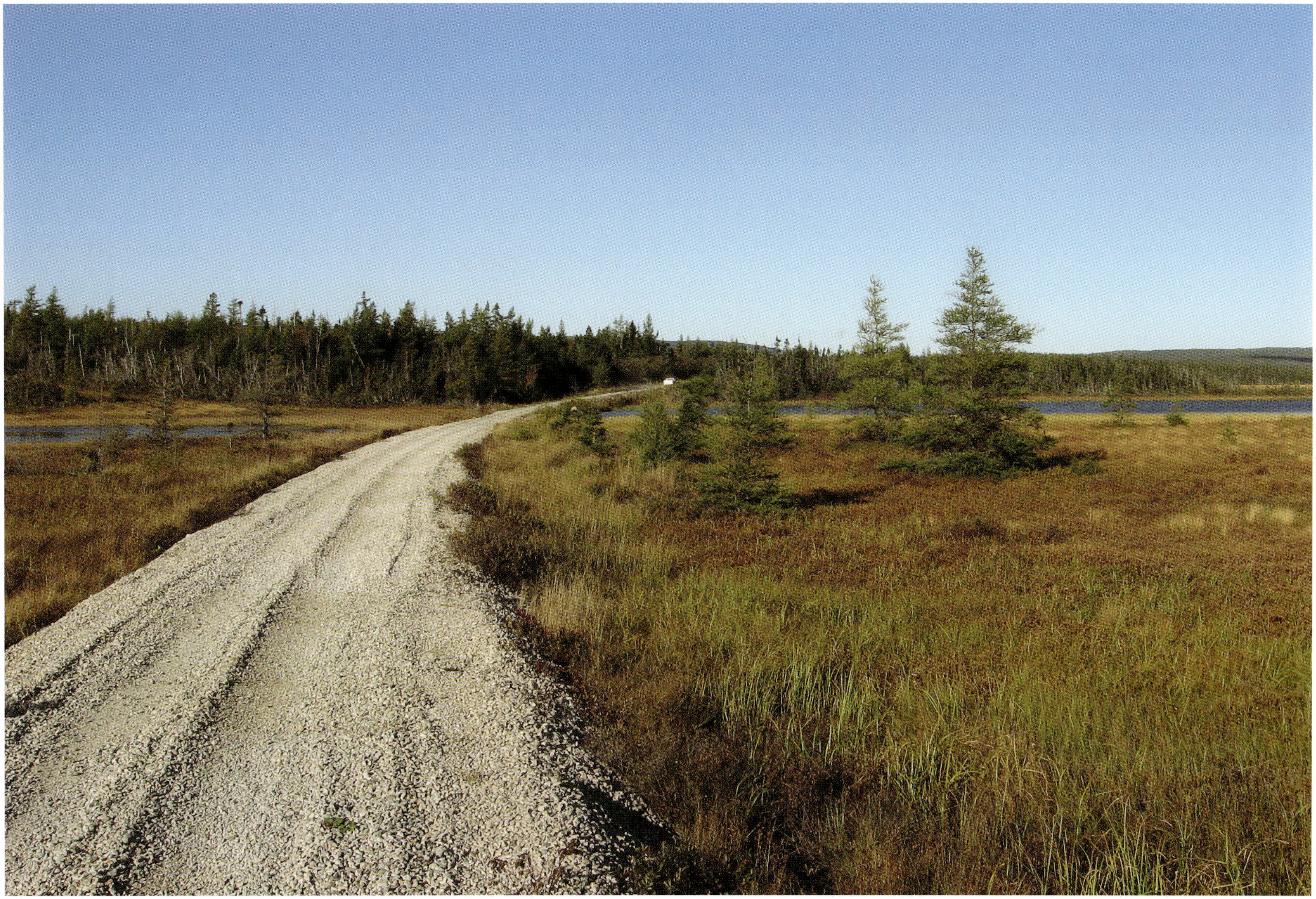

SOUTH BRANCH TODAY
South Branch came into existence as a community for those building the railway, with section foreman Dick Wells being the first settler. Nowadays, the road bed, which remains in excellent condition, allows access of nearly every type of motorized equipment as can be seen by the Ford pickup off in the distance, following the trail of the *Caribou*. The 'Clarenville' would survive the end of passenger service and be converted to Work Car 5012 in 1970. *Author photo*

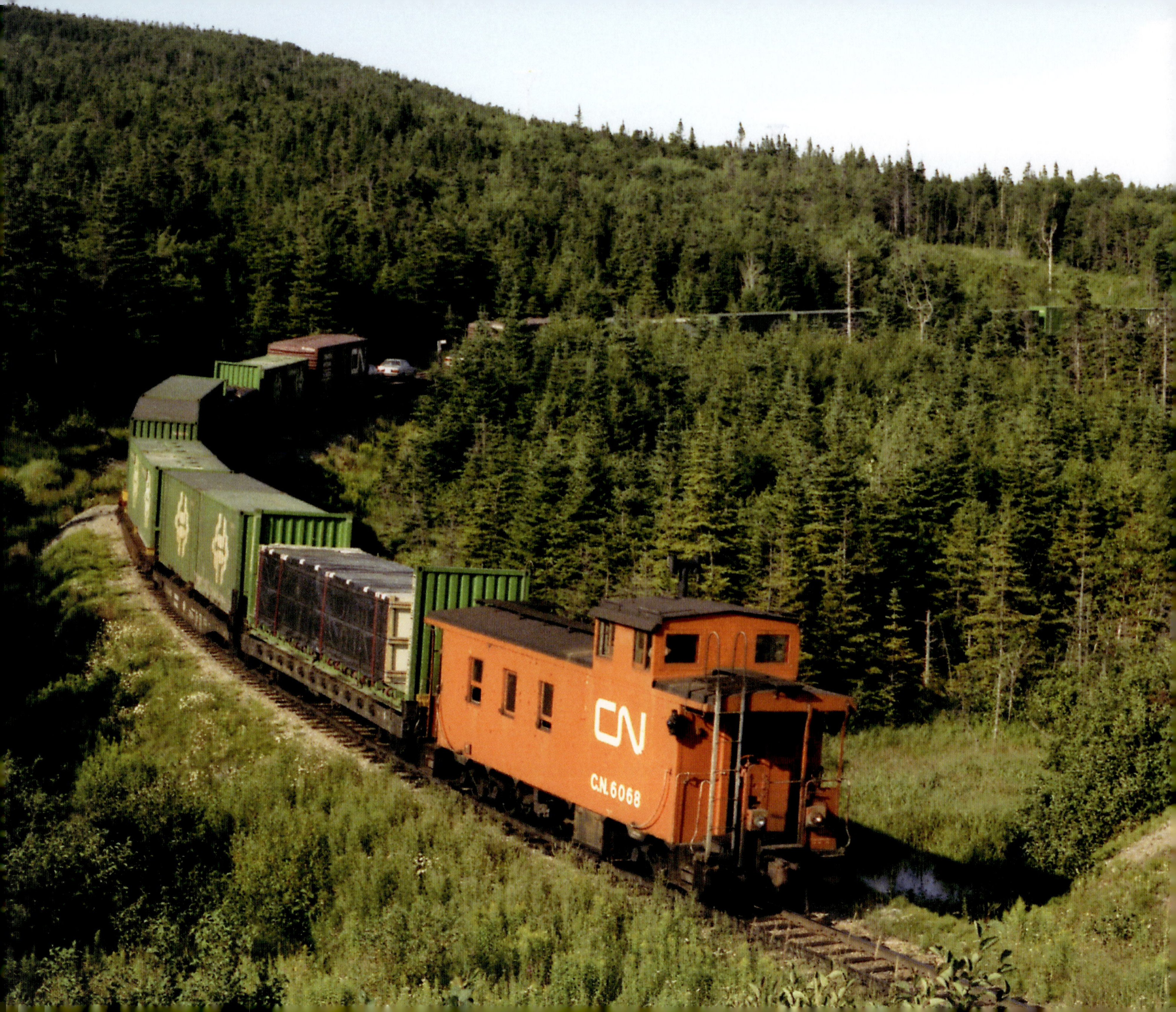
CN
C.N. 6068

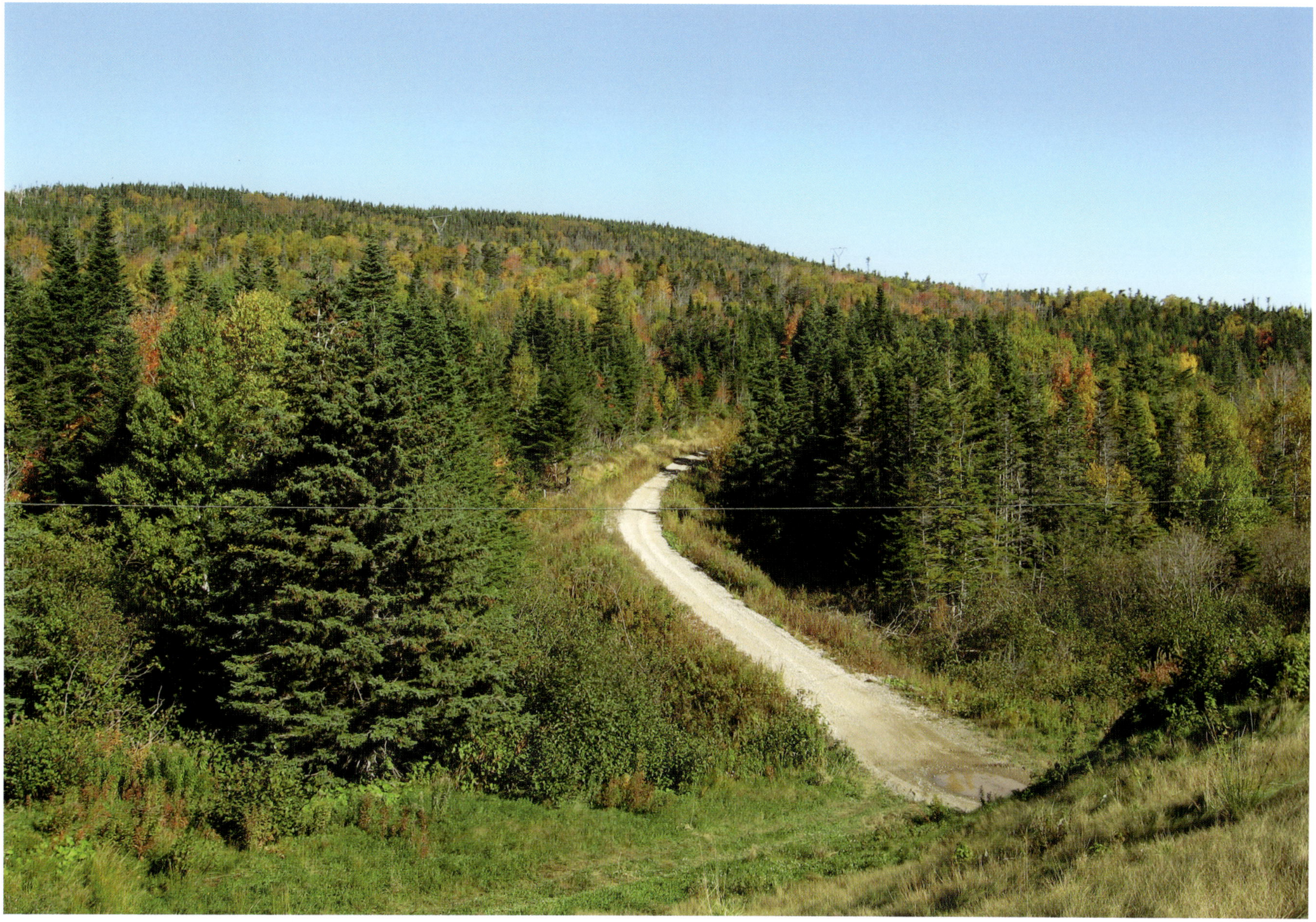

CODROY POND OVERPASS 1984
Terra Transport Train 204, with a combination of 40-foot steel boxcars and the new bright green intermodal containers, heads east at the Codroy Pond overpass on August 7, 1984. At this time full containerization was not yet achieved and the standard boxcar was still required for some customers. Steel caboose 6058 and her sisters remained in use until the very last train. *Dan Rowsell photo*

CODROY POND OVERPASS TODAY
The autumn colours are ablaze with the reds, browns and yellows of the trees surrounding the Codroy Pond area. The old concrete overpass has since been replaced with a corrugated steel tunnel. In the days of steam, due to the many grades, this was a necessary water stop to allow the engines leaving from Port aux Basques to continue their journey eastward. *Author photo*

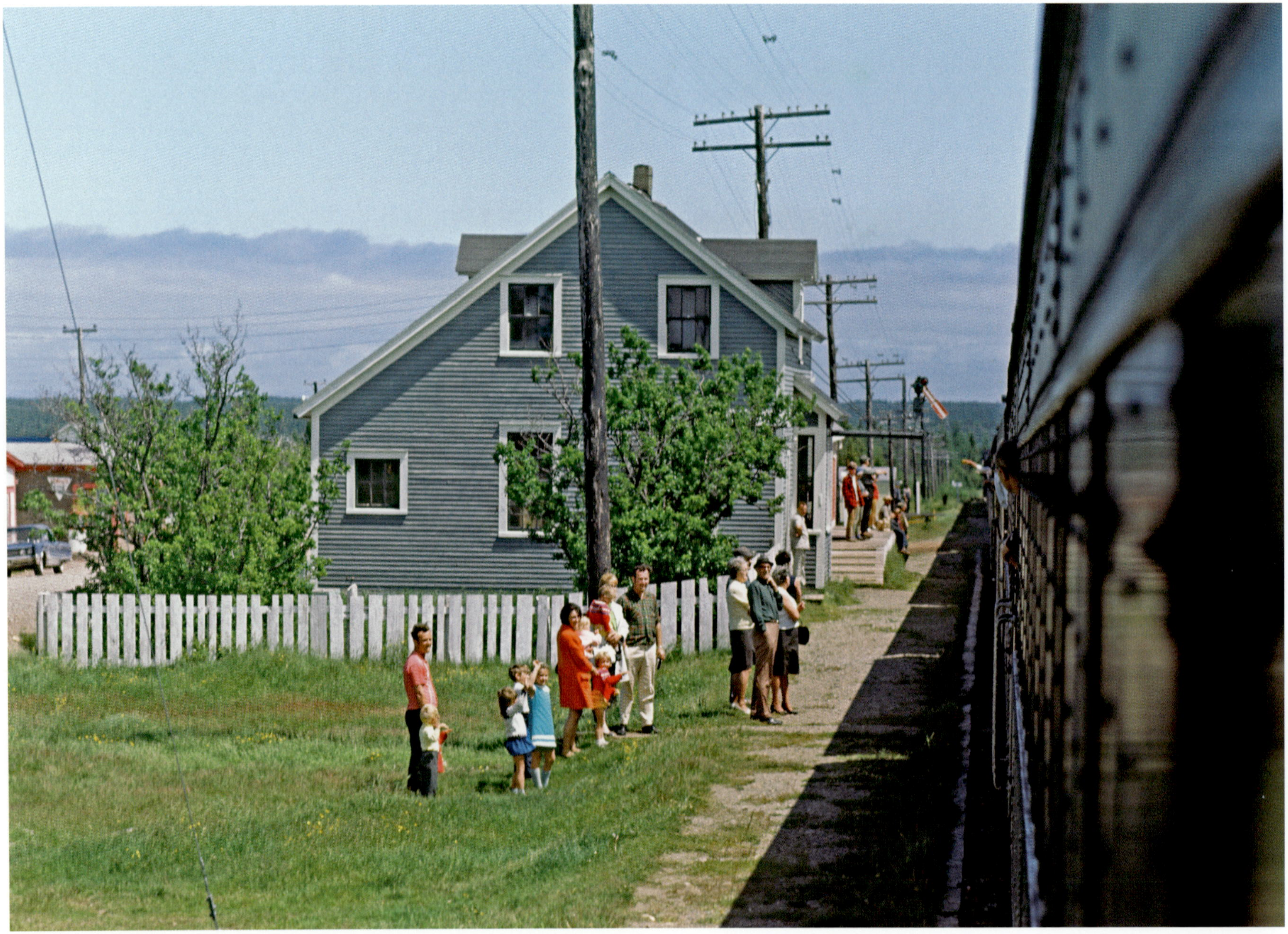

ST. FINTAN'S 1969
Residents of the village of St. Fintan's, most of whom descended from the Scots that moved from Cape Breton, bid farewell to the last *Caribou*, Train 102 as she passes through on July 2, 1969. On that same day, but out of sight from this view the engineer was advised by Train Order No. 382 that twenty-five freight cars were on the passing track. *Robert J. Sandusky photo*

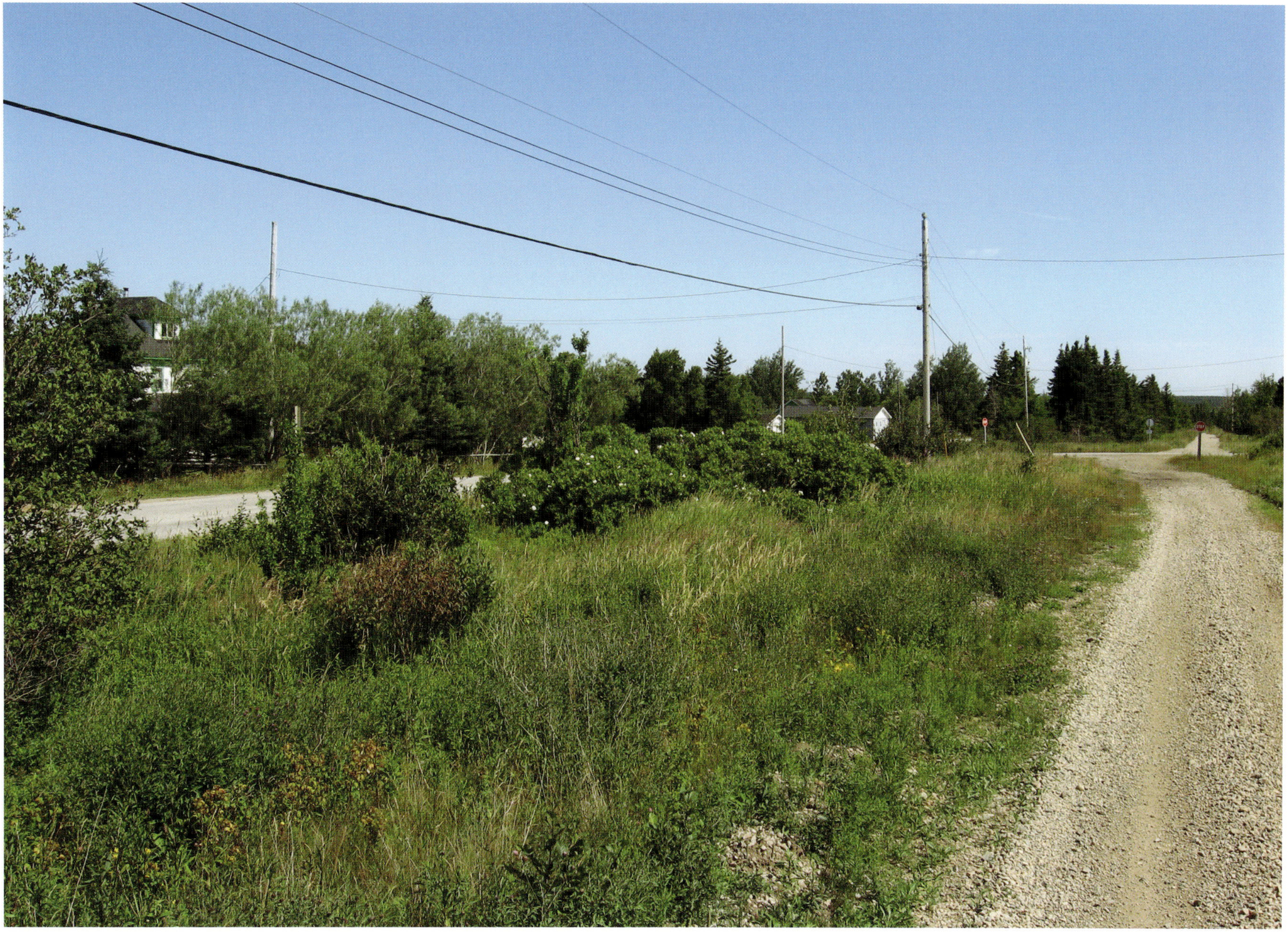

ST. FINTAN'S TODAY
The wild white roses have clearly covered the site of the old station in St. Fintan's, once known as Crabbes Station when railway employee Bill Quilty settled there in the early 1900's. Roadmaster Tom Wells lived in the white house on the left when stationed at St. Fintan's. Farms and small businesses still provide a living in this community with the most Scottish of names. *Author photo*

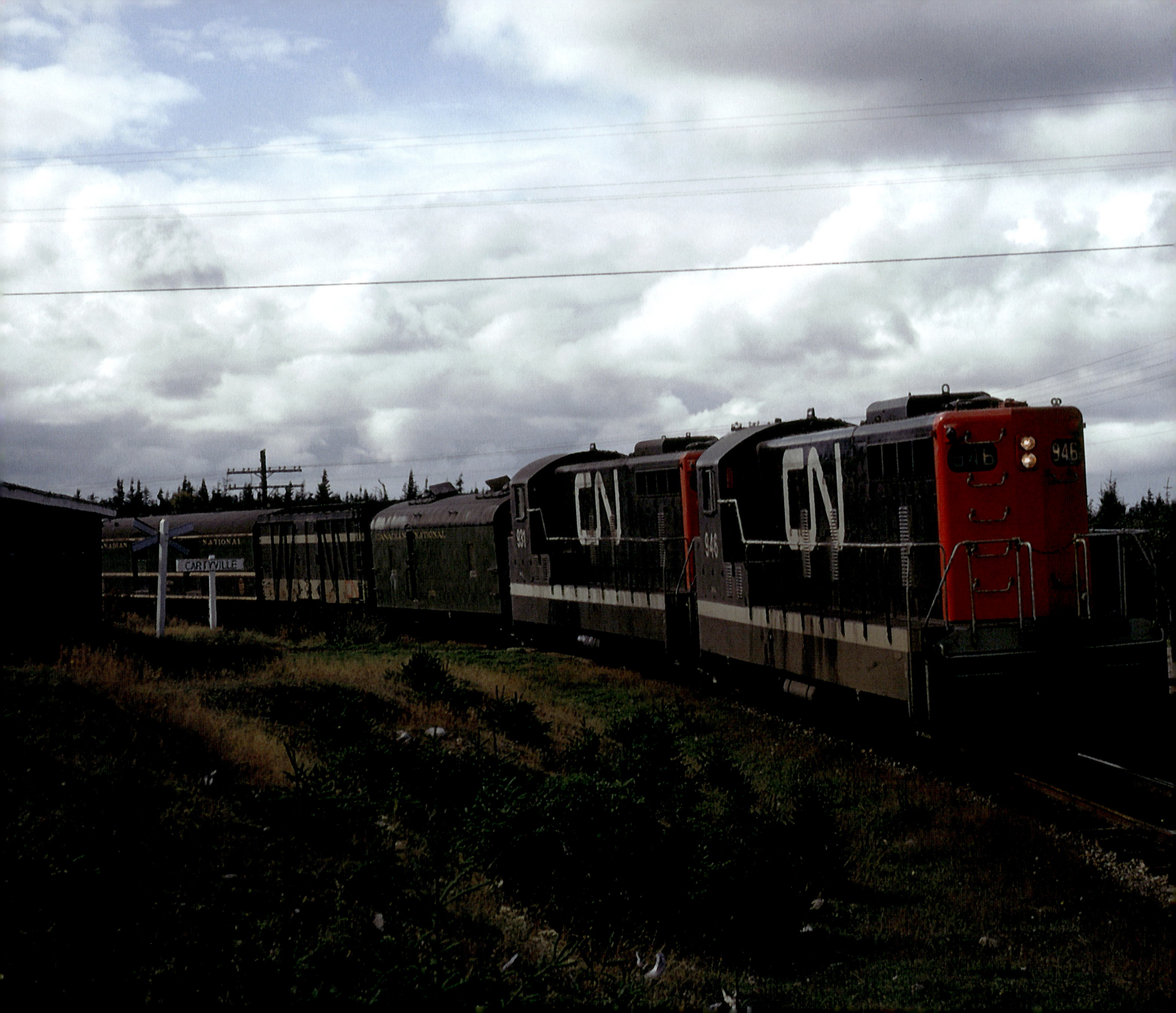
CARTYVILLE
CN
CN
946

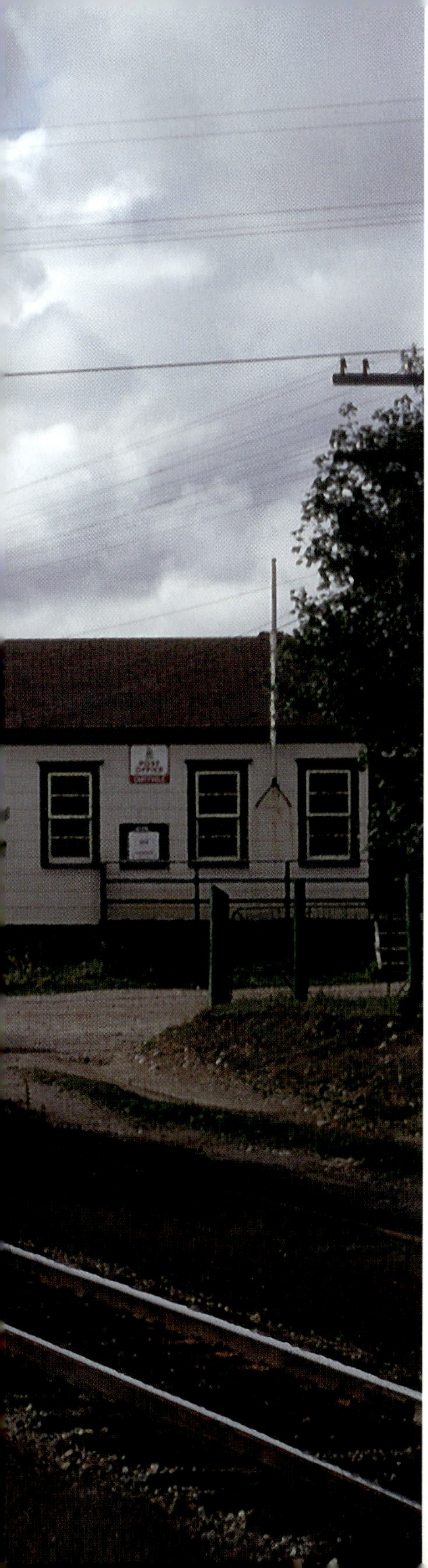

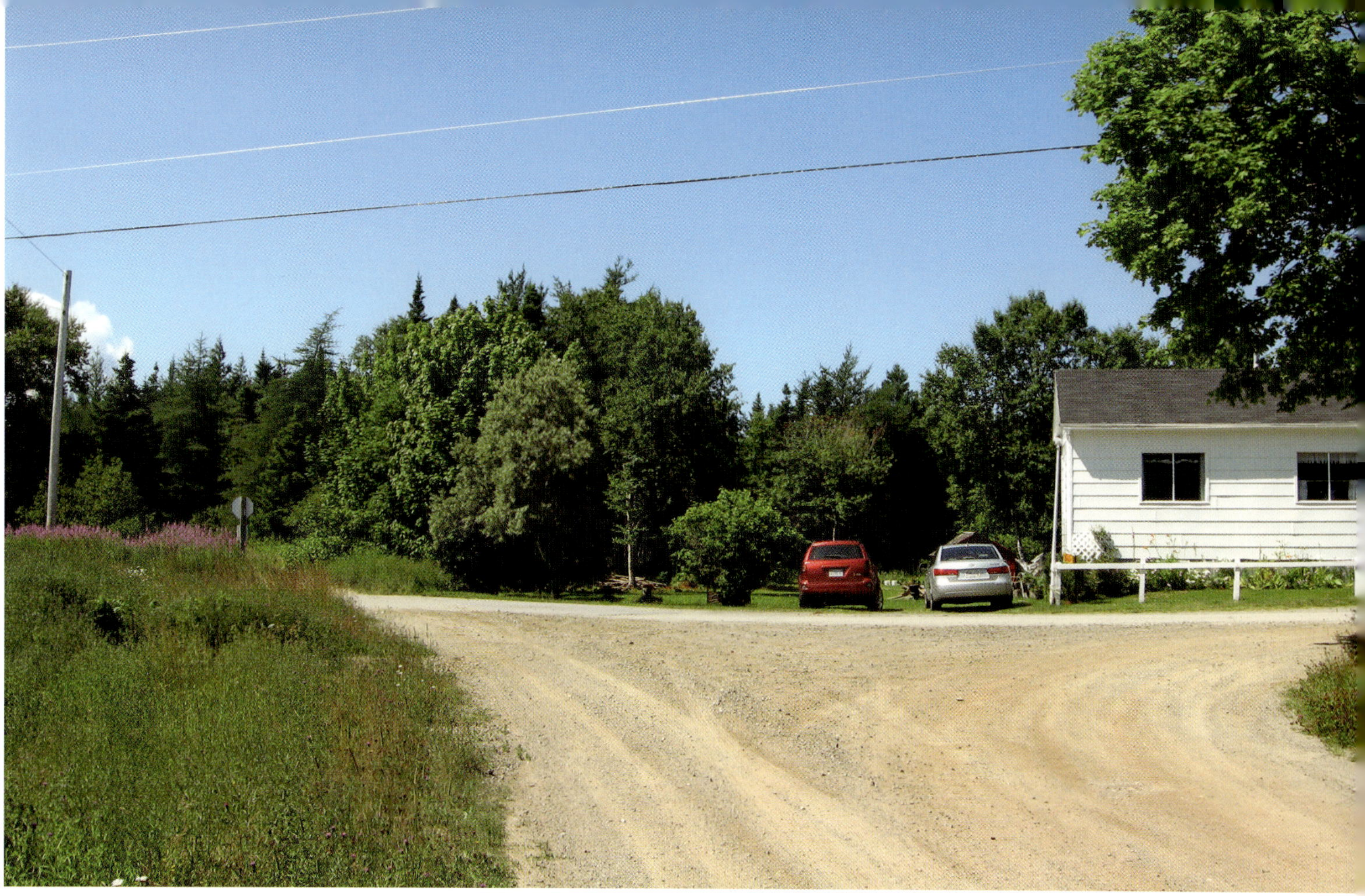

CARTYVILLE 1968
Engineer Kevin Byrne takes CN Train 102, the eastbound *Caribou* with NF210s 946 and 931, through Cartyville without stopping on October 6, 1968. Photographer Bill Linley with his friends Ted Wickson and Terry Thompson began chasing the *Caribou* from Port aux Basques in the morning and would continue to capture her until dusk fell at Deer Lake that evening. *Bill Linley photo*

CARTYVILLE TODAY
This small farming community was originally settled in 1830 by fishermen from Cape Breton and the Channel Islands. With the coming of the railway, people moved inland from the ocean shore and supplemented their livelihoods by growing crops and hay. In 1939, the Commission of Government built a freight-vegetable warehouse of which the farmers brought shares. *Author photo*

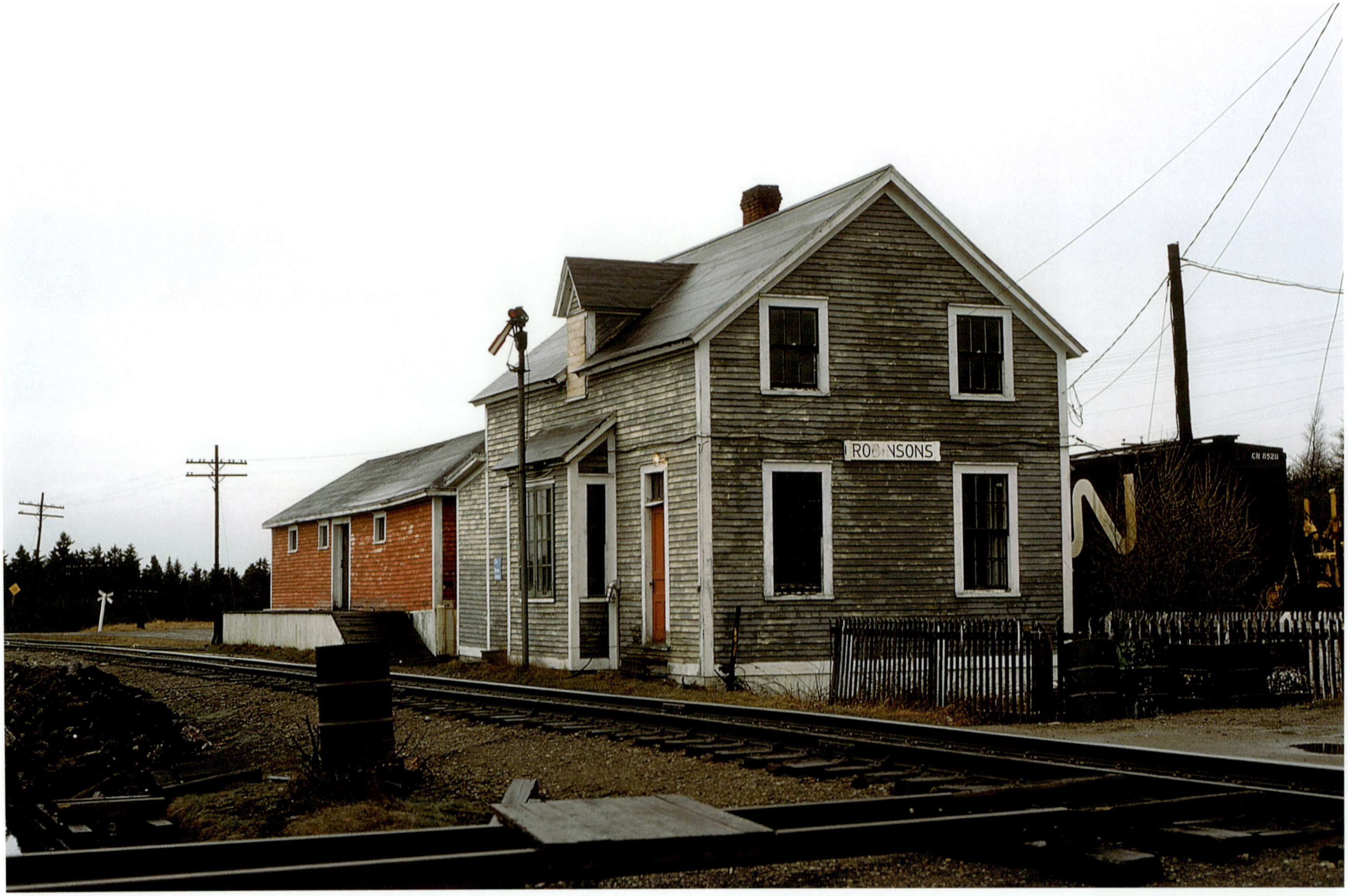

ROBINSONS 1975
Forty-foot steel boxcar CN 8528 keeps a lonely vigil behind the station and freight shed at Robinsons on a wet and rainy spring afternoon on May 8, 1975. This two storey station design, typically seen at many communities along the Newfoundland Railway, often had a siding run behind the building. It was in 1913 that Prince Albert, later to be King George VI, travelled by train to Robinsons River to catch a seven-pound salmon. *Phil Mason photo*

ROBINSONS TODAY
A small dog watches the author cautiously, daring not to proceed further near the site of the former station and freight shed where boxcar 8528 has long since been picked up. Originally called Second Barrisway, the early settlers were fishermen of Scottish and English decent. Many of their descendents moved to Robinsons Station in the 1890's and became involved with livestock and root farming because of the fertile ground in the area. *Author photo*

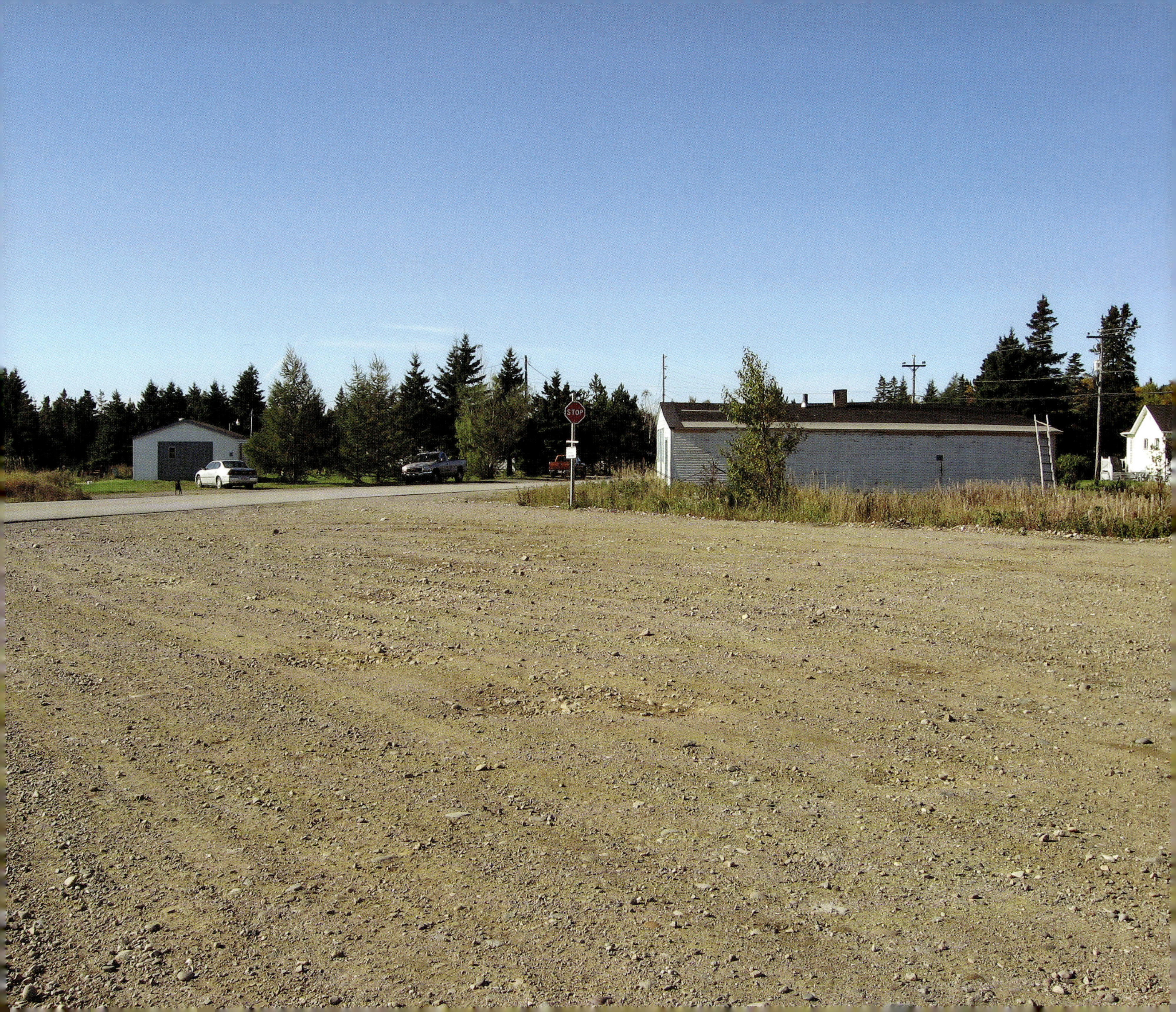
STOP

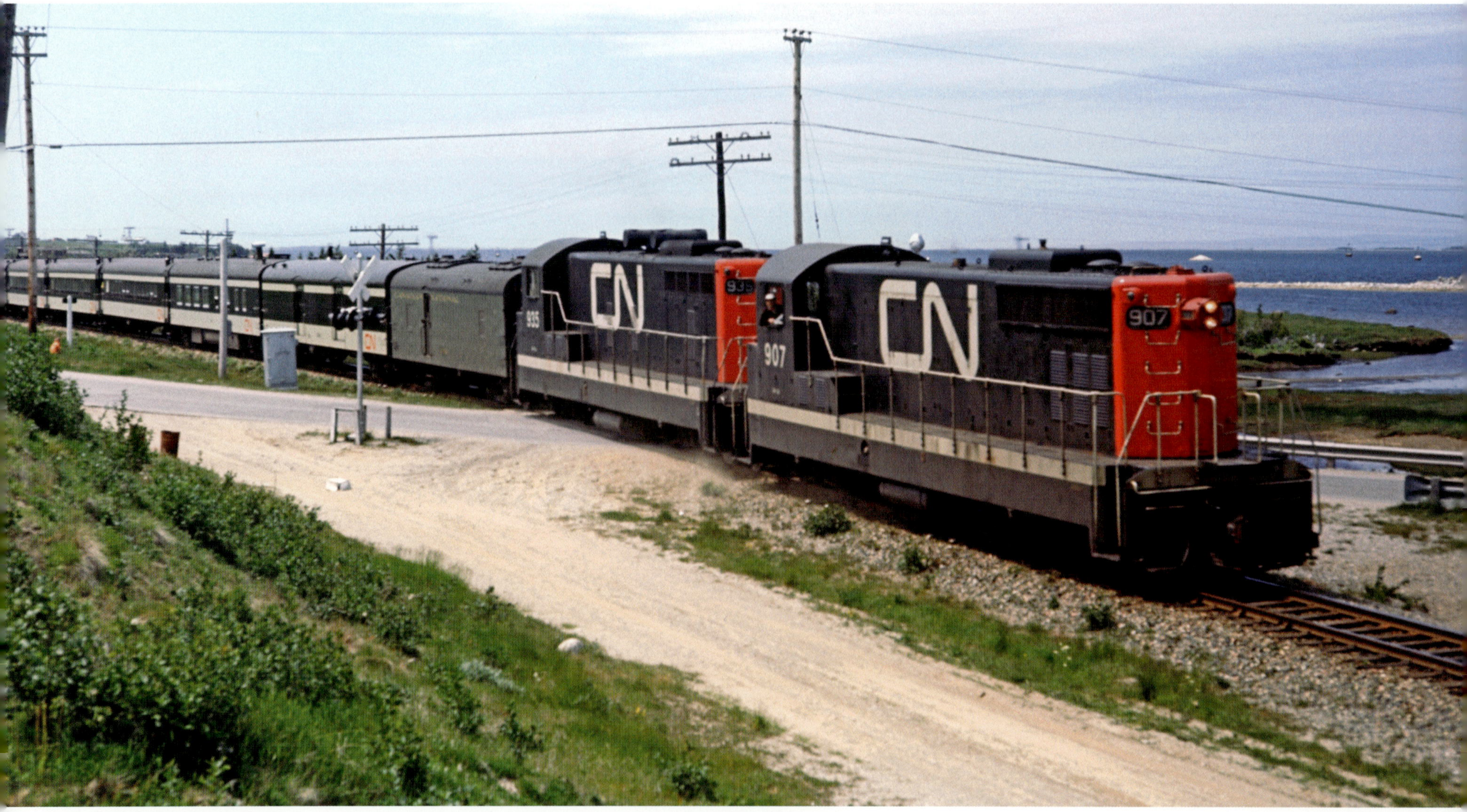

ST. GEORGE'S 1969
Engineer David Dicks opens the throttle on eastbound CN Train No. 102 hauled by NF110 907 and NF210 935 while crossing Highway 60 at St. George's on June 29, 1969, the last weekend for the *Caribou.* The Flinkote 'bucket line' which carried gypsum from Flat Bay for shipment and Sandy Point can be seen in the background. St. George's was the site of both the eastbound and westbound vegetable train due to the many farms nearby. *Robert J. Sandusky photo*

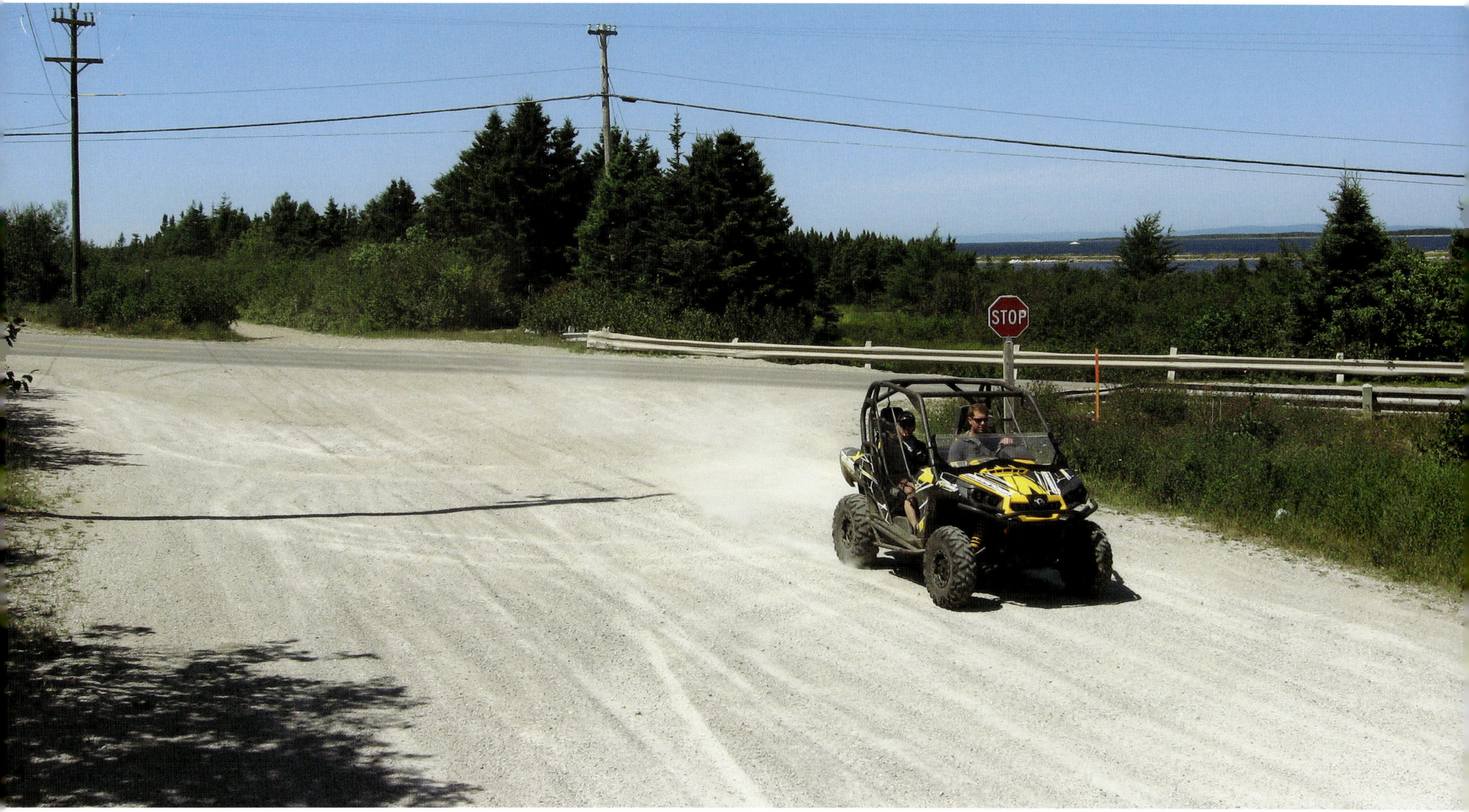

ST. GEORGE'S TODAY

As a warm summer breeze from the Gulf of St. Lawrence blows over Bay St. George, the driver of an all terrain side by side crosses route 60 and proceeds on the former right of way. Until the US Air Force Base was constructed in Stephenville in 1941, St.George's was the major centre of the entire bay. It was here in 1975 at age 12 that the author took his first ever train photograph, with a Brownie 127 camera. *Author photo*

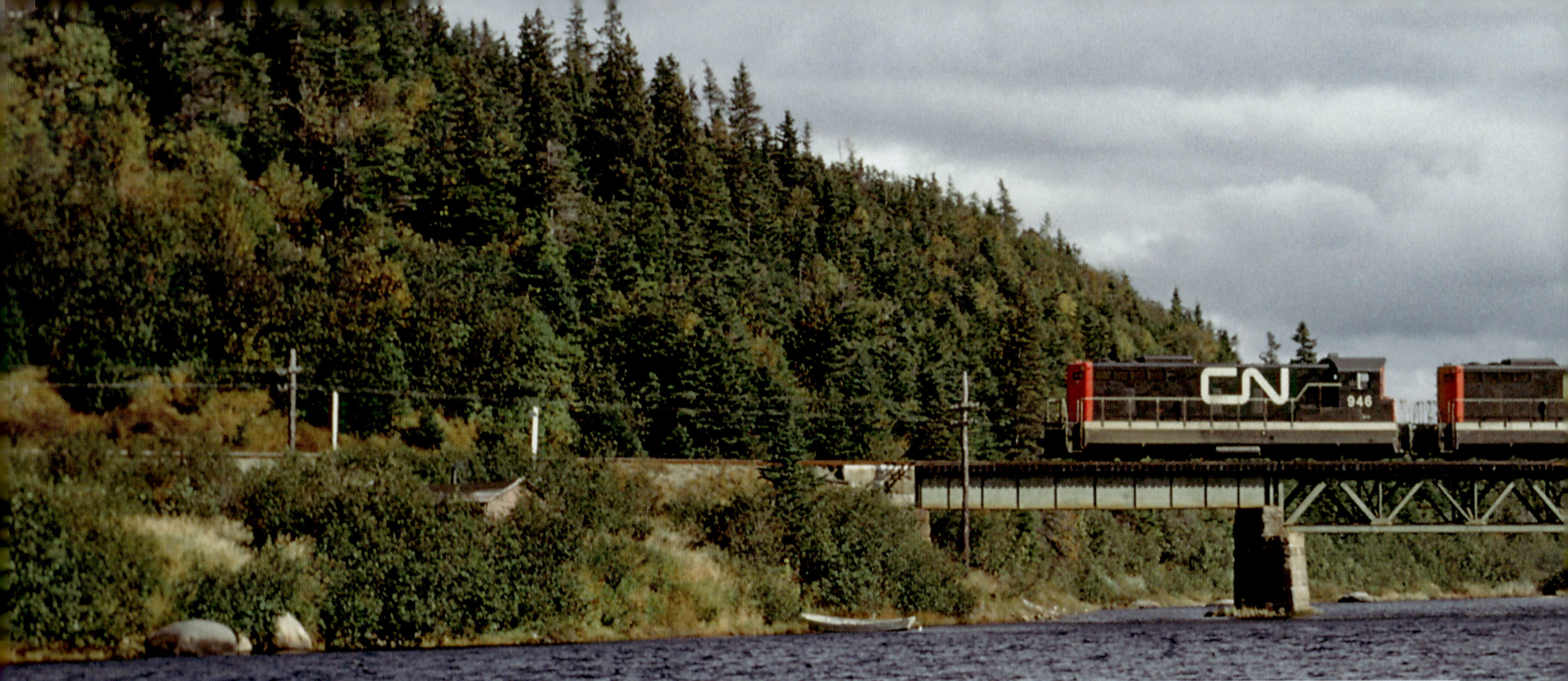
CN
946
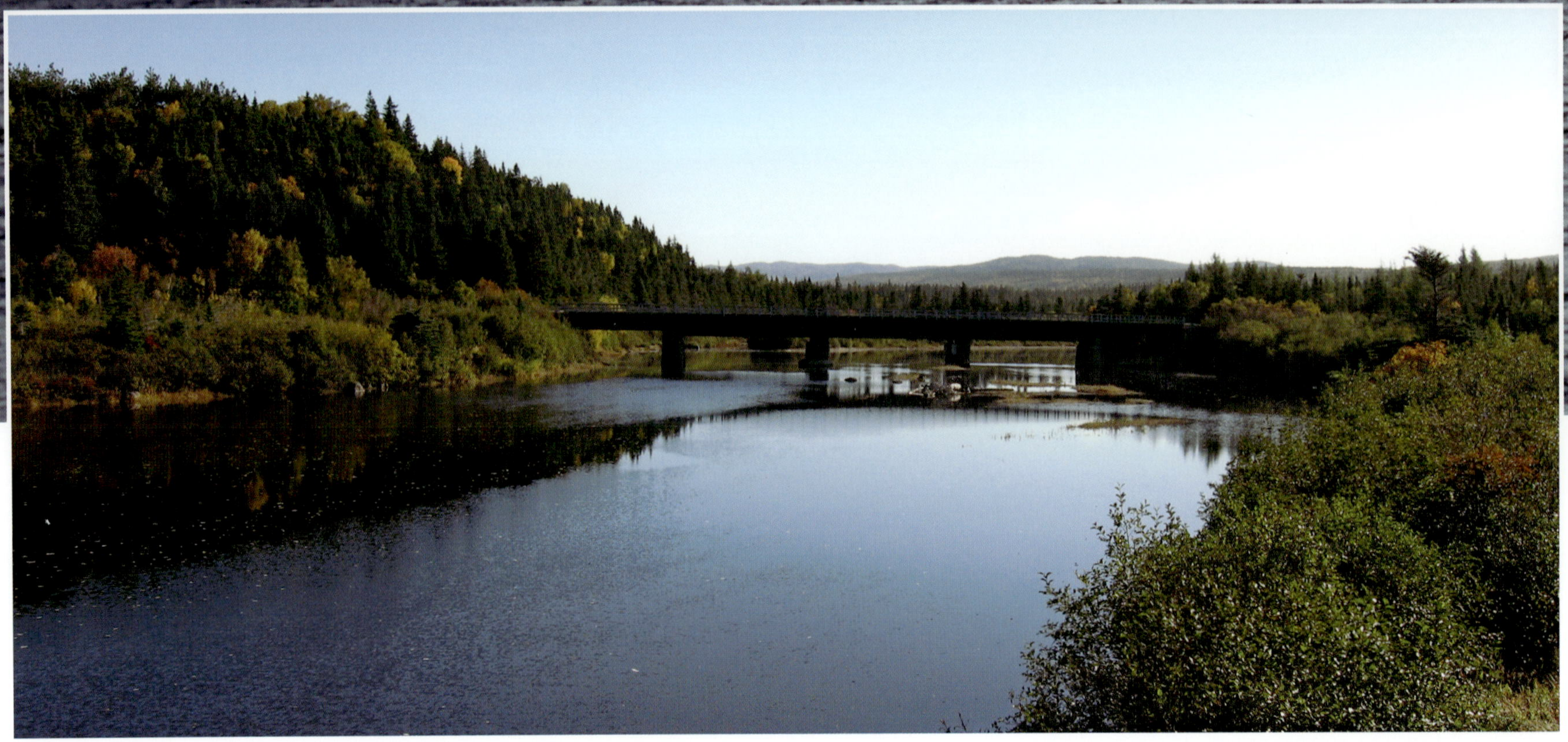

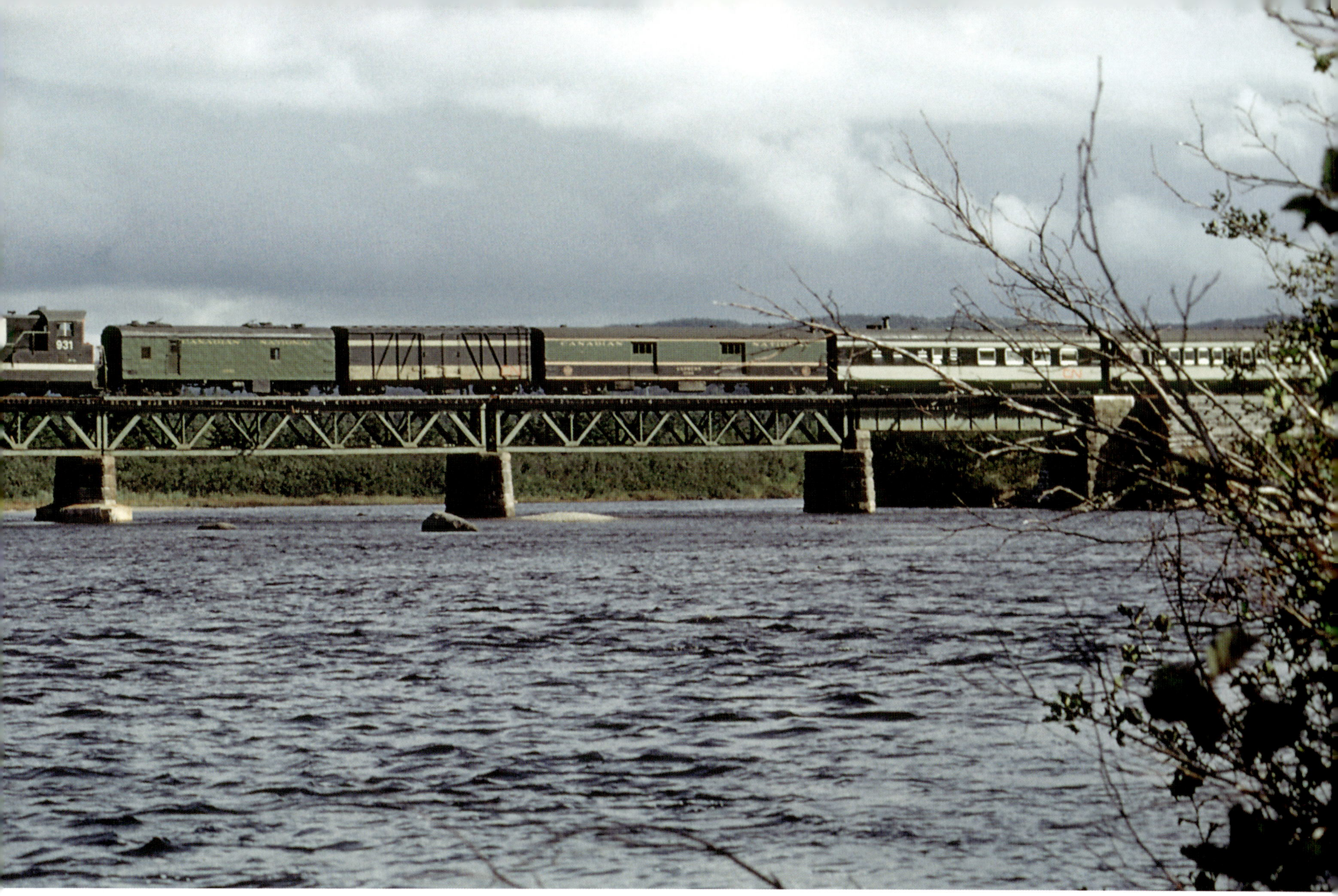

BARACHOIS BROOK TODAY

The steel trusses in the railway bridge over Barachois Brook Bridge have since been replaced. With the wooden safety rails updated post-shutdown, it is perfectly suited for pedestrians crossing on this calm and cool October morning. This tiny community, with a population of 300 recorded in the latest census, until recently was the location of the RCMP Detachment for the surrounding area. Back in the day, the trains ran right in front of it. *Author photo*

BARACHOIS BROOK 1968

CN Train No. 102, the eastbound *Caribou* with locos 946 & 931, catches the late afternoon sun on the 5 span Little Barachois Bridge on October 6, 1968. Photographer Ted Wickson would continue to chase and photograph this train until he boarded it at Deer Lake later in the evening for a meal in the diner and a ride to Windsor. *Ted Wickson photo*

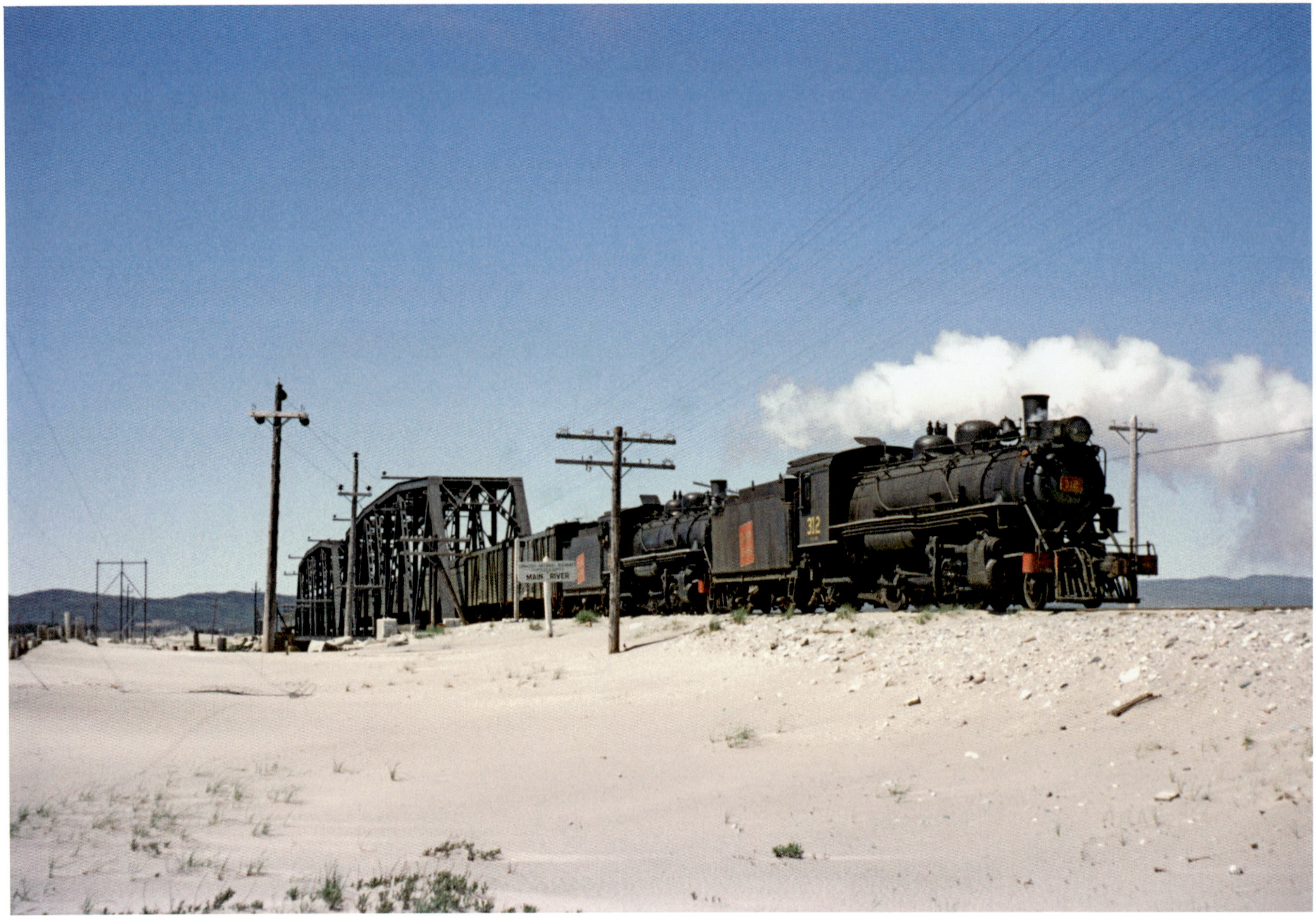

MAIN RIVER 1956

CNR Train No. 1 with 2-8-2 Mikado's 312 and 317 leading the passenger consist across the Main River on June 24, 1956. The sandy soil is typical for this part of Bay St. George and the Mikado's would continue operating until the arrival of five steam generator cars later that summer. Built by CNR Moncton, they would provide heat to the coaches to allow the new diesels to head the trains. *Robert J. Sandusky photo*

MAIN RIVER TODAY

A famous landmark in the Stephenville Crossing area, the old 'Gut Bridge,' rebuilt in the 1940s, still stands proudly. A testament to the engineering spirit of the early days of railroading, it had a lift span in operation until 1901. Until completion of the new parallel highway bridge in 1972, autos crossed the river one at a time by way of a single lane wooden attachment to the former. *Author photo*

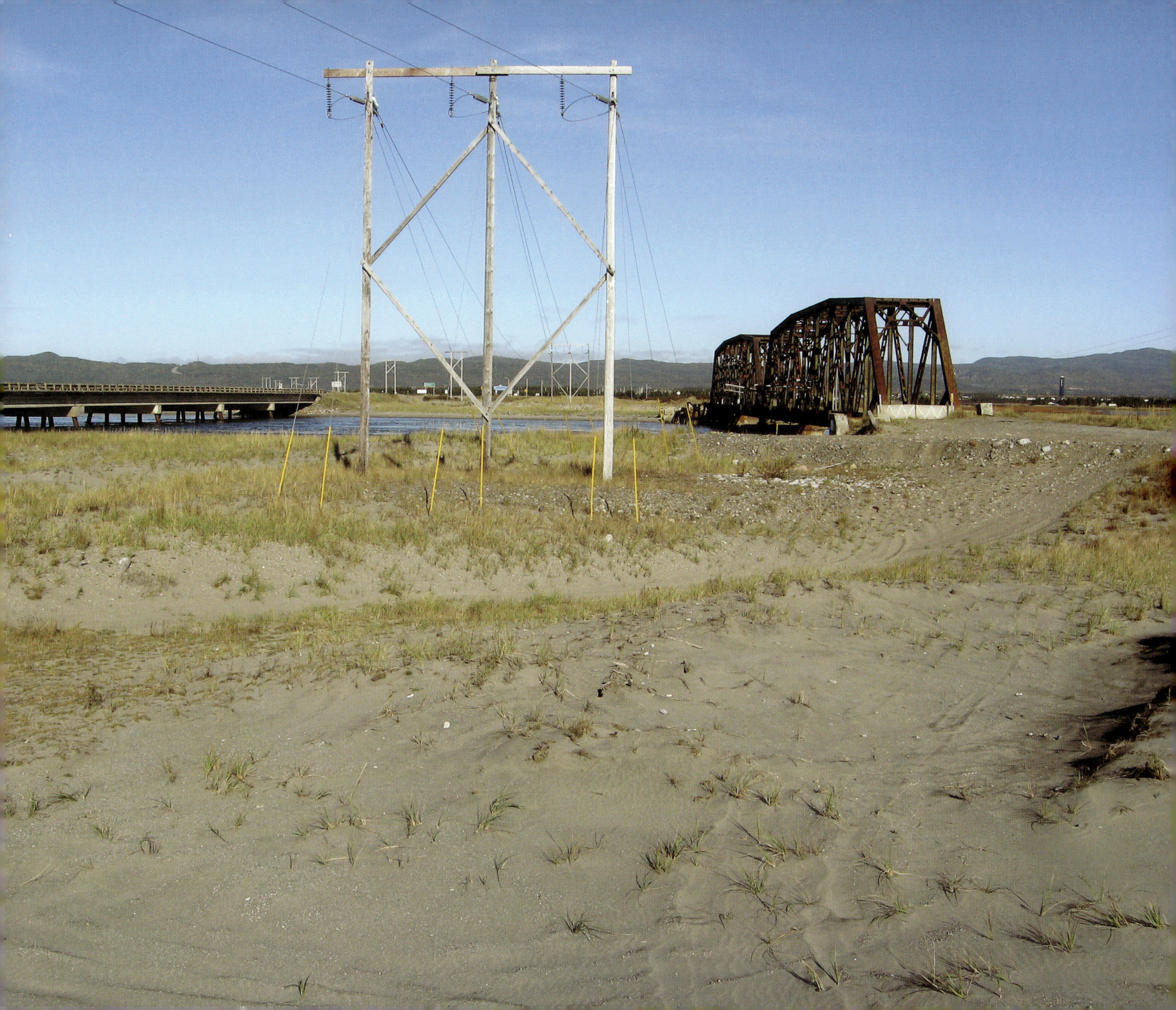

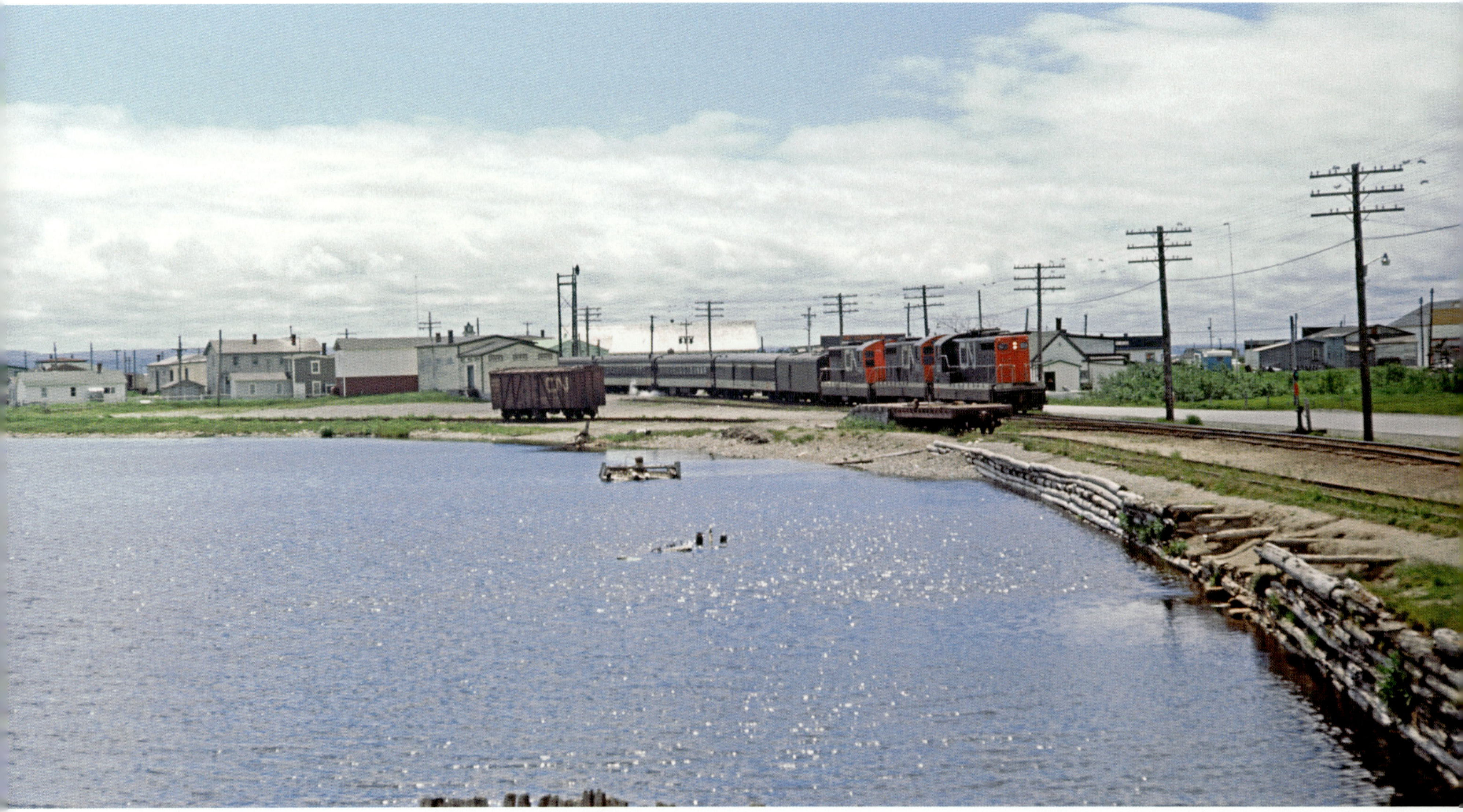

STEPHENVILLE CROSSING 1969

Locos 923, 910 & 906 leave Stephenville Crossing with the last 102 on July 2, 1969. The consist for the run included a steam generator car, one baggage car, four coaches, two dining cars and eight sleeping cars. A sole boxcar to the right has been pushed off its truck, almost as a silent protest to the loss of passenger service. *Robert J. Sandusky photo*

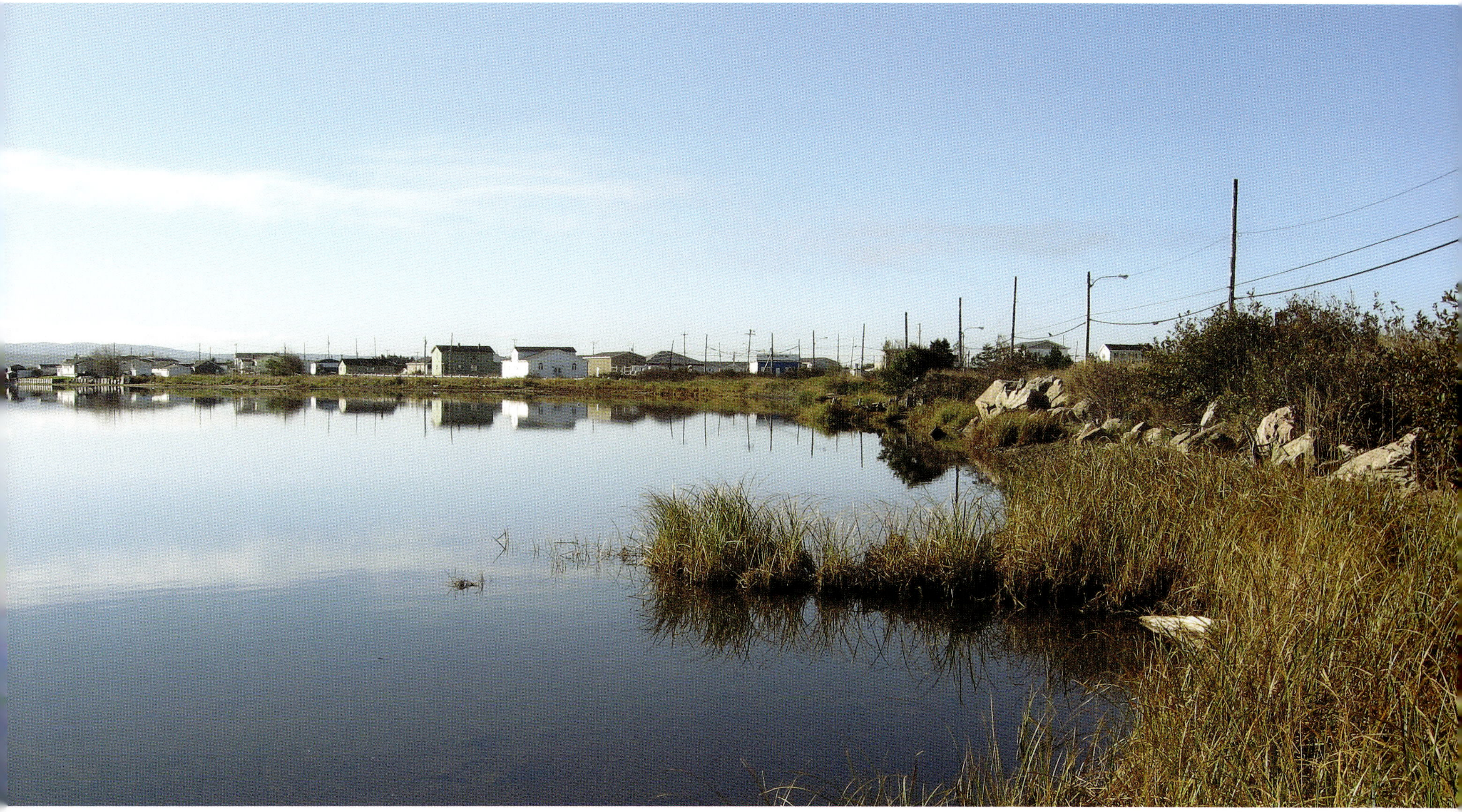

STEPHENVILLE CROSSING TODAY

The houses of Stephenville Crossing are reflected in an almost perfect mirror image early on a cool crisp fall morning. Although the railway station was demolished, the adjacent Canadian National Telegraph building has been expanded as the home of the Barachois Ground Search and Rescue unit. This area is known for its wetlands habitat and conservation of protected species such as the endangered Piping Plover. *Author photo*

WHITE'S ROAD 1975

With the white flags on the nose of NF210 914 indicating its designation, CN Extra 914 West passes through the mainline at White's Road, the junction for the 9-mile branch to Stephenville, on May 8, 1975. Constructed by the USAF to connect the Earnest Harmon Air Force Base to the CNR, and officially the Gull Lake Railway, it was locally known as the 'Loose Moose Line'. *Phil Mason photo*

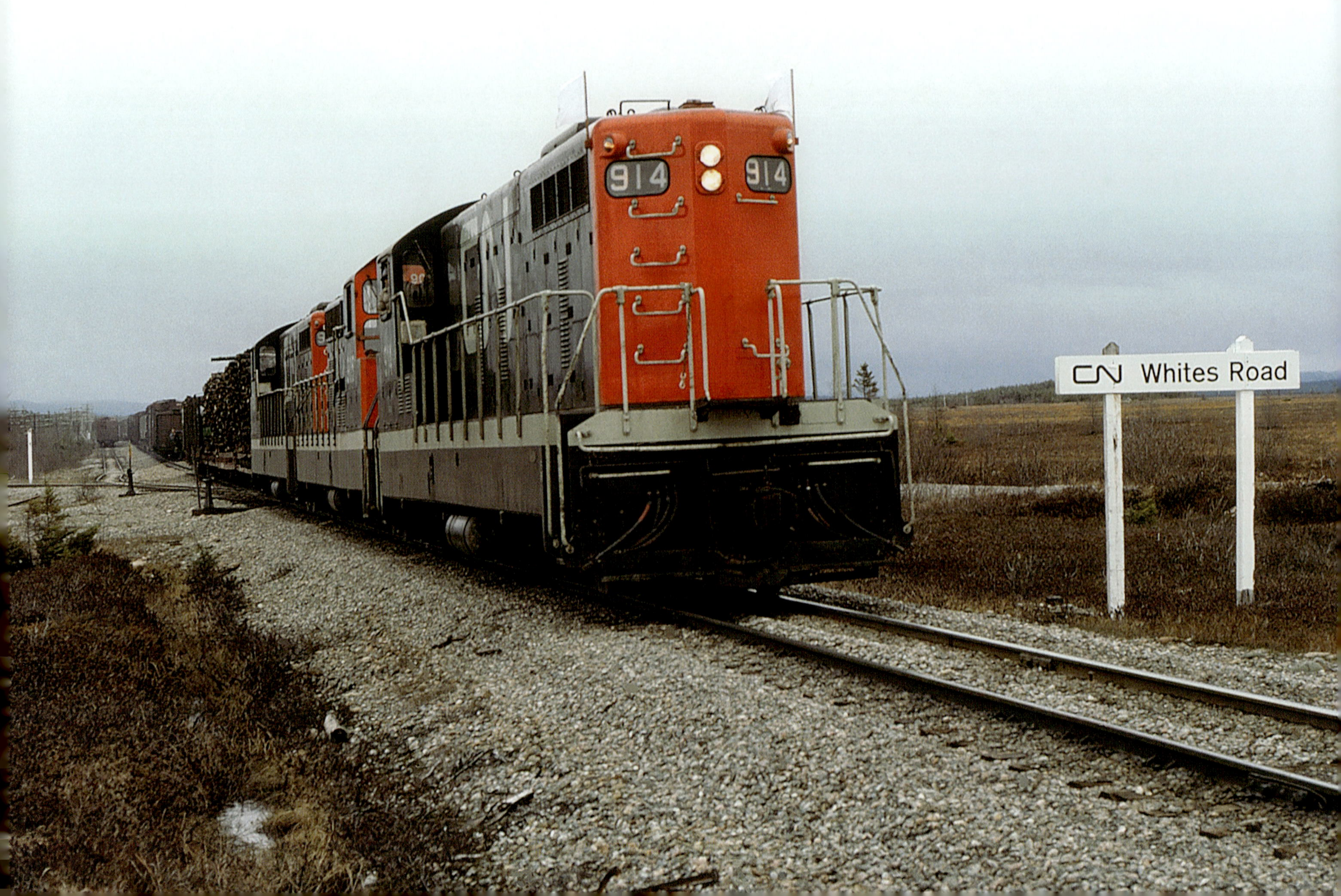

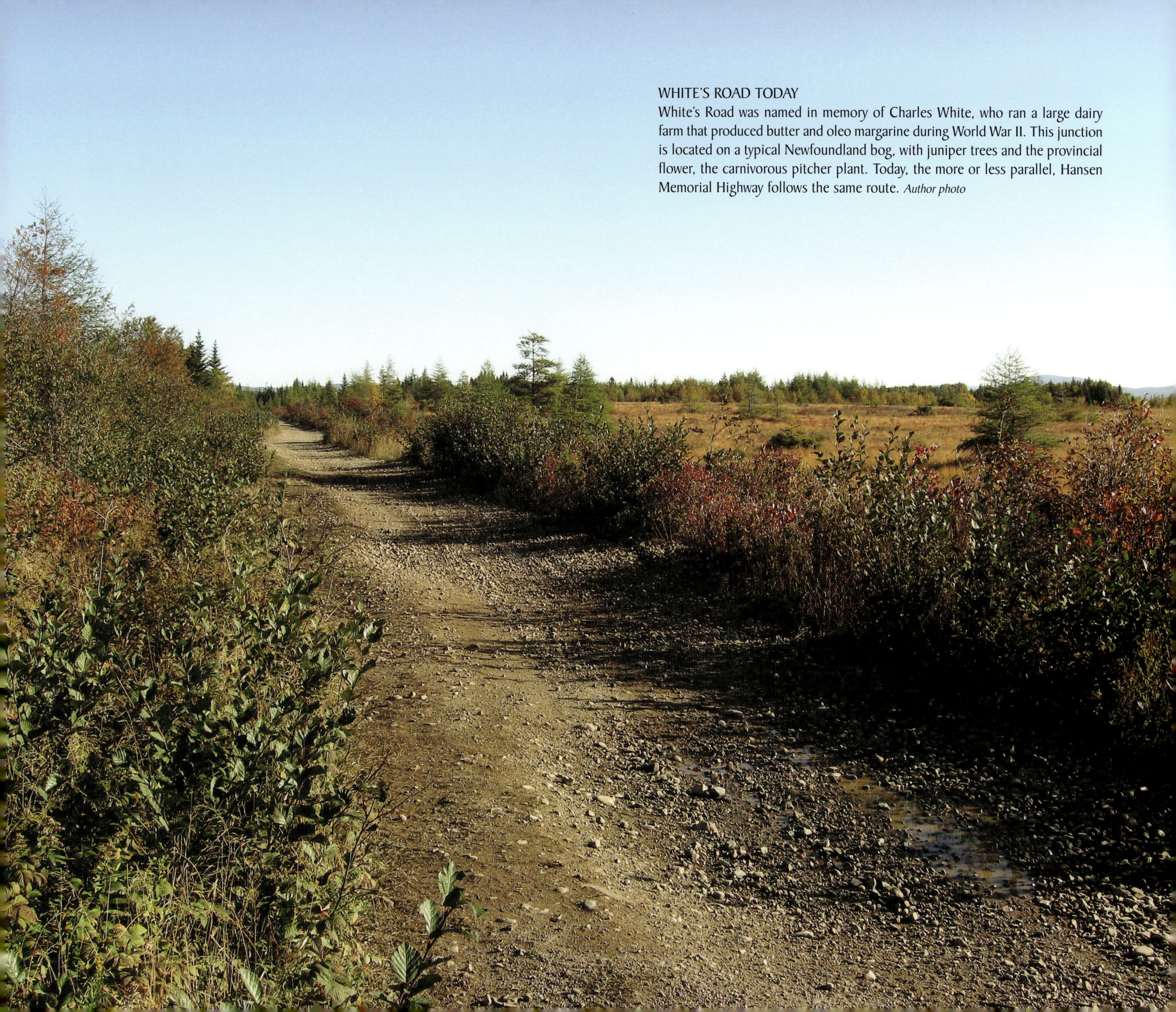

WHITE'S ROAD TODAY

White's Road was named in memory of Charles White, who ran a large dairy farm that produced butter and oleo margarine during World War II. This junction is located on a typical Newfoundland bog, with juniper trees and the provincial flower, the carnivorous pitcher plant. Today, the more or less parallel, Hansen Memorial Highway follows the same route. *Author photo*

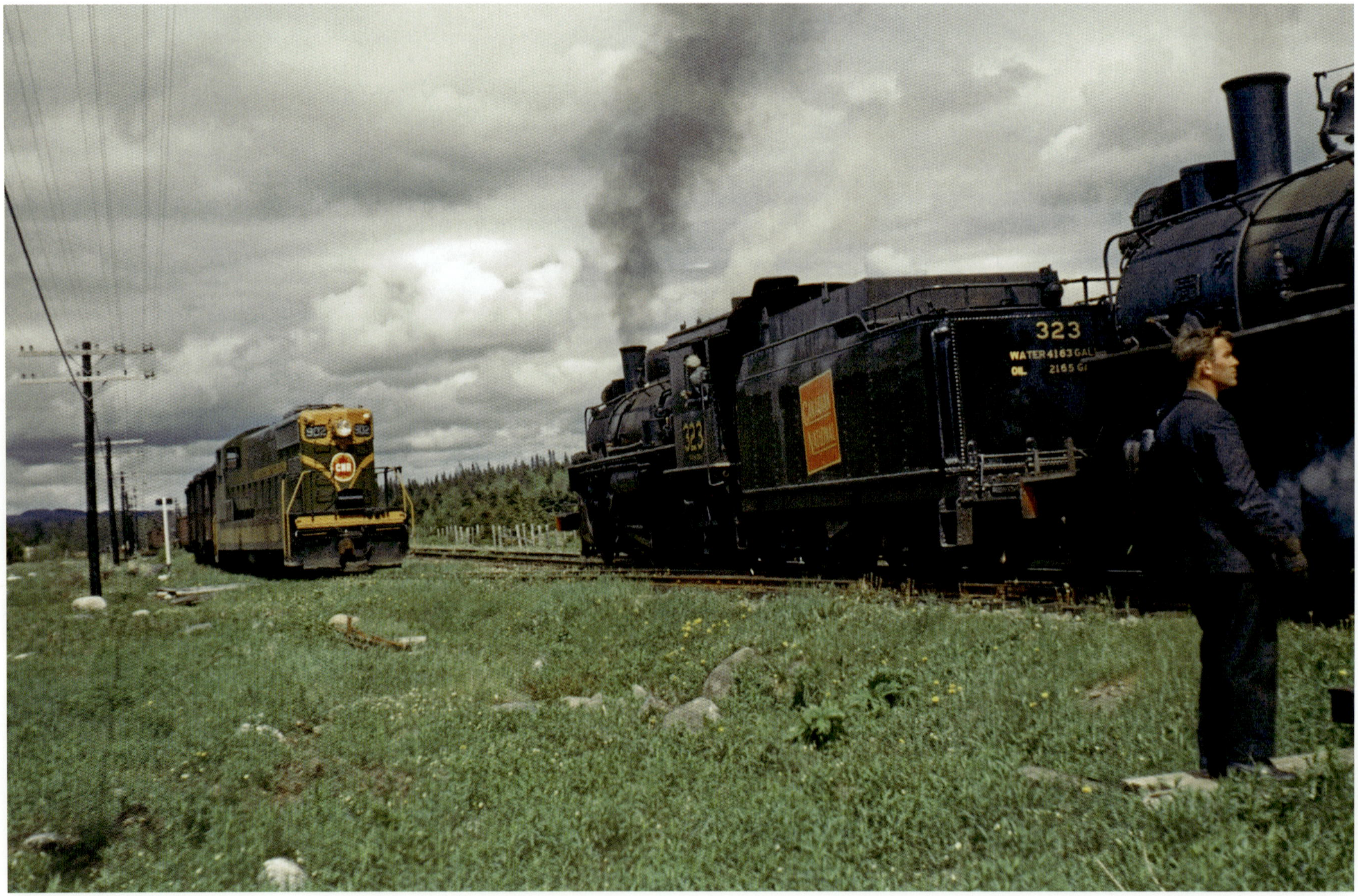

HARRY'S BROOK 1956
NF 110 902 meets the eastbound *Caribou* headed by 2-8-2 Mikado 323, while trainman Bert Kelly keeps a watchful eye, on June 24, 1956. This was part of a four way meet involving two passenger trains and two freights. 902 was the third of three diesels to arrive in January of 1953 and would forever change the face of railroading in Canada's newest province.
Robert J. Sandusky photo

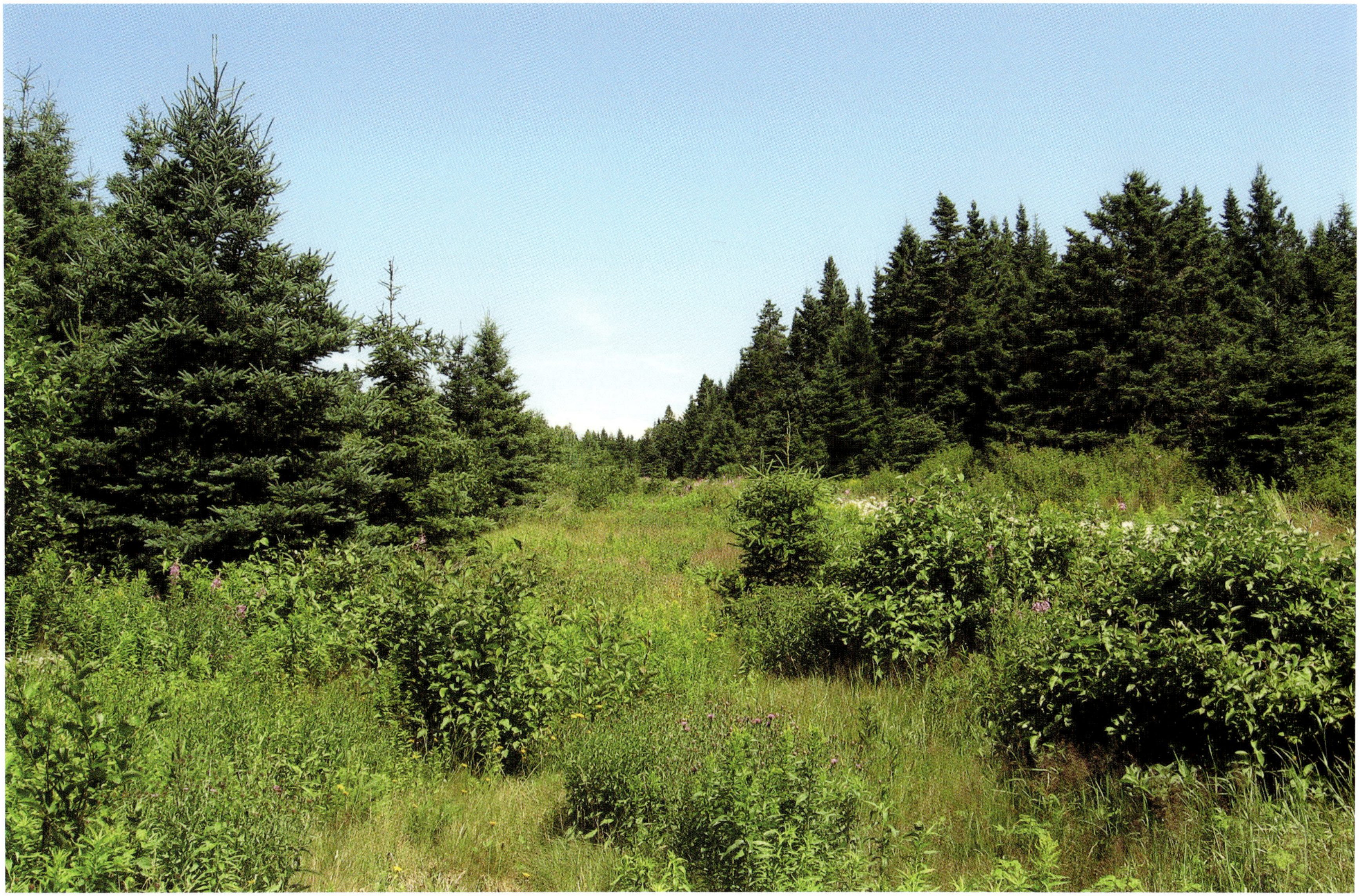

HARRY'S BROOK TODAY

Sixty years of fir and spruce growth have made the Harry's Brook area nearly unrecognizable, were it not for the odometer reading taken on the author's pickup at the Gallants Bridge and using the timetable as a reference. Known as the 'River Run', today the forests have obscured the view of one of Newfoundland's most famous salmon rivers. The two Mikados were sent to the scrap heap by 1957 but 902 lives on in a static display at the Lewisporte Train Park. *Author photo*

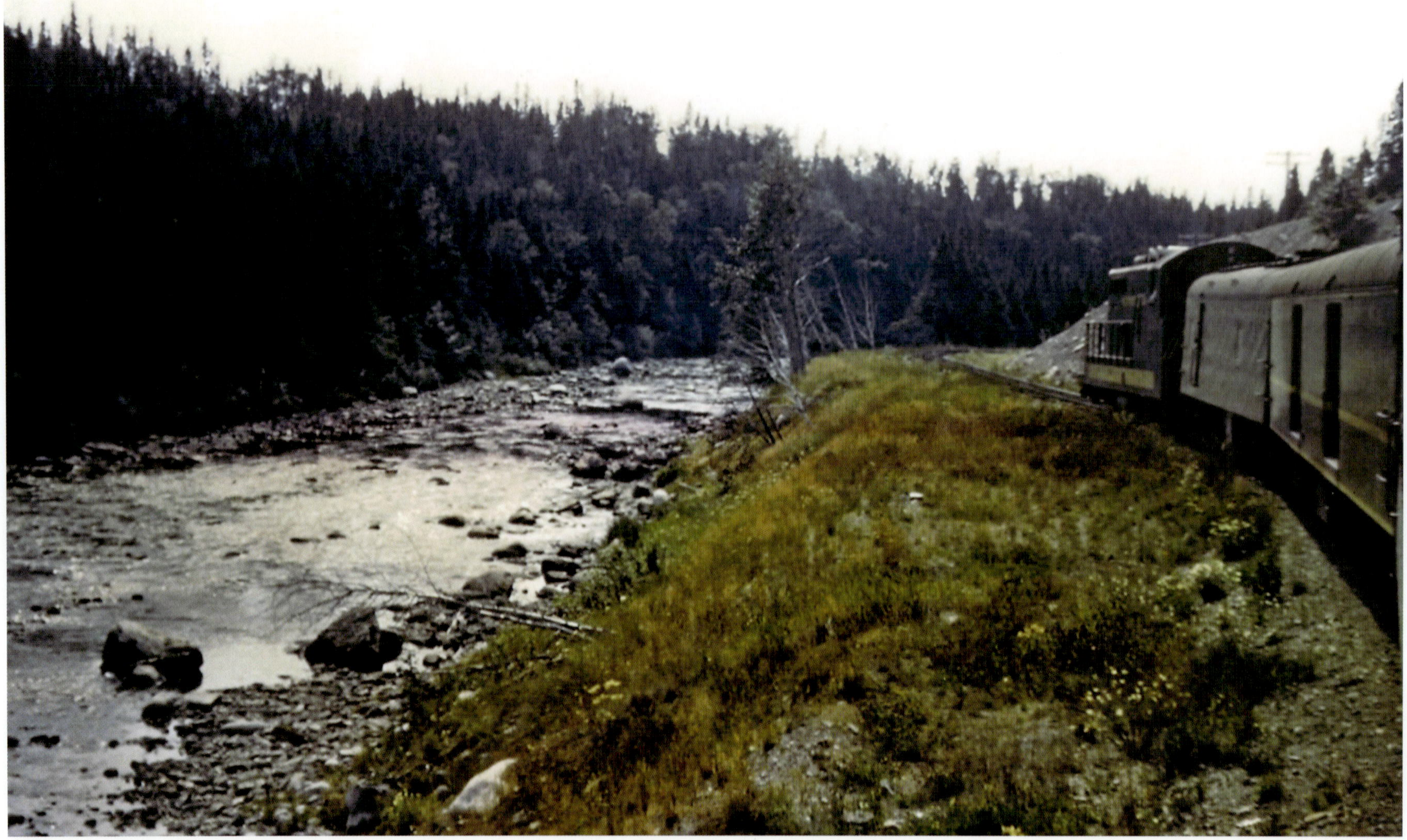

GALLANTS 1961
CNR Train No. 1 with single unit NF210 926 on the head end meanders around Harrys River near Gallants in August of 1961. Sixteen-year-old Bob Coolidge, en route to Boston after a week of visiting his Newfoundland relatives, captured the *Caribou* in her most handsome paint scheme of green, black and yellow. The train was already several hours behind schedule due to the terrible forest fires that ravaged the province in 1961, but none the less still managed to carry 150,000 passengers that year. *Bob Coolidge photo*

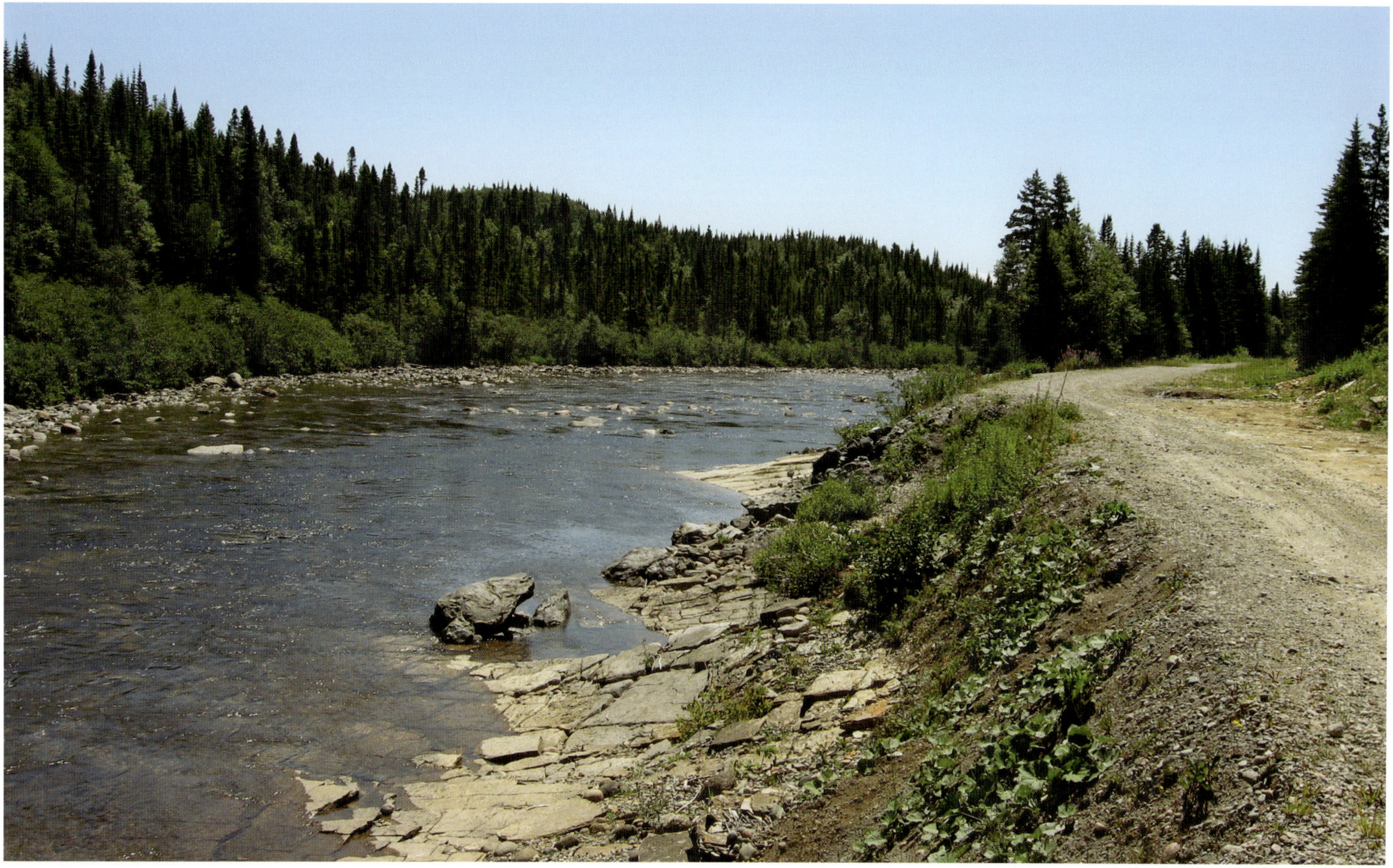

GALLANTS TODAY

Fifty years of storms and the effects of nature have eroded the right of way near Ledge Pool. Ice jams even relocated some of the boulders further downstream in this very popular crystal-clear fishing spot, often teeming with wild Atlantic salmon. The logging community of Gallants was home to a siding called Cleary in which trains were loaded with pulpwood for the mill in Corner Brook. *Author photo*

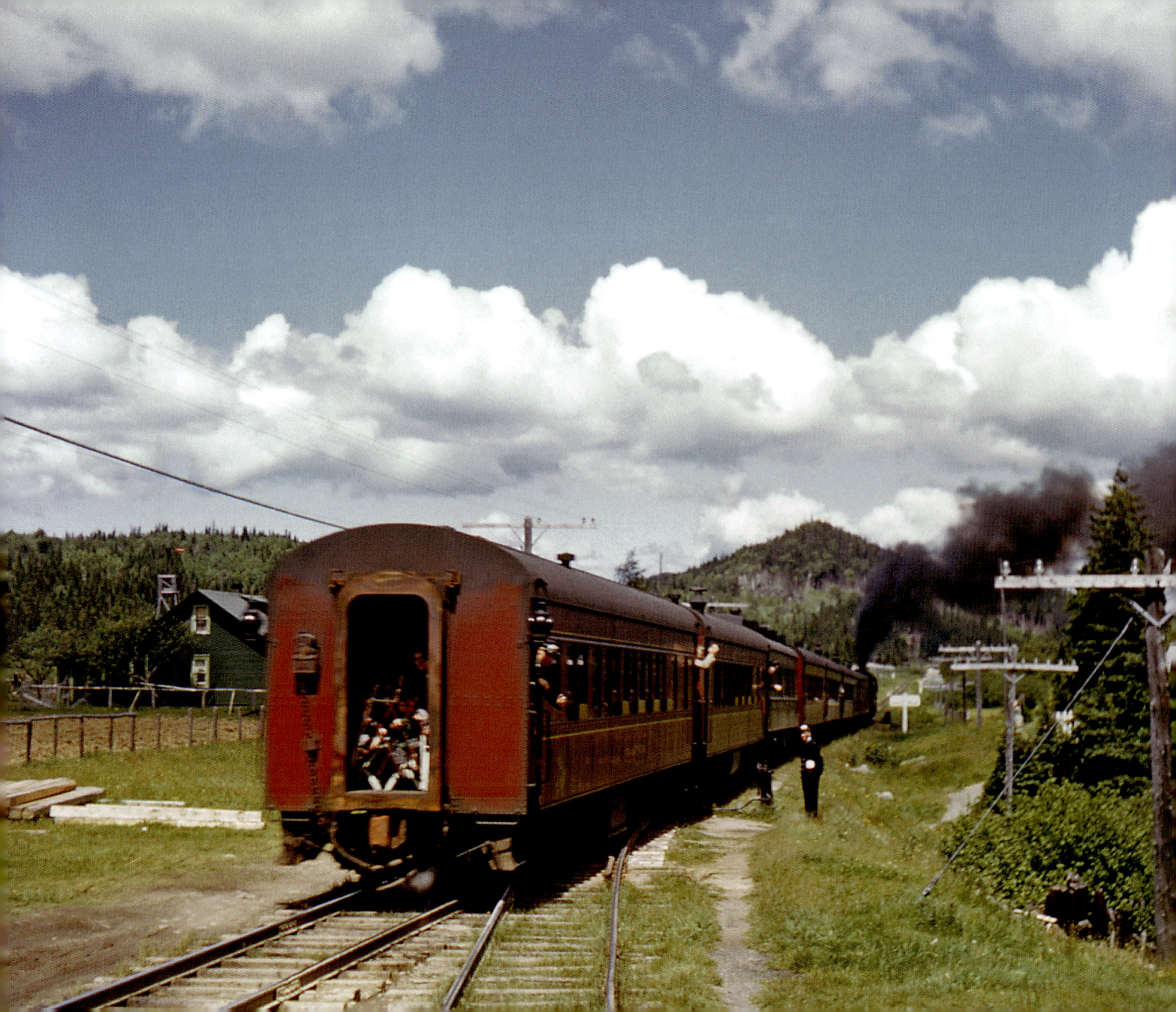

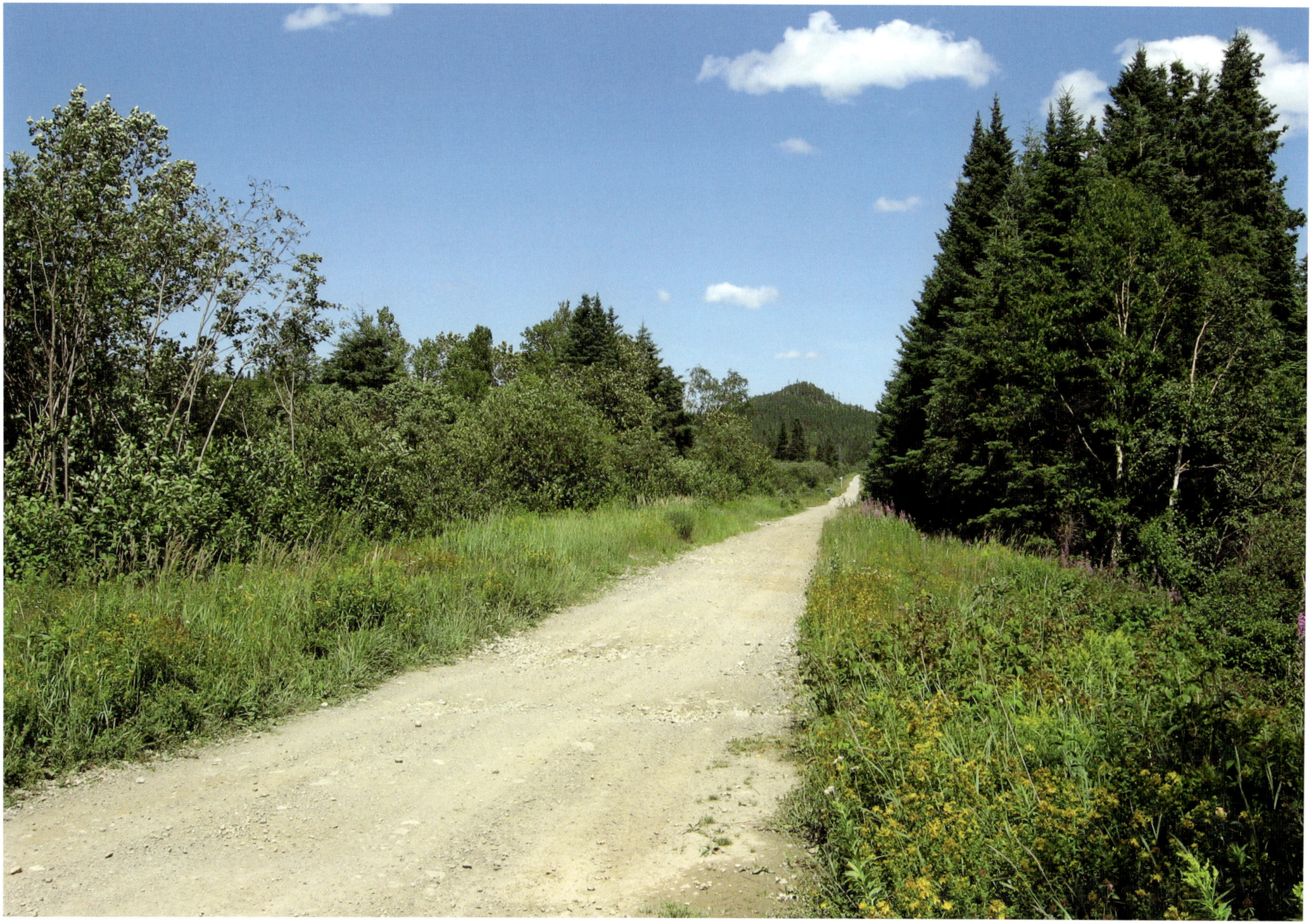

SPRUCE BROOK 1952

CNR Train No. 2 with nearly all the cars in the red livery of the pre-Confederation Newfoundland Railway, clears the mainline at Spruce Brook while No. 1 holds the siding on June 25, 1952. Omer Lavellee of Quebec, one of Canada's most distinguished railway historians, captures this scene during his first of two visits to record in colour the final years of steam operations in Newfoundland. *Omer Lavelle photo*

SPRUCE BROOK TODAY

The tiny community that housed seventeen families in the 1945 census has become home to many cottages and cabins for those wishing to escape the often hectic urban lifestyle. Spruce Brook once had a spur for loading wood for the Bowaters operation. It is also here that railway machinist Ted Hickey built a working model of NF210 943 that runs on 1800 feet of track. *Author photo*

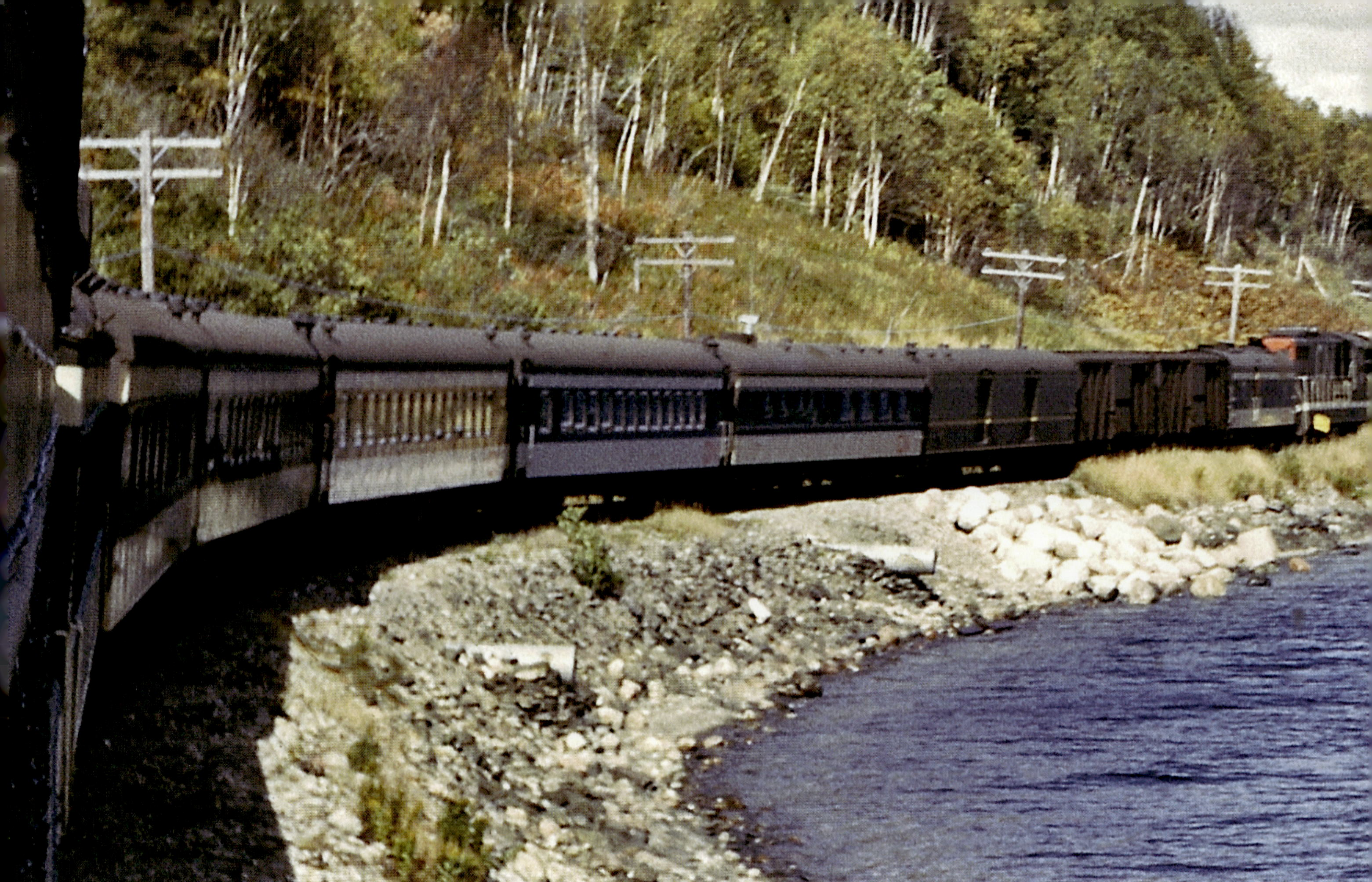

GEORGE'S LAKE 1966

The *Caribou* follows the shores of Georges Lake on route to Corner Brook on September 13, 1966. Upon arrival, a third diesel and four additional coaches will be added to handle the many students returning to Memorial University in St. John's. Eminent railway historian Jim Scribbins, who spent a career with the Milwaukee Road, would travel and photograph along the entire route of No. 102 with his wife. *Jim Scribbins photo*

GEORGES LAKE TODAY

The lush green forested hills tower over the right of way near one of the most pristine lakes in the Province. A boaters paradise, it is one of the most desired locations for a cottage on the west coast. Just around this turn was the station of Howards where wood trains were dispatched from Humbermouth to pick up pulpwood from the summer and fall loading camp operated by George Rowe. *Author photo*

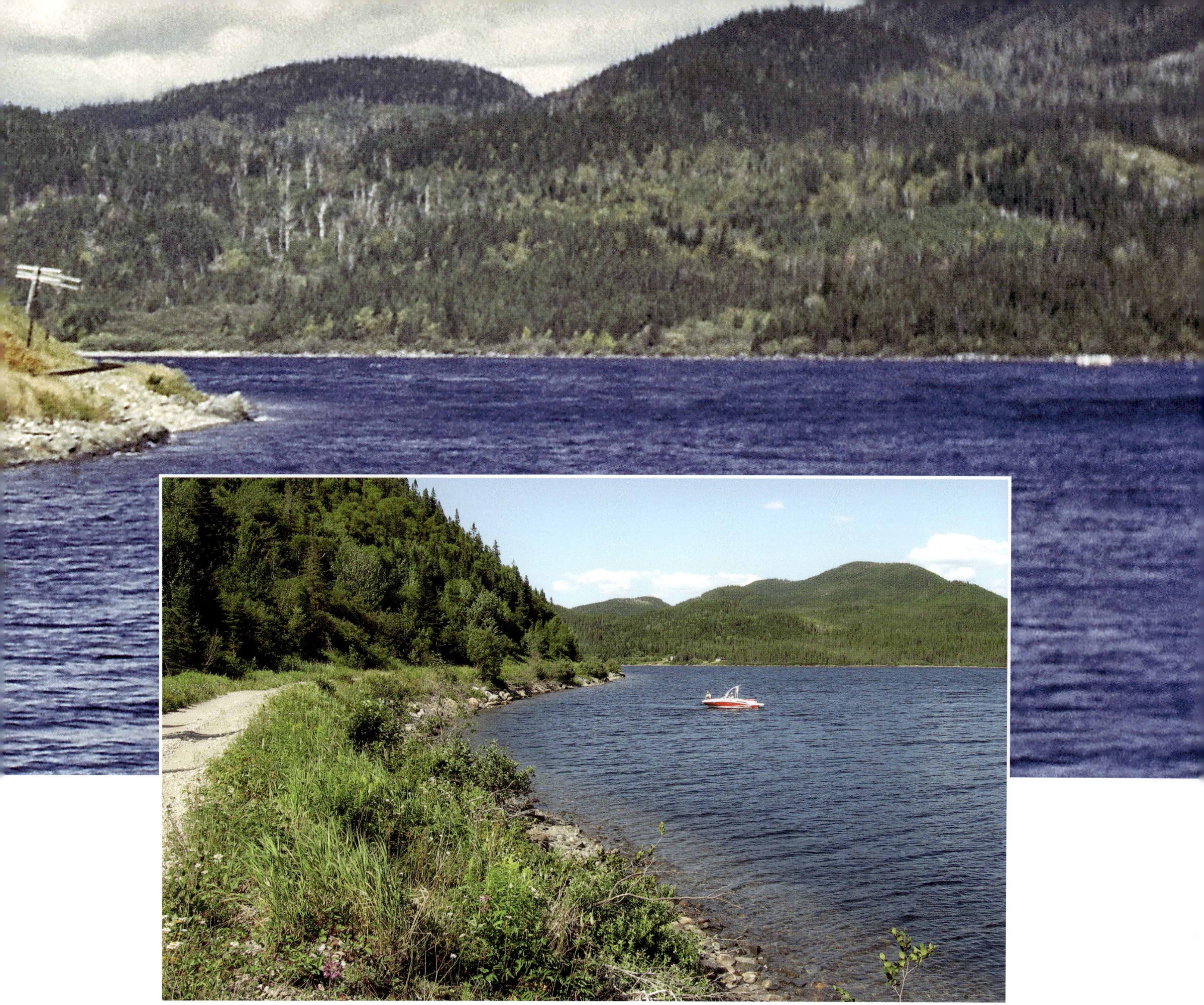

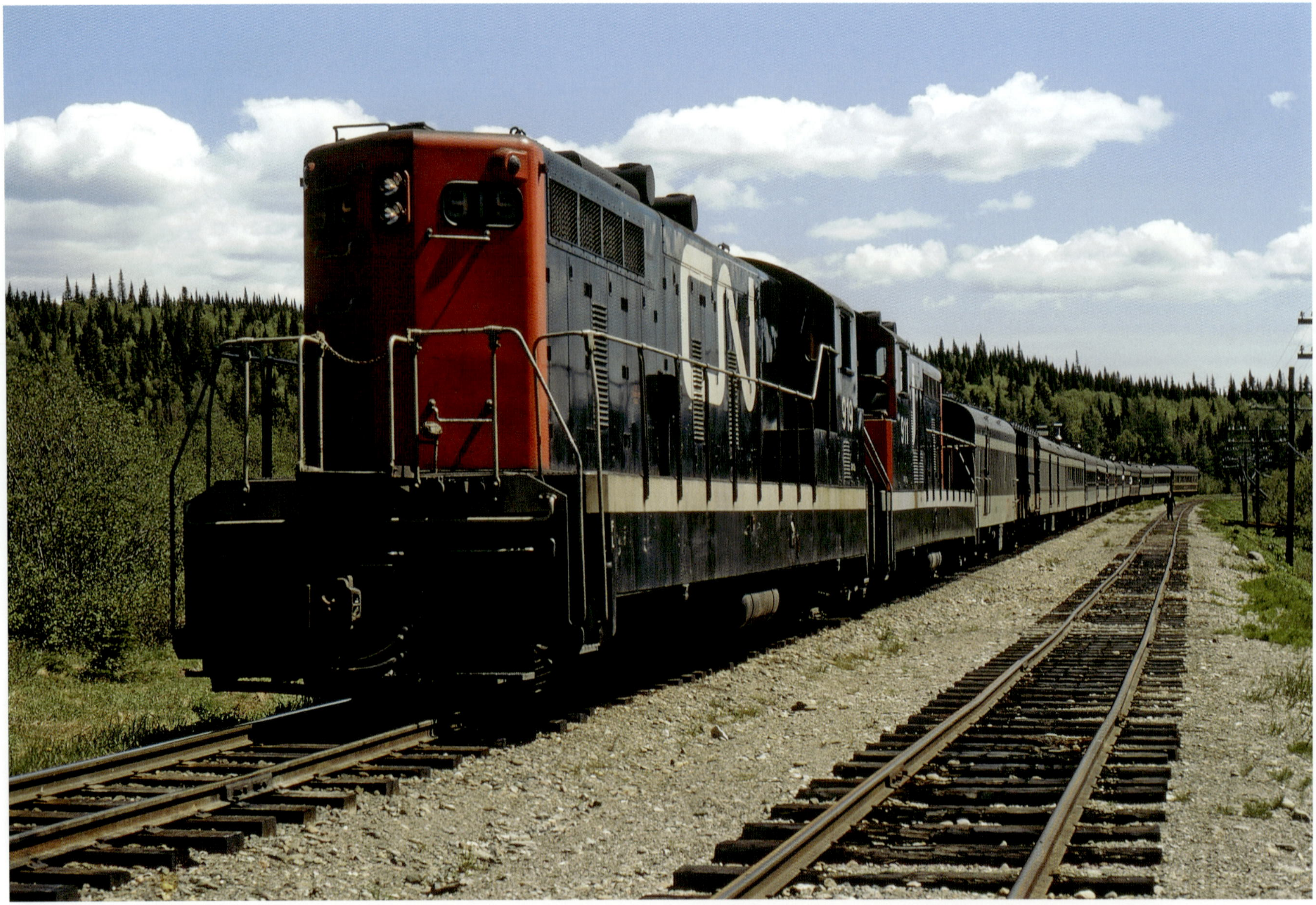

COOKE 1967

NF210's 919 and 911 head the eastbound *Caribou* at Cooke on June 20, 1967. No. 102, with a 13-car consist, waits on the mainline for its designated timetable meet with westbound No. 101 before proceeding on to Corner Brook. Before long, NF210 925, adorned in the green and gold, will appear and lead 101 on to the siding, allowing engineer Kevin Byrne and 102 to resume their trans-Island journey on this beautiful day. *James A. Brown photo*

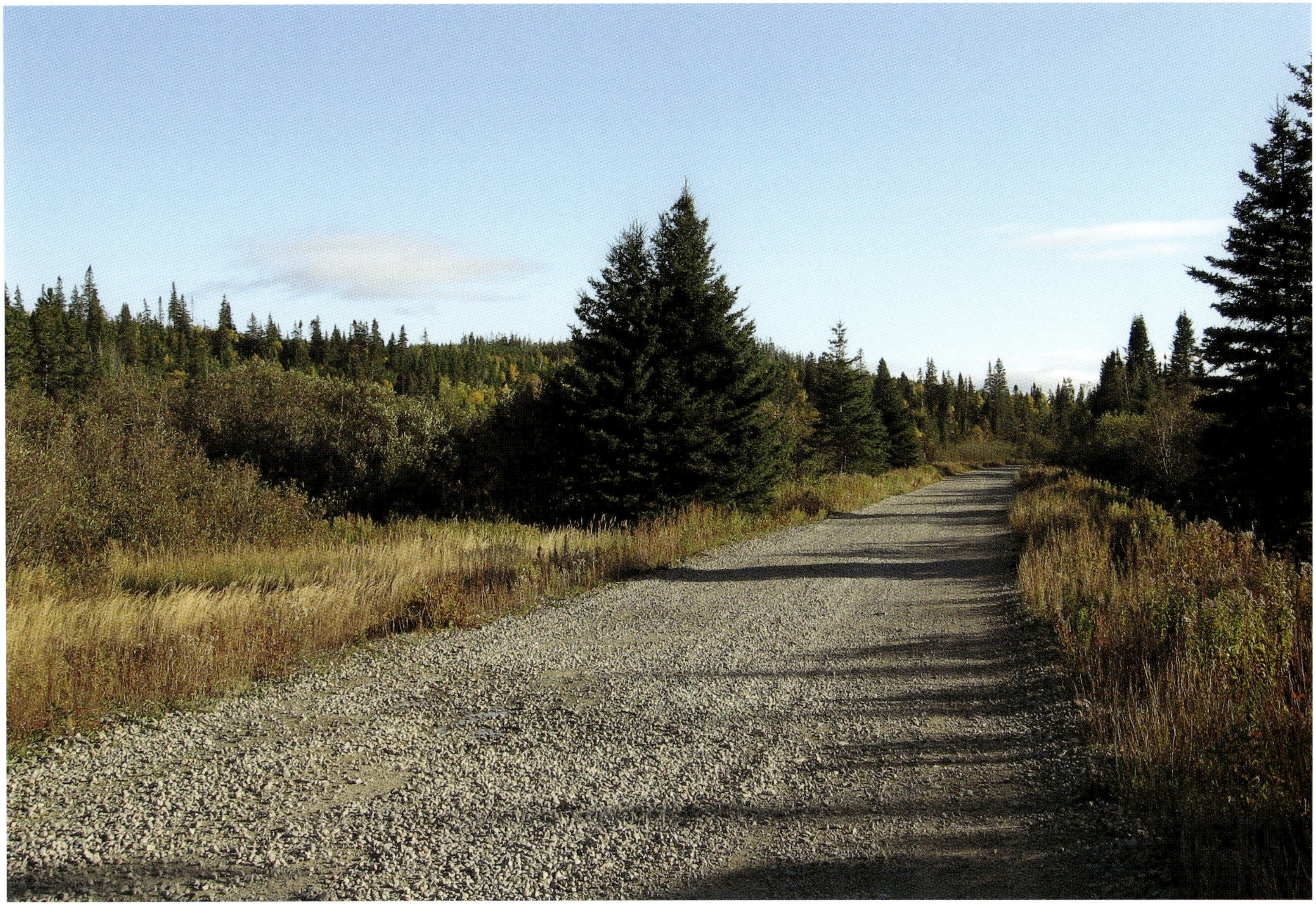

COOKE TODAY
The late autumn sunset casts long shadows on the former meeting place of the east and westbound *Caribou* as the running waters of nearby Cooks Brook breaks the silence of an otherwise still evening. Located in a beautiful valley, the water flows into the Humber Arm of the Bay of Islands. Besides an area for train meets, the former siding here had capacity for 100 cars. *Author photo*

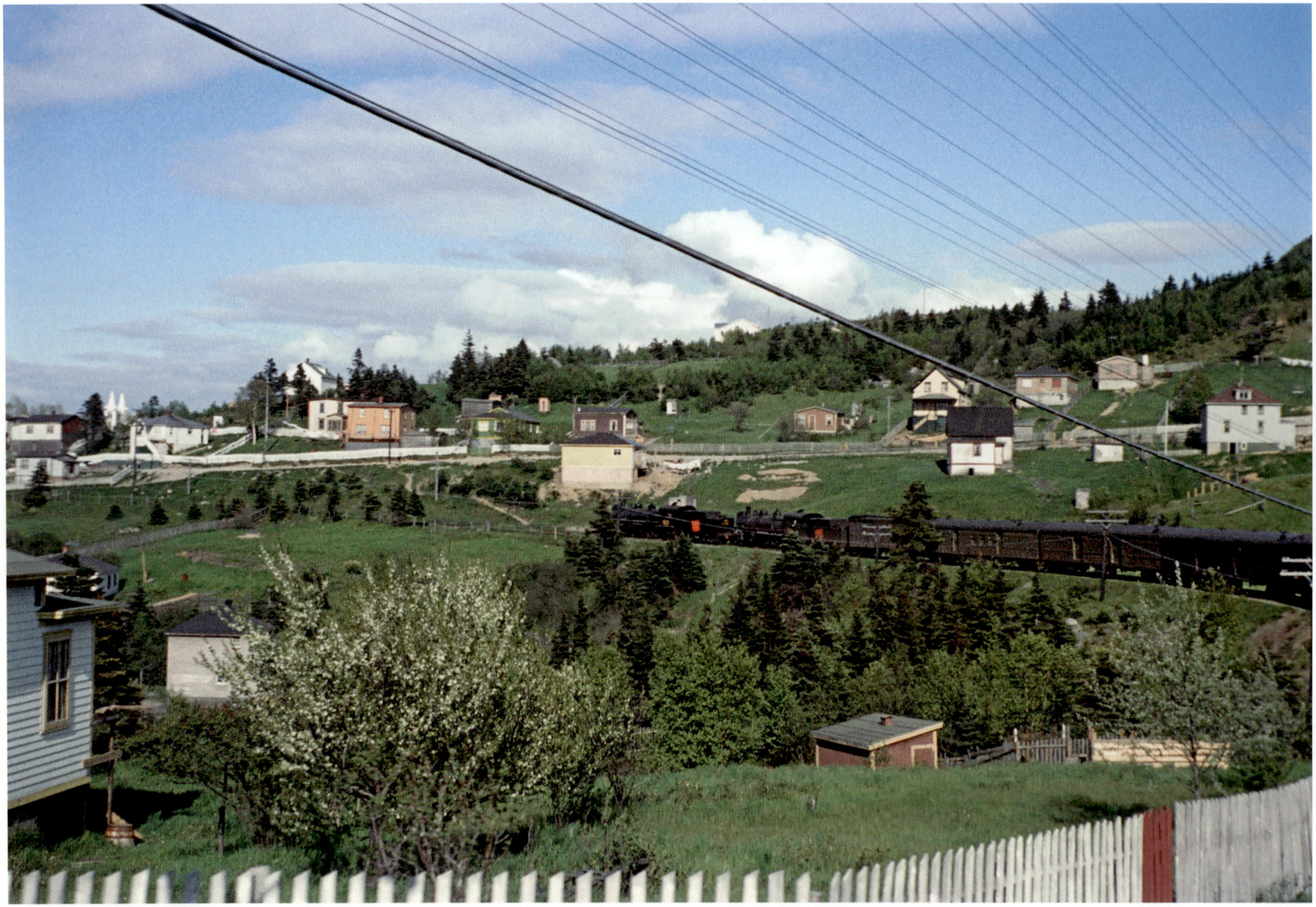

CURLING 1956
A lengthy CNR Train No. 2 with double headed Mikados rounds the sharp curve near Petries on the beautiful sunny afternoon of June 19, 1956. In addition to the passenger trains, Curling was a very busy spot for the railway's yard switchers with the three oil distributers, perishable seafood as well as lumber business all in the local area. *Robert J. Sandusky photo*

CURLING TODAY
Severe weather, certainly not evident in this scene, has washed away the right of way, thus making it impossible to traverse. That, along with the subsequent development that came with amalgamation with Corner Brook in 1954, has justified this view with the twin steeples of Sacred Heart Church barely visible. Up until 1939, Sentinel Steam Coach 'B' operated every hour on the hour from Humbermouth to Sopers with a stop at Petries Crossing in Curling. *Author photo*

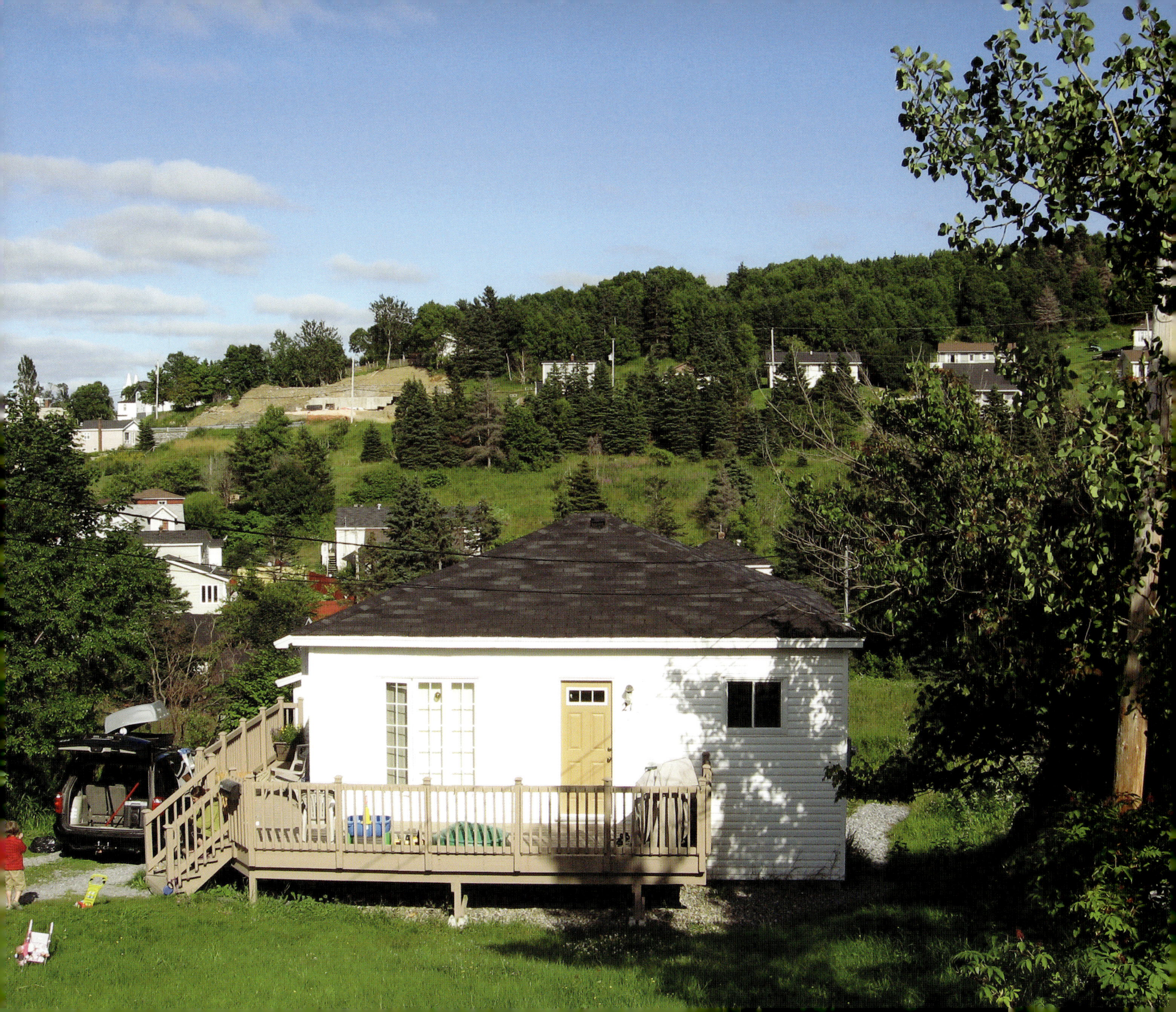

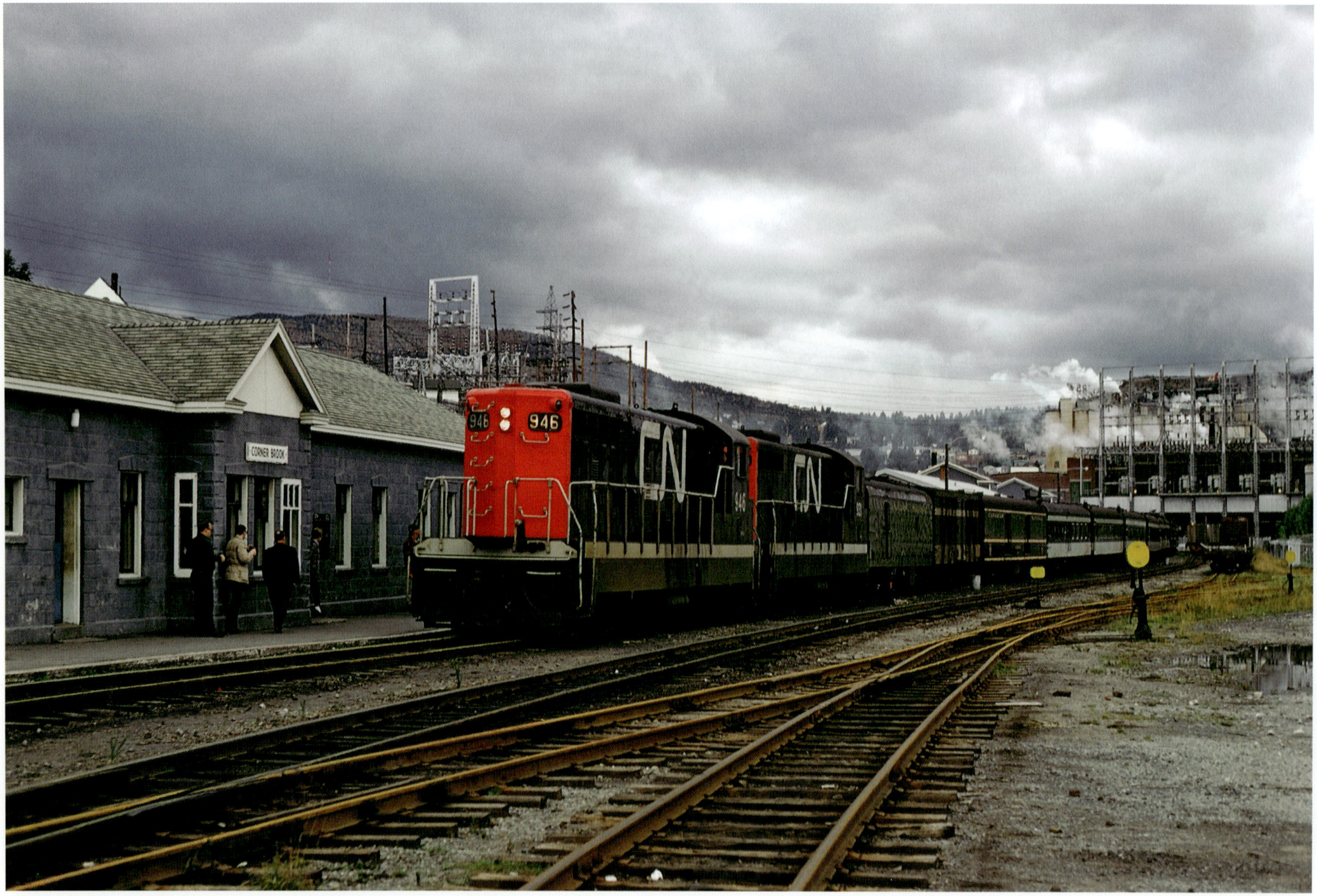

CORNER BROOK 1968
CN Train 102, the eastbound *Caribou*, with NF210's 946 and 931, gracefully glides to a stop at the Corner Brook station on October 6, 1968 as steam pours from the nearby Bowater's paper mill. Engine 946 was the last of the series delivered by GMD of London in 1960 and was later sold to F.C. del Pacifico of Nicaragua. Number 931 has been preserved with its prime mover intact by the Railway Society of Newfoundland, also located in Newfoundland's second city. *Bill Linley photo*

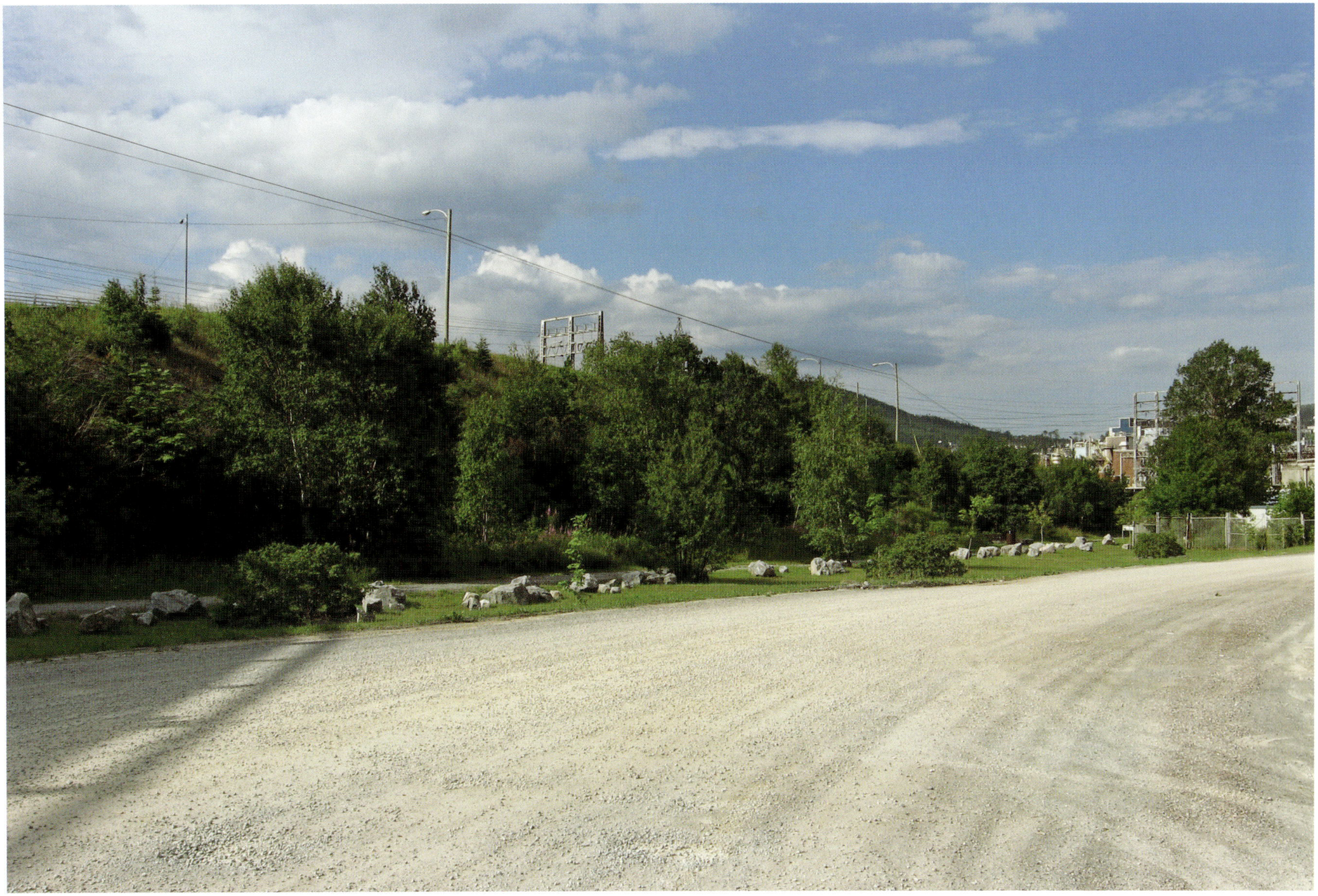

CORNER BROOK TODAY
At the site of the former train station, steam continues to spew from the nearby paper mill, now owned by Kruger Inc. of Montreal. When built in 1924, it was the largest of its kind in the world and, for many decades that followed, was one of the biggest customers of the railway with dedicated pulpwood trains. The area behind the former station site is now part of the Lewin Parkway cloverleaf, built in the 1970s. *Author photo*

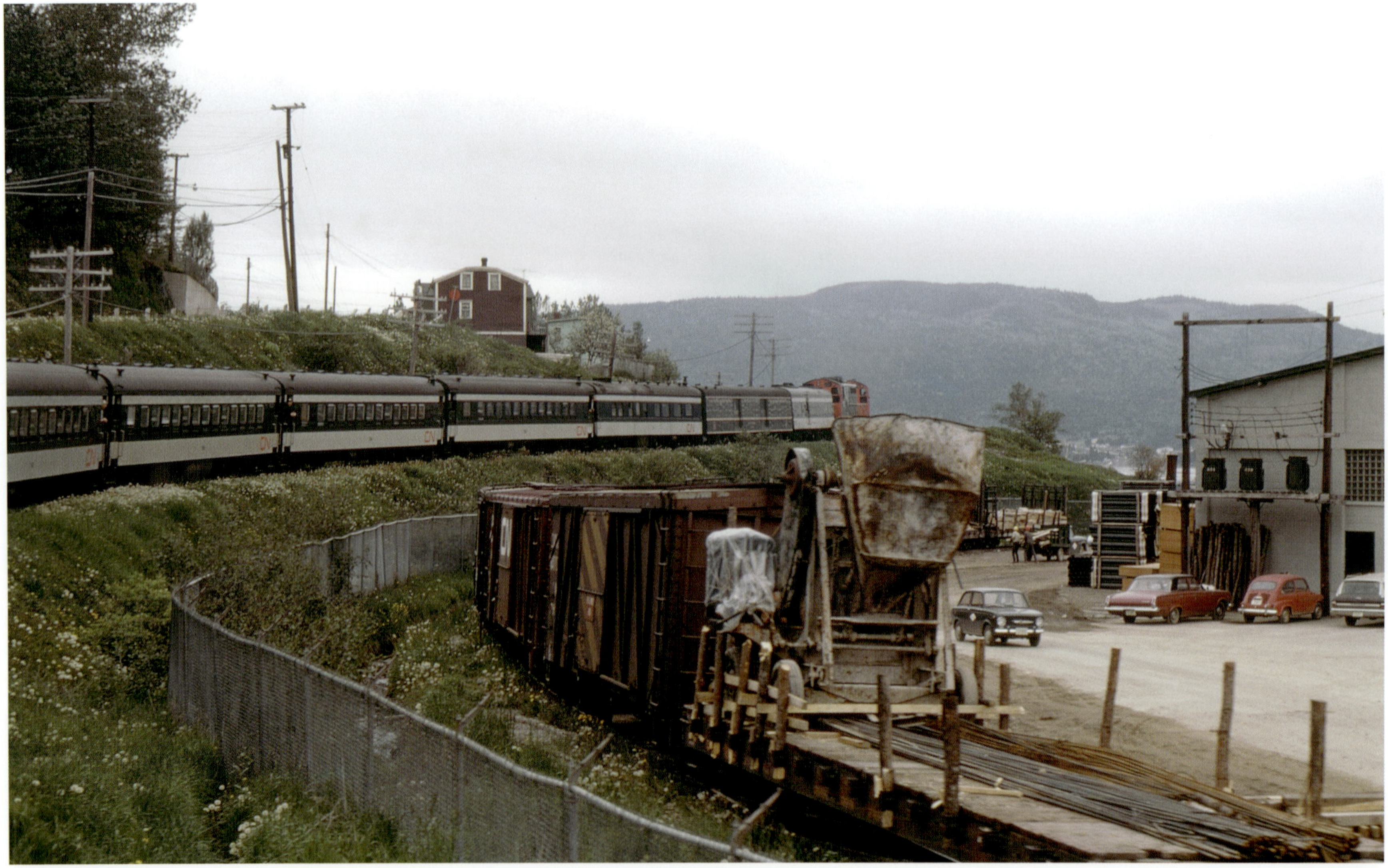

HUMBERMOUTH 1967

Train 101, the westbound *Caribou,* rounds the sharp curve at Brakes Cove in Humbermouth, moments before the next stop at Corner Brook on June 23, 1967. Once a hub of railroading, the last passenger train stopped at Humbermouth on October 24, 1959. The nearby cars on the siding indicate the industrial business nature of the massive Lundrigans Company.
James A. Brown photo

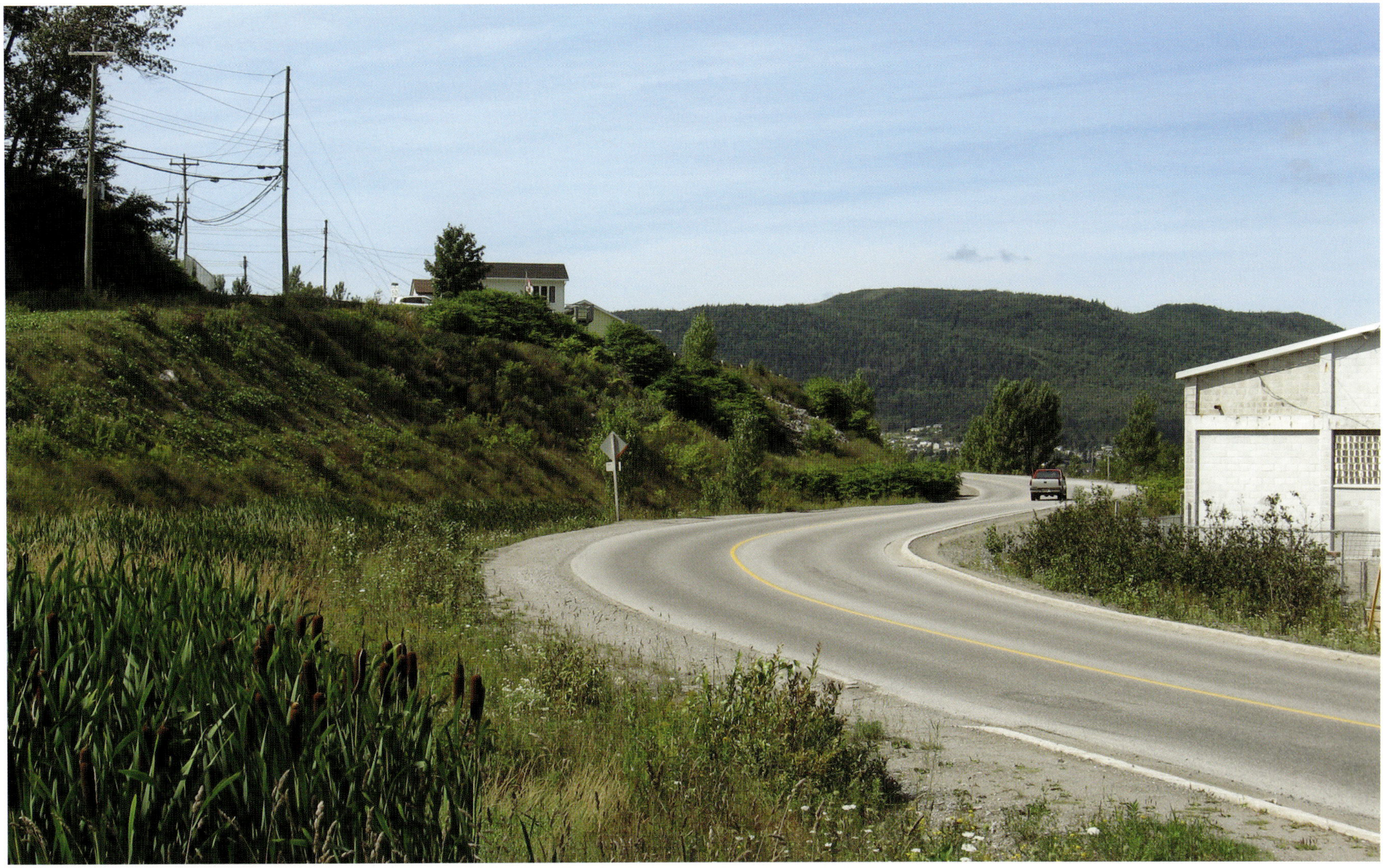

HUMBERMOUTH TODAY
Cattails and cars fill the space where the ribbons of steel once ran. Riverside Drive links Humbermouth to downtown Corner Brook while the concrete building serves as a reminder of the former Lundrigans Empire. Just around the turn is the Railway Society's static display, including 4-6-2 Pacific # 593. Built by Baldwin of Philadelphia in 1920, it remains the only surviving steam locomotive from the Newfoundland Railway. *Author photo*

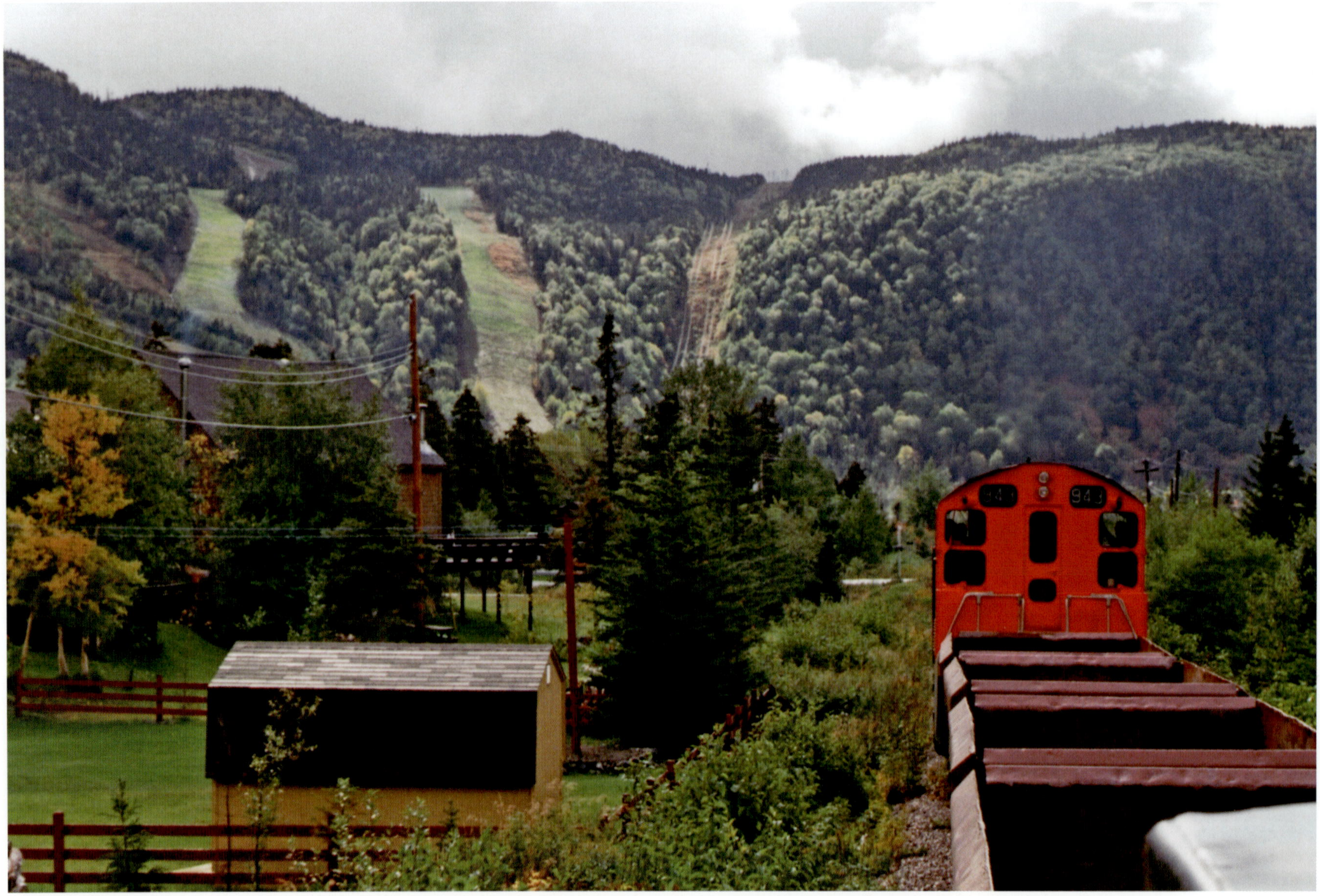

STEADY BROOK 1988
Just a day before the shutdown, maintenance still had to be carried out. Gander photographer Charlie Falk spent several months shooting the final rail operations in the province. Here, Extra 943 West, with only four cars, has finished dumping crushed stone and is photographed from the caboose while passing through Steady Brook on Sept 29, 1988. *Charlie Falk photo*

STEADY BROOK TODAY
The former railbed is now a new street called Marble Drive, which motorists in Steady Brook use to access both the TCH and Marble Mountain. With its 1600-foot vertical drop, it is purported to have 'the best skiing East of the Rockies'. It was near this site on April 15, 1946 that Train No. 2 derailed, tearing up the tracks and sending several cars over on their sides. It took work crews four days of working around the clock to reopen the line. *Author photo*

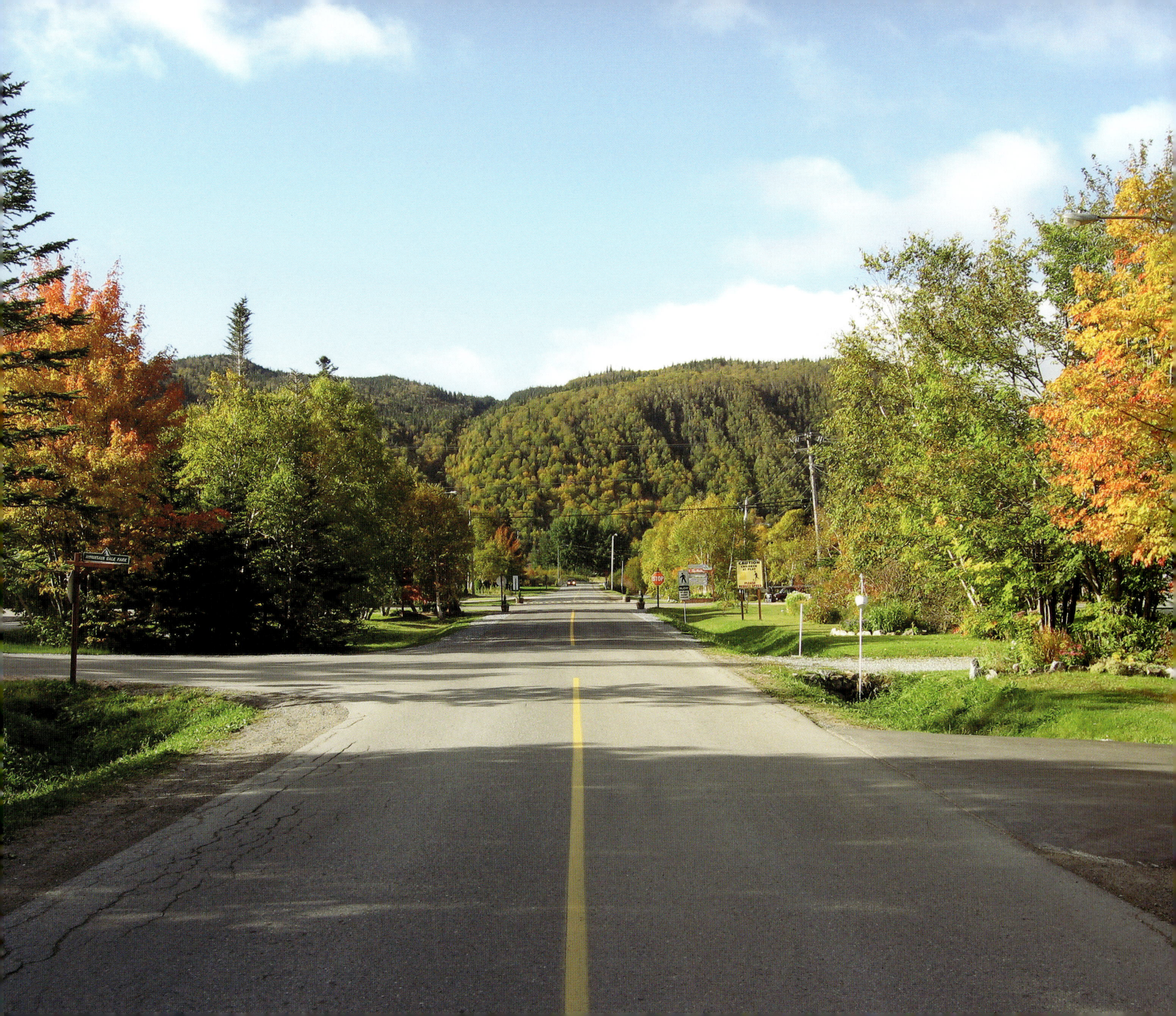

STOP
CAUTION

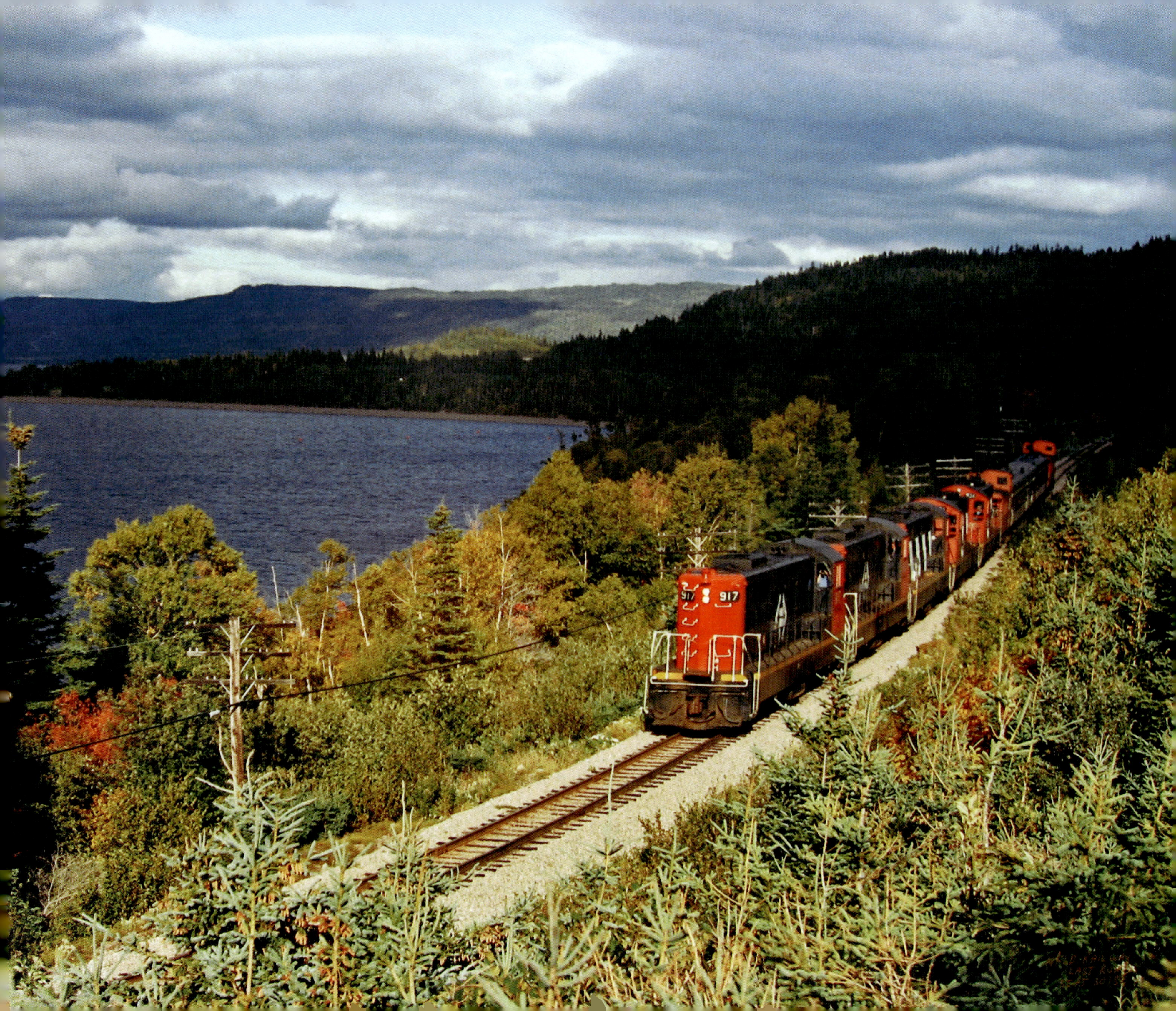

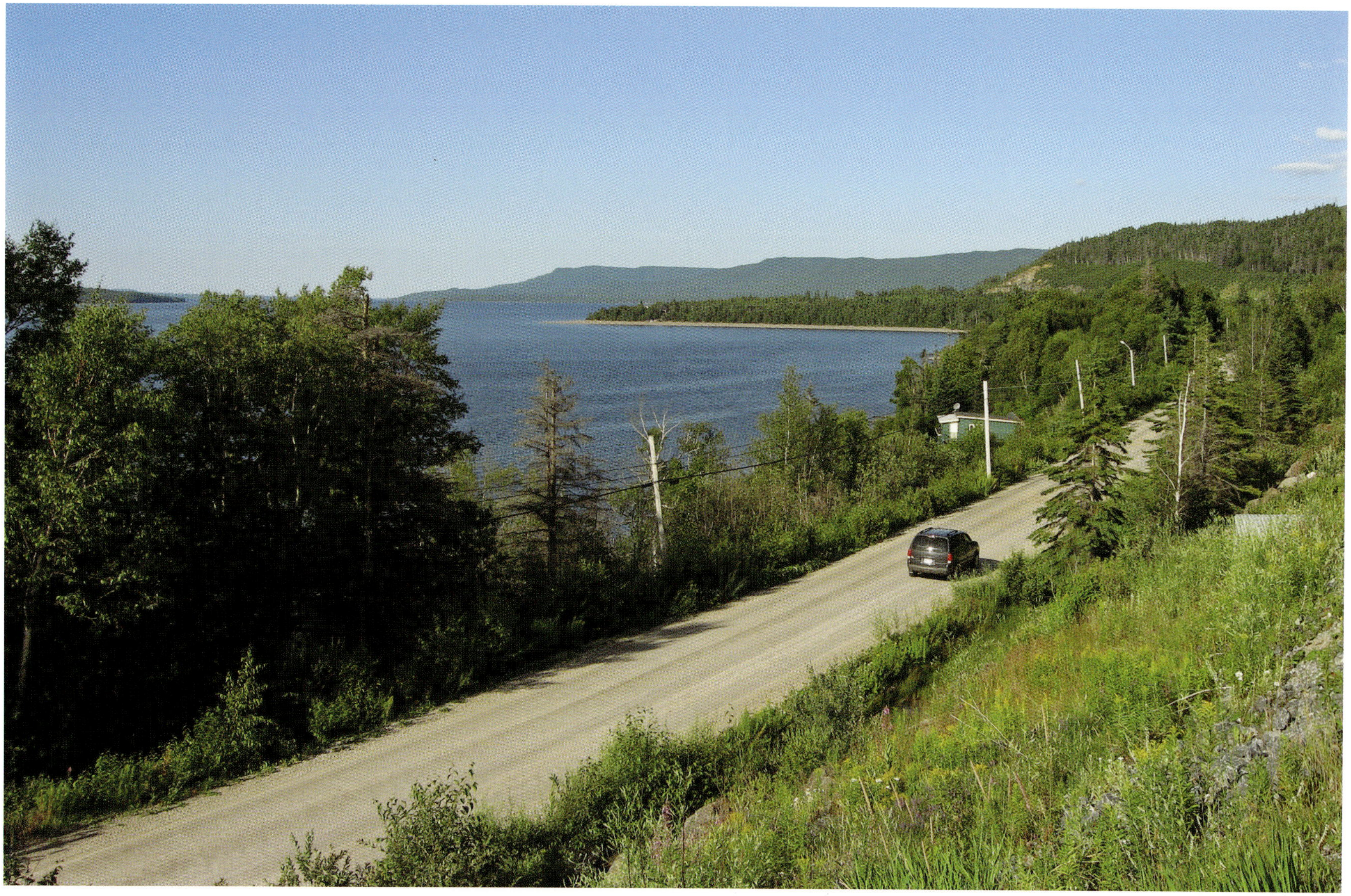

PASADENA 1988
Extra 917 West, the final No.203, has finished passing Pasadena and South Brook Park. The sun has just broken out, accentuating the little train with five NF210s, three pieces of passenger equipment and two cabooses on September 30, 1988. It was at South Brook Park that steam locomotive 593 was on display from 1957 until its move by rail to Corner Brook twenty years later. *Charlie Falk photo*

PASADENA TODAY
The former rail bed is now a gravel access road linking the many cabins from South Brook to Little Rapids. The closure permitted the expansion of the TCH to four lanes to accommodate the additional trucks and other vehicles in this busy area. South Brook Park has since been sold and is now the site of a new high end luxury housing development called South Brook Point. *Author photo*

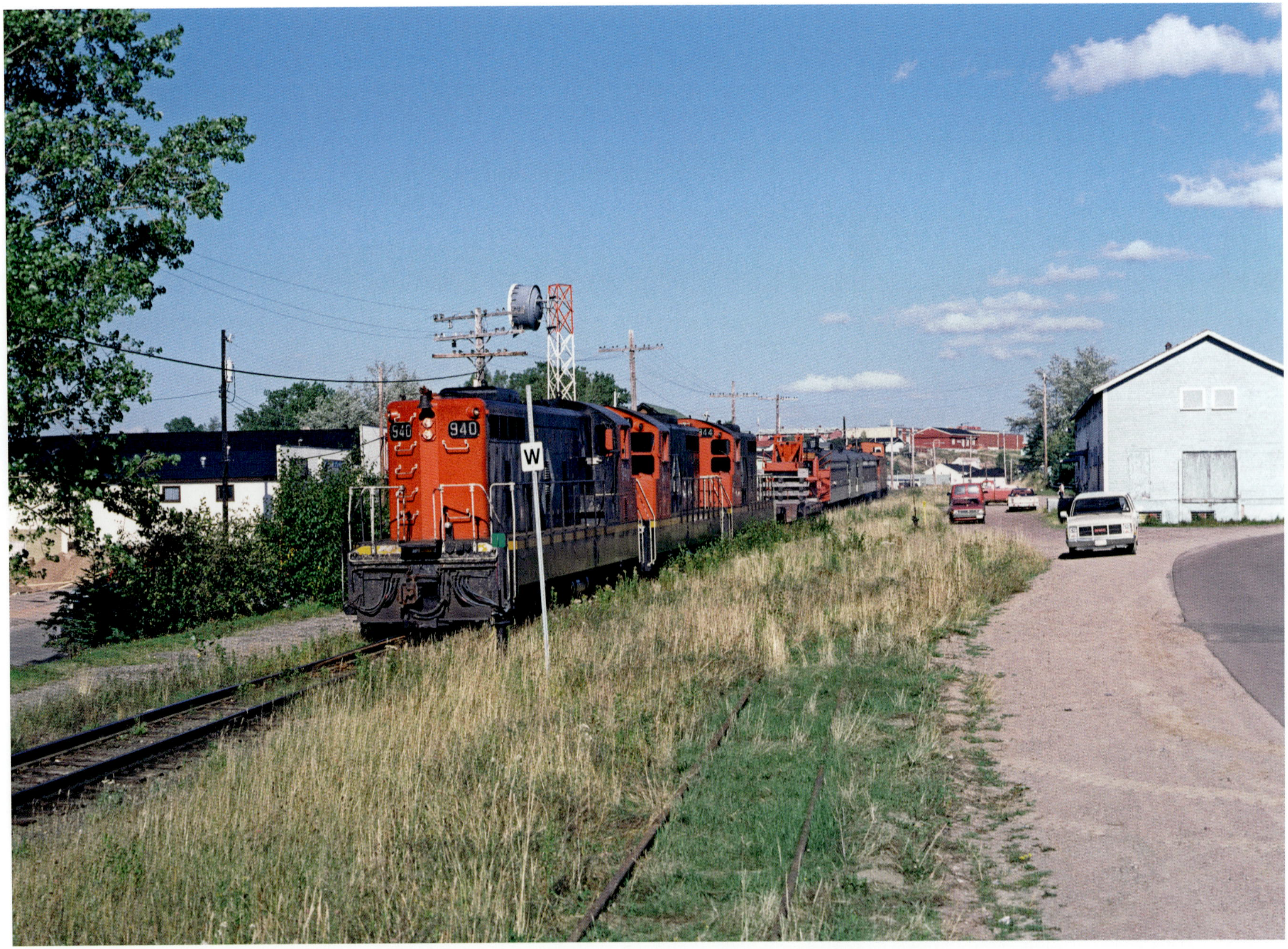

DEER LAKE 1988

Before returning to Toronto, CN engineer David Whitnall photographs Terra Transport Train #203 with NF210's 940,941 & 944, a depressed centre flatcar, regular flatcar, two coaches, baggage car and caboose approaching the station at Deer Lake on September 21, 1988. Amazingly, all three engines have survived. 940 is on static display in Whitbourne, Newfoundland while sister 941 was sold to F.C. del Pacifico of Nicaragua and 944 to F.C Antofagasta Boliva of Chile. *David Whitnall photo*

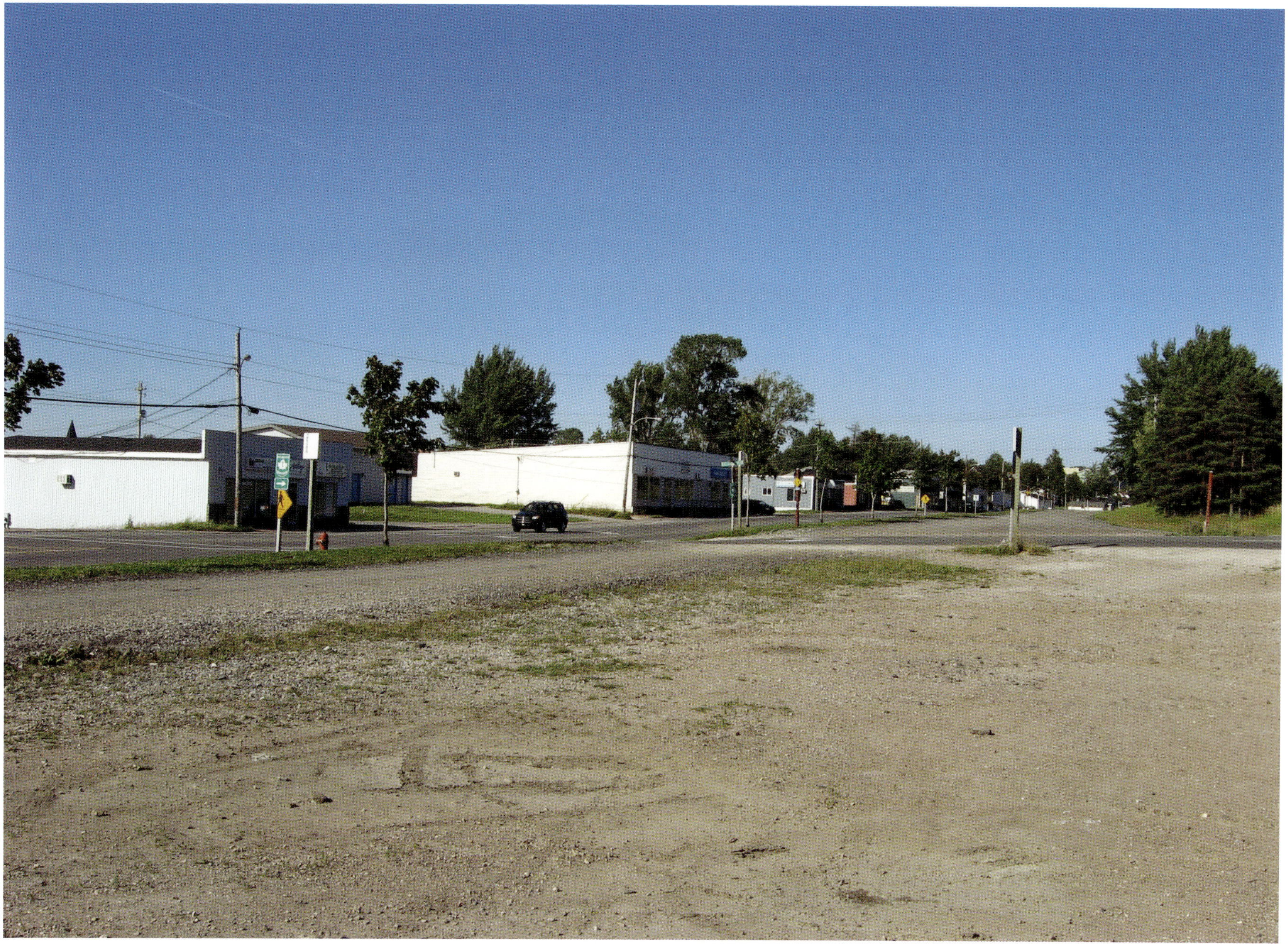

DEER LAKE TODAY
Businesses along the former right of way still flourish in downtown Deer Lake. Founded in 1864 by settlers from Cape Breton, this town of 5000 is home to the Humber Valley Strawberry Festival and boasts the most sunshine hours in the province. A branch line to Bonne Bay from Deer Lake was planned in 1910 but never proceeded further than some grading. *Author photo*

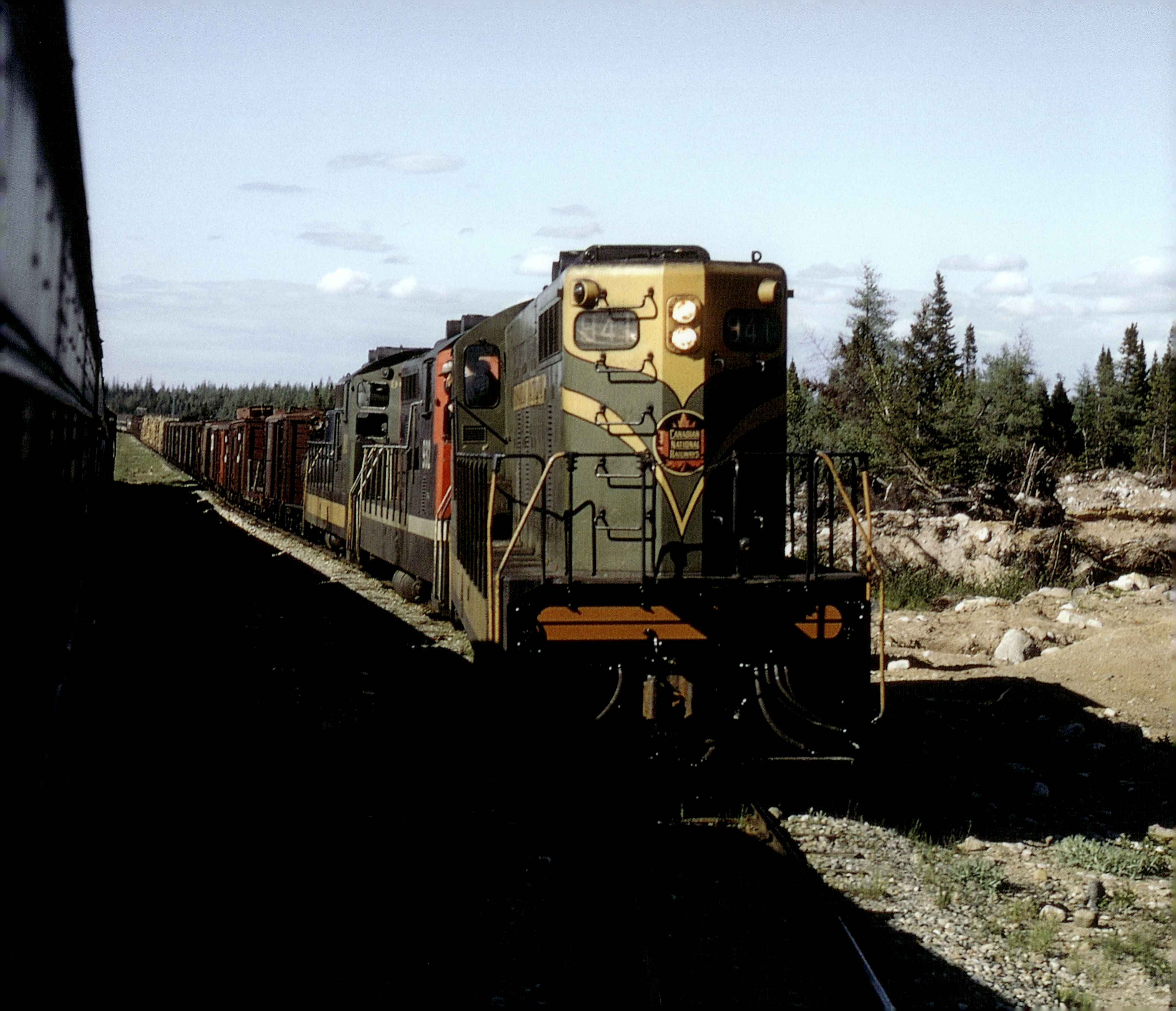
941
941
CANADIAN NATIONAL RAILWAYS

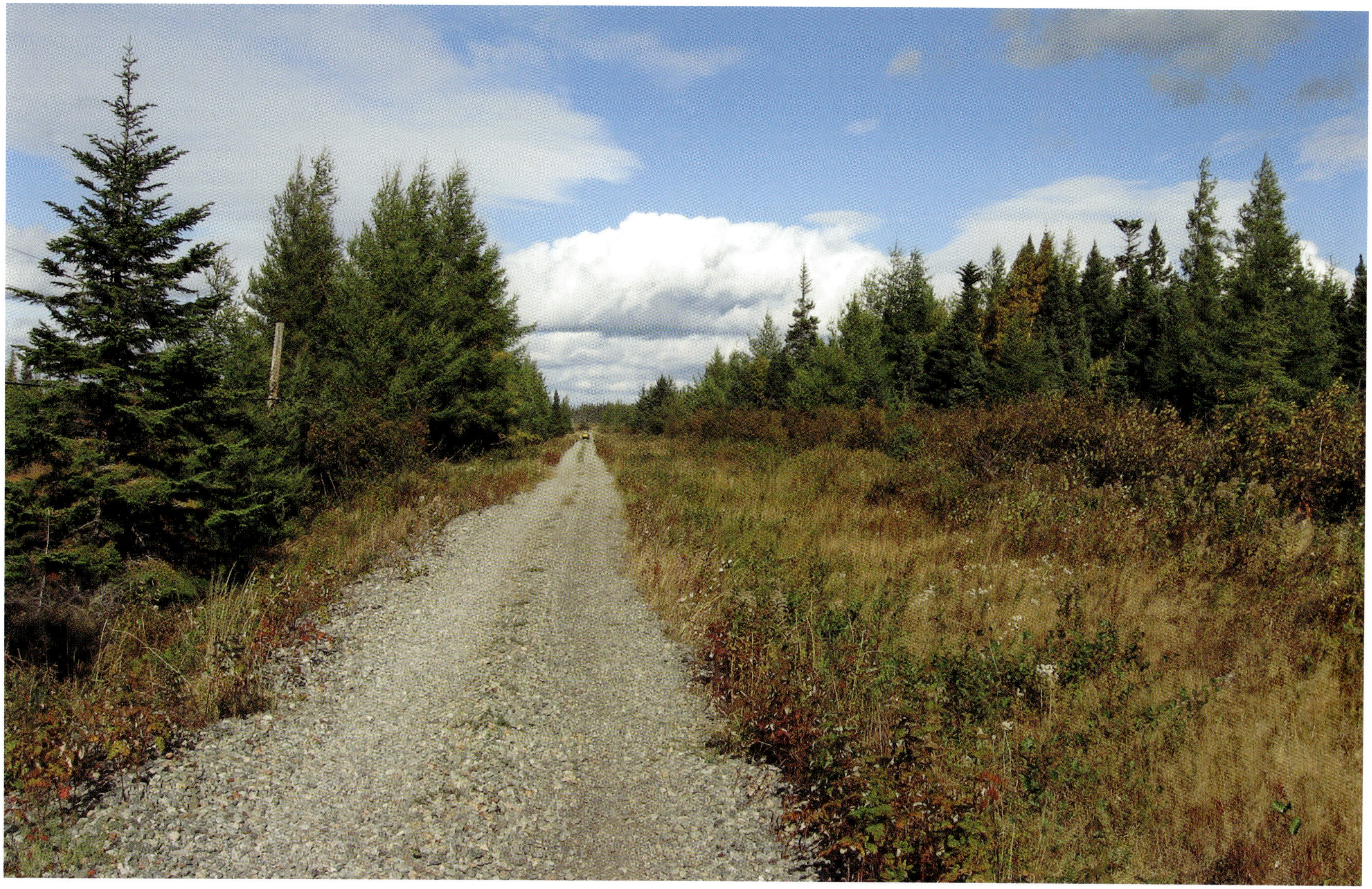

NORTHERN 1967
Mixed train #203 with NF210 941 takes to the siding at Northern while Train 102, the *Caribou*, continues eastward on the main line on June 20, 1967. Still wearing her handsome green and gold paint scheme and with a CN class of GR-12-x, 941 was one of nine in the final order of NF210 locomotives delivered to Newfoundland by GMD of London in 1960. *James A. Brown photo*

NORTHERN TODAY
Off in the distance, an ATV carrying an adventurous young couple heads eastward on the former mainline. Enjoying the fine weather and warm temperatures of a mid-October afternoon, they probably never knew that the overgrown parallel siding ever existed. Let alone know, that once upon a time, not so long ago, a train was the only means of travel to this very spot. *Author photo*

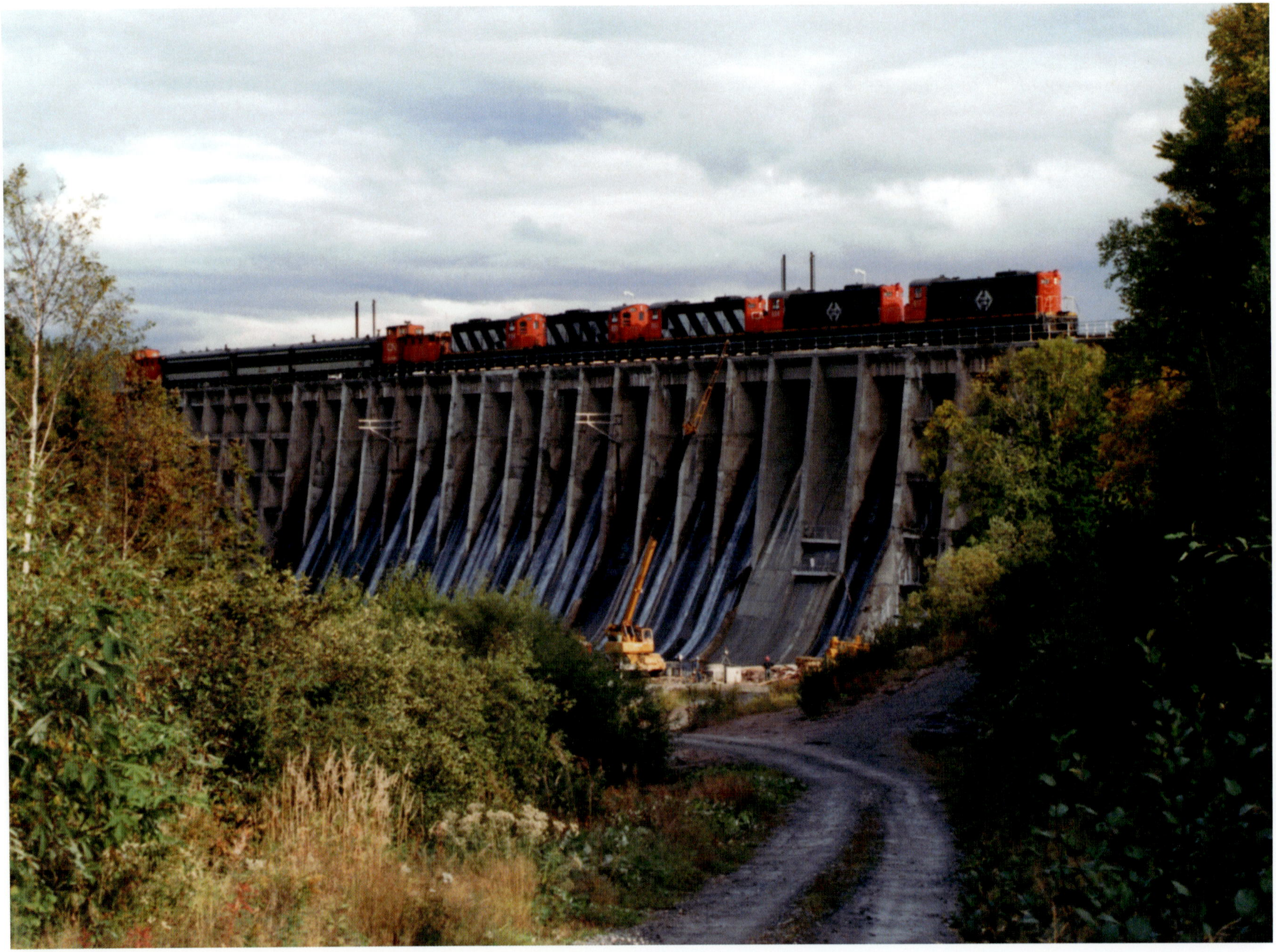

MAIN DAM 1988

Terra Transport Extra 917 West, the last scheduled mixed train, with five NF210s, two coaches, one baggage car and two cabooses crosses Main Dam at the restricted speed of 15/mph on September 30, 1988. Passengers on the right side have a splendid view of the Junction Brook valley 75 feet straight down below while those on the left side can watch the water almost lap up against the rails. *Charlie Falk photo*

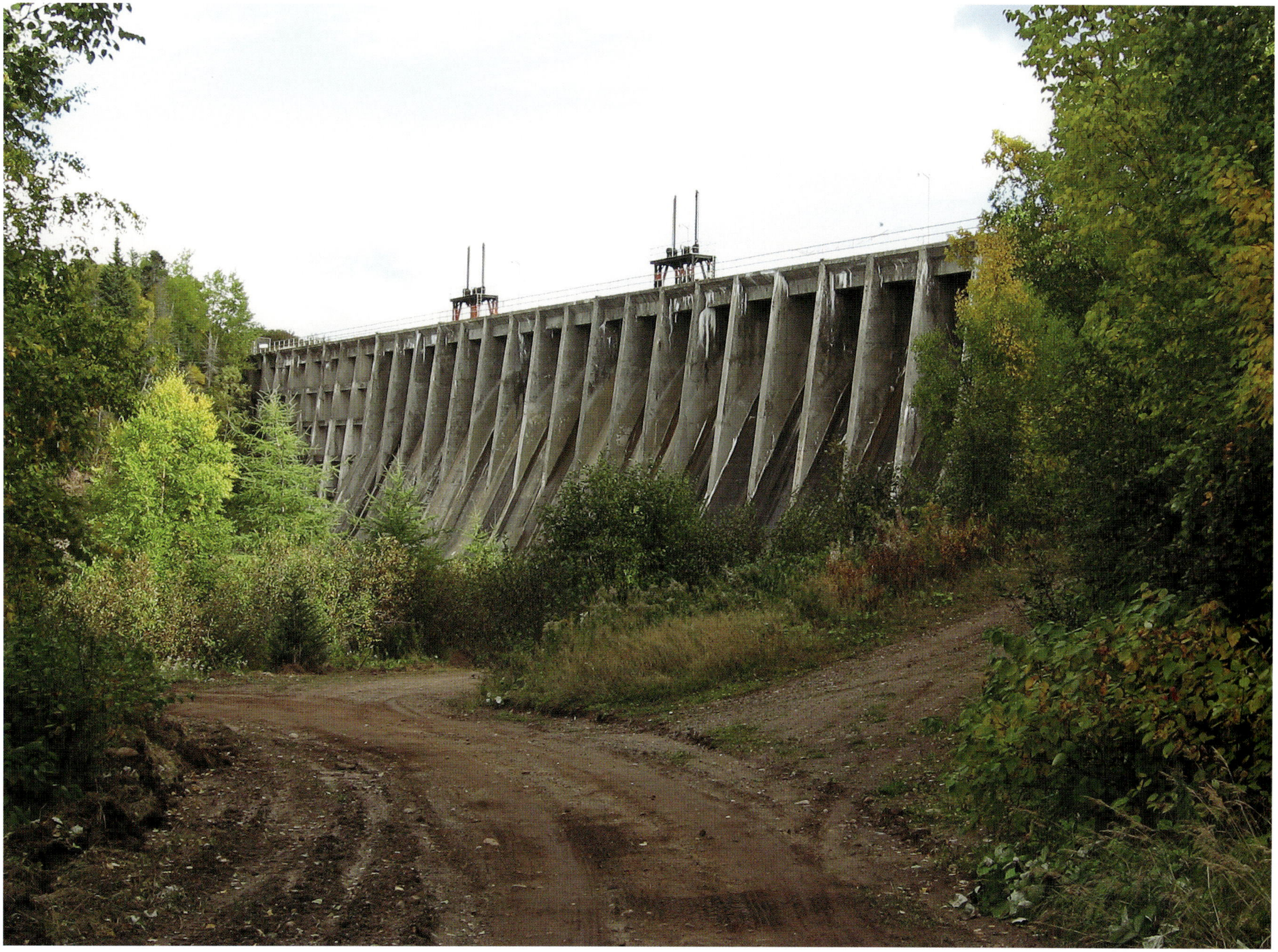

MAIN DAM TODAY
Built in 1924 to provide electricity to the paper mill in Corner Brook, this 244 metre long and 24 metre high concrete structure backs up water in Grand Lake to 130 kilometres when full. This 5,030 square kilometer watershed has become one of Canada's finest wildlife, bird and fish regions. Both big and small game can thrive in this area that is far removed from the towns, cities and highways. *Author photo*

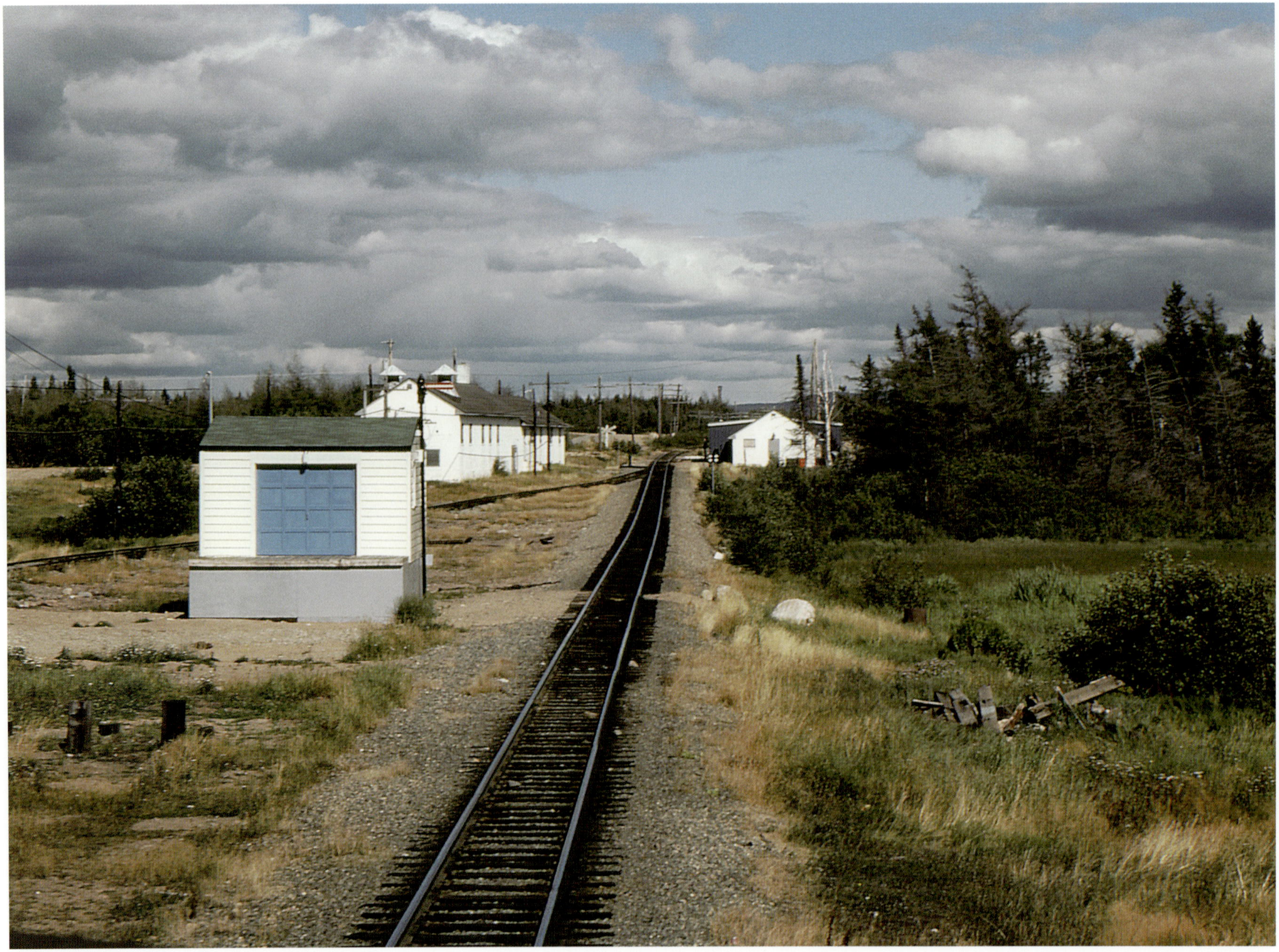

HOWLEY 1978

The narrow gauge rails shine from the steel wheels of CN mixed train 203 as it pulls away from the tiny freight shed at Howley following a long downgrade from the Gaff Topsails on August 28, 1978. This line is part of an eleven mile diversion paid for by the Newfoundland Pulp and Paper Company in 1924 after the damming of Grand Lake in which the original station and track were flooded. *Rich Taylor photo*

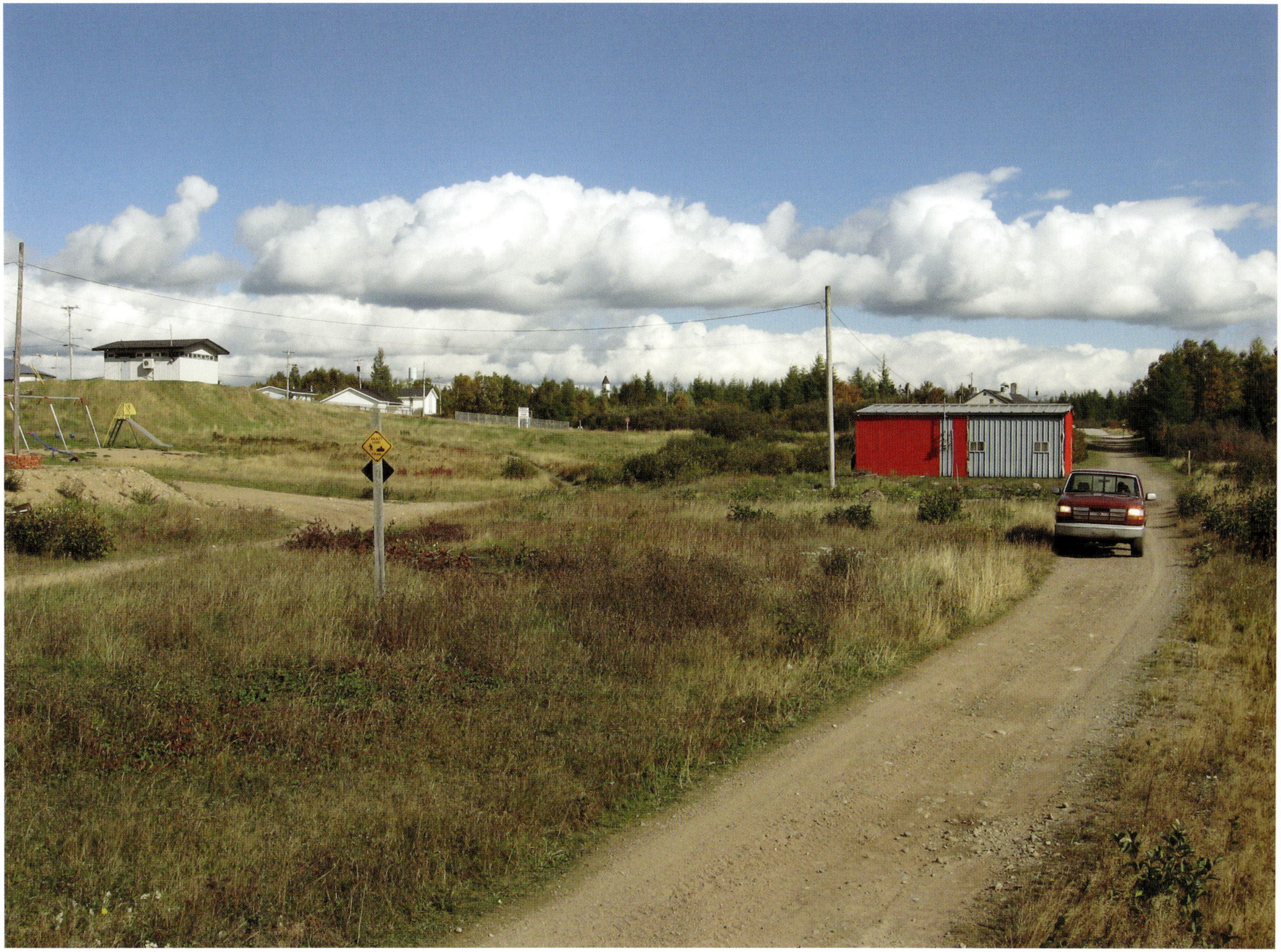

HOWLEY TODAY

A late model Ford pickup bounces by the site of the old freight shed. Still dependent on a rail link after the termination of the passenger service in 1969, Howley could only be accessed by mixed train service until a road was built to the Trans Canada Highway some time later. This community, named after surveyor James P. Howley, was where four moose from New Brunswick were released from a boxcar in 1904, introducing that species to Newfoundland. *Author photo*

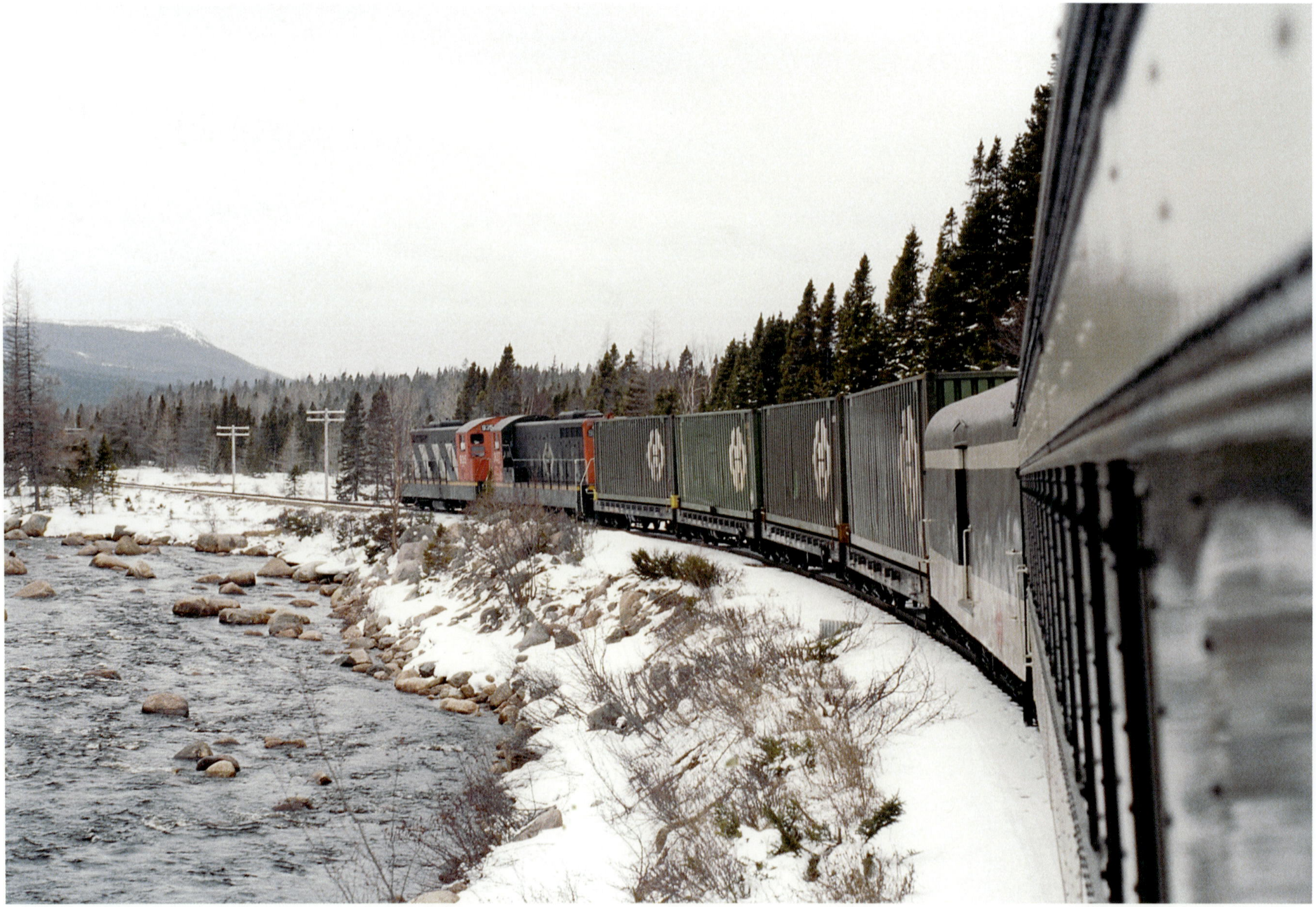

KITTY'S BROOK 1988

Terra Transport mixed train #203 follows Kitty's Brook to the flag stop bearing the same name on April 16, 1988. This was the author's third of five trips by train over the line during the last two years of operation and the first on the recently refurbished coach. Departing Bishop's Falls with only passenger equipment, the two NF210s picked up the four containers at Grand Falls, thus making it a true mixed. *Author photo*

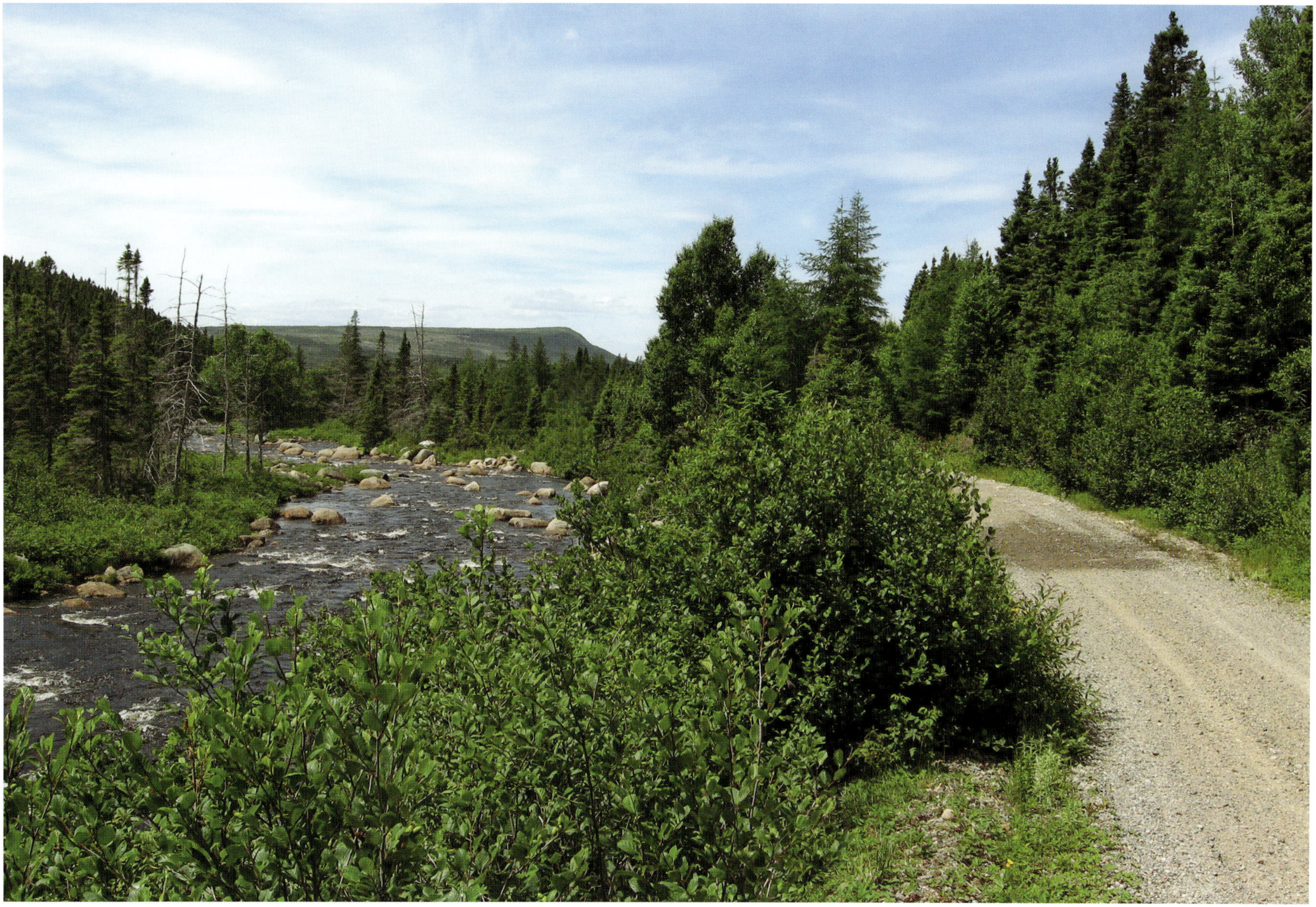

KITTY'S BROOK
Settled in 1903, Kitty's Brook had both a long siding and a wye to turn around plow trains that cleared snow from the Gaff Topsails. The snowfall was so excessive that in 1903 an express train was stuck at Kitty's Brook for seventeen days. In 1935 the community had a population of 11 souls but was abandoned by 1945 except for railway use. *Author photo*

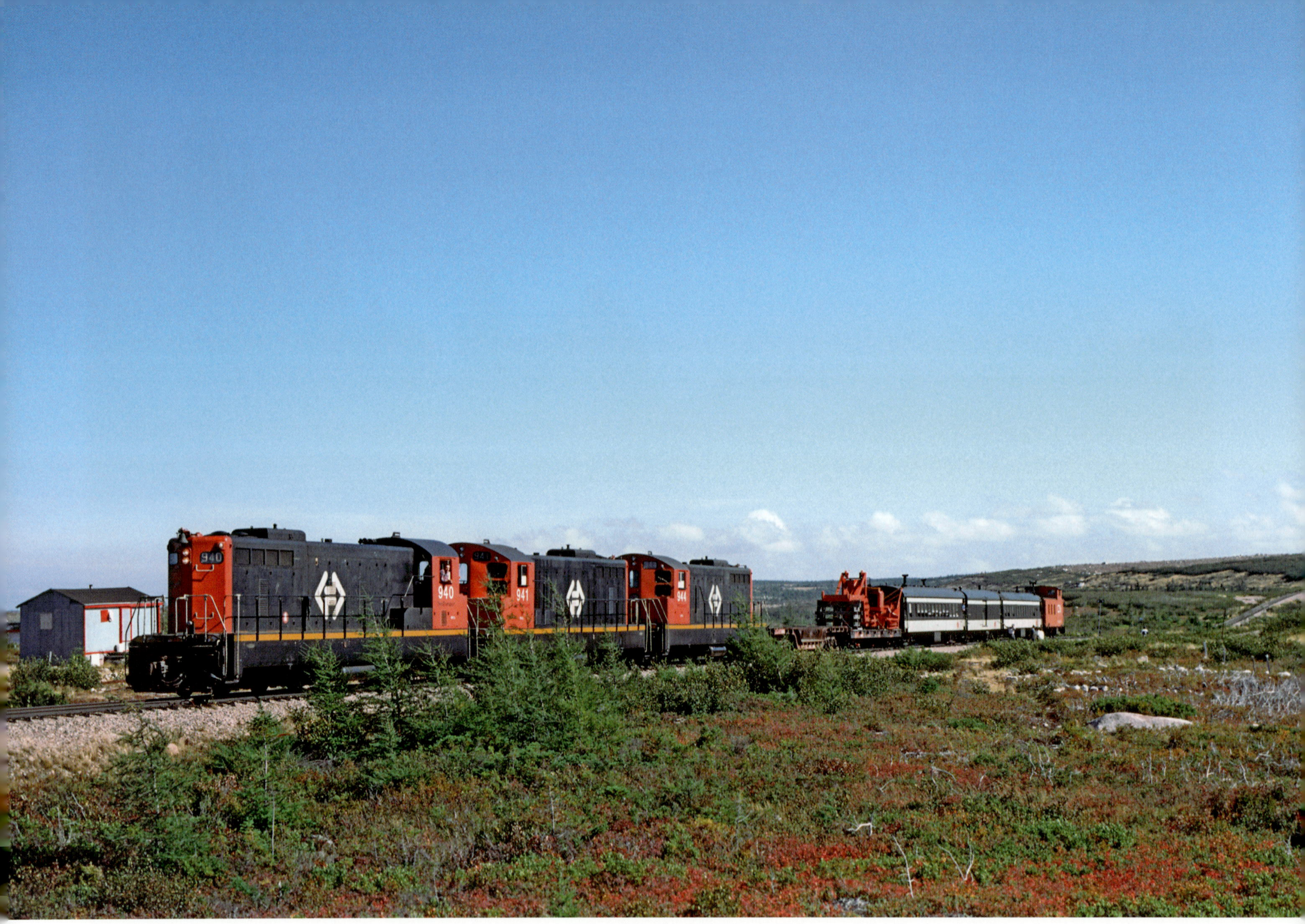

POND CROSSING 1988
After freight service terminated, there were still a few mixed runs over the Gaff Topsails and rail fans Gary Zuters and David Whitnall travelled from Ontario to observe them. Here Terra Transport locos 940, 941 & 944 with a depressed centre flat, regular flat, two coaches, baggage car and caboose stop at Pond Crossing on a crystal-clear September 21, 1988.
Gary Zuters photo

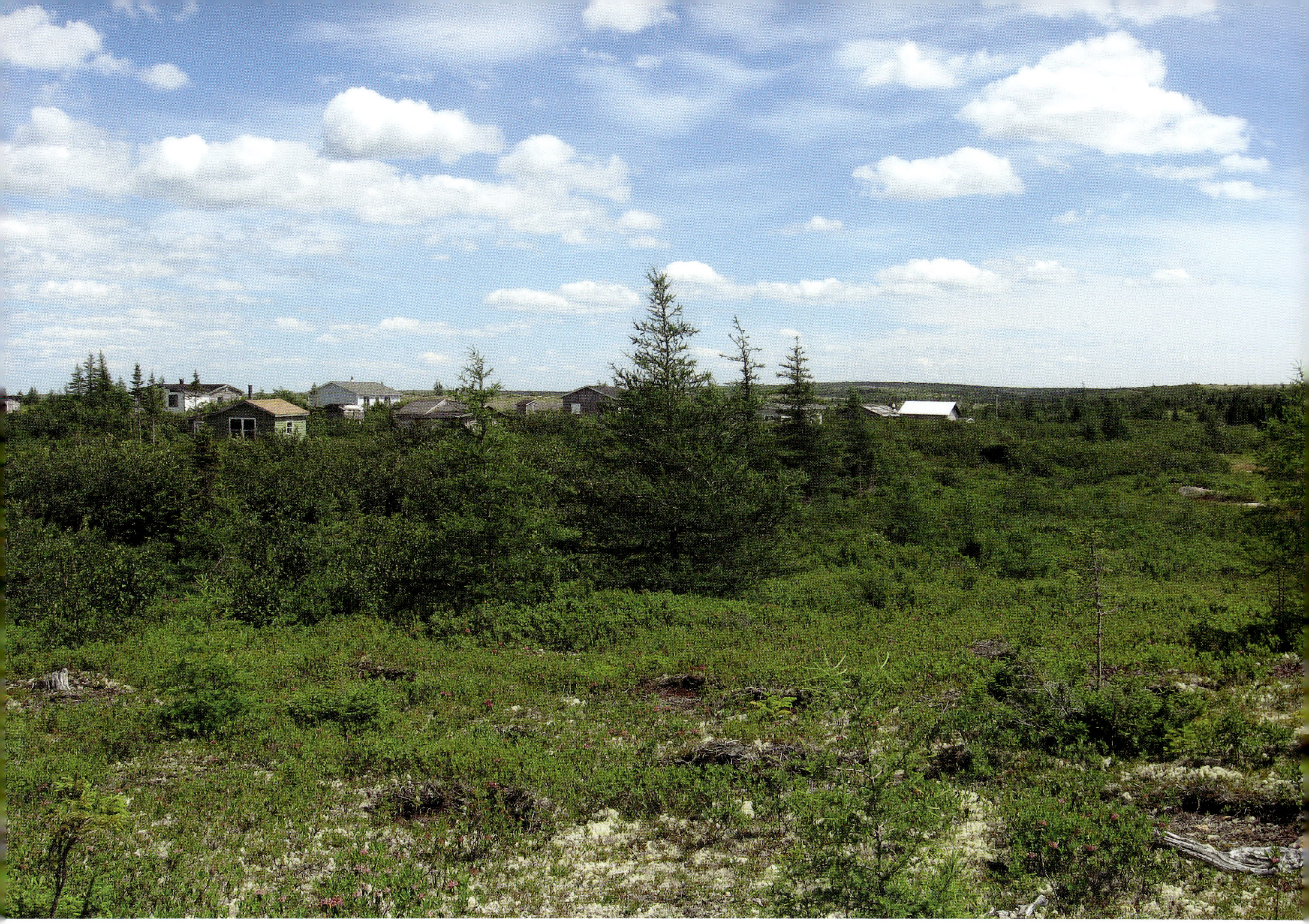

POND CROSSING TODAY
The juniper trees have grown rapidly since 203 stopped here in 1988, nearly obscuring Pond Crossing from view. However, the number of cabins has surprisingly increased, perhaps due to accessibility on the excellent roadbed. At 1350 feet above sea level, and with the Chain Ponds nearby, it is a hunter and fisherman's paradise. *Author photo*

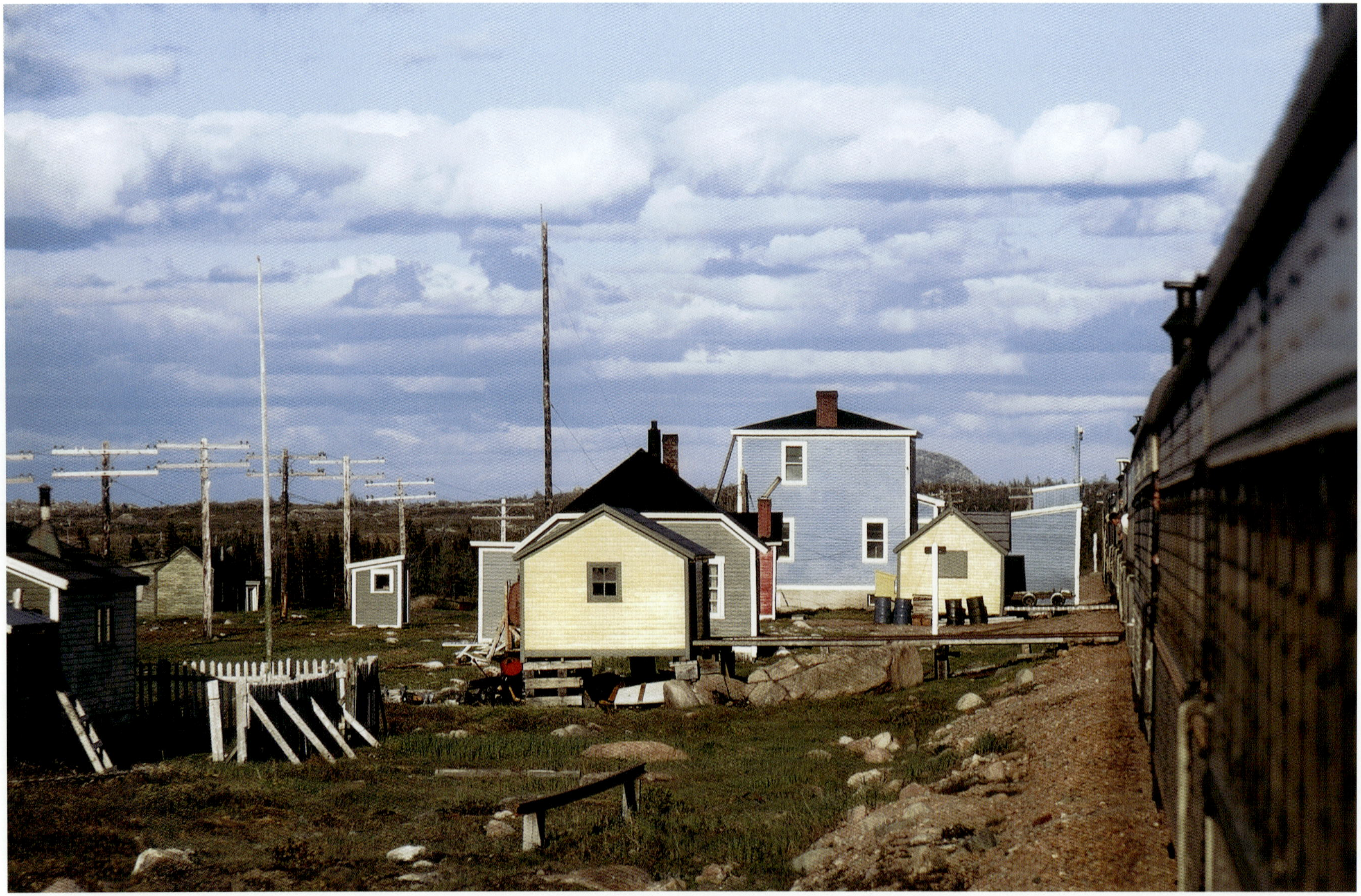

GAFF TOPSAIL 1967

The last rays of the setting sun, on one of the longest days of the year, accentuate the colourful houses at Gaff Topsail on June 20, 1967. CN Train 102, the eastbound *Caribou*, resumes the remainder of its journey overnight towards St. John's, with folks bedding down in the sleepers 'Princeton', 'Twillingate', 'Whitbourne' and 'Clarenville'. *James A. Brown photo*

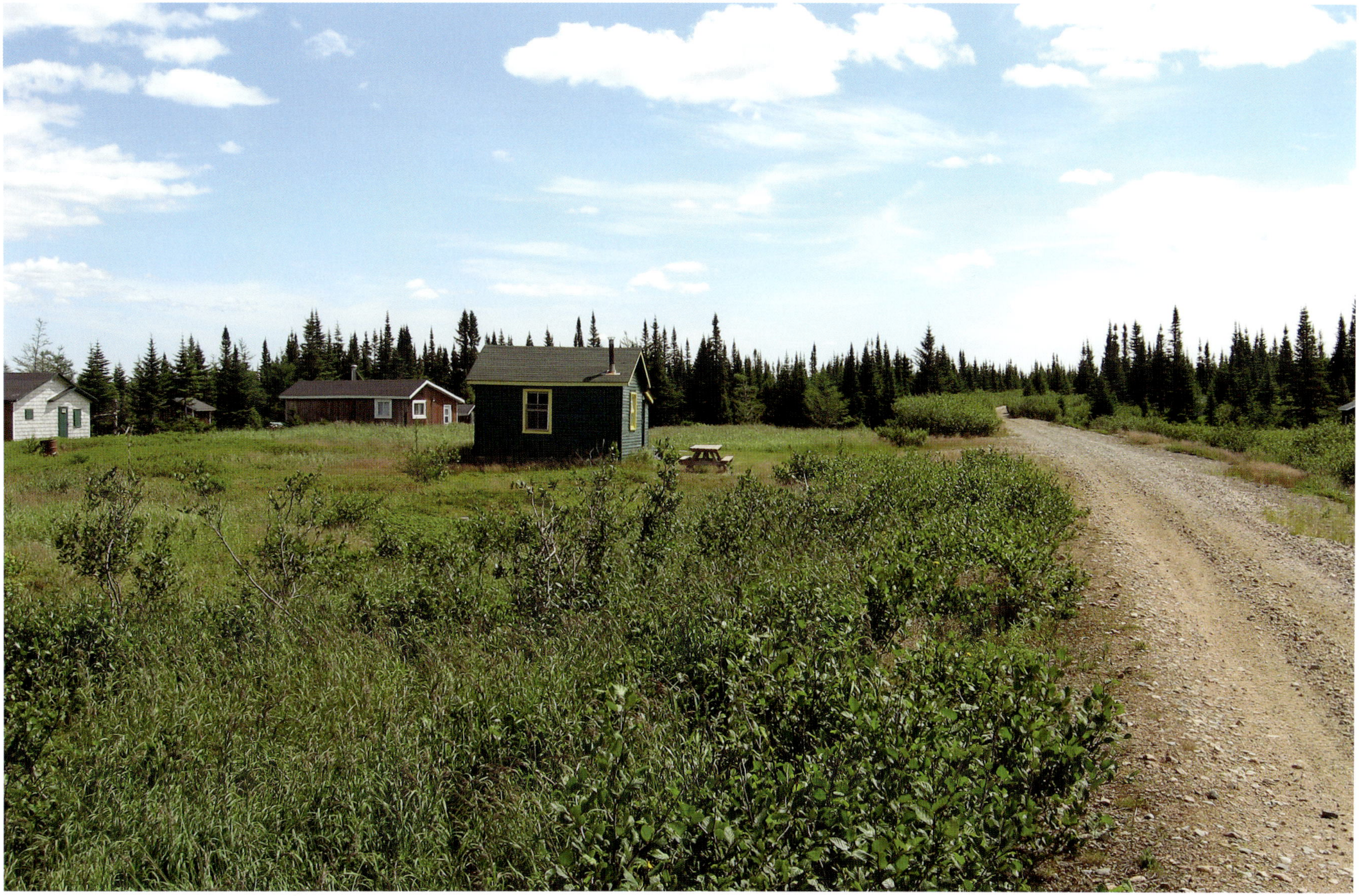

GAFF TOPSAIL TODAY

One of the few surviving structures is the little green cabin that once belonged to roadmaster J.T. Hannon. With lots of vehicular traffic over the railbed, the signs at the eastern approach say 'Welcome to The Gaff' and 'Caution - Children and Pets Present'. The Gaff was once site of a Frontier College operation in the 1950s and 1960s where male university students worked alongside and taught academic skills to labourers in remote settings. *Author photo*

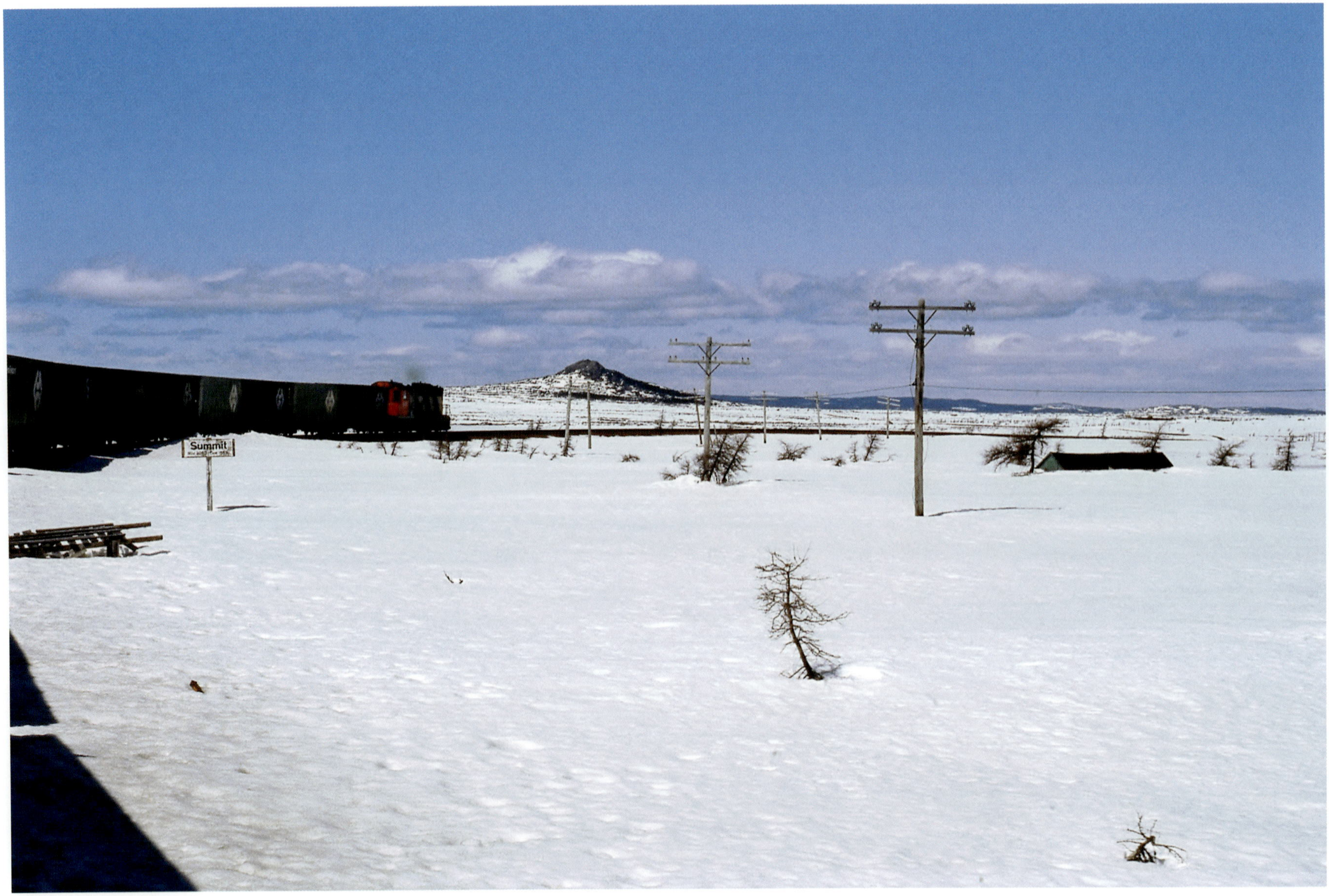

SUMMIT 1987

Terra Transport mixed train 203 with single unit NF210 945 arrives at Summit on April 20, 1987. The heavy snowfall from the winter is still piled several feet high, belying the fact that spring is well underway elsewhere on the Island. At 1555 feet above sea level, it was the highest point of the railway. The only passengers to travel there that day were the author and his girlfriend on their first trip on a Newfoundland train. *Author photo*

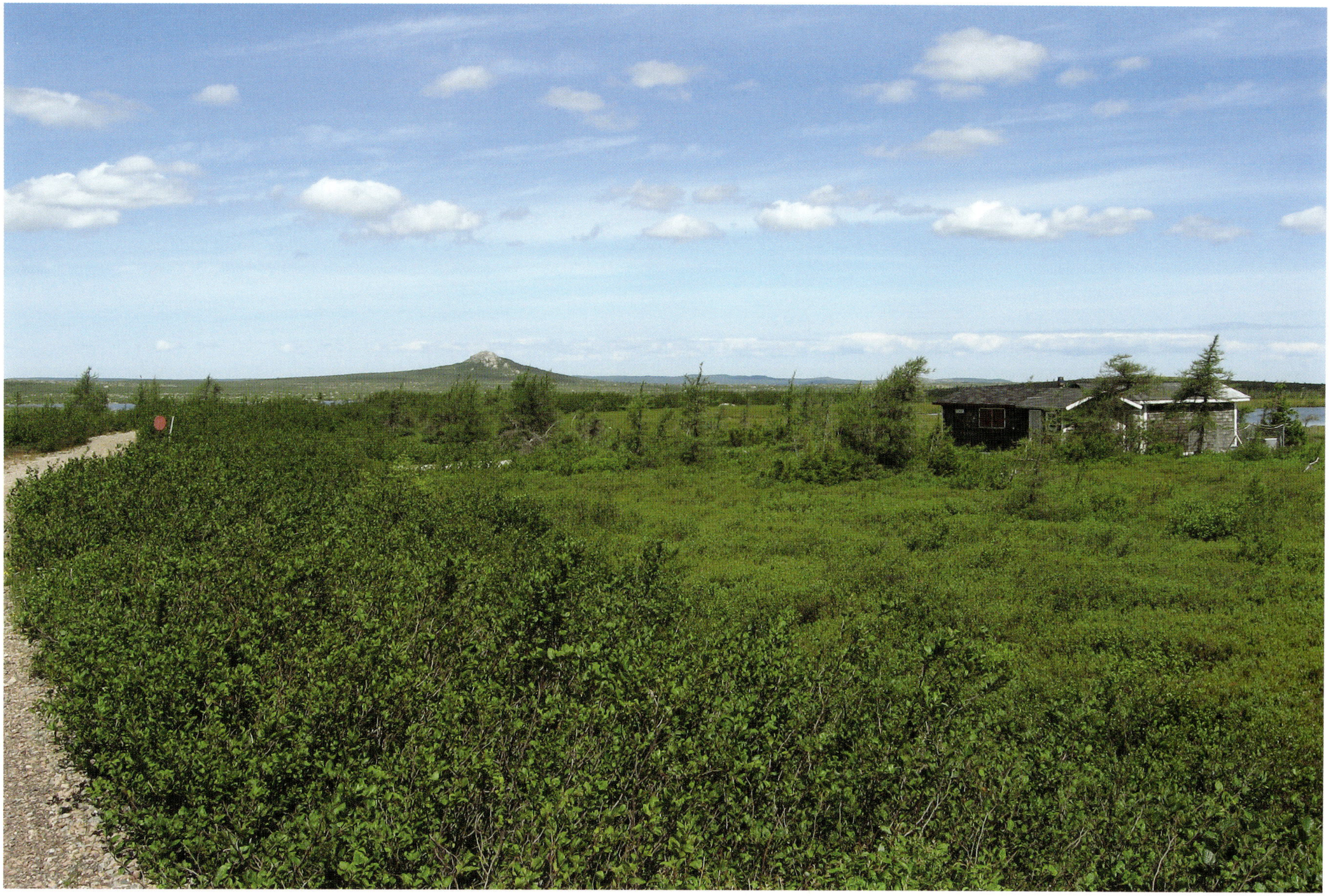

SUMMIT TODAY
By late July, any snow remaining from the previous winter has long since melted and the tundra-like vegetation has turned a rich green. Summit provides a perfect view of the four Topsail Mountains nearby named after the sails on a ship; Gaff, Mizzen, Main and Fore. Like the trains of yesterday, any vehicles navigating the roadbed have a steep descent both east and west of this point. *Author photo*

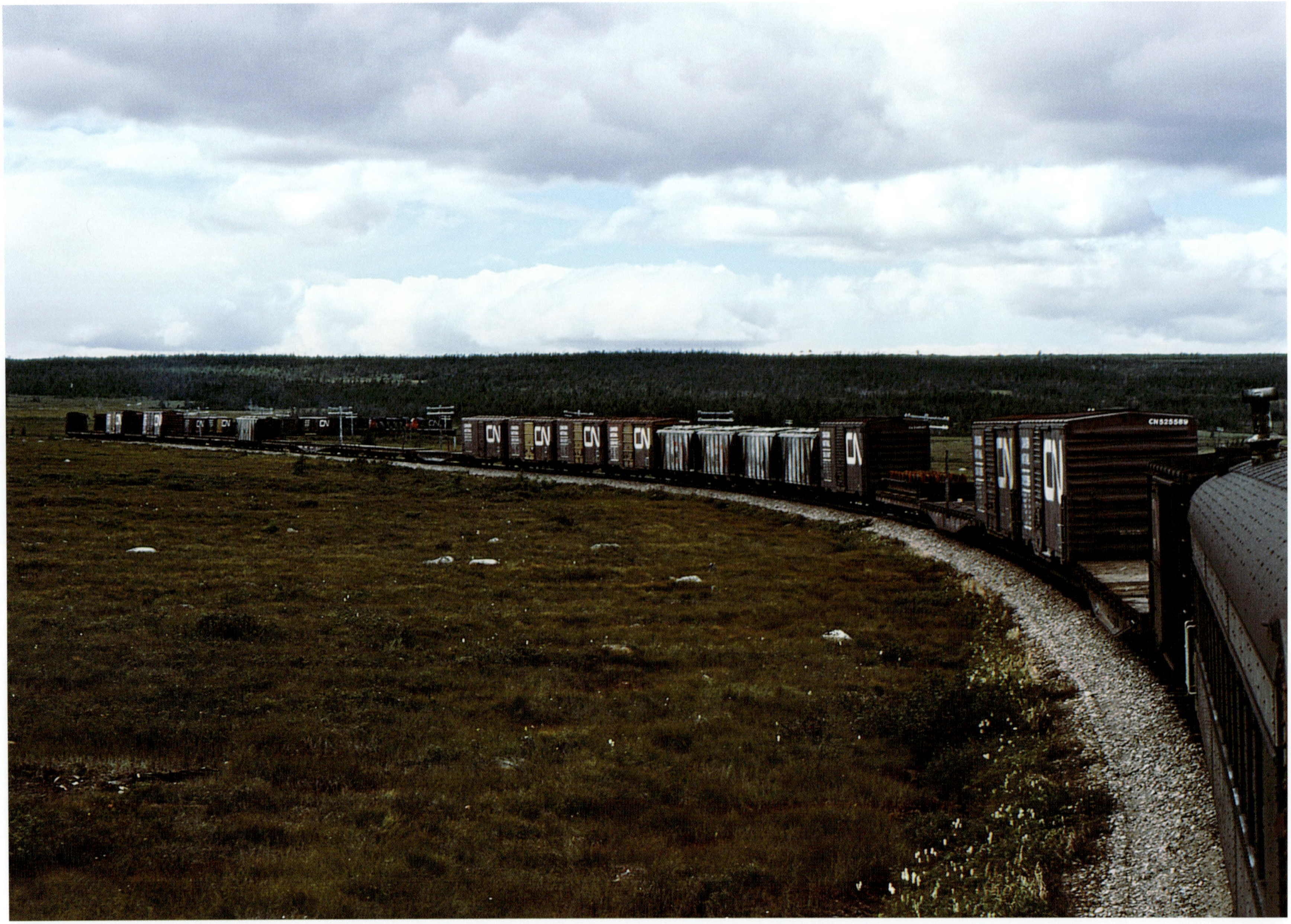

QUARRY 1978
CN mixed train 203 with three NF210s rounds Blaggards Curve near Quarry on August 28, 1978. Caribou roam the barrens here in great numbers and engineer Bren Dicks once photographed a huge herd walking along the main line in front of his train. Quarry used to be the site of an inexhaustible source of granite and blocks from here were used to build the Victorian Station in St. John's in 1902. *Rich Taylor photo*

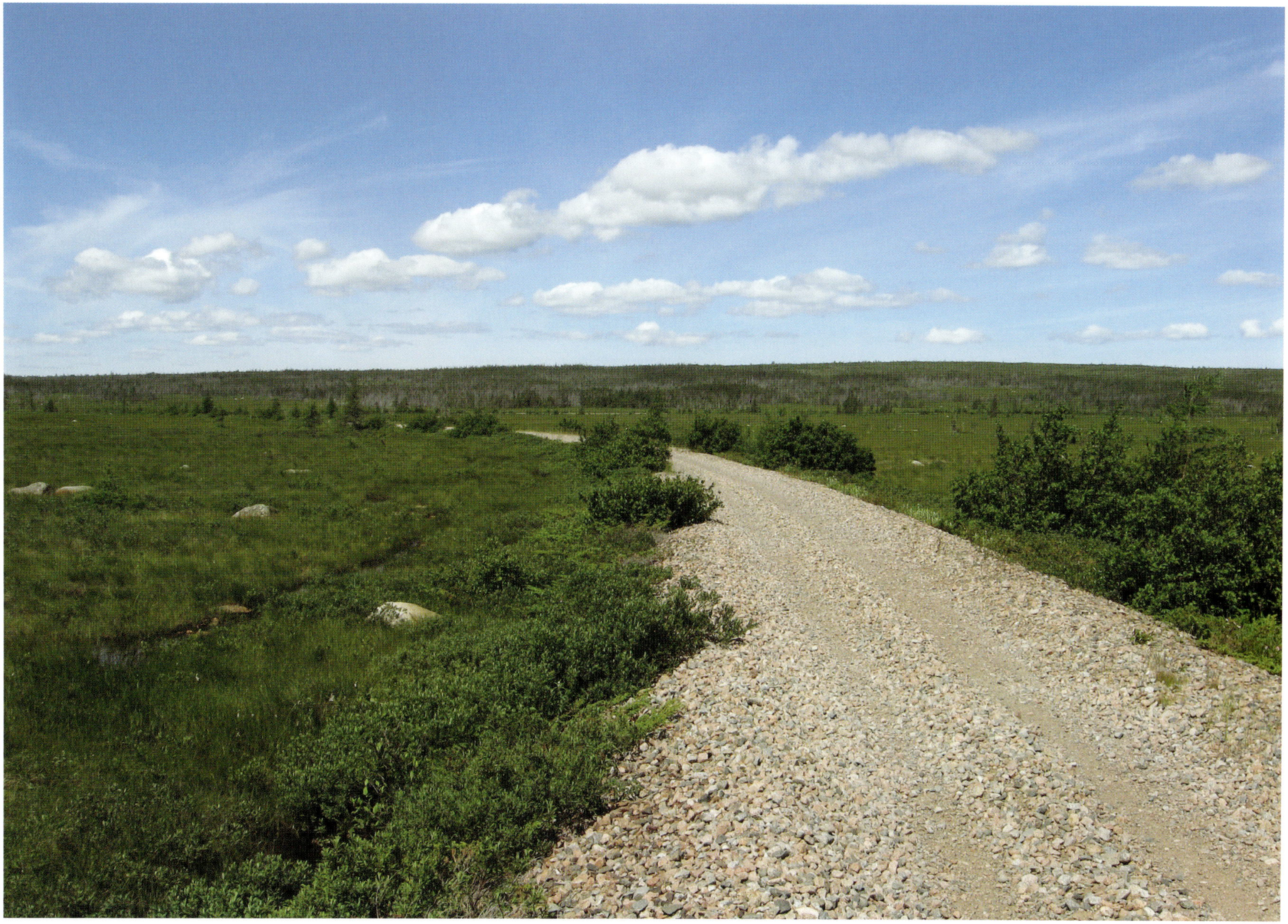

QUARRY TODAY
The sharp 'S' curve is still evident on a hot July day. The huge granite deposit, used to pave Water Street in St. John's at the turn of the last century, may one day be declared a provincial historic site. Built by the C.C.&F. in 1943 as the sleeper 'Buchans', Bunk Car 5023 of the White Fleet (to accommodate work crews), has found a third lease on life as a cabin of sorts in Quarry. *Author photo*

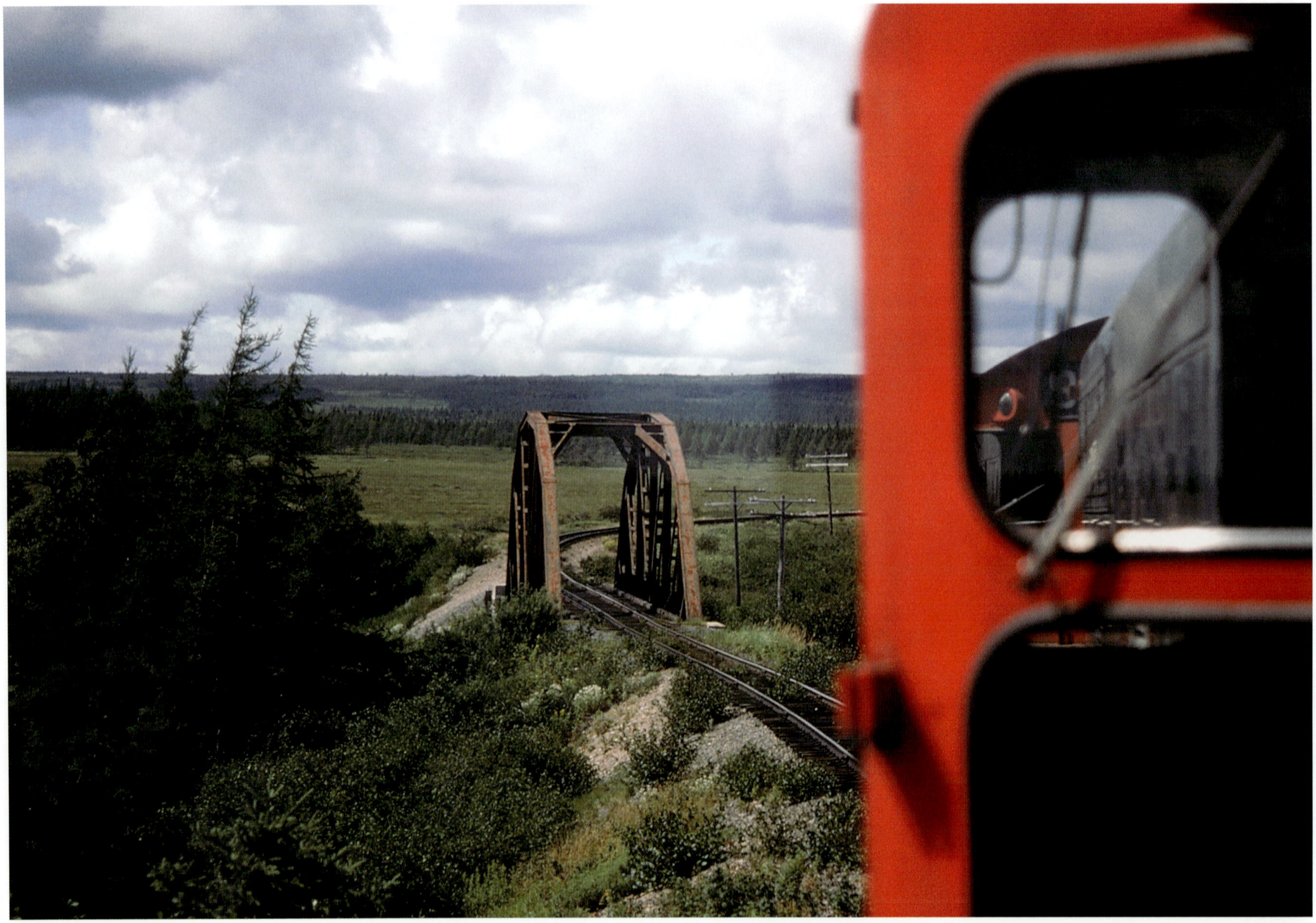

MARY MARCH 1985

Terra Transport mixed 203 approaches the Mary March River Bridge on August 13, 1985. Photographed from the cab of the third diesel on one of five trips from 1977 to 1988, Wendell Lemon will ride this unit all the way to Deer Lake where he will make a Roadcruiser connection to the ferry in Port aux Basques. A 'ghost train' event occurred in 1945 when the section men, after hearing a train cross this bridge, moved a speeder to allow it to pass but it never did appear. *Wendell Lemon photo*

MARY MARCH TODAY

An overgrowth of alders has restricted view of the bridge until the straight approach. A Trans Canada Trail marker at this location tells the user that the former Newfoundland Railway is now part of its 16,500 km coast to coast network. Mary March was the site of a huge shed that held the railway's rotary plow, two steam engines, three tenders and a cook/ bunk when not clearing snow. *Author photo*

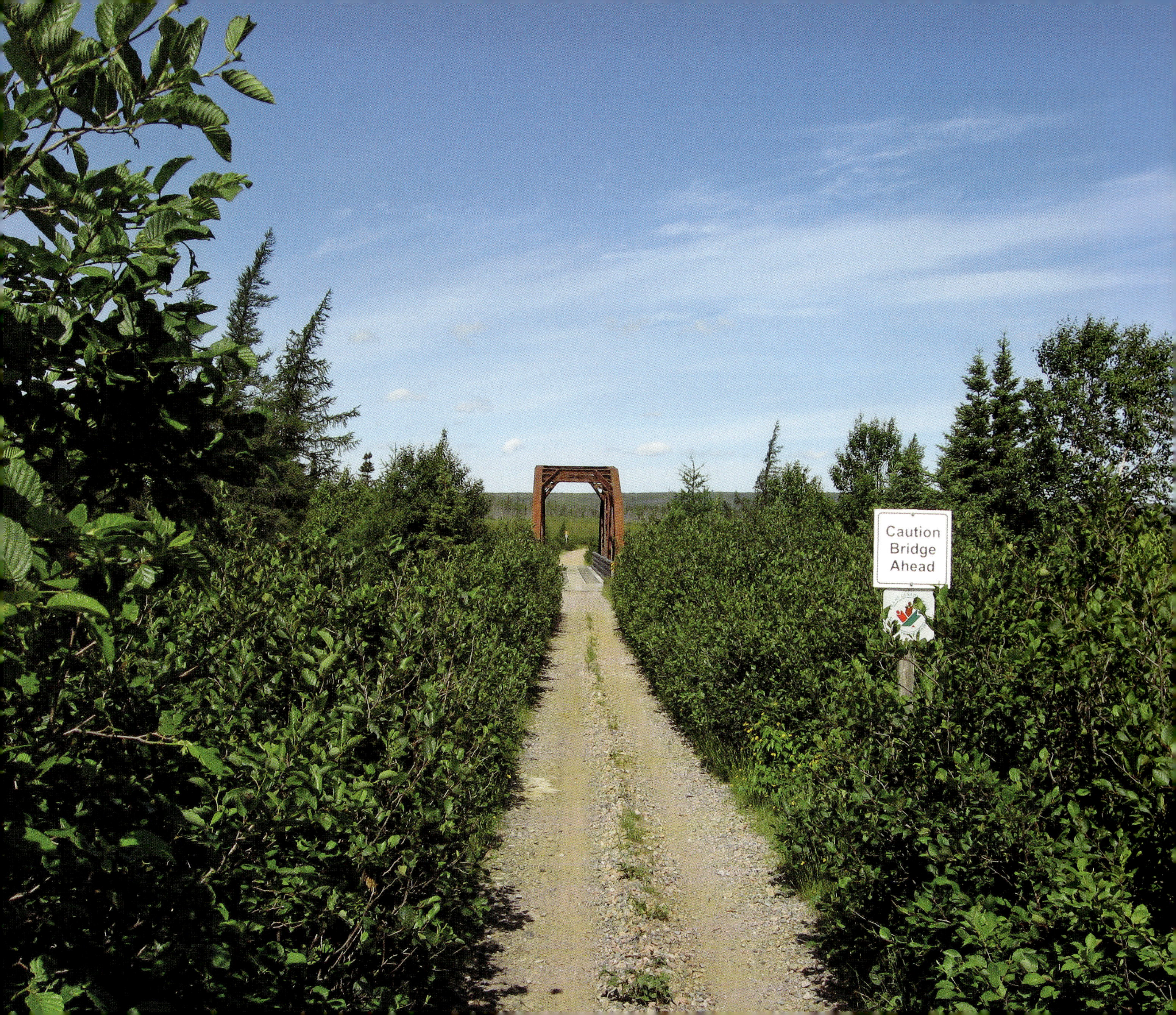
Caution
Bridge
Ahead

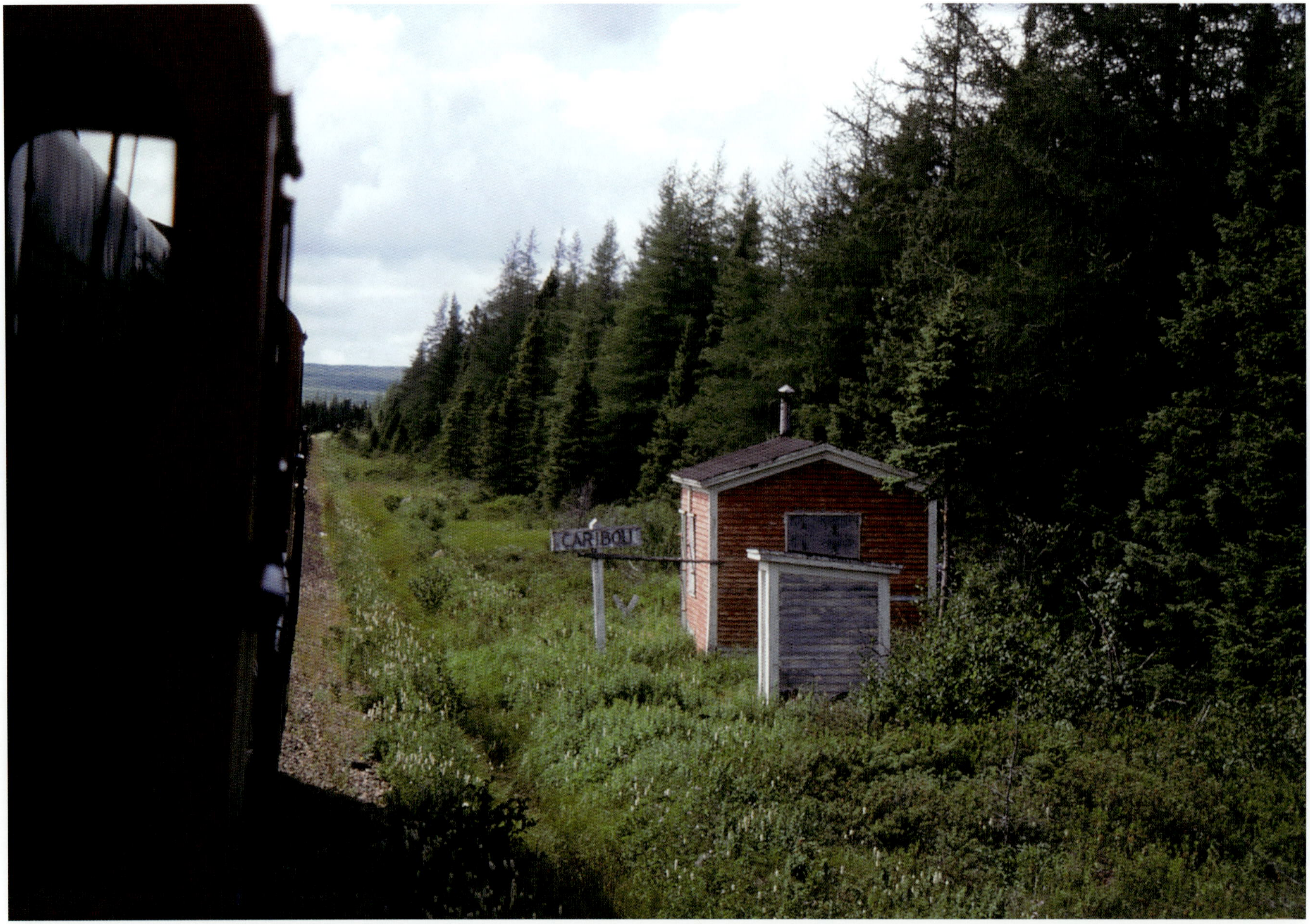

CARIBOU 1985

As the diesels of Terra Transport Train 203 roll and list somewhat to the right, the photographer captures the section men's shack and cut-in house at Caribou, MP 319.2 on August 13, 1985. Operators used this building until the 1960s to ensure train movement over the Topsails in winter and it was moved from mile 312 to Mary March and finally to Caribou.

Wendell Lemon photo

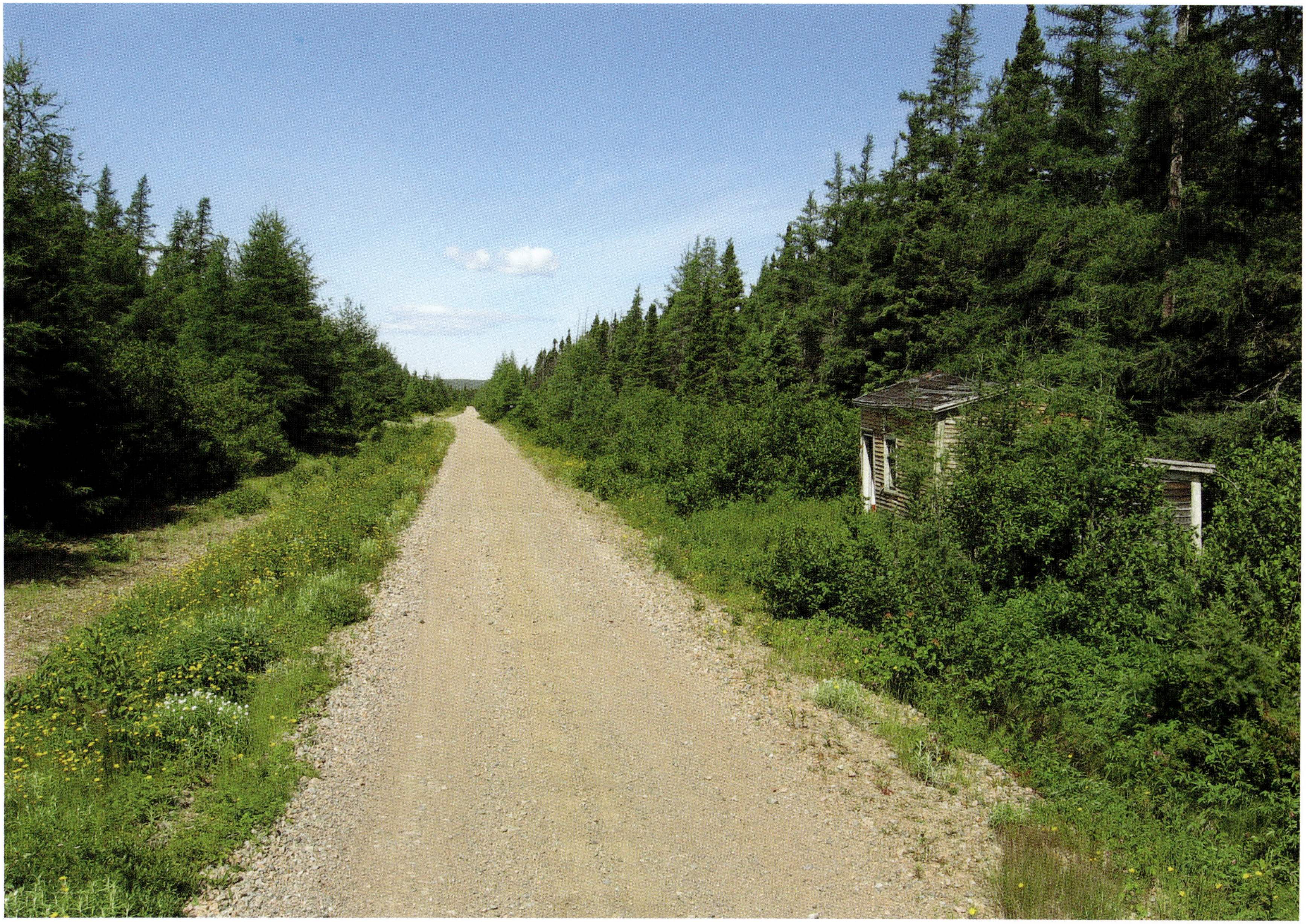

CARIBOU TODAY

Several decades later, the roadbed remains in excellent shape and the long siding can be easily seen on the left. The shack and cut-in house, used in the event of radio failure with the dispatcher, still stands despite the weight of the heavy winter snow. It was at Caribou that the crew of the last westbound 203 stopped the train to join their wives and friends in the caboose for a special celebration with a cake in the shape of a train. *Author photo*

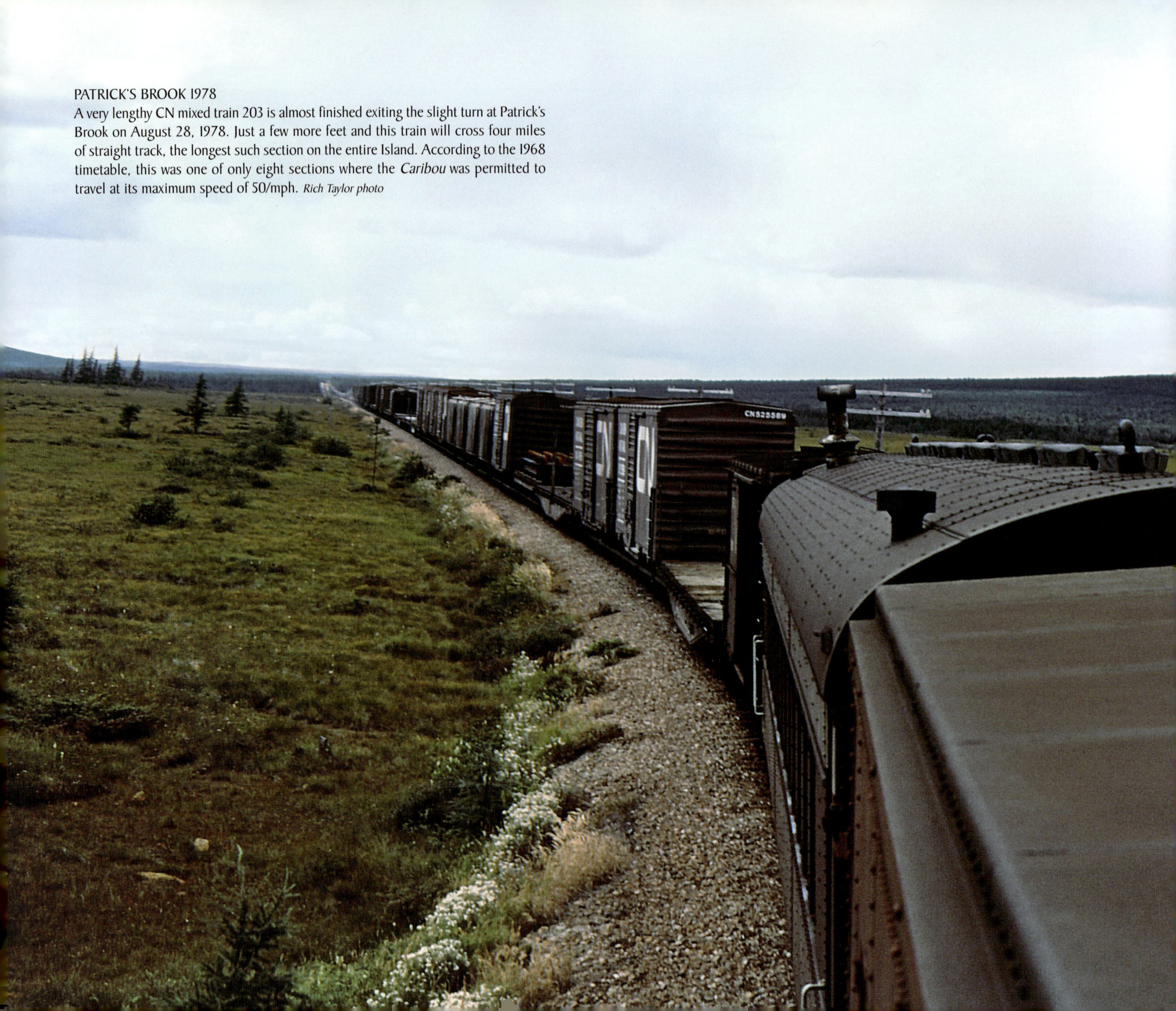

PATRICK'S BROOK 1978

A very lengthy CN mixed train 203 is almost finished exiting the slight turn at Patrick's Brook on August 28, 1978. Just a few more feet and this train will cross four miles of straight track, the longest such section on the entire Island. According to the 1968 timetable, this was one of only eight sections where the *Caribou* was permitted to travel at its maximum speed of 50/mph. *Rich Taylor photo*

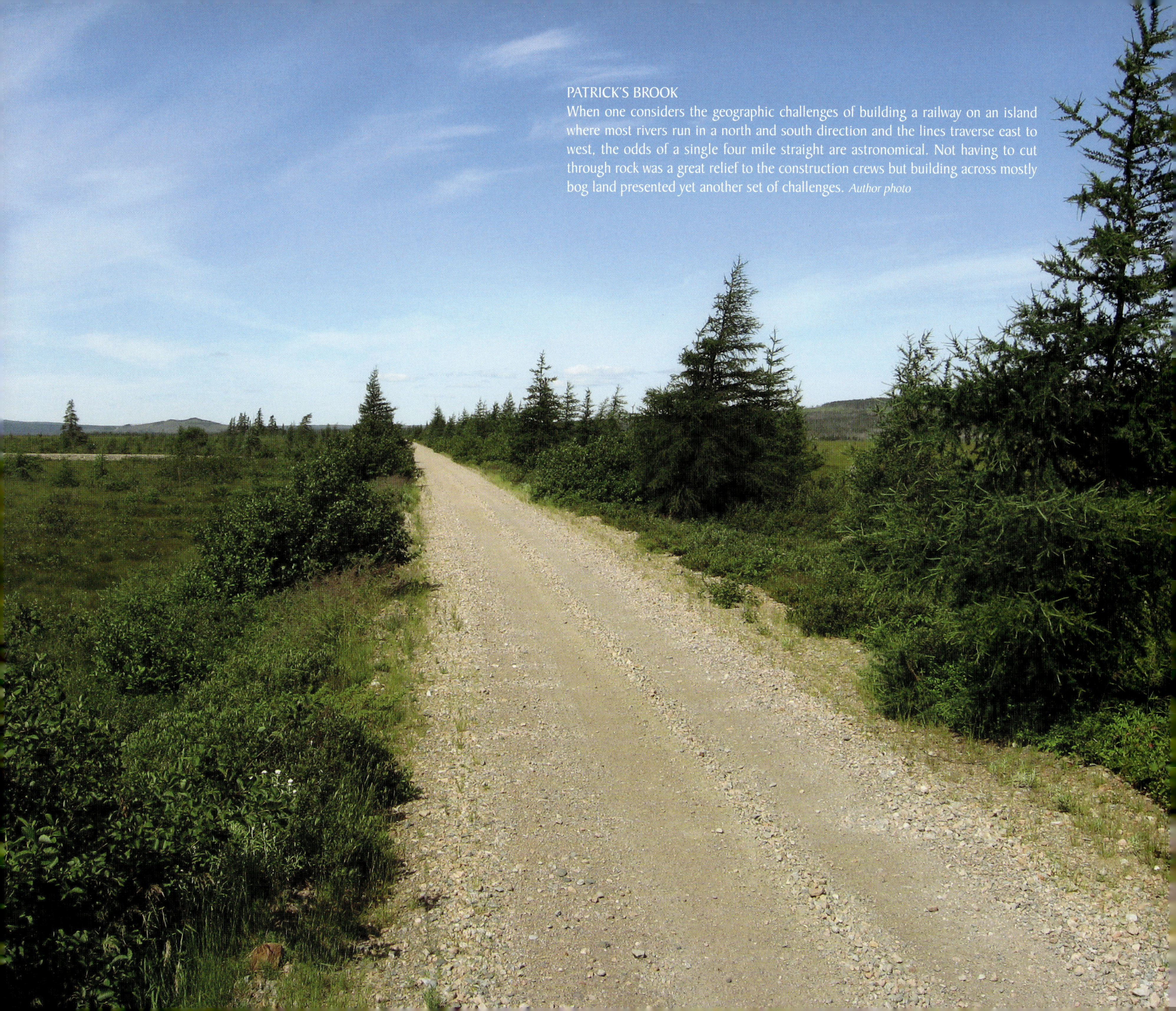

PATRICK'S BROOK

When one considers the geographic challenges of building a railway on an island where most rivers run in a north and south direction and the lines traverse east to west, the odds of a single four mile straight are astronomical. Not having to cut through rock was a great relief to the construction crews but building across mostly bog land presented yet another set of challenges. *Author photo*

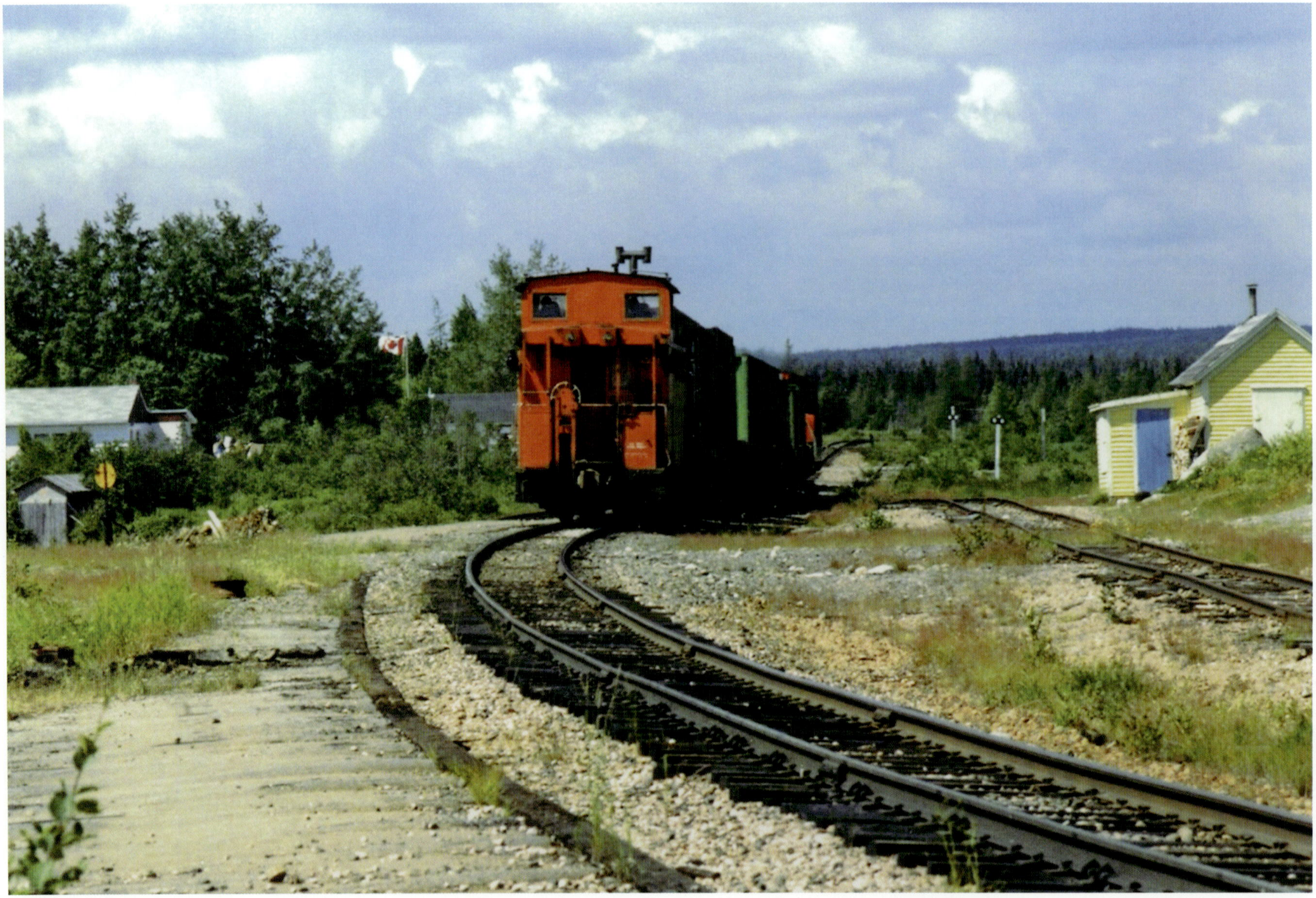

MILLERTOWN JUNCTION 1988

Late in the summer of 1988, Terra Transport Train 203 with NF210 941, five containers and a caboose pass through Millertown Junction. At this time the railway was winding down and the mixed service was offered only three days a week. Educator and photographer Mike Shufelt of Maine discovered the Newfoundland Railway in 1986 and spent the next three summers recording it for posterity. *Mike Shufelt photo*

MILLERTOWN JUNCTION TODAY

The bright yellow section men's shack is a reminder of the railway presence in the beautiful and flourishing Millertown Junction area. Railway author and historian Mont Lingard still lives in the red roof cabin to the left, on the edge of Joe Glodes Pond, and photographer Mike Shufelt has returned to his cabin here for several weeks every year since the closure. *Author photo*

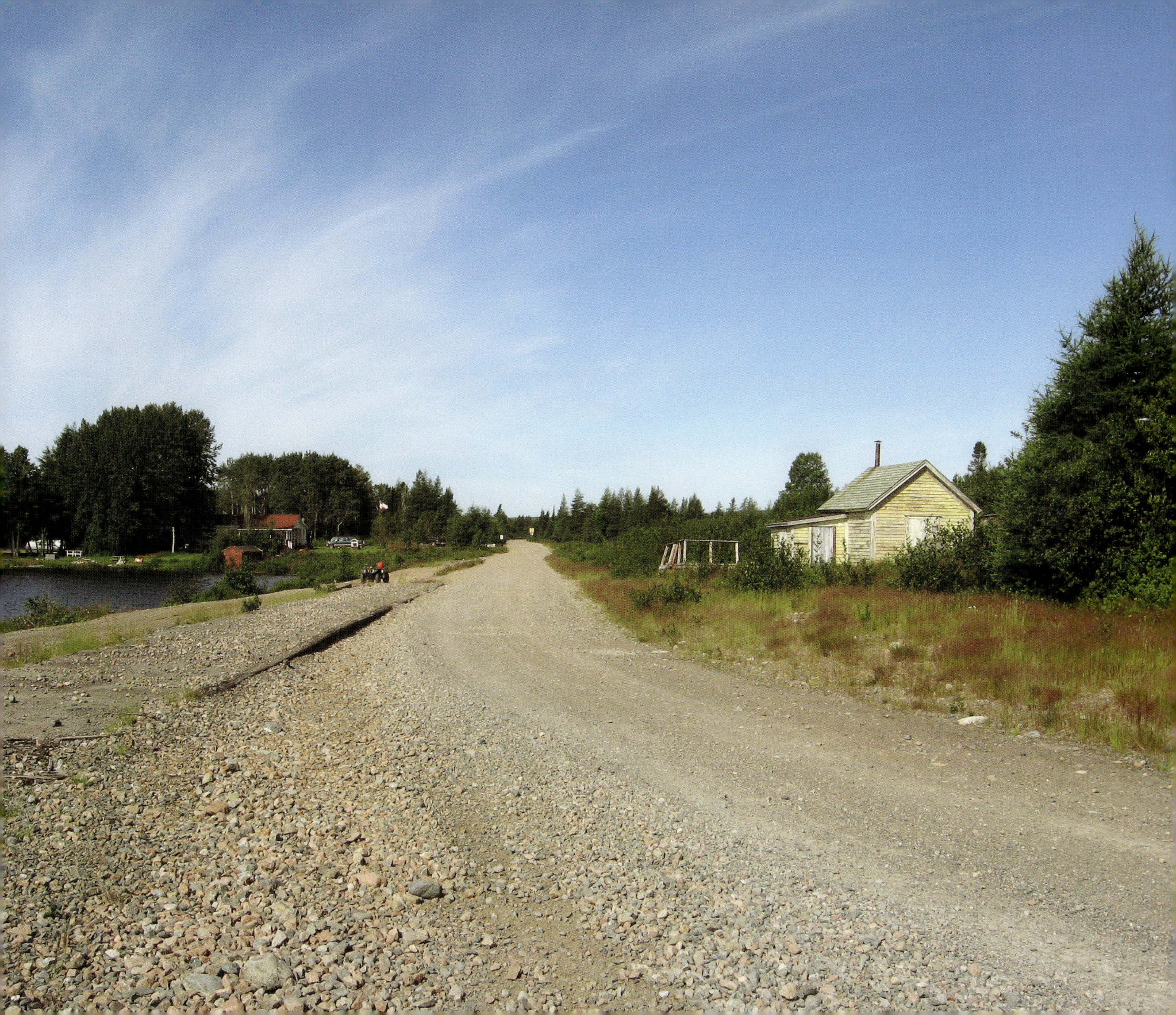

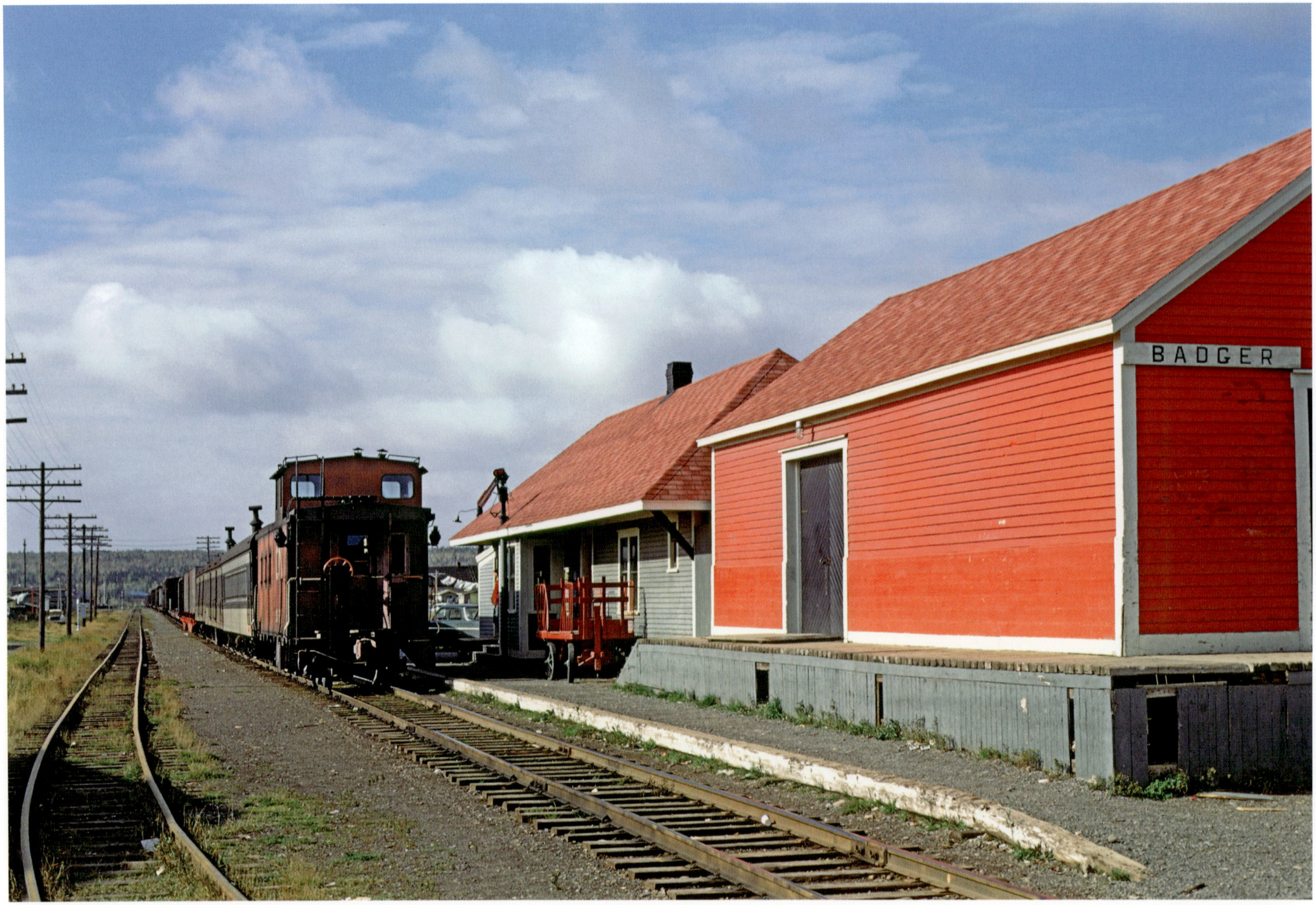

BADGER 1968

CN mixed train 203 with three pieces of passenger equipment stops at Badger before heading over the Gaff Topsails on October 9, 1968. This would be the last area connected with the Trans Canada Highway until arrival in Deer Lake, 80 miles west. In 1968, 203 operated as a mixed over the entire line, taking just short of thirty hours to make the complete trans-Island journey. *Ted Wickson photo*

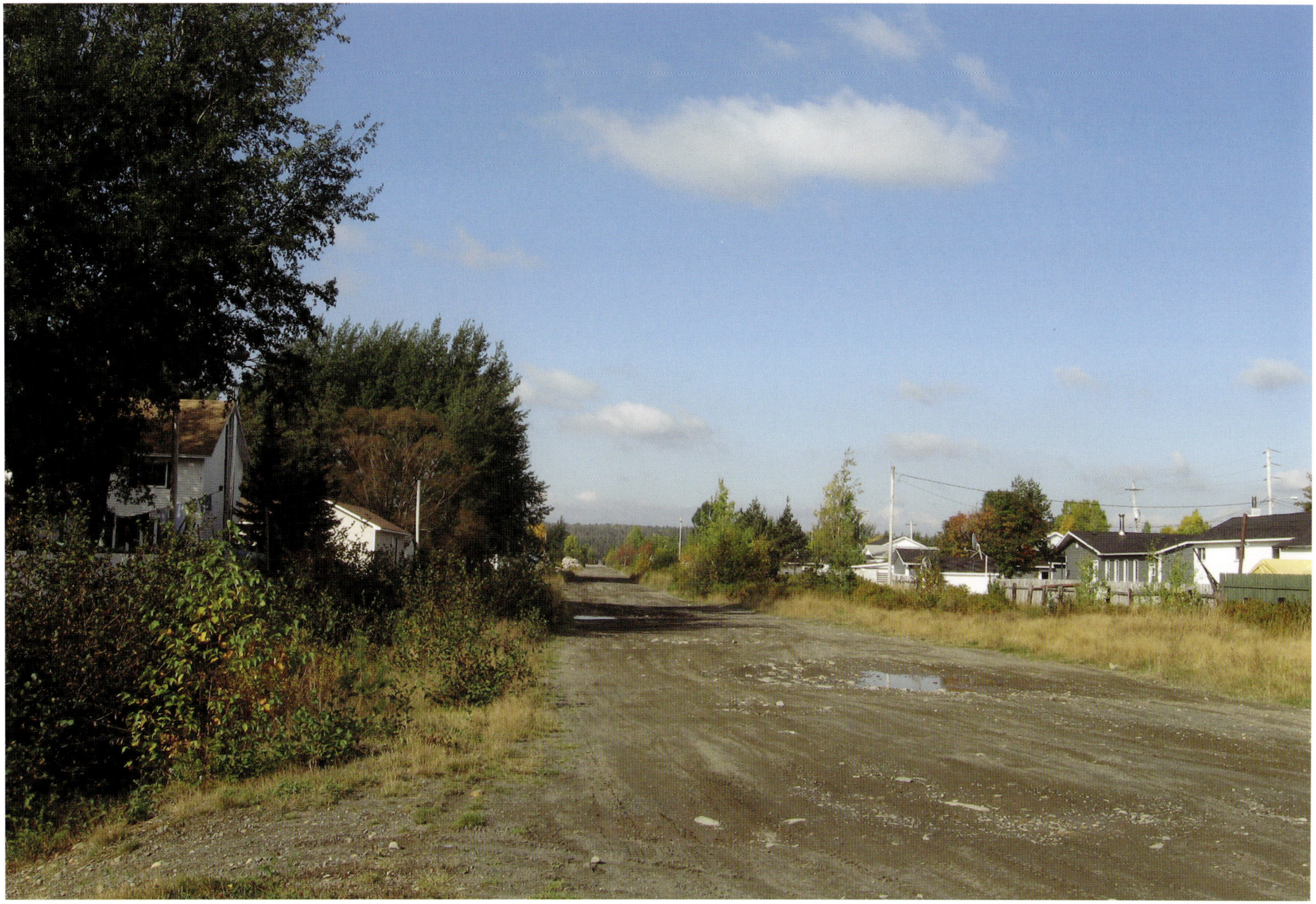

BAGDER TODAY

Looking west towards the Gaff Topsails, the town of Badger was nearly lost when the Exploits, Red Indian and Badger Rivers overflowed on February 15, 2003. The former rail yard was under 2.5 metres of water and thousands of residents were evacuated. Fortunately, the little station also survived as it was previously relocated near the Trans Canada Highway as a take-out restaurant. *Author photo*

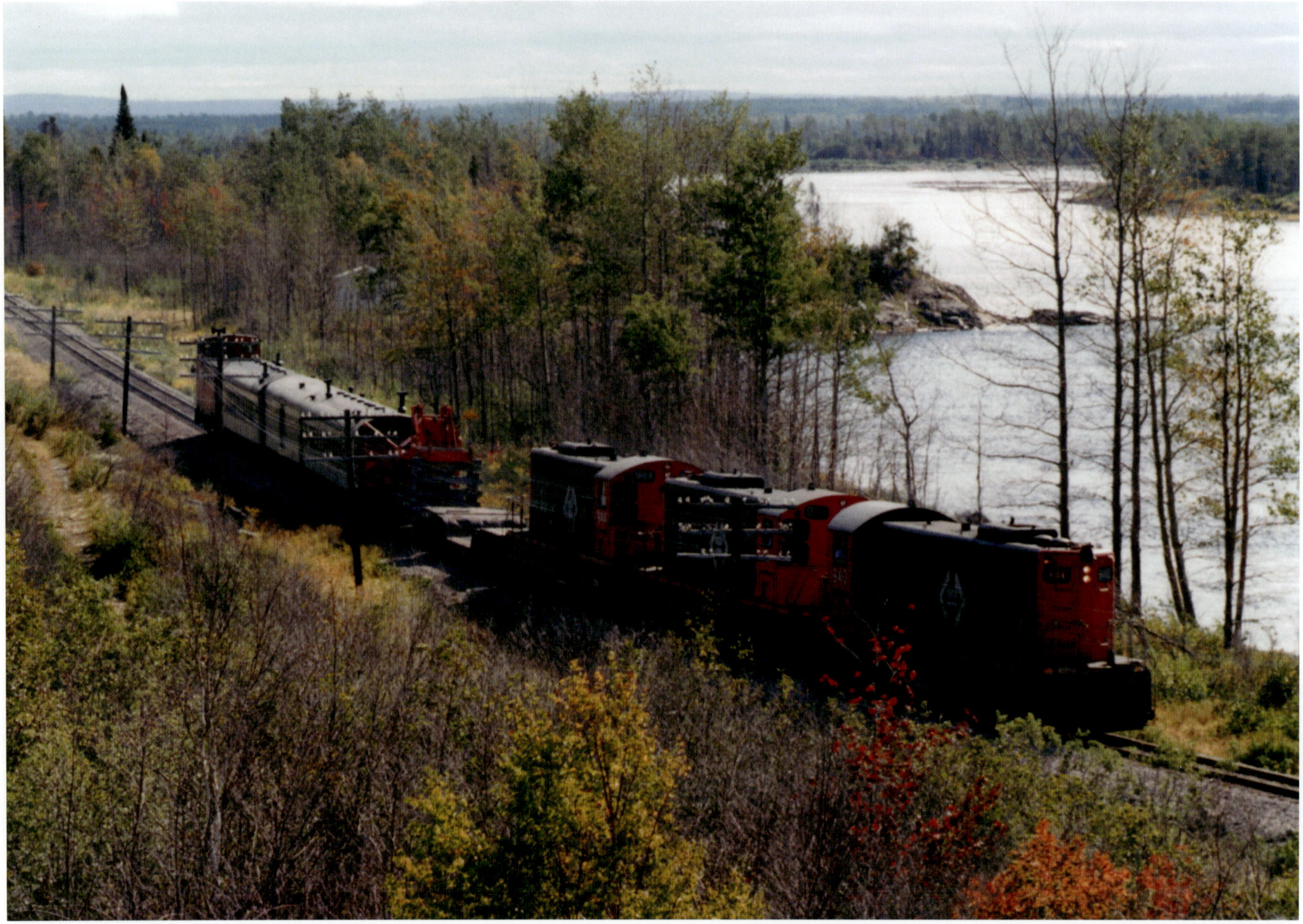

EXPLOITS RIVER 1988
Terra Transport mixed train 203 with NF210's 940, 941 and 944 along with a depressed centre and regular flat for freight skirts the shore of the Exploits River on September 21, 1988. With only a few more runs left, trains such as these often were used to place rail removal equipment at stategeic points on the line.
Charlie Falk photo

EXPLOITS RIVER
At 246 kms, the Exploits River is the longest on the Island and drains an area of 11,000 square kilometres. Nearby is the halfway mark of the Island's Trans Canada Highway, and when opened by Prime Minister Lestor B. Pearson in 1965, a huge stone monument once marked the spot. The railbed is now nearly invisible from this section of the parallel TCH. *Author photo*

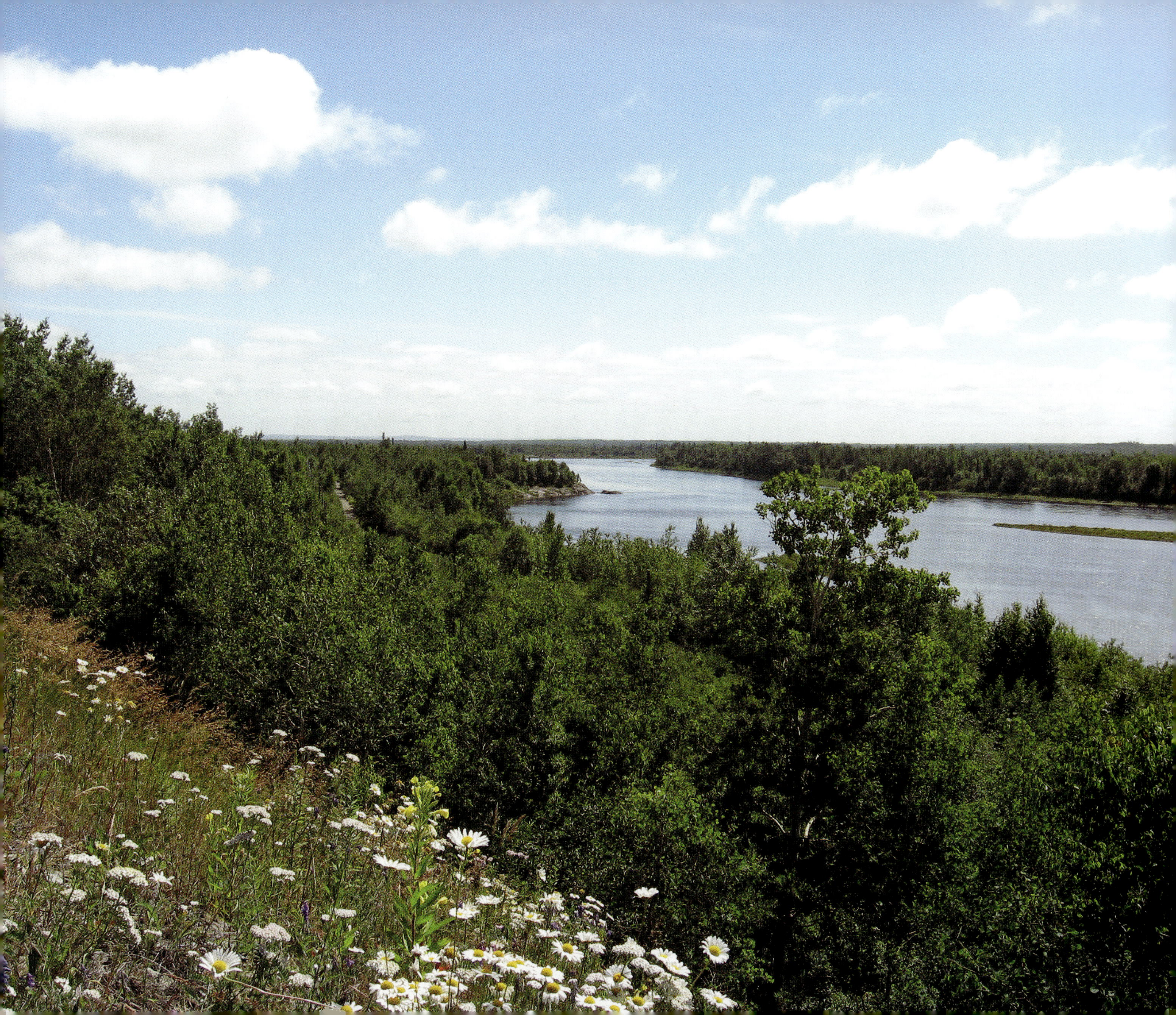

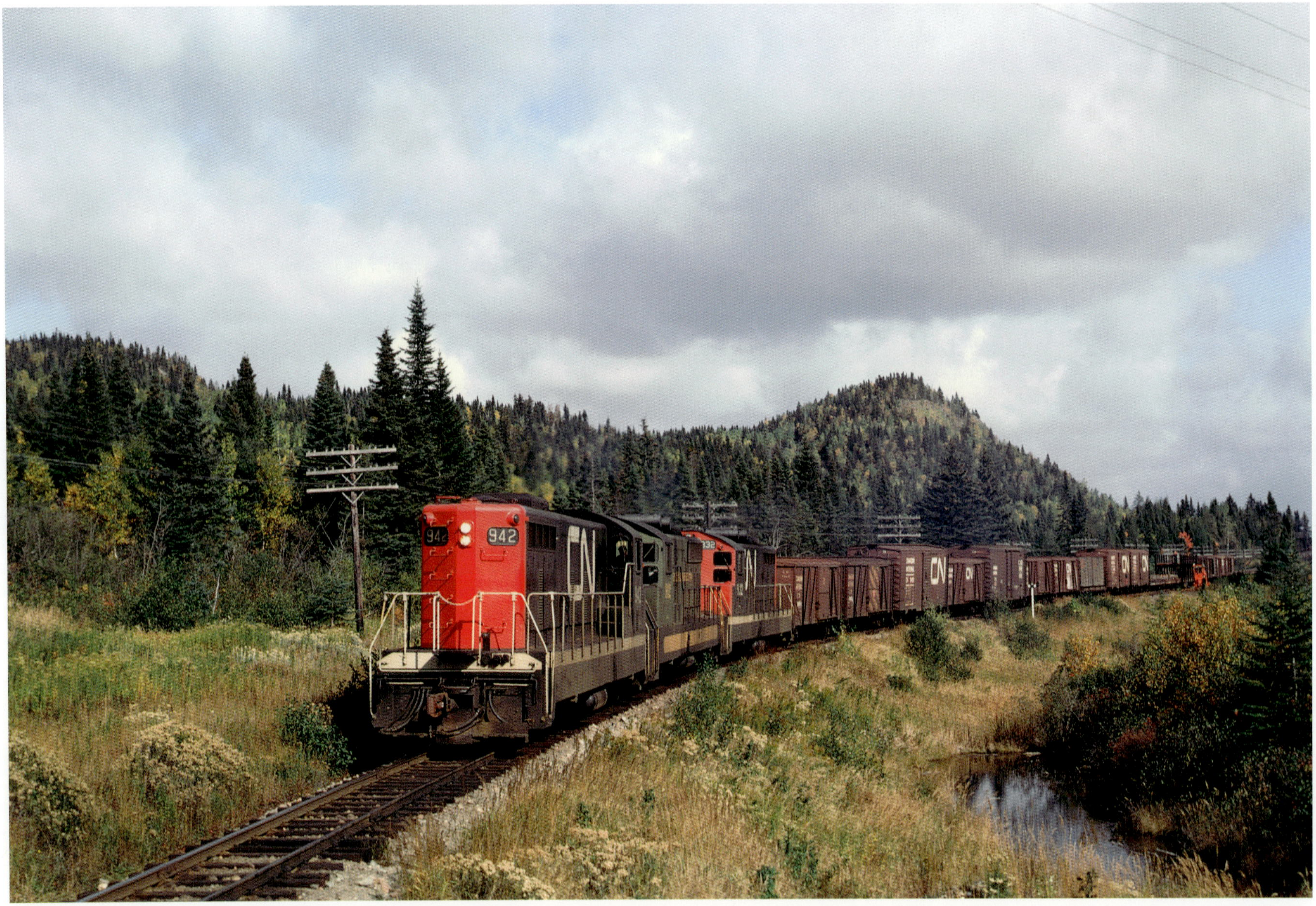

RED CLIFF 1968

Canadian National mixed train 203 with locomotives 942,902 and 932 is captured approaching the TCH from Red Cliff on October 9, 1968. This mixed train has both standard mainland boxcars as well as the smaller former Newfoundland Railway outside braced ones. As part of the consist, the rear of the train includes, but out of sight from this view, two baggage cars and a coach. *Ted Wickson photo*

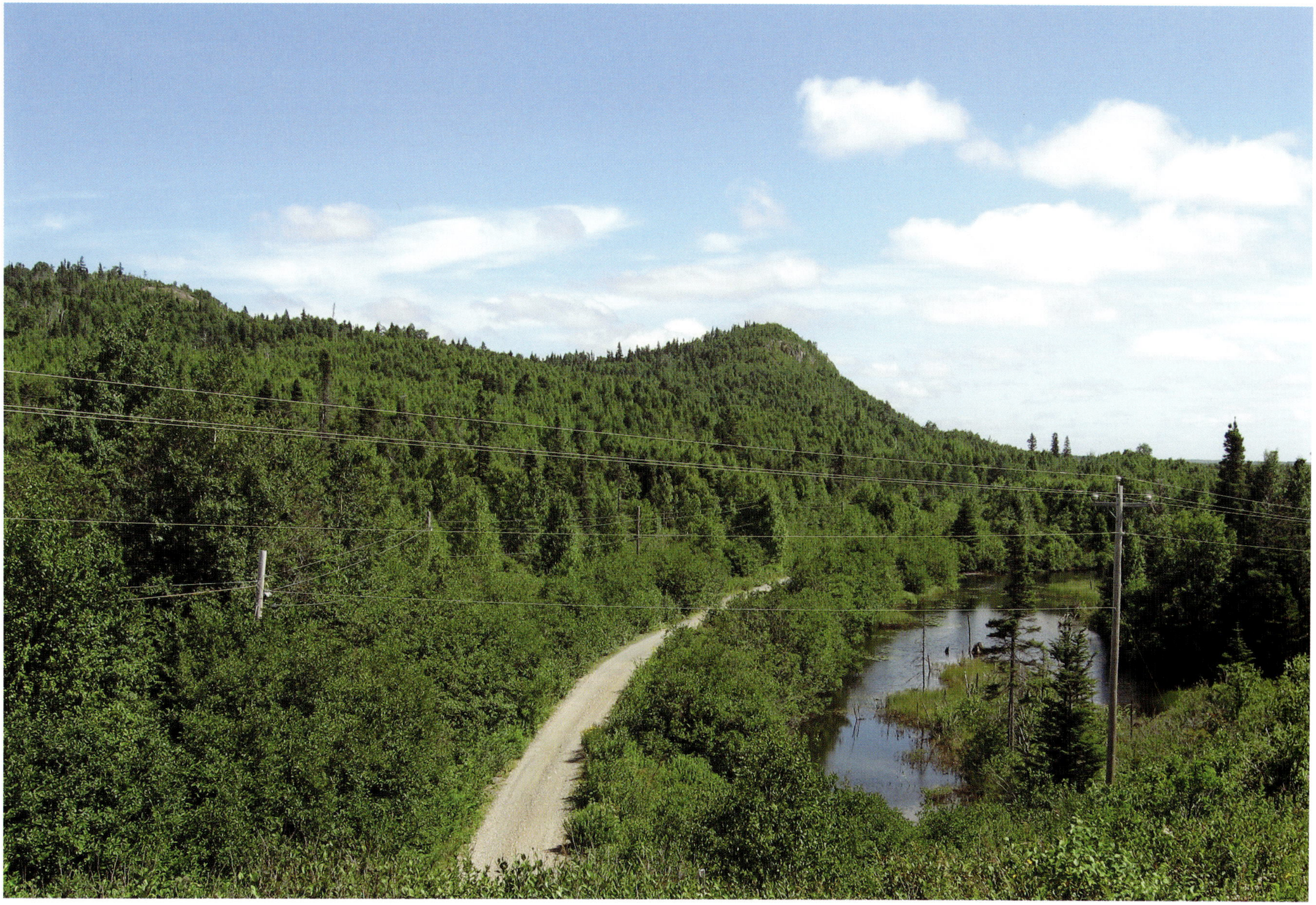

RED CLIFF TODAY
With all its rich greenery and looking somewhat like a scene from an Amazon jungle, any visitor to the Island could be mistaken for thinking they were not in Newfoundland as they drove past Red Cliff, home of the only drive-in theatre in the province. The Red Cliff camp grounds can accommodate up to 1400 tents, just perfect for the thousands who attend the nearby Exploits Valley Salmon Festival. *Author photo*

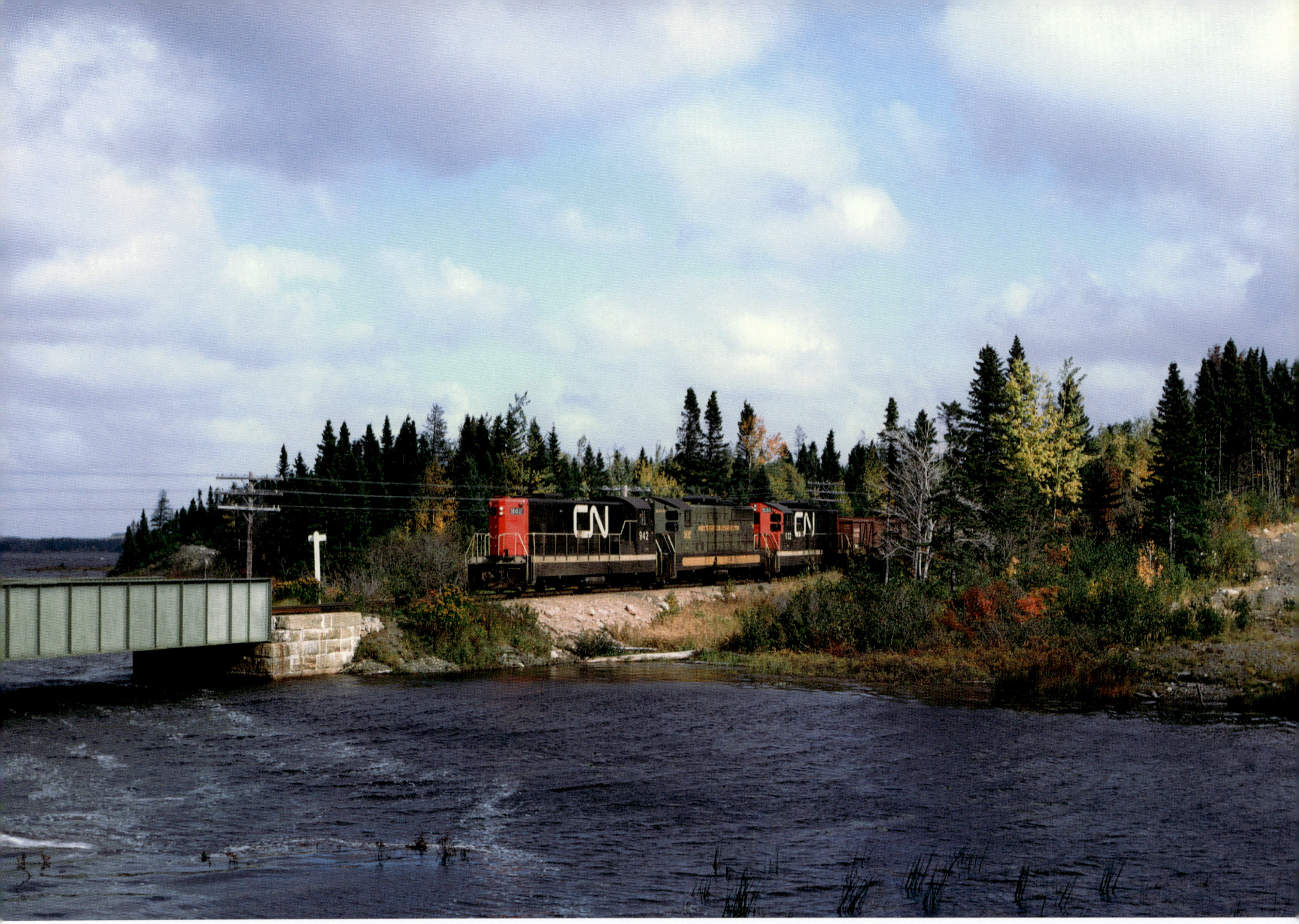

RUSHY POND 1968

Canadian National mixed train 203 with locomotives 942, 902 and 932 prepare to cross the trestle at Rushy Pond on October 9, 1968. NF110 902 was still wearing the original green and gold paint scheme from her delivery in 1953. One of the last units still in that livery, she would soon be wearing the new image CN black and red of her sisters. *Ted Wickson photo*

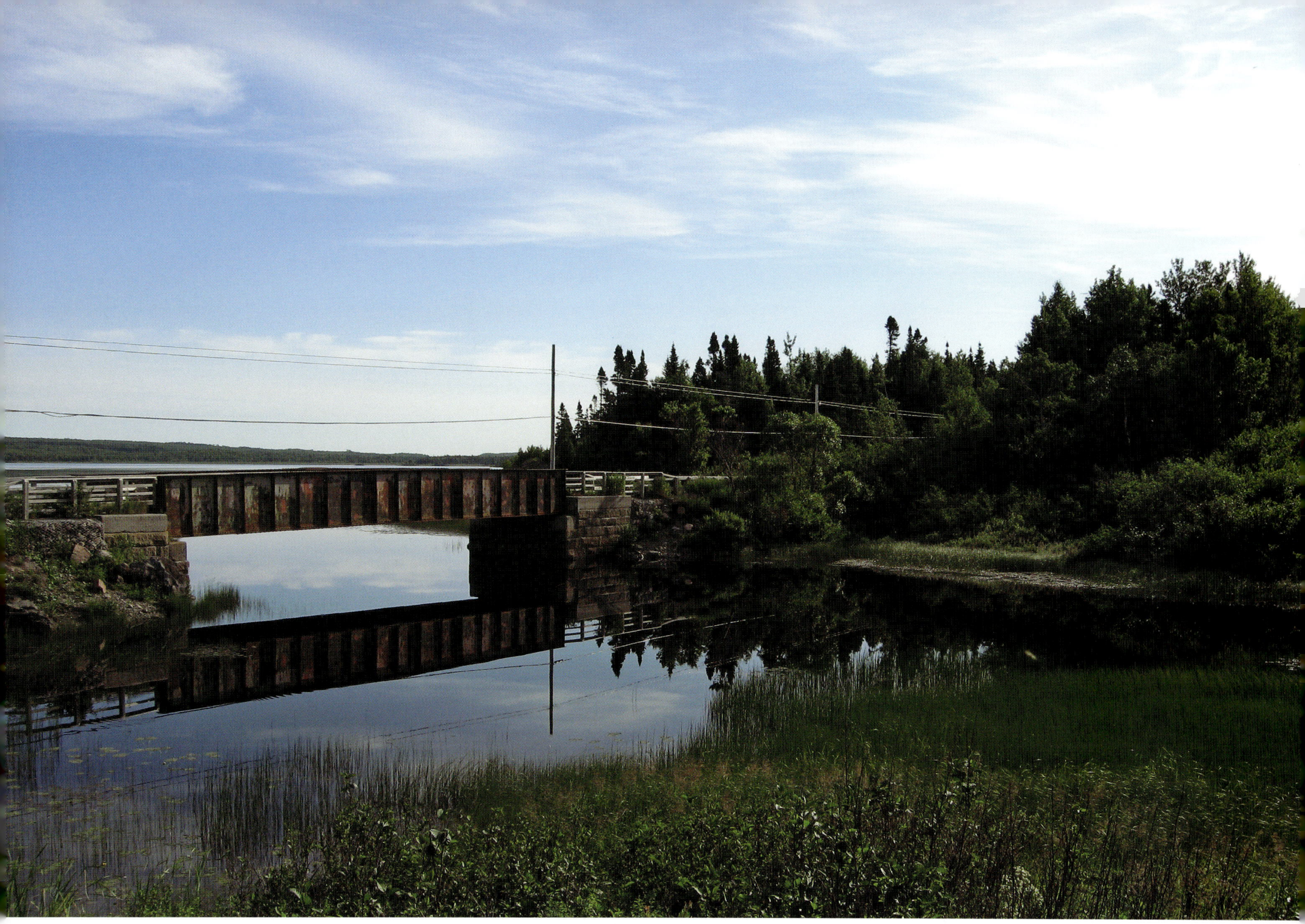

RUSHY POND TODAY
The trestle at Rushy Pond makes a picture perfect reflection on an early July morning. Golfers playing at the nearby Grand Falls Golf Club are witness to this scene on every visit to the course that has been open since 1924. Engineers at this point would slow their eastbound train for the Grand Falls yard limit speed. *Author photo*

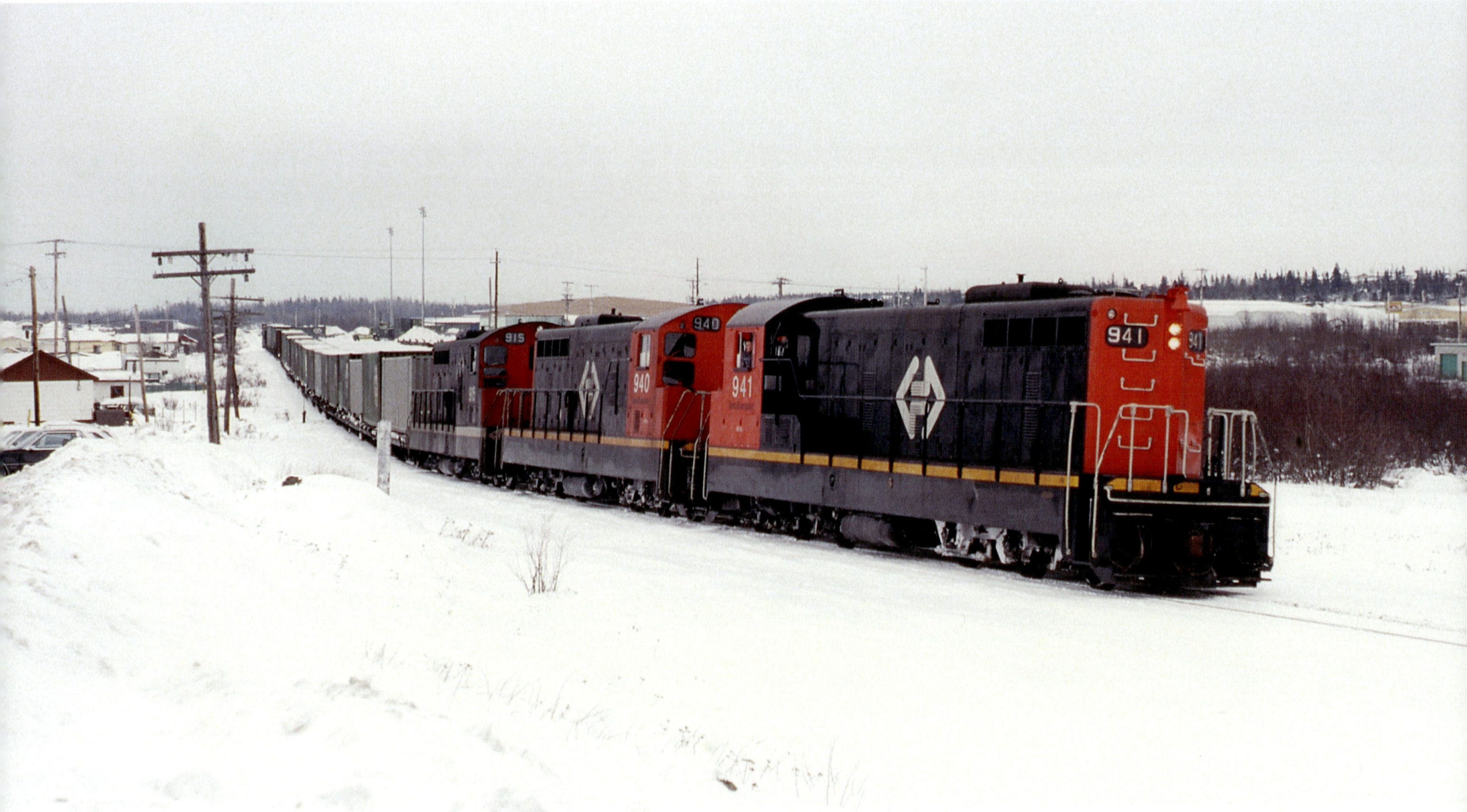

GRAND FALLS 1987
Terra Transport mixed train 203, with engineer Ray Boyd at the controls of NF210 941, prepares to depart from Grand Falls during Christmas week 1987. Just days after this photo, a CTC rule saw the coach service removed from the consist until the following April. For the first three months of 1988, 203 would run as a freight only service. *Author photo*

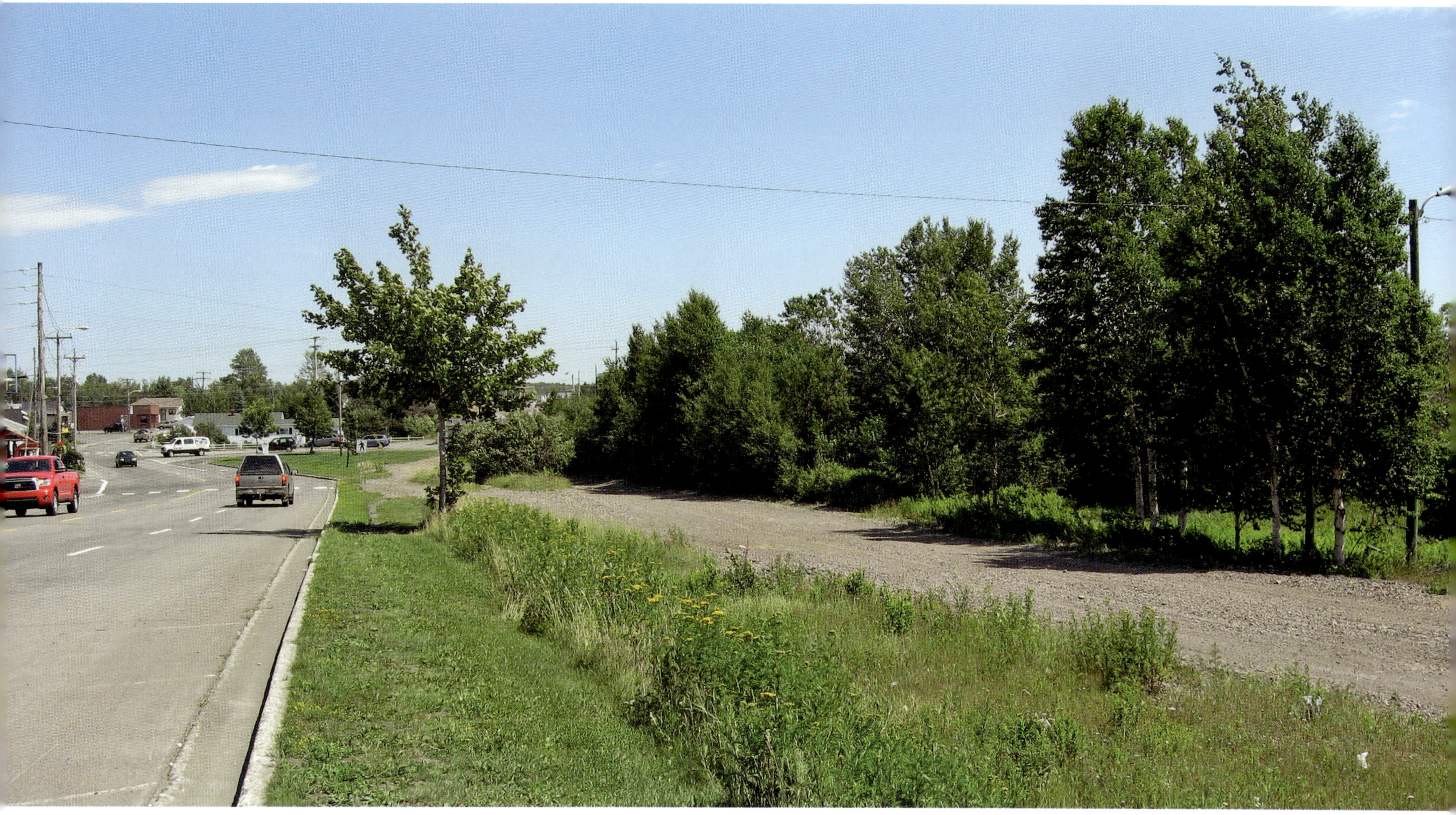

GRAND FALLS TODAY

With the removal of the tracks that separated the two towns, Grand Falls and Windsor amalgamated in 1991 to form the new municipality of Grand Falls-Windsor, now comprising over 13,000 residents. Its annual summertime Exploits Valley Salmon Festival attracts some of the biggest names in musical entertainment, from Great Big Sea to Aerosmith.
Author photo

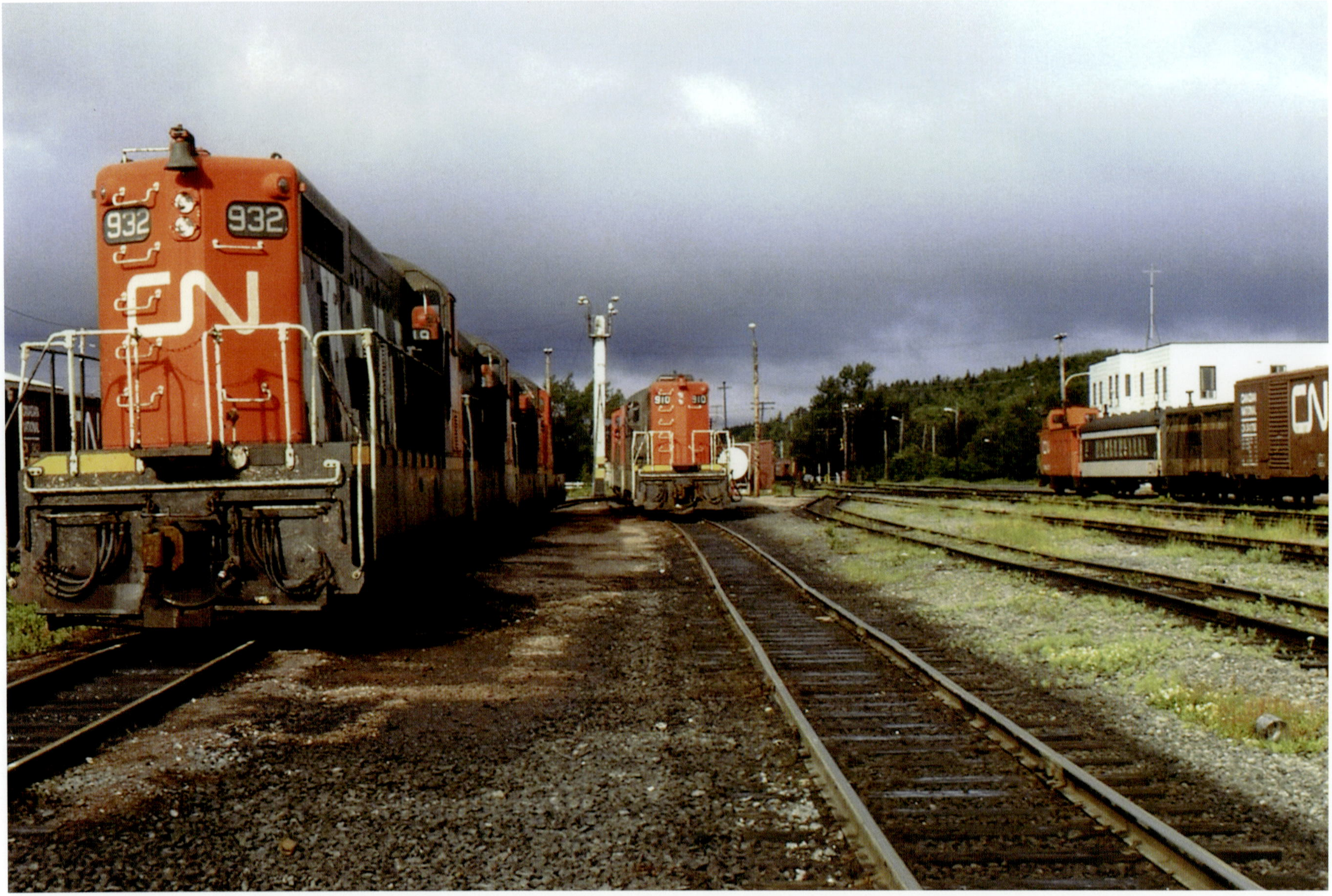

BISHOP'S FALLS 1986
With dozens of NF210s awaiting the call to duty, plenty of motive power is evident in this scene taken at the Bishop's Falls yard on July 5, 1986. The passenger equipment on the rear of Train 204, which had arrived hours earlier from Corner Brook, will be shunted for the return trip on 203 later that morning. *Mike Shufelt photo*

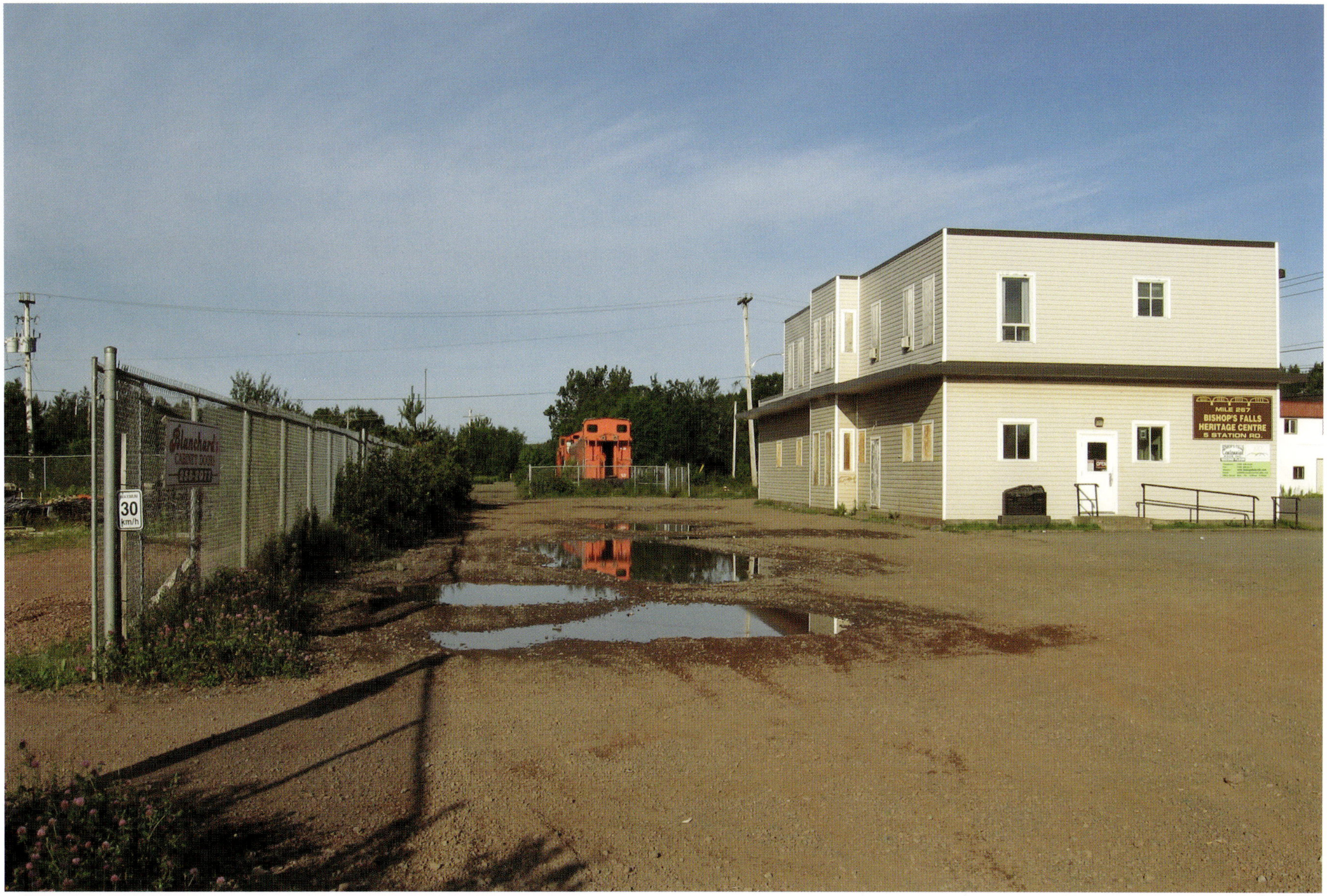

BISHOP'S FALLS TODAY
The old station which saw much activity has been preserved and is now home to the Bishop's Falls Heritage Centre. It keeps a watchful eye over a static train display with locomotive NF210 924, snowplow 3454, baggage car 4149 and caboose 6057. When placed there in November 1990 by engineer Bren Dicks, 924 was the last such engine to operate on mainline trackage. *Author photo*

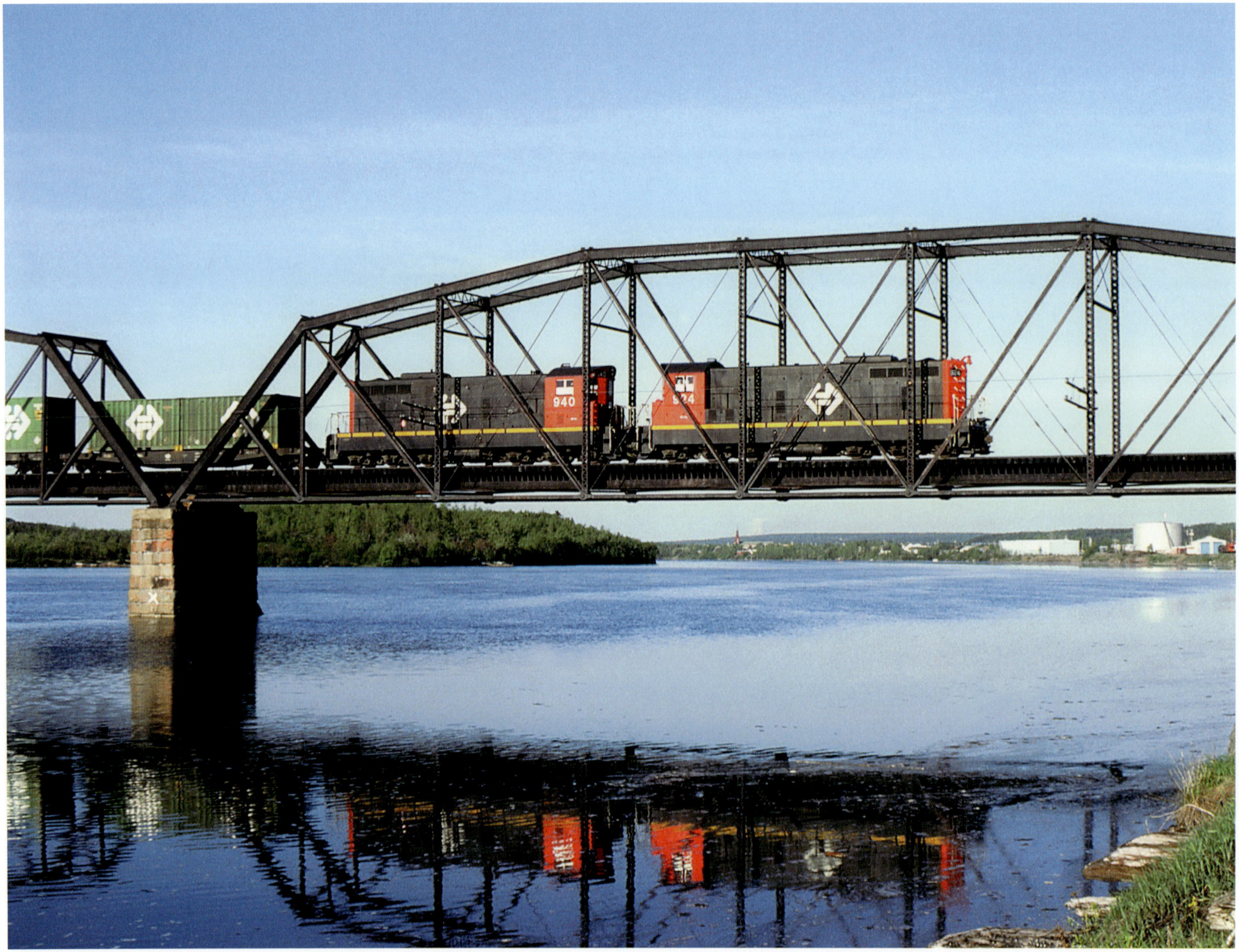

EXPLOITS BRIDGE 1985

Terra Transport train 203 with NF210s 924 and 940 enter the fourth and final span of the longest bridge on the Newfoundland Railway early in the morning of May 31, 1988. A coach will be added upon arrival at Bishop's Falls, making it a mixed run to Corner Brook and then removed for the remainder of the journey to Port aux Basques. *Wendell Lemon photo*

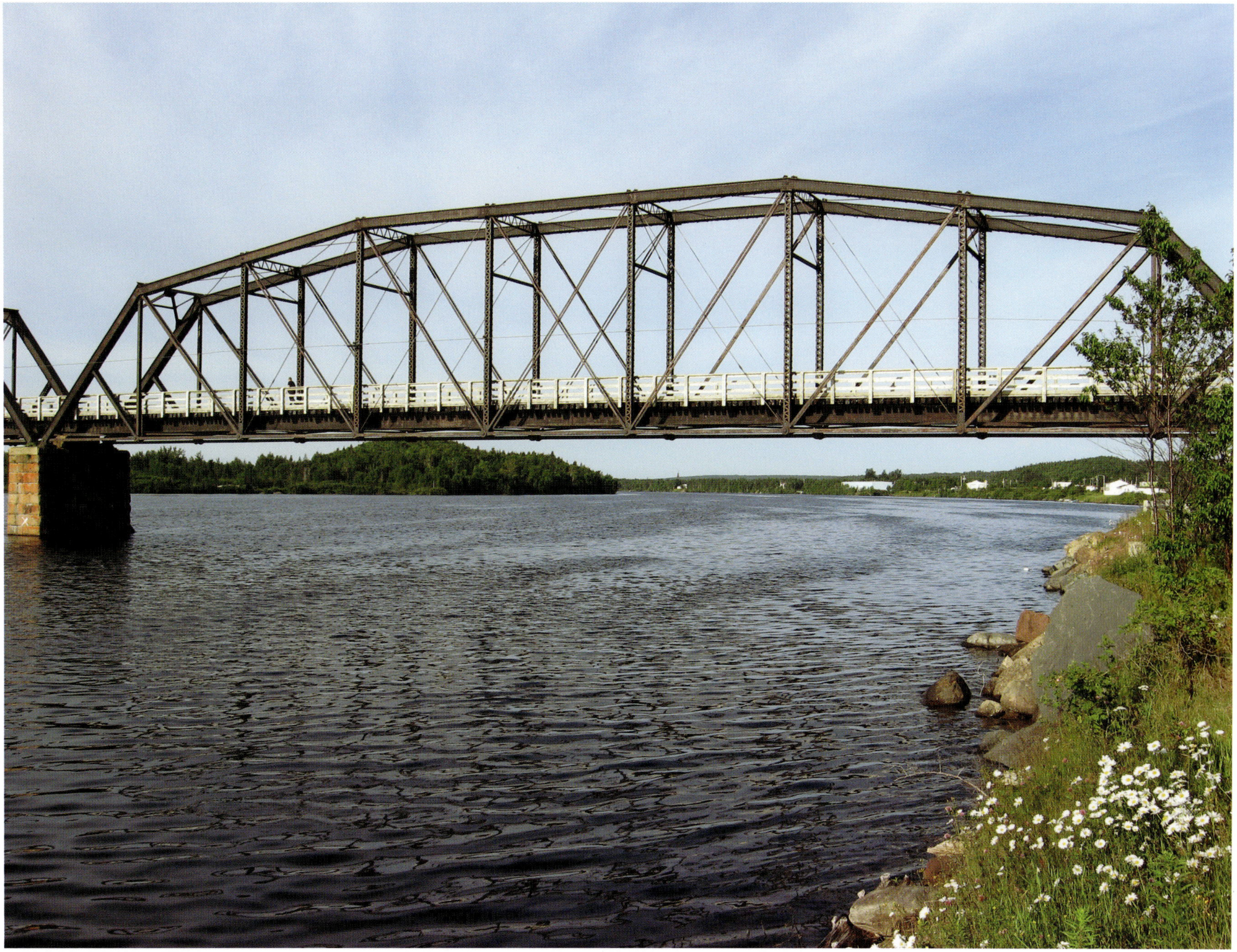

EXPLOITS BRIDGE TODAY
A hiker strolls across the 927-foot bridge that was completed in 1901 by Dominion Bridge Company. This was the fourth bridge to cross the Exploits River; the previous three, all about a half mile below this spot, were washed away by ice. Built on abutments of granite from Quarry, the massive bridge makes for a most impressive sight when lit on special occasions such as Come Home Year. *Author photo*

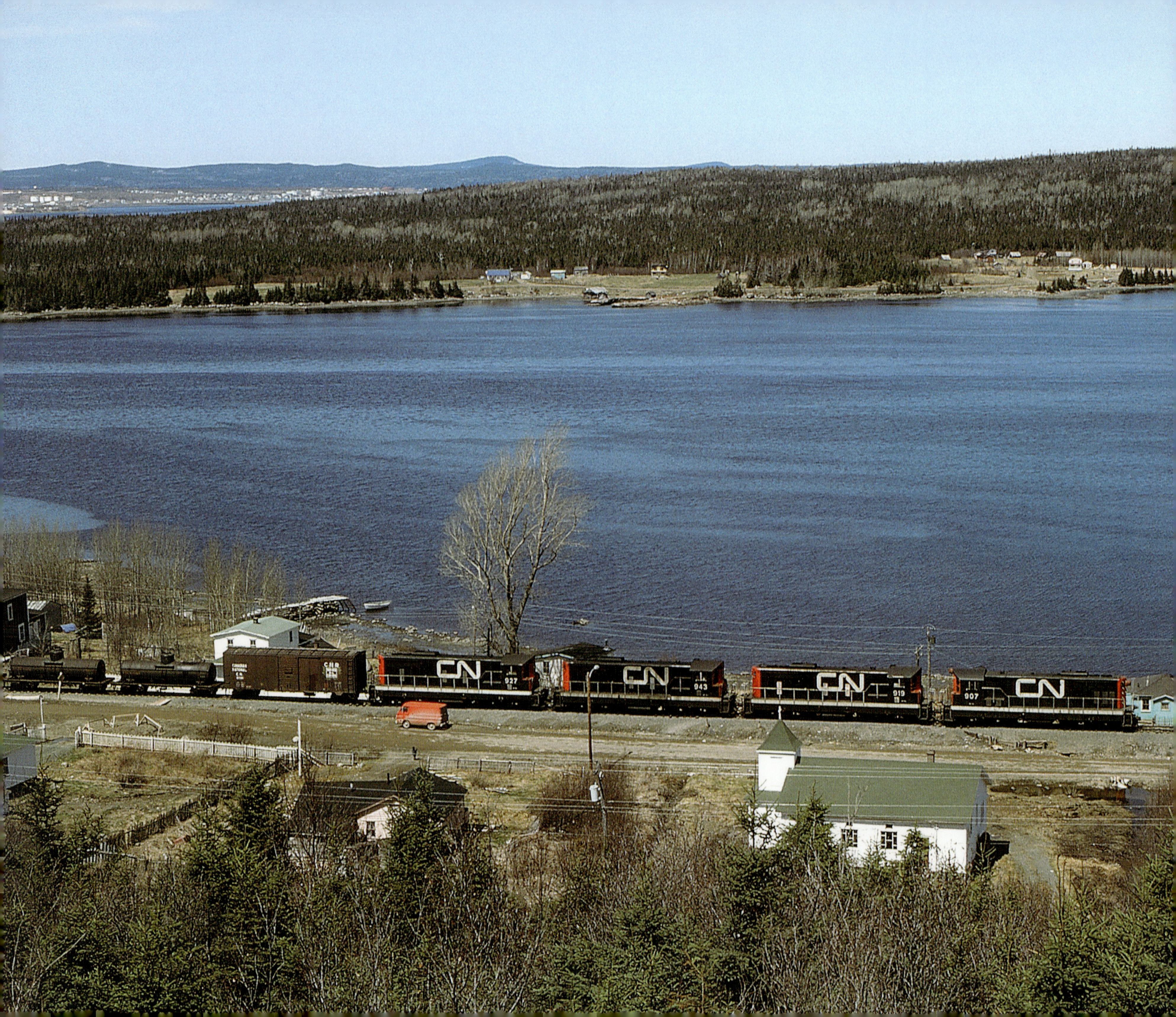
927
943
919
907

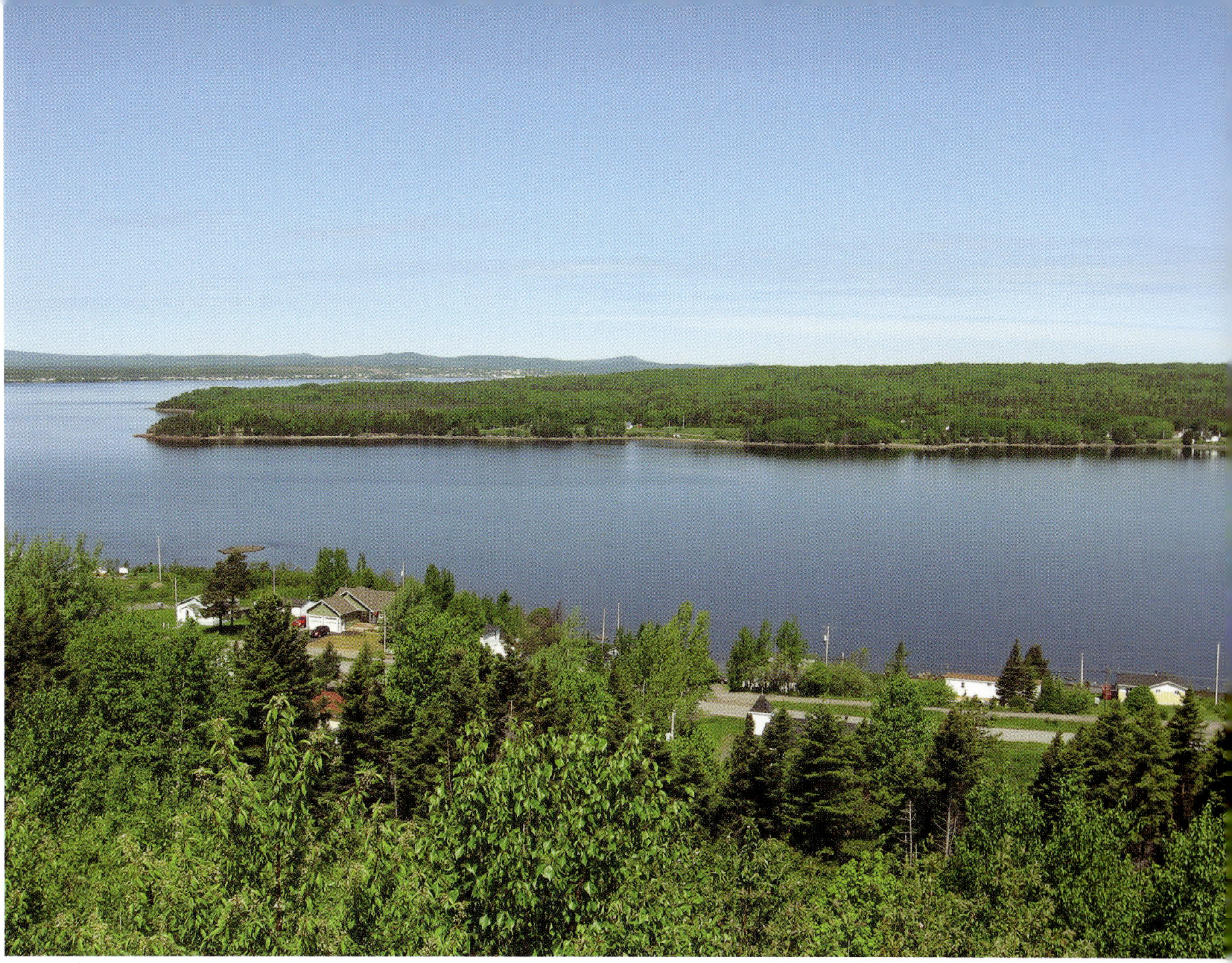

NORRIS ARM 1975
Four locomotives, a mix of NF110s and 210s and all wearing the black and red CN 'noodle' paint scheme, are photographed hauling eastbound freight 204 past the United Church in Norris Arm. With the rumble of a total of 4800 horsepower from all four engines and the sound of the whistle, the silence of this peaceful community is broken early in the morning of May 10, 1975. *Phil Mason photo*

NORRIS ARM TODAY
Norris Arm, once the terminus of the Hall's Bay Railroad, boasts one of the most scenic lookouts in the entire province. With the port town of Botwood as a backdrop, sunsets viewed from this vantage point on the former Trans Canada Highway are nothing short of spectacular. Drivers on the present day TCH totally bypass Norris Arm and miss this unique view. *Author photo*

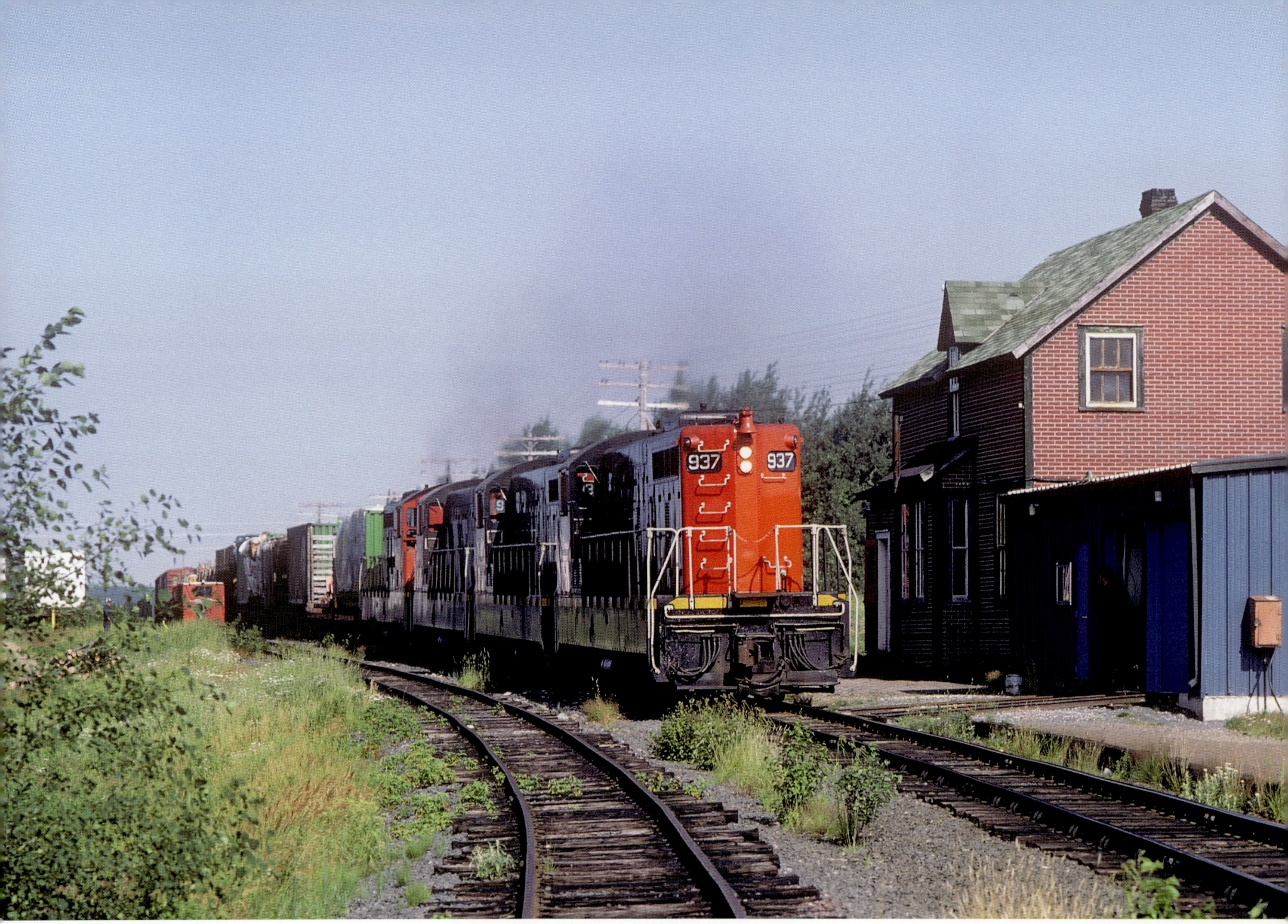

NOTRE DAME JUNCTION 1980
On one of his multiple trips to Newfoundland from 1977 to 1984, former Sante Fe Railway employee and owner of McMillan Publications Joe McMillan shoots Terra Transport Train 204 at Notre Dame Junction. NF210 937 on the head end looks resplendent in a coat of fresh paint on this sunny July 31, 1980. Behind the station lies the nine-mile branch to the port at Lewisporte. *Joe McMillan photo*

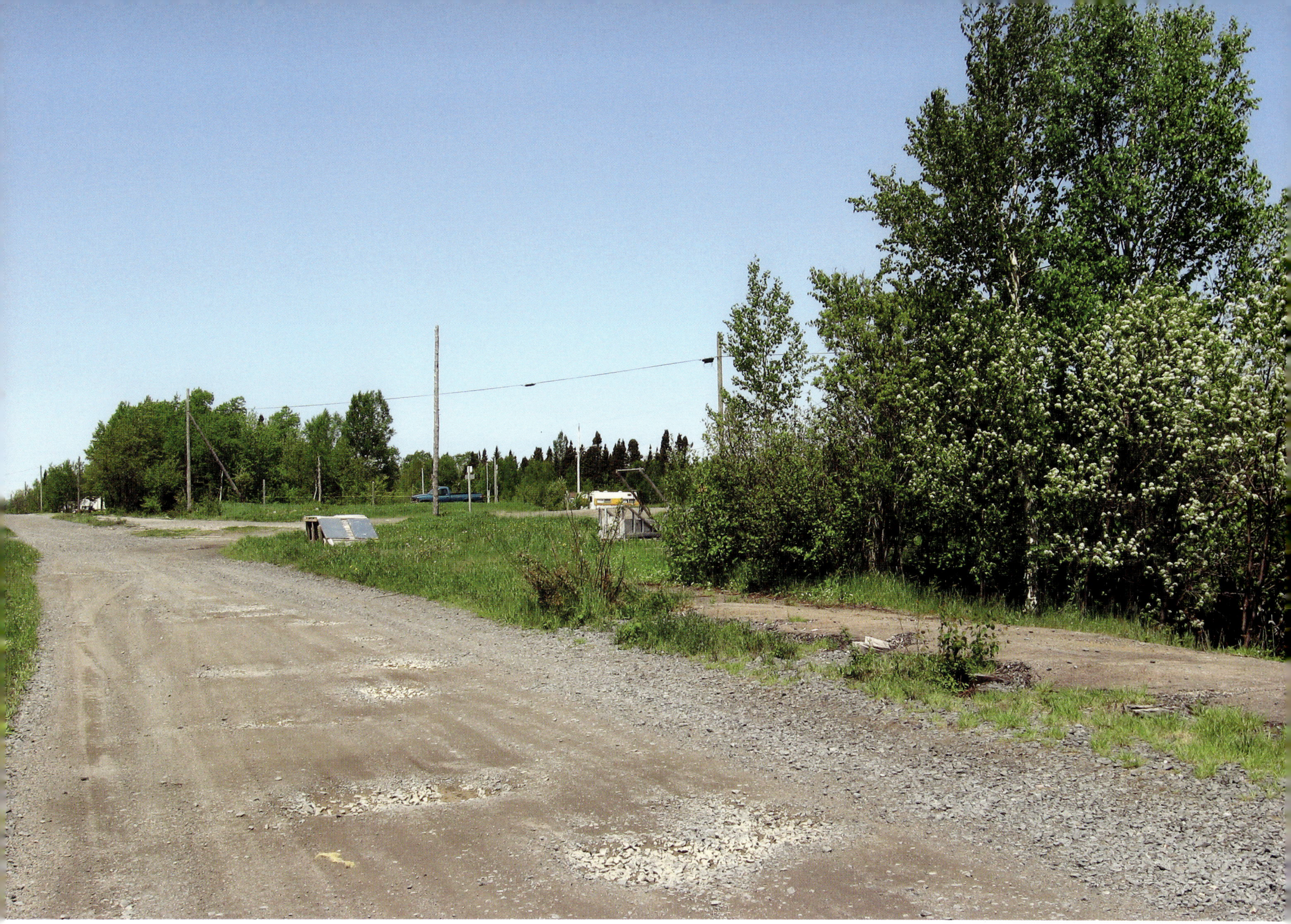

NOTRE DAME JUNCTION TODAY

A beautiful cherry blossom tree has sprouted up along the paved station walkway. Notre Dame Junction is a very busy spot for the Newfoundland and Labrador Snowmobile Federation, with signage trails and a loading ramp for Lewisporte travellers. Engine 937 also survived and was sold in 1991 to SQM, a private mining company in Chile, the only NF210 to that railway. *Author photo*

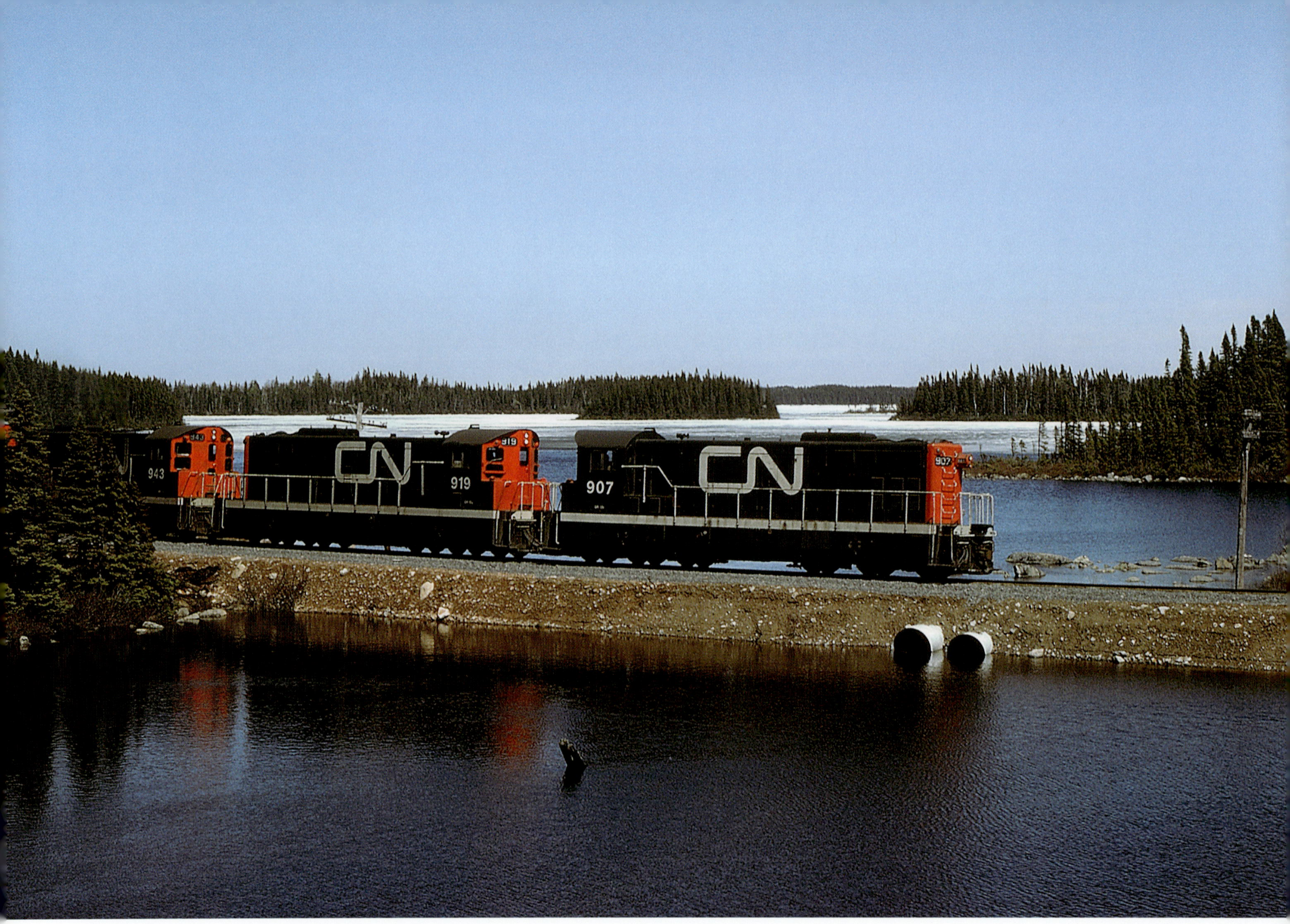

LAKE O'BRIEN 1975
With the winter ice still in abundance in the background, NF110 907 leads the consist of eastbound CN Train 204 at Lake O'Brien on May 10, 1975. This scene is typical of how close the railway ran next to the, more or less parallel, Trans Canada Highway. The only major exception to this is the eighty mile stretch between Badger and Deer Lake where the highway abruptly heads north to Hall's Bay. *Phil Mason photo*

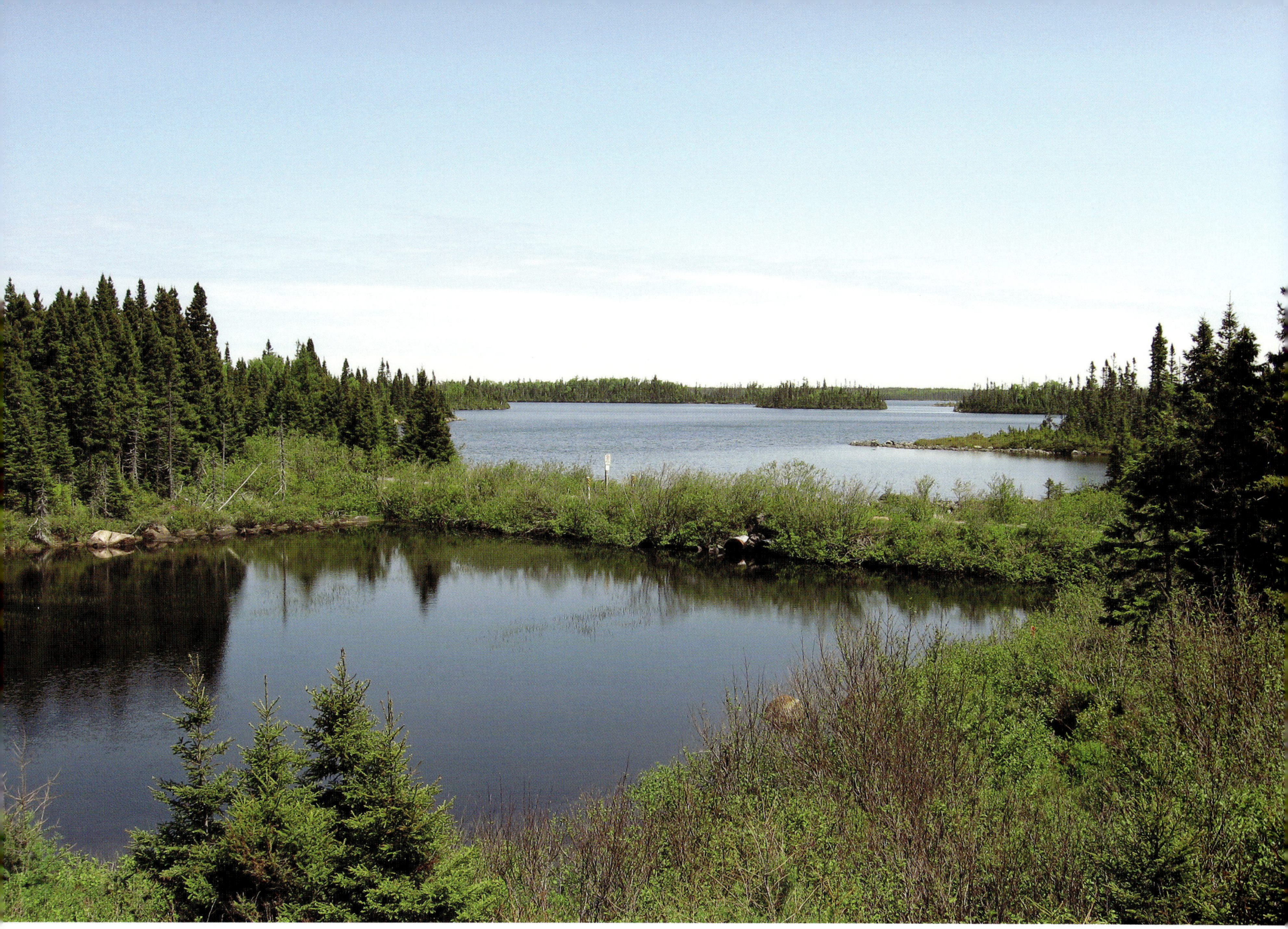

LAKE O'BRIEN TODAY
Nestled between Grand Falls-Windsor and Gander, this beautiful lake has become home to many cottages and cabins. It was near here on the night of July 29, 1954 that an eastbound passenger train with steam engine number 308 collided head on with diesel number 908 on a westbound wood train. Nearly all cars derailed, but amazingly with no loss of life or major injuries. *Author photo*

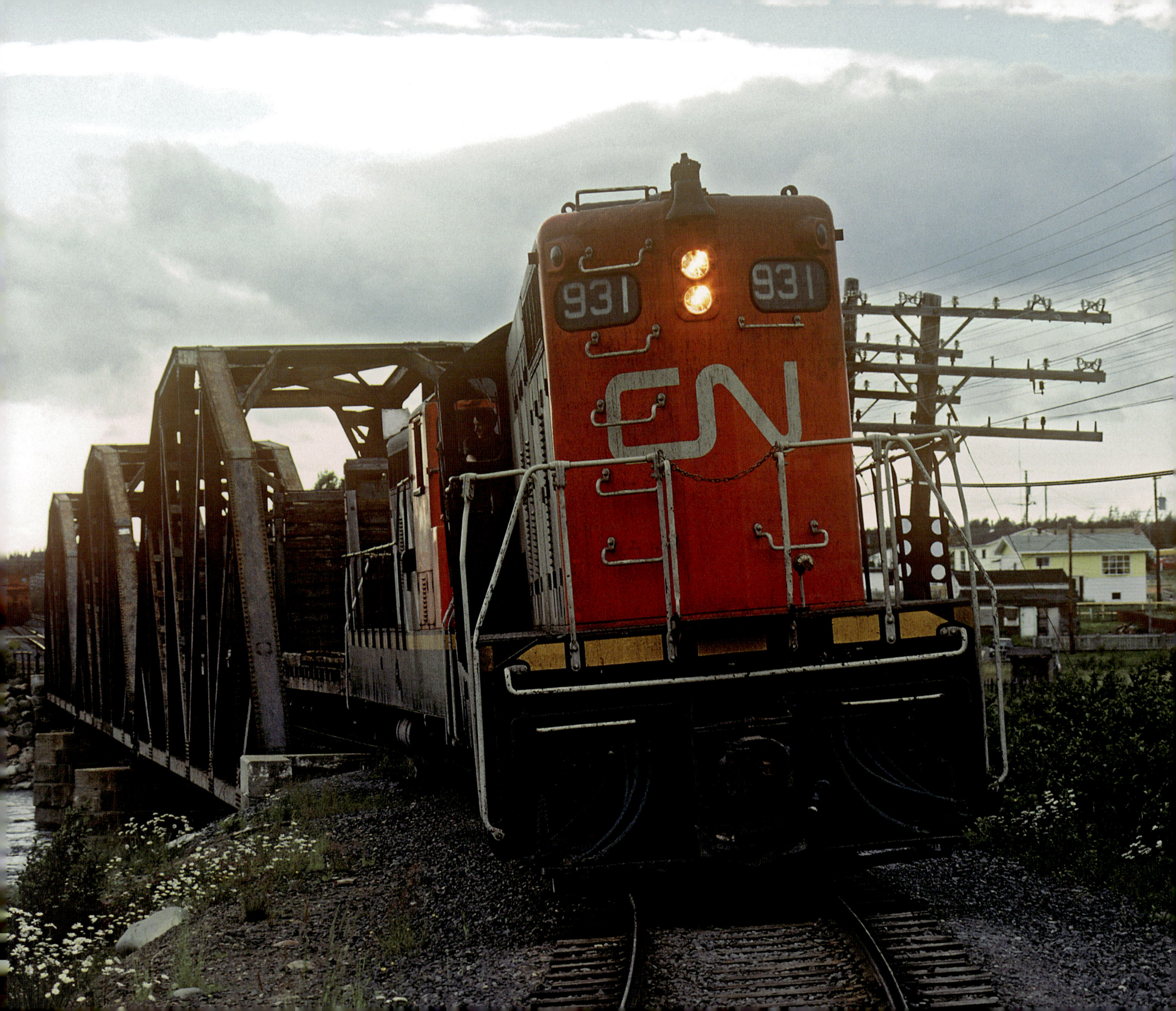
931
931
CN

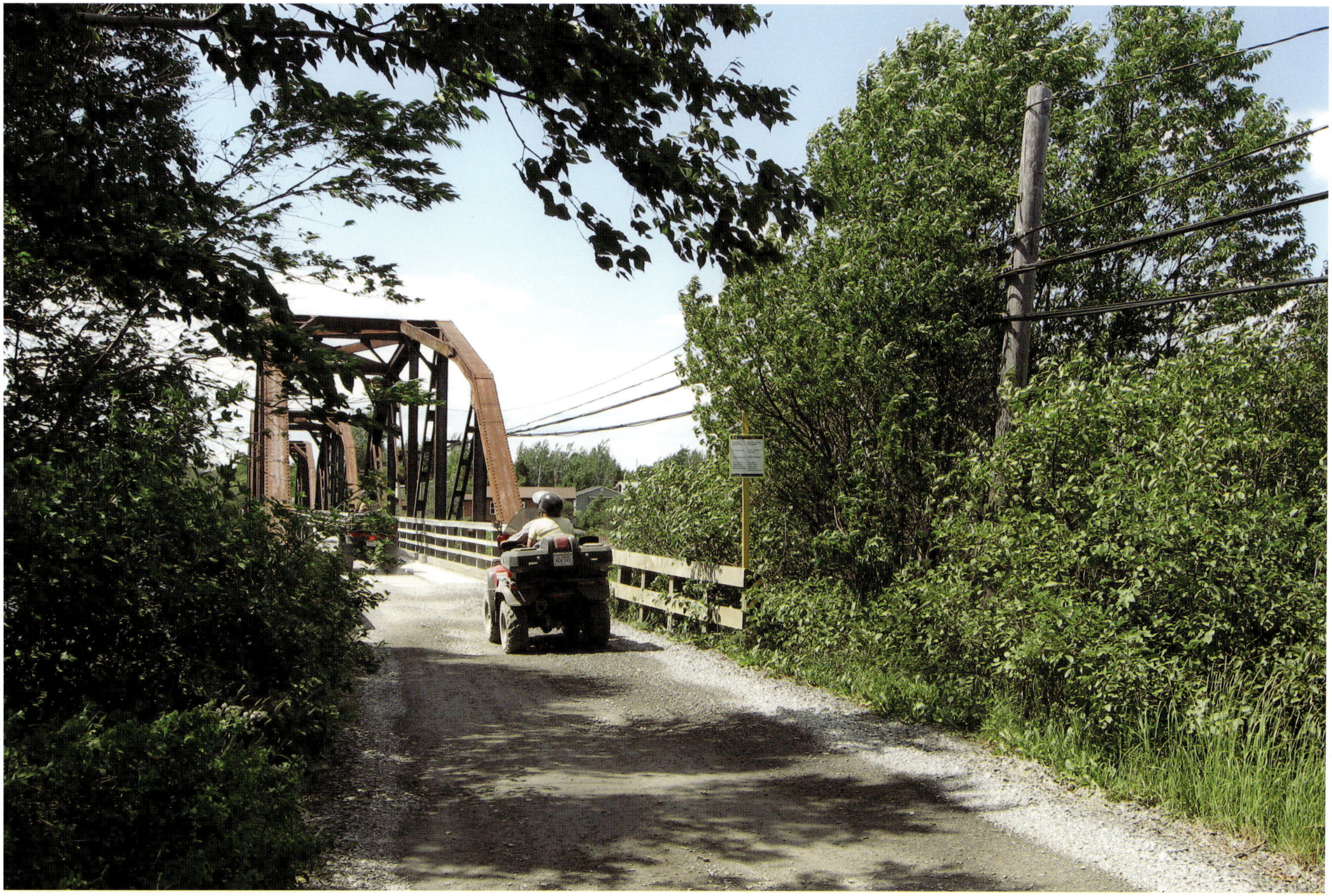

GLENWOOD 1980

NF210 931 and sister pause on the eastern side of the three span railway bridge over the Gander River on July 31, 1980. The engineer will soon back the two NF210s with multiple pulpwood cars past the station to the spur for loading with pulpwood destined for the Bowaters Mill in Corner Brook. Glenwood was the site of a major woods operation and the various sidings and spurs could hold 372 cars. *Joe McMillan Photo*

GLENWOOD TODAY

The railway bridge is a major landmark in the Glenwood area and is located just a few hundred feet upstream from the Queen Elizabeth II highway bridge. It allows ATV users and pedestrians to safely cross the mighty Gander River. In addition to the preserved station, 931 also survived and is on display in Corner Brook, the only such engine with its prime mover still operational. *Author photo*

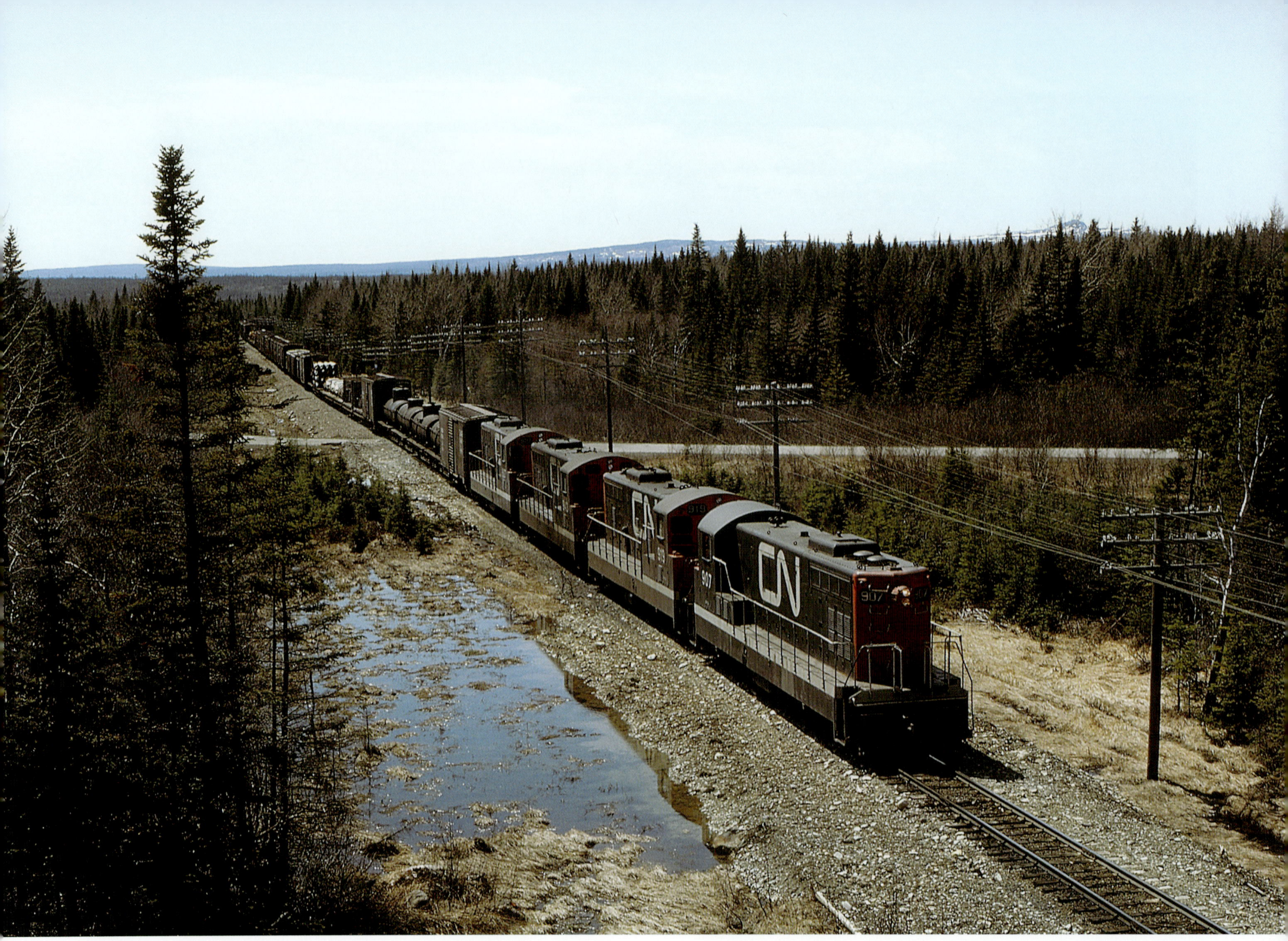

GLENWOOD OVERPASS 1975

CN Train 204 crosses the former Trans Canada Highway as it approaches the overpass just east of Glenwood on May 10, 1975. With signage proclaiming the motto "We'll Finish The Drive in '65", the Newfoundland portion of the TCH was completed by 1965. This necessitated the building of several railway overpasses across the mainline during that decade to eliminate the grade crossings. *Phil Mason photo*

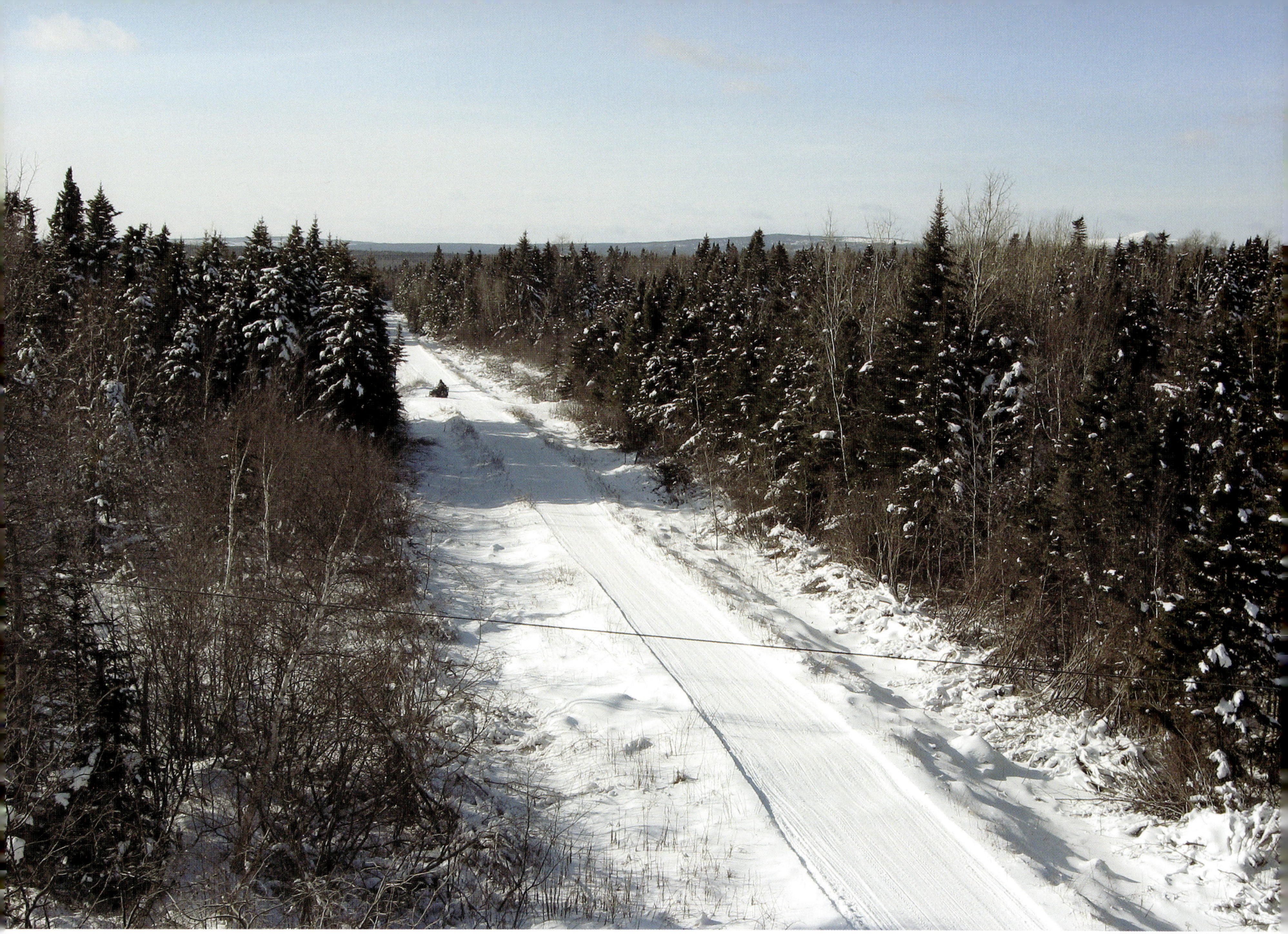

GLENWOOD OVERPASS TODAY

A snowmobiler leaves the perfectly groomed trail right at the former TCH. The abandoned right of way makes for a perfect all season recreational trail. The snow capped 342 metre high Mount Peyton as well as endless miles of uninhabited wilderness can still be viewed from this vantage point. *Author photo*

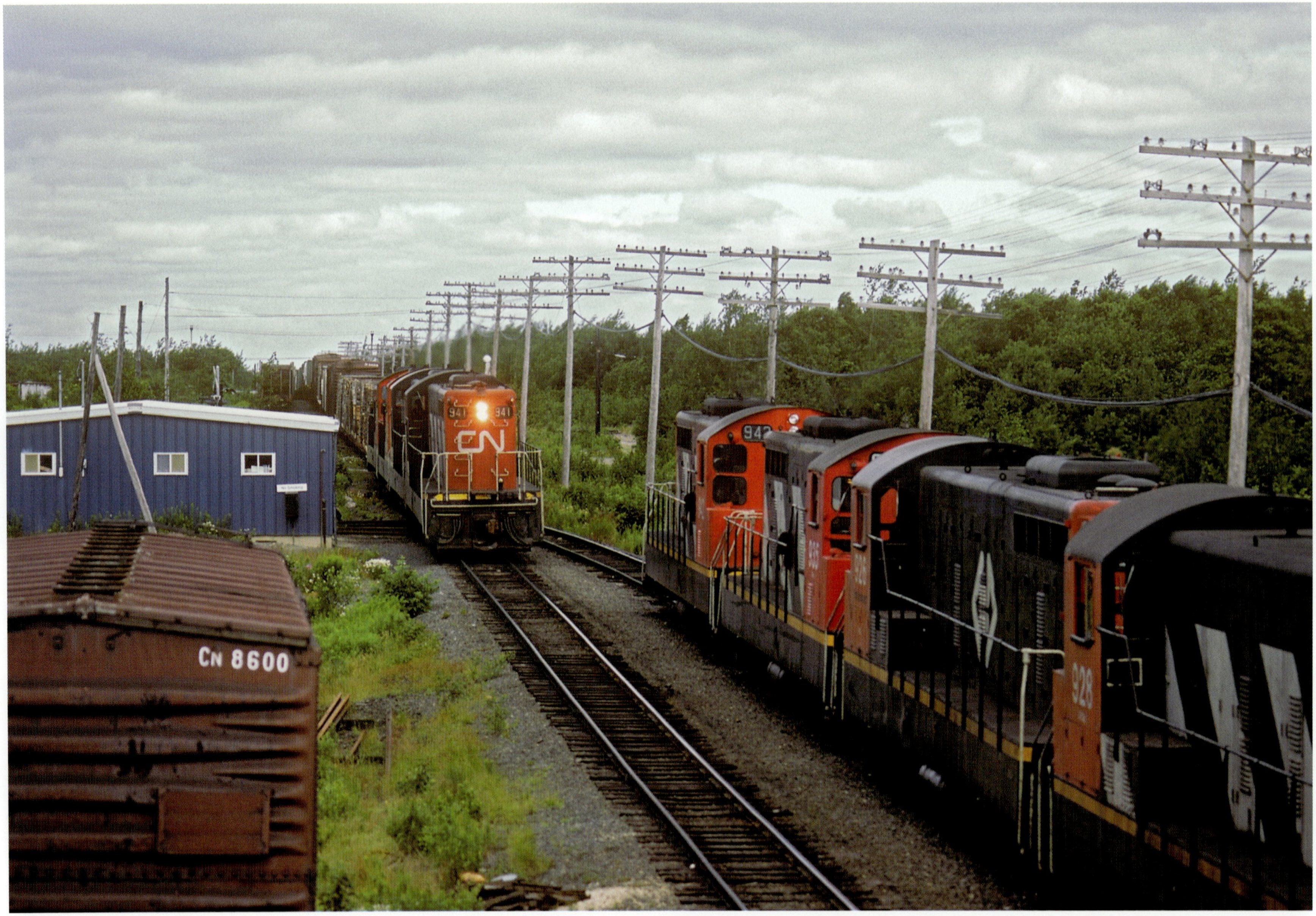

GANDER 1984

Westbound Terra Transport freight 203 holds the siding at Gander on July 25, 1984. This will allow 204 to continue the superior direction eastward journey on the mainline. With 204 safely out of the way, 203 will proceed to Bishop's Falls where it will pick up a coach and become a mixed. With a total of four NF210s at 1200 horsepower on each train, they effortlessly moved to their destinations. *Joe McMillan photo*

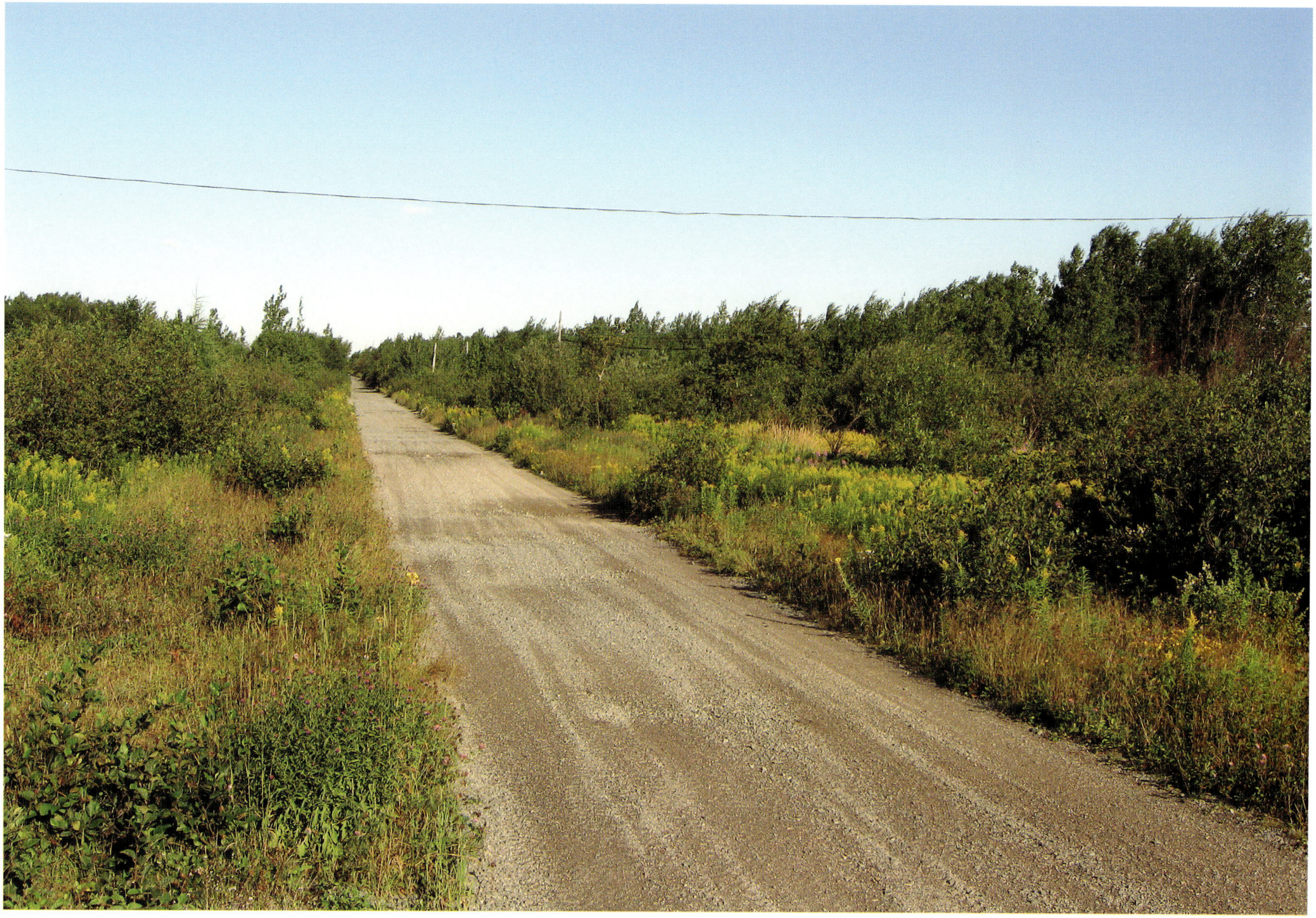

GANDER TODAY

Gander, once known in aviation circles as 'The Crossroads of the World', saw over 20,000 Allied planes delivered overseas by RAF Ferry Command during World War II. Construction of the Newfoundland Airport commenced in 1938 at Milepost 213. The Newfoundland Railway was a vital part of its construction, bringing all the workers, as well as hundreds of trainloads of crushed ore and other vital supplies to the site. *Author photo*

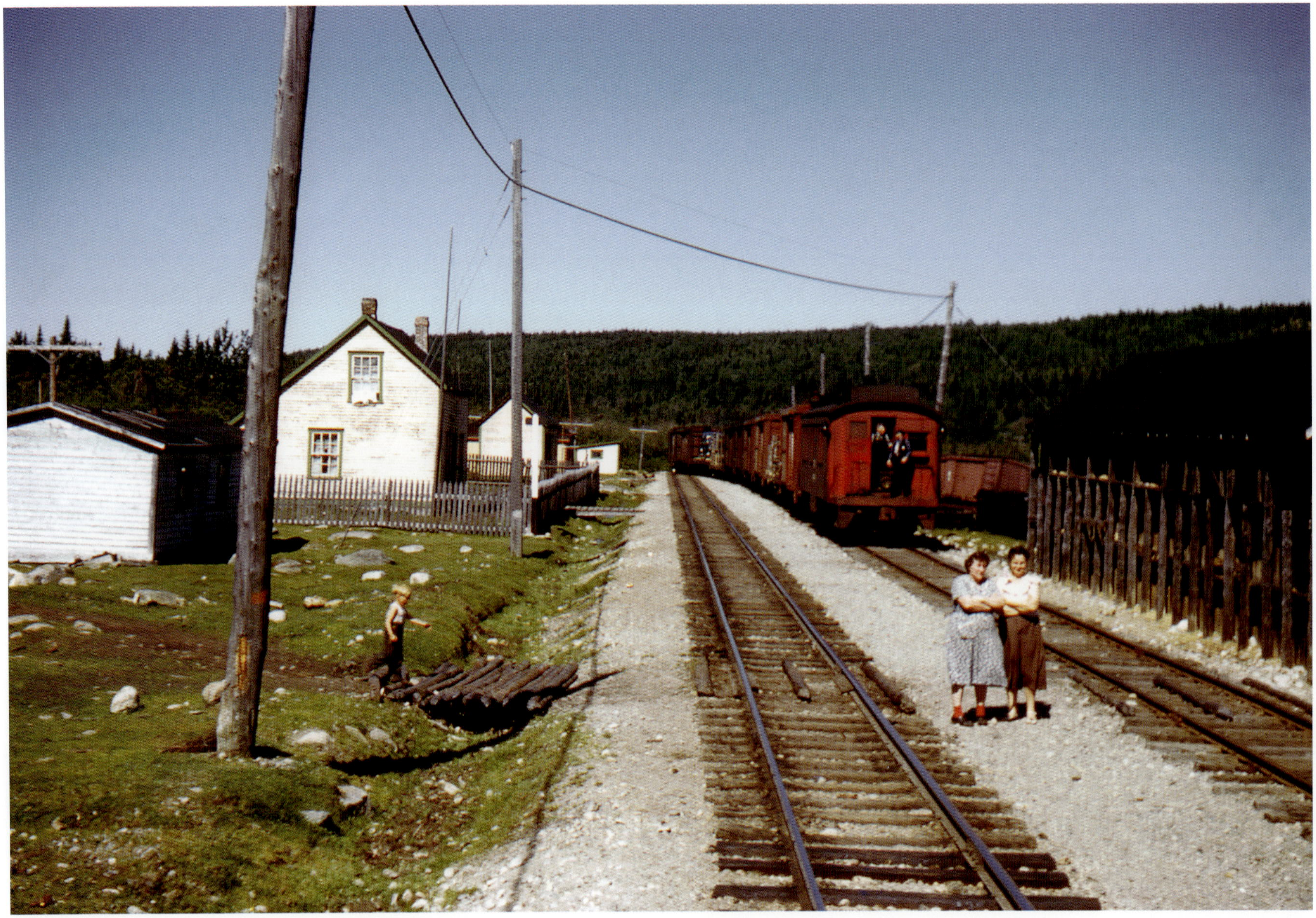

BENTON 1952

As seen from the rear platform of passenger Train #2, the westbound CNR fourth class way freight leaves the siding at Benton on June 24, 1952. The way freight trains, numbers 33 and 34 in the 1952 timetable, made flag stops virtually everywhere along the line. The two ladies watch the departing train head east towards the next station stop at Gambo, while the young boy crosses the log bridge to reach them. *Omer Lavallee photo*

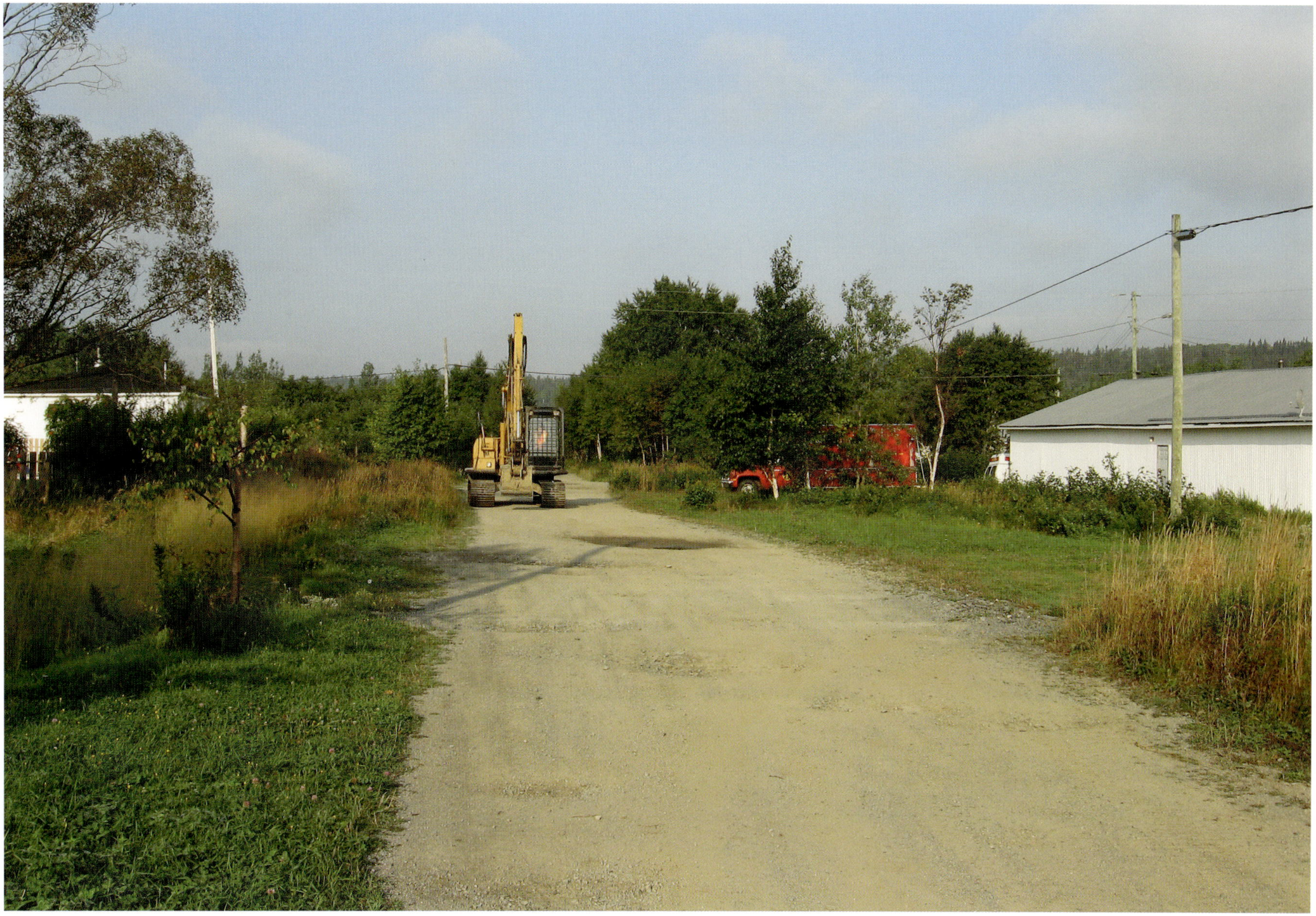

BENTON TODAY

A large excavator slowly proceeds eastward on the former mainline past the town hall and fire department early in the morning. Benton, once a major player in the woods operation with a 100 car siding and sawmill operations, was nearly destroyed by a major forest fire in August, 1961. Even the telegraph poles along the tracks caught fire.
Author photo

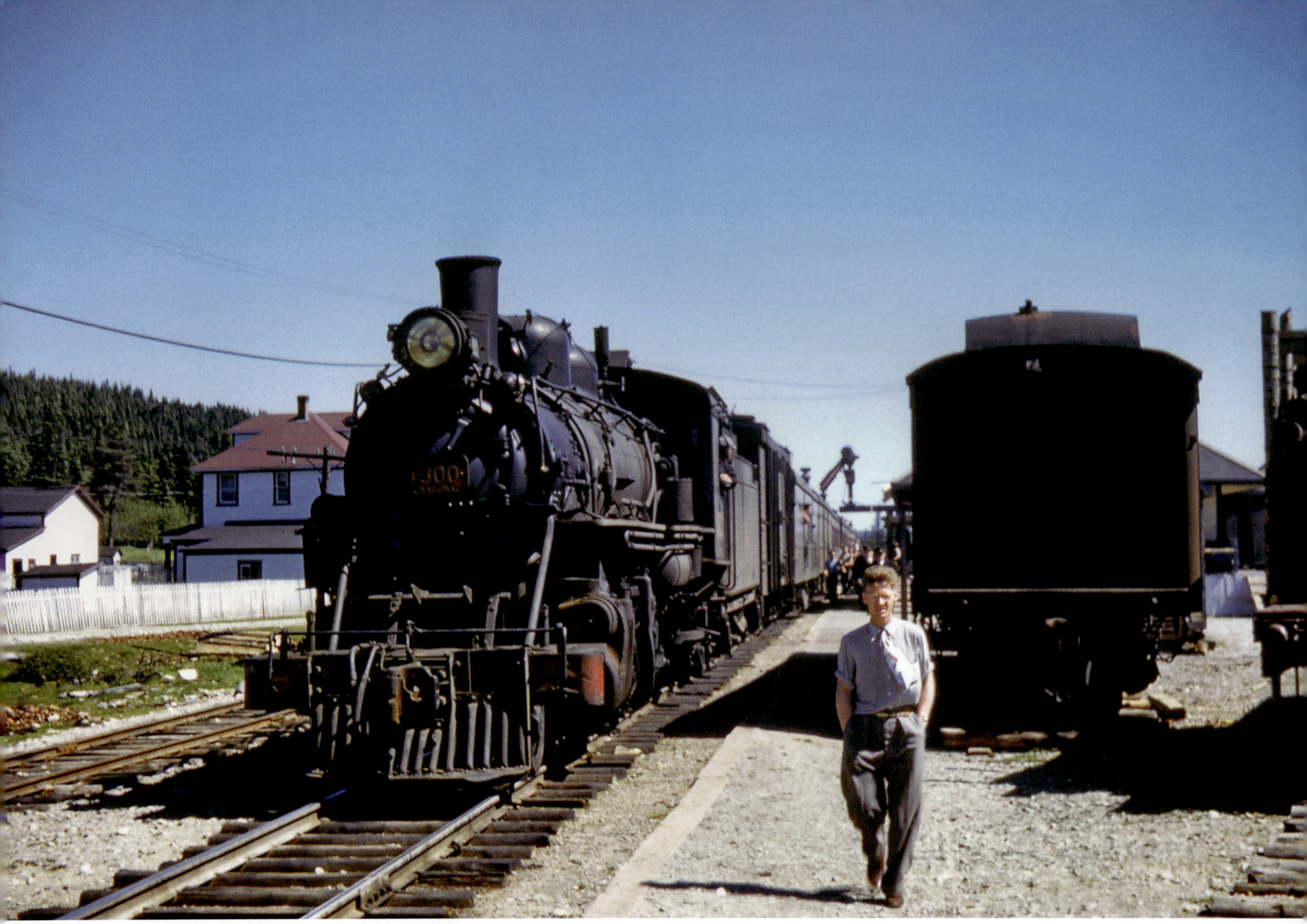

GAMBO 1952

2-8-2 Mikado #300, built in 1930 by Alco of Schenectady, New York and formerly #1000 under the Newfoundland Railway is the only motive power on CNR Train No. 2 at Gambo on June 24, 1952. Just a year earlier on May 17th, one of the worst train wrecks in Newfoundland history occurred west of this point. Making a run for the hill, engines 1017 and 305 of the westbound wood train derailed, killing engineer Ted Stanley and seriously injuring fireman Frank Cole. *Ron Ritchie photo*

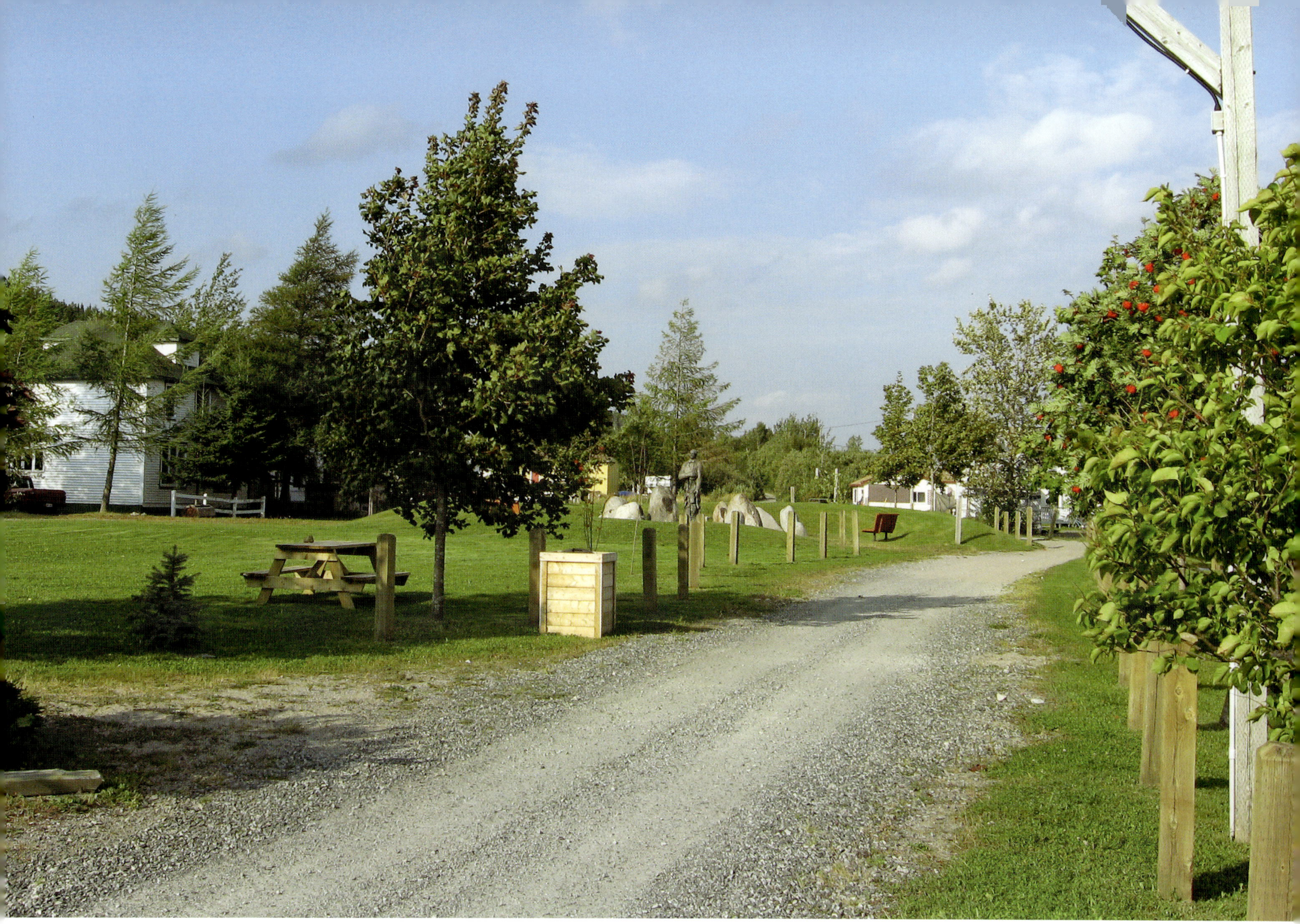

GAMBO TODAY
A statue of Gambo native Joey Smallwood, once the only living Father of Confederation, keeps watch over the area known as the 'Village Green'. Gambo's rich railway heritage is preserved at this site with a speeder display, a steel boxcar and a station designed as a stage for musical performers. The still-standing white house is now home to the very popular Cashin's Chestnut Tree Cafe. *Author photo*

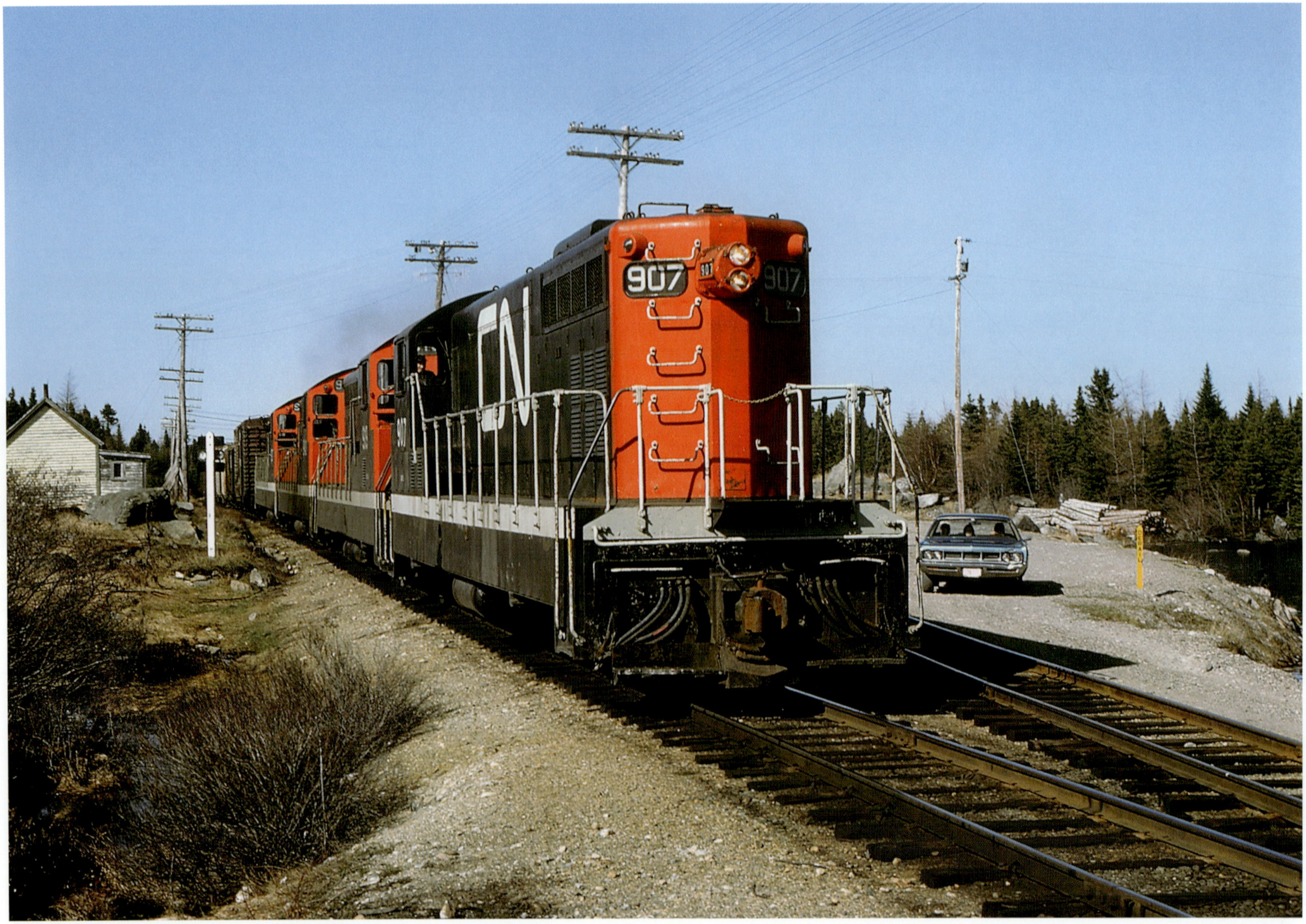

ALEXANDER BAY 1975

With NF110 907, a GMD London product of 1953 on the head end, Canadian National Train 204 speeds past the old railway shack at Alexander Bay on May 10, 1975. Obstructed by 204 is the freight shed and adjacent two story station where one could still obtain a CN money order. Located just three miles east of Glovertown, it served all the communities on the scenic Eastport Peninsula. *Phil Mason photo*

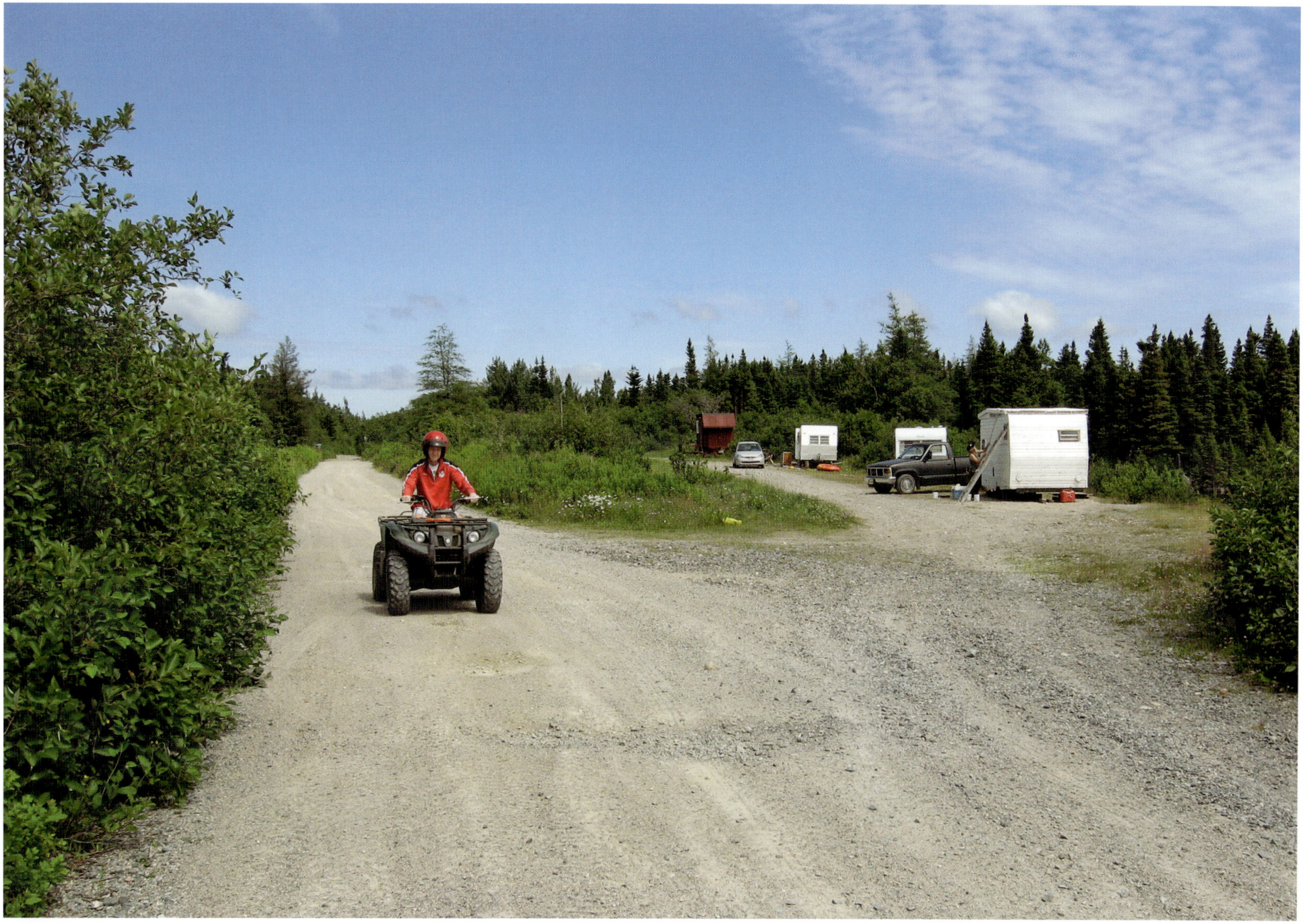

ALEXANDER BAY TODAY

The author's son, Thomas, paused the ATV at the same spot where 907 rumbled past several decades earlier. Along with the track, gone too is the shack, the shed and the station, replaced by a bunch of vintage camper trailers alongside the pond. The coming of the railway in 1894 helped establish Glovertown as the main service center for the Eastport Peninsula. *Author photo*

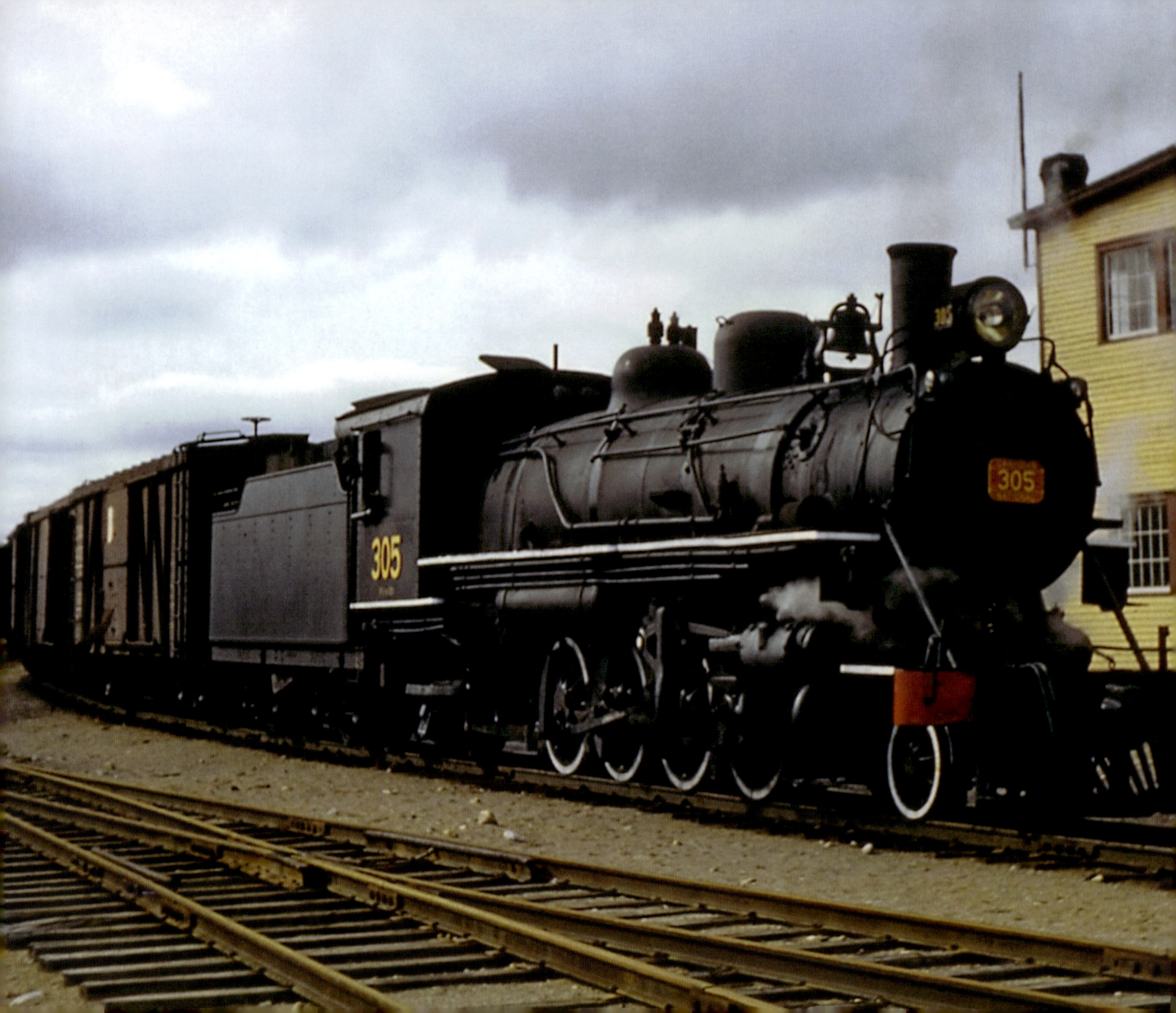
305
305
305

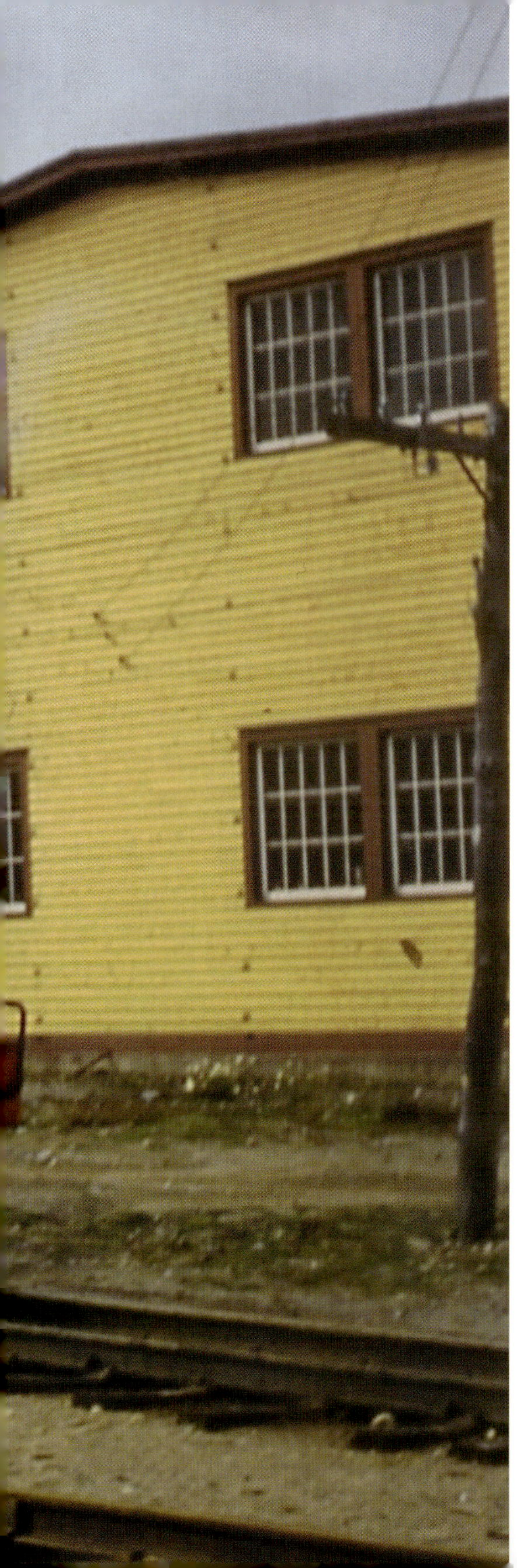

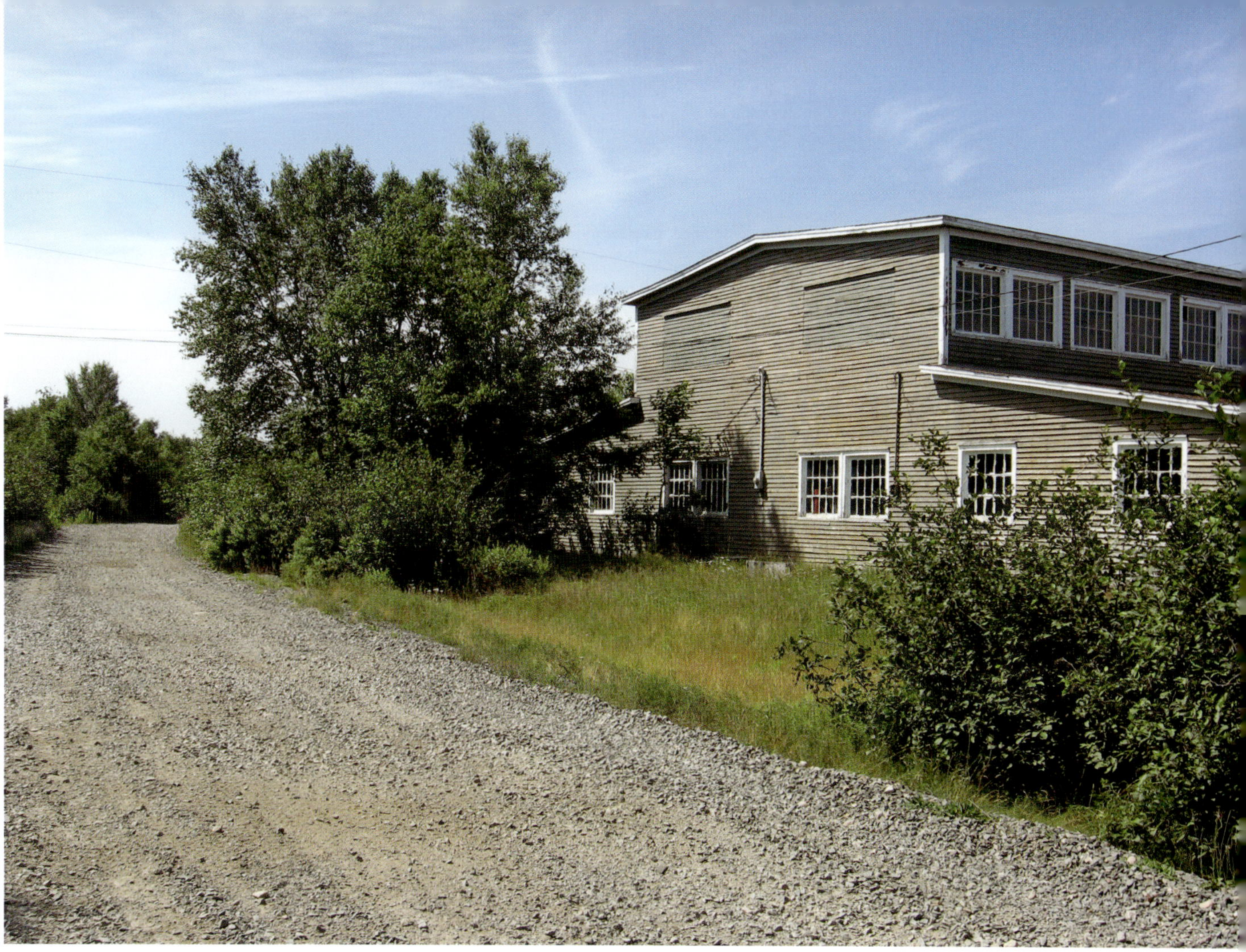

TERRA NOVA 1953
Freshly painted CNR 2-8-2 Mikado #305 (formerly Newfoundland Railway 1005), built in 1938 by North British Locomotive Works of Glasgow, Scotland, pauses with a westbound freight at the Gray Stores Ltd. building in Terra Nova during the summer of 1953. USAF Airman Jerome Young, assigned to Newfoundland from 1952-54, captured this scene near their camp. The buffer beams of CN steam engines in Newfoundland continued to be painted a crimson red, like their European counterparts. *Jerome Young photo - Merritt C. Scharnweber collection*

TERRA NOVA TODAY
Terra Nova was the Anglo Newfoundland Development Company's eastern headquarters for a network of camps that supplied wood to the paper mill in Grand Falls. The Grey Stores building, which sold goods such as boots and outerwear to the woodsmen, still stands in this small community of 68 residents. With hundreds of cottages built around Terra Nova today, there are weekends when the population swells many times this amount. *Author photo*

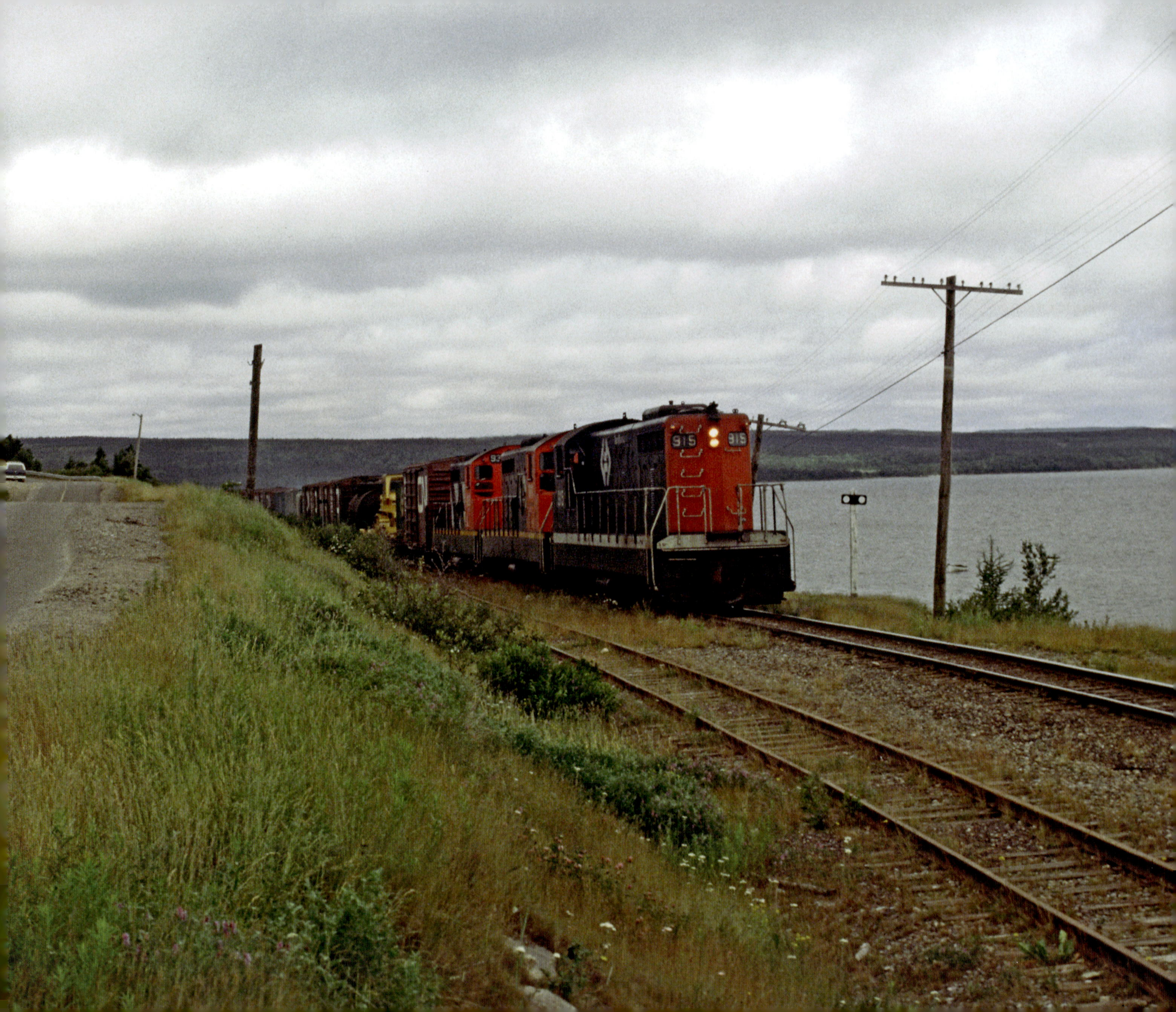
915
915

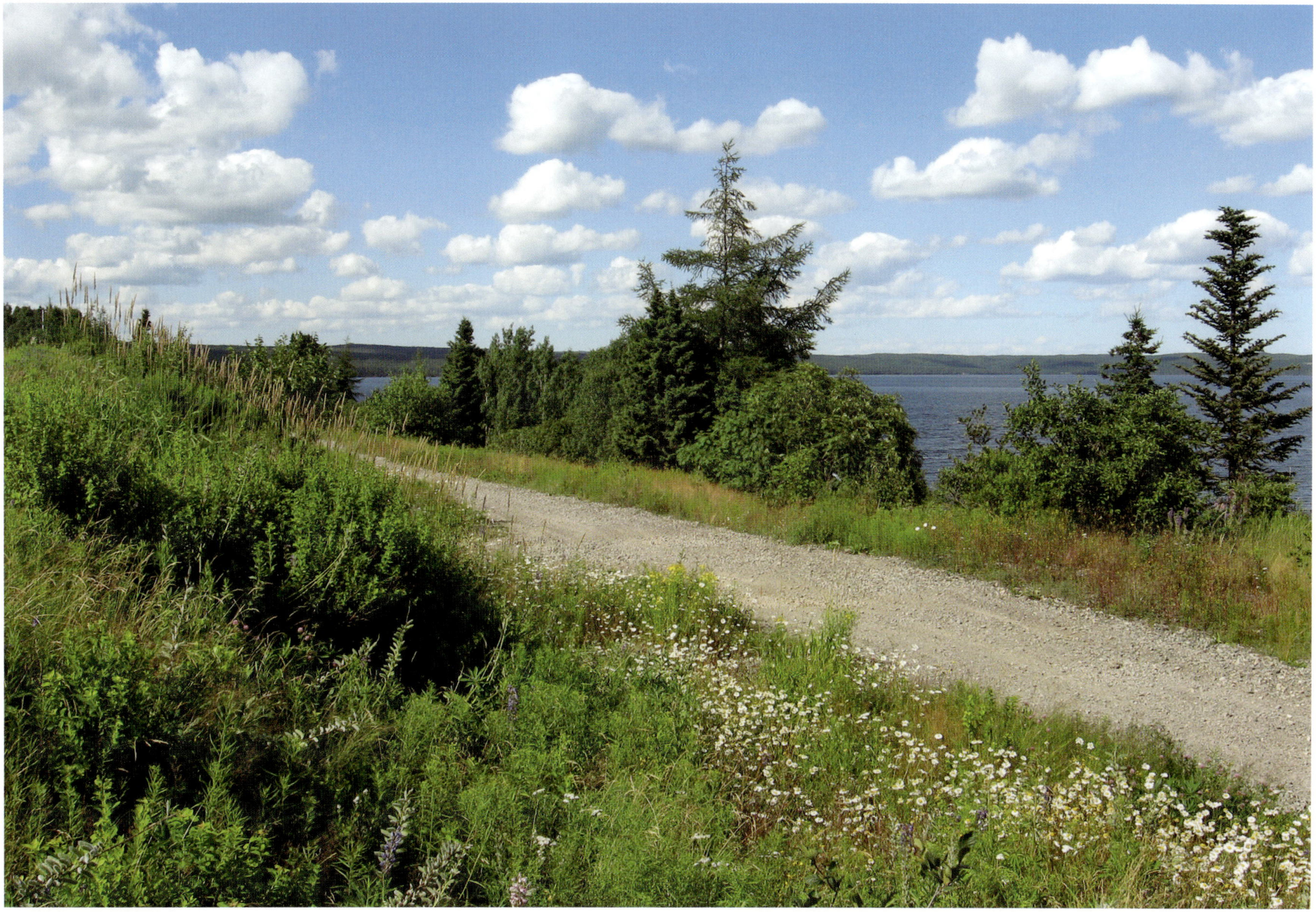

PORT BLANDFORD 1984

Terra Transport Train 204 with NF210 locomotives 915, 911 and 935 are passing Port Blandford beside Clode Sound on an overcast July 11, 1984. NF210 915 was one of only two such engines to have the Terra Transport bi-directional arrow applied towards the top of the hood. Prior to the building of the Bonavista Branch railway, Port Blandford was the railhead for steamers servicing the Bonavista Peninsula. *Robert J. Sandusky photo*

PORT BLANDFORD TODAY

The wild flowers and other vegetation are in full bloom at Port Blandford, and before long the trees will obscure the view of Clode Sound. With the three rivers, Southwest, Salmon and Northwest flowing into the Sound, the Port Blandford area is an angler's delight. Along with the year round trailway for ATVs and snowmobiles, there are plently of recreational activities. *Author photo*

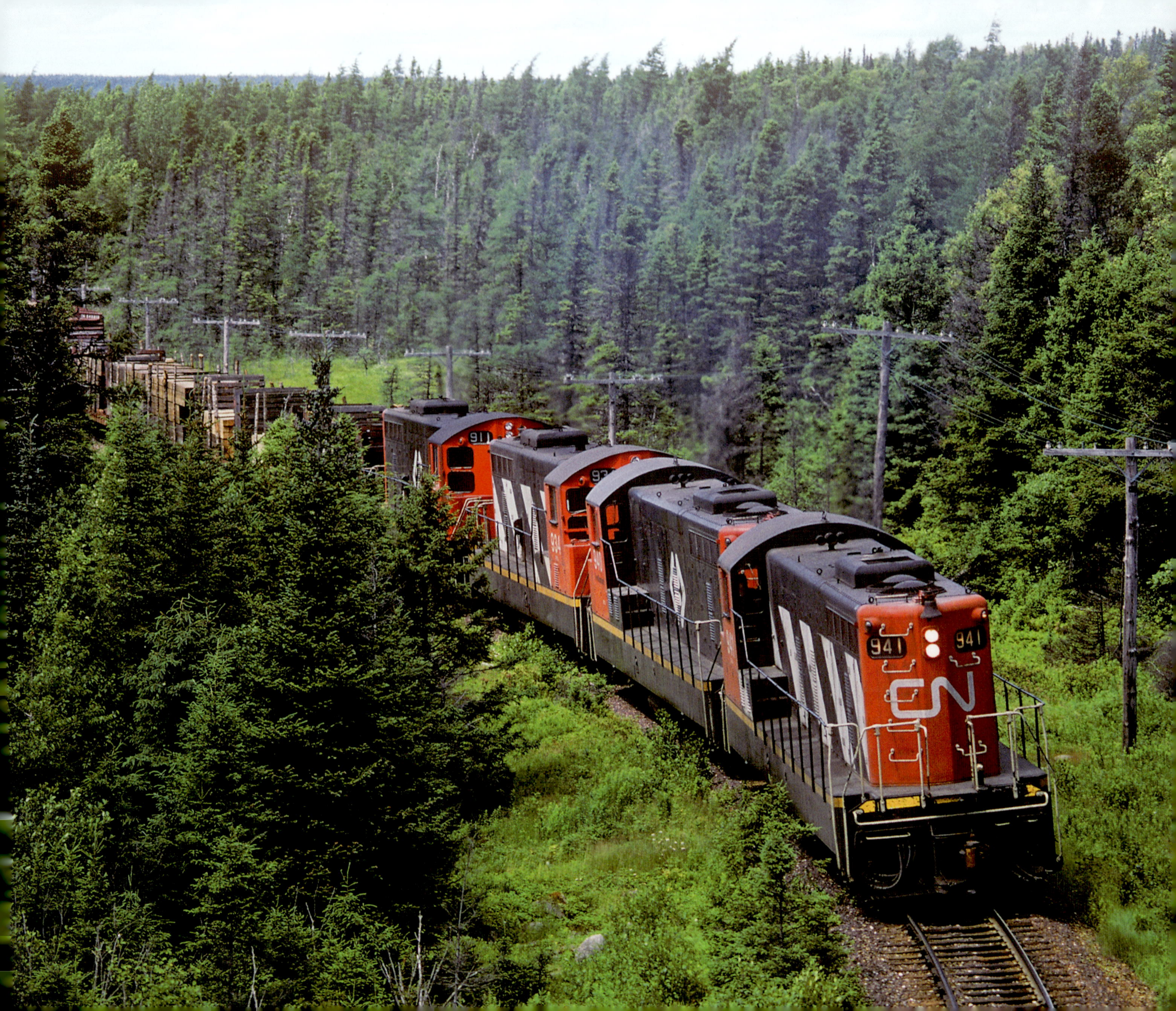
941
941
CN
911

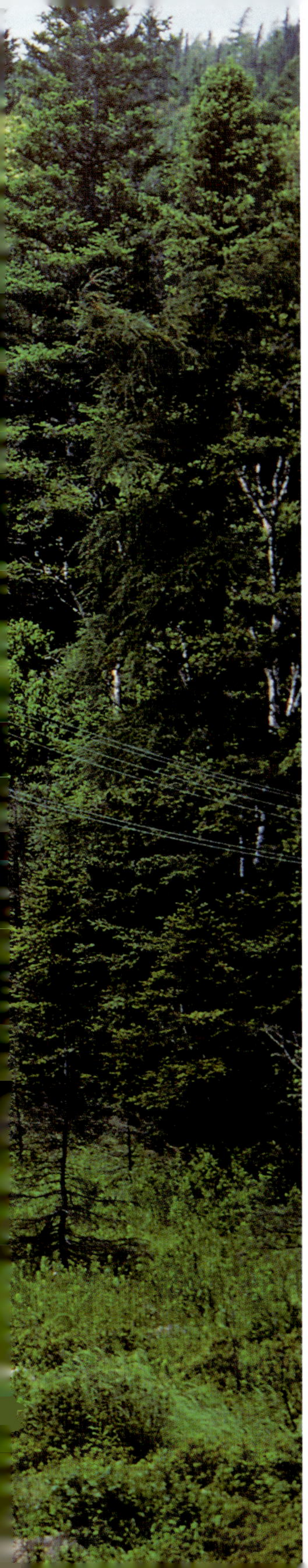

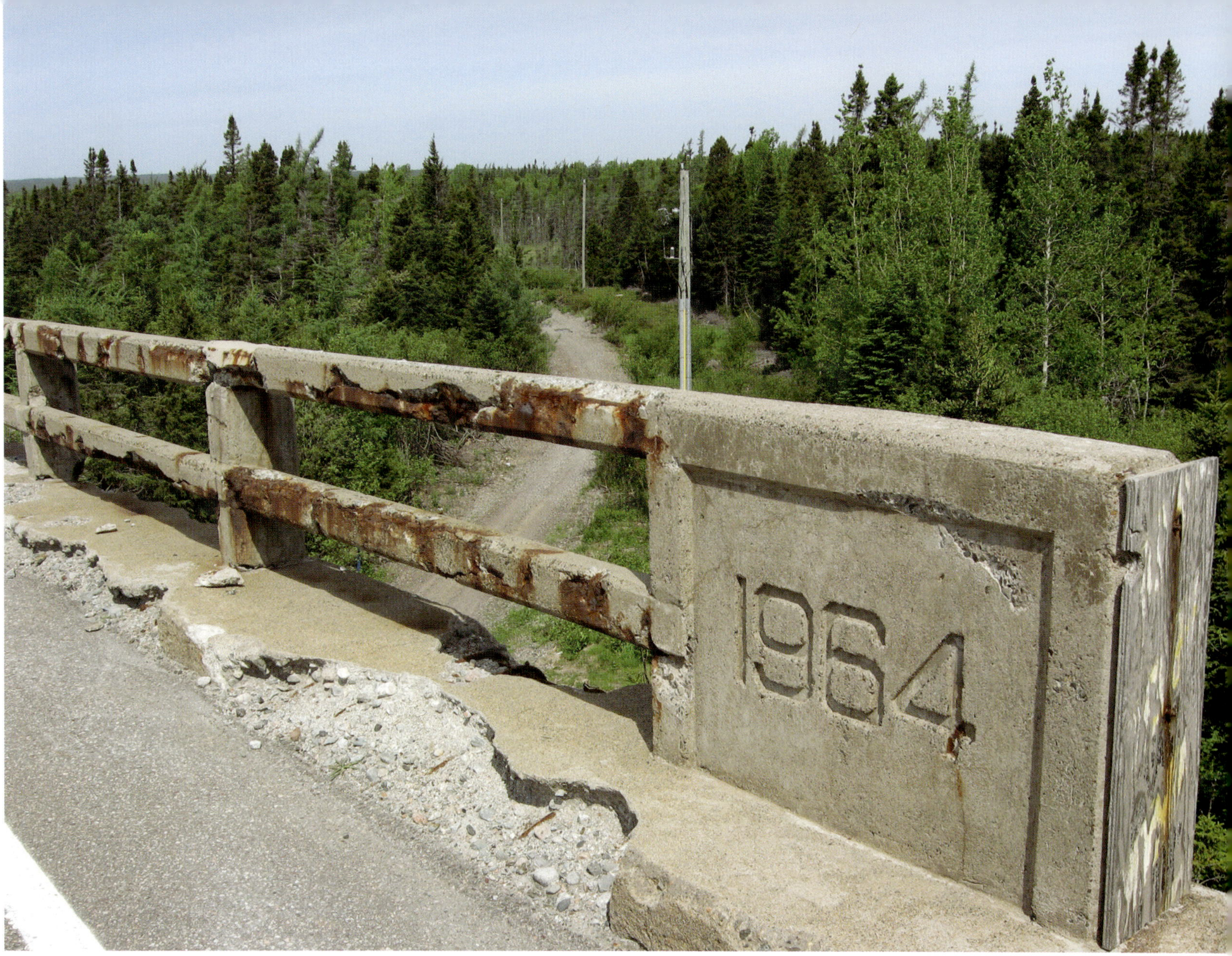

THORBURN LAKE OVERPASS 1984
Terra Transport eastbound freight 204, led by NF210 941 and three sisters, approach the overpass at Thorburn Lake on July 25, 1984. At the time of this photo, the railway was in the process of applying the engines final paint scheme. Soon, most engines would wear a red nose and cab with a black body and the white bi-directional Terra Transport arrow applied to it. *Joe McMillan photo*

THORBURN LAKE OVERPASS TODAY
Constructed in 1964 and clearly showing signs of deterioration from the salt and sand applied during the harsh Newfoundland winters, this is one of few remaining intact original overpasses. With the money from the Rails for Roads Agreement and the resulting improvements to the highway, most of the overpasses were replaced by large corrugated culverts over the right of way. *Author photo*

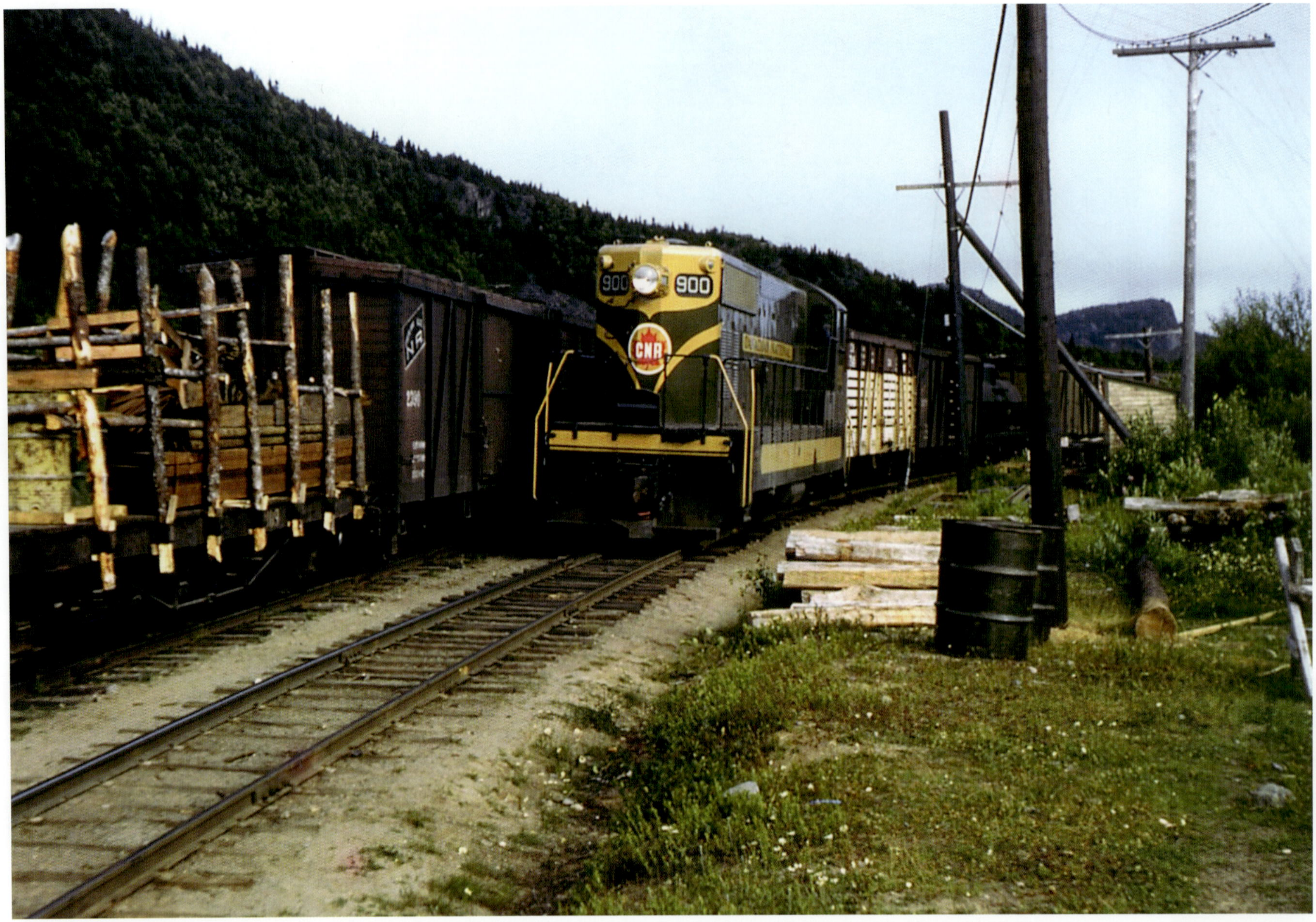

SHOAL HARBOUR PIT

NF 110 #900, the first 1200 HP road switcher delivered by GMD of London, ON aboard the *S.S. Brigus* to Argentia in January 1953, pulls an eastbound freight at the Shoal Harbour Pit in the summer of 1953. Originally equipped with single lamp Pyle headlights, the 110s were later changed to a double headlight. At only six months old, the nearly mint 900 passes an area once known as 'Rioux' in the timetable while the outside braced boxcar on the left still wears the pre-Confederation N.R. logo. *Jerome Young photo - Merritt C. Scharnweber collection*

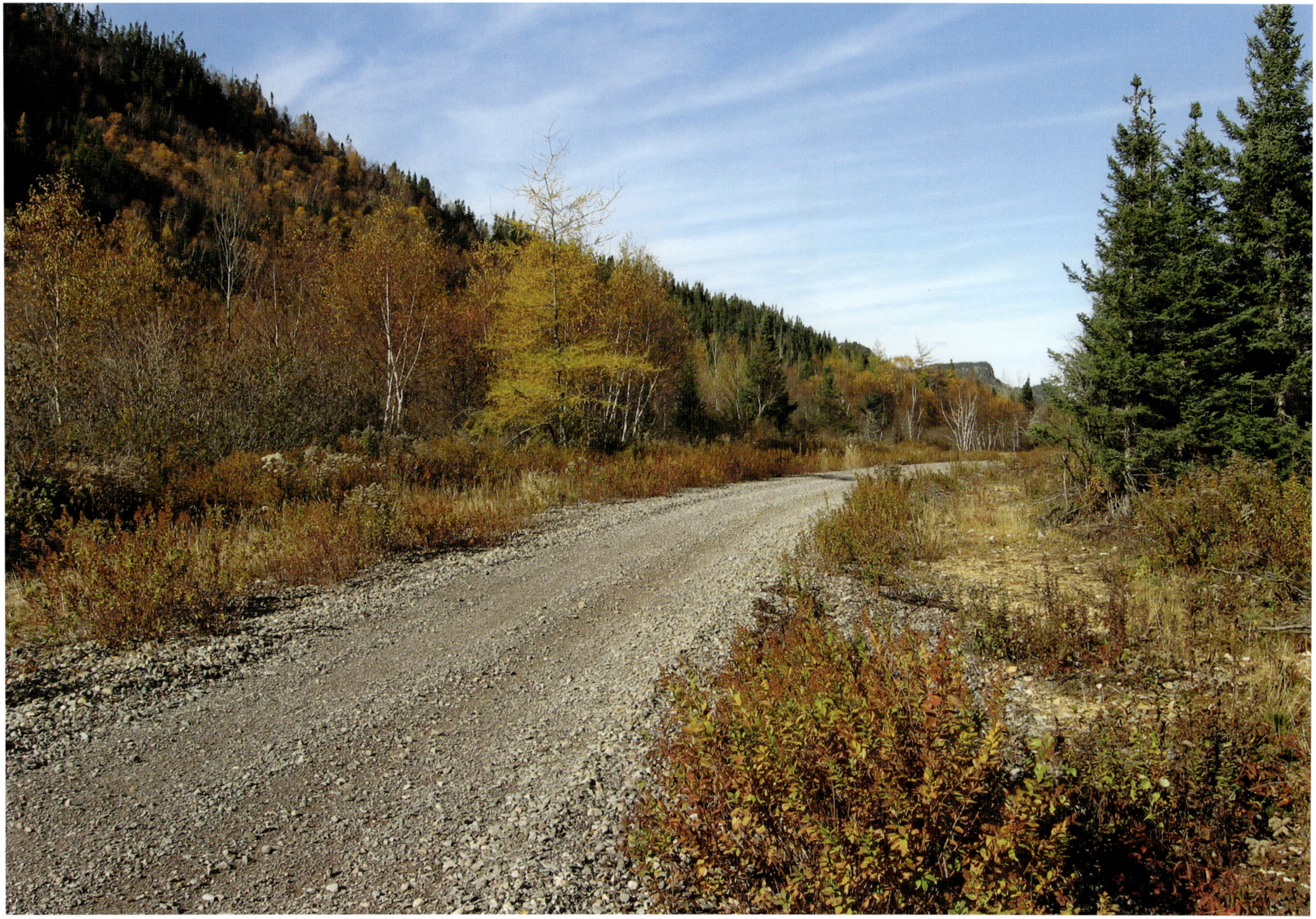

SHOAL HARBOUR PIT TODAY

Once used for railway ballast, the Shoal harbour Pit became Camp 1 for the 1ST Communications Construction Squadron of the US Air Force in 1953, responsible for construction and maintenance of communications for the Northeast Air Command. Other camps were located at Port Blandford, Terra Nova, Goobies and Rantem. NF110 900 has been restored and preserved in nearby Clarenville. *Author photo*

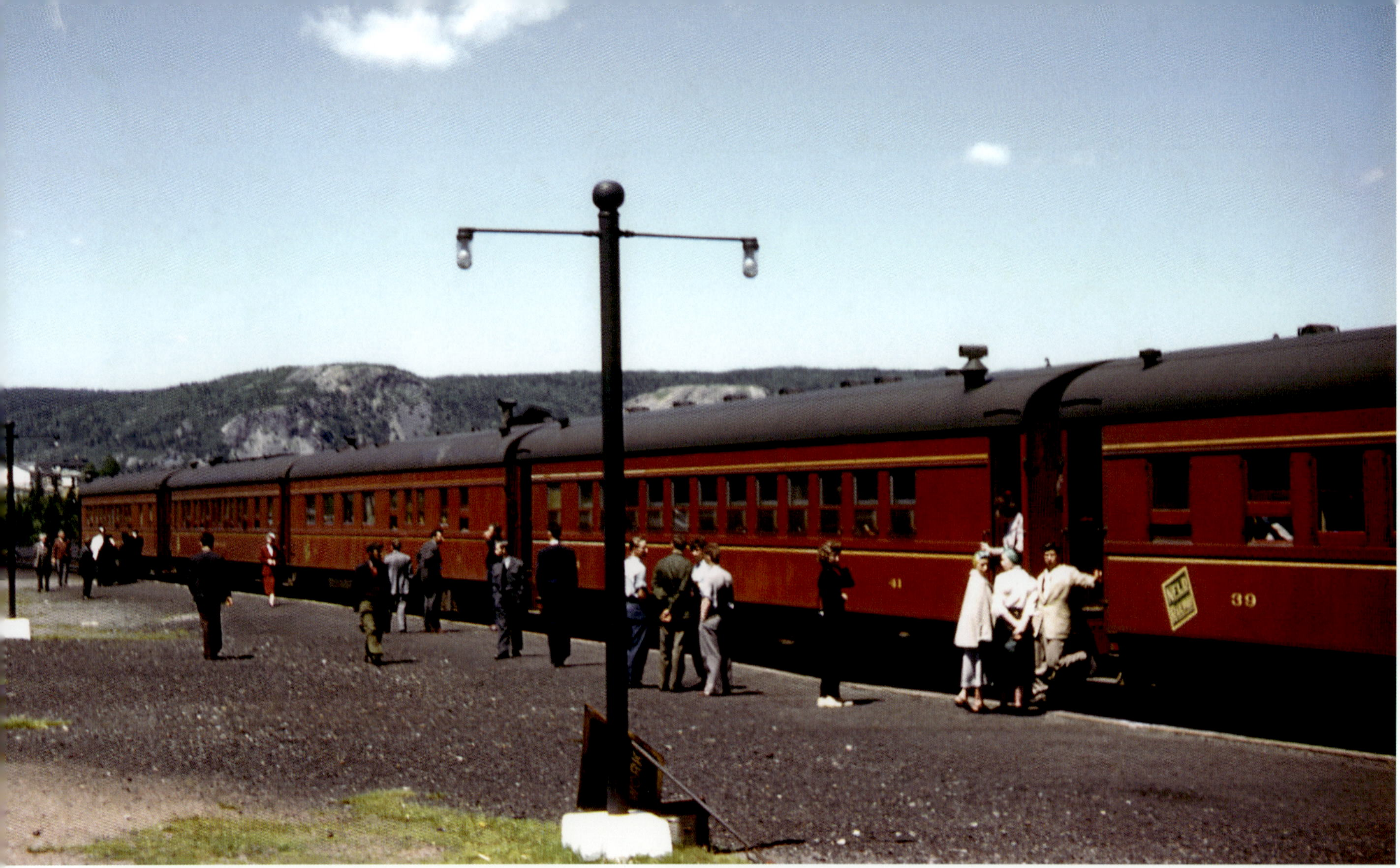

CLARENVILLE 1952

The dapper passengers of CNR Train No. 2 step off to stretch their legs during her twenty-minute stop in Clarenville on June 25, 1952. Still adorned in the beautiful red livery of the Newfoundland Railway, these cars will soon be painted in the olive green of their new operator. At the time of this photo, passengers could travel from here to Bonavista on No. 11, the third class tri-weekly mixed train over the 80-mile branch line. *Omer Lavallee photo*

CLARENVILLE TODAY

The Clarenville Heritage Society boasts one of the Island's best displays with ownership of NF110 900, Diner 176, Caboose 6061 and working equipment from the Newfoundland Hardwoods Company next to the preserved Clarenville station. A former shipyard for the Newfoundland Railway, this bustling and vibrant town has become the major service centre for the Bonavista Peninsula and surrounding area as well as the booming oil industry. *Author photo*

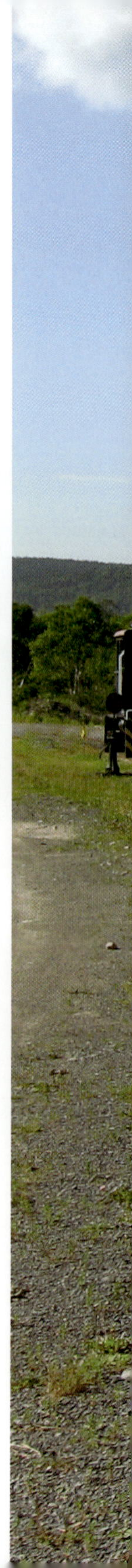

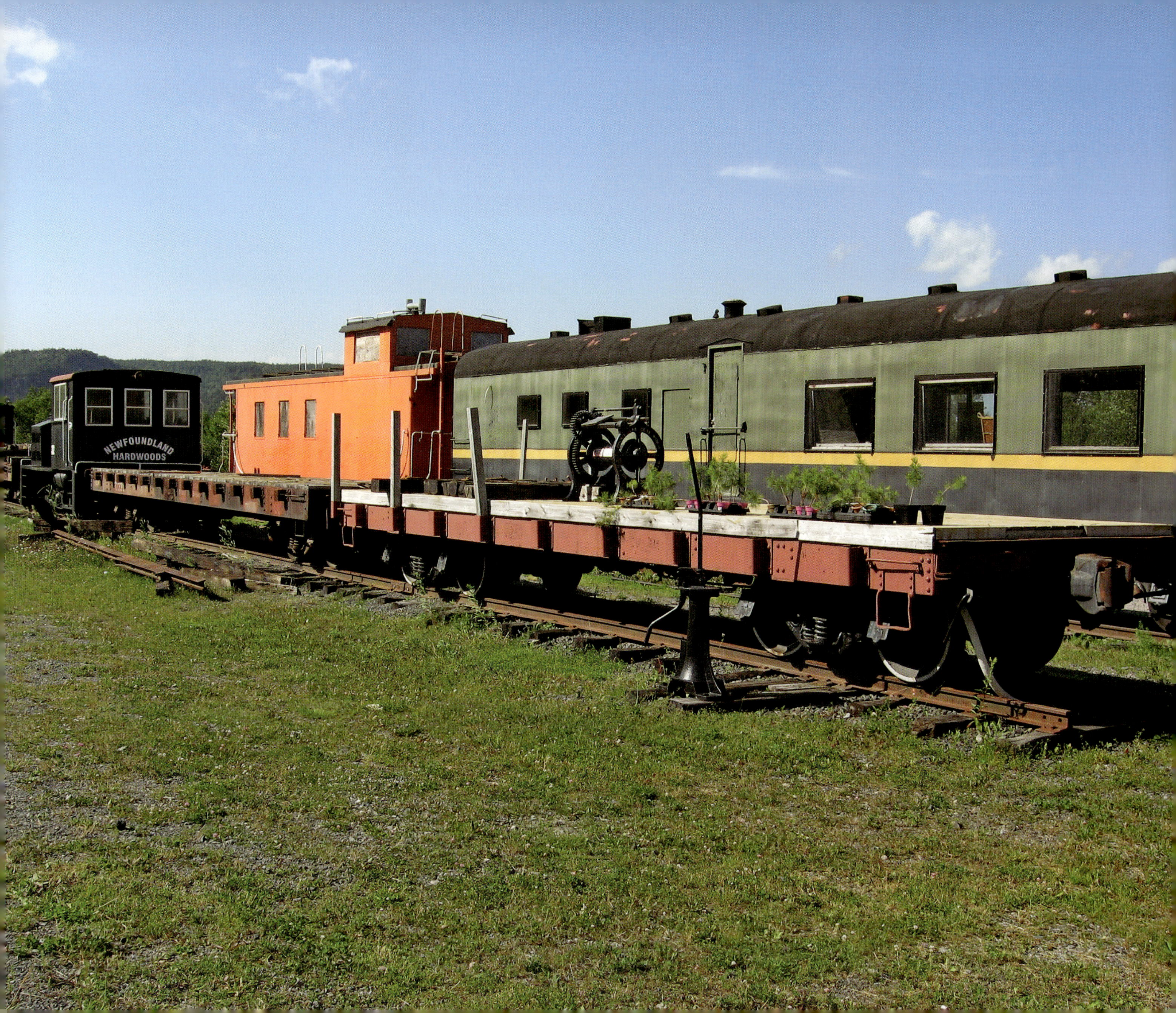
NEWFOUNDLAND
HARDWOODS

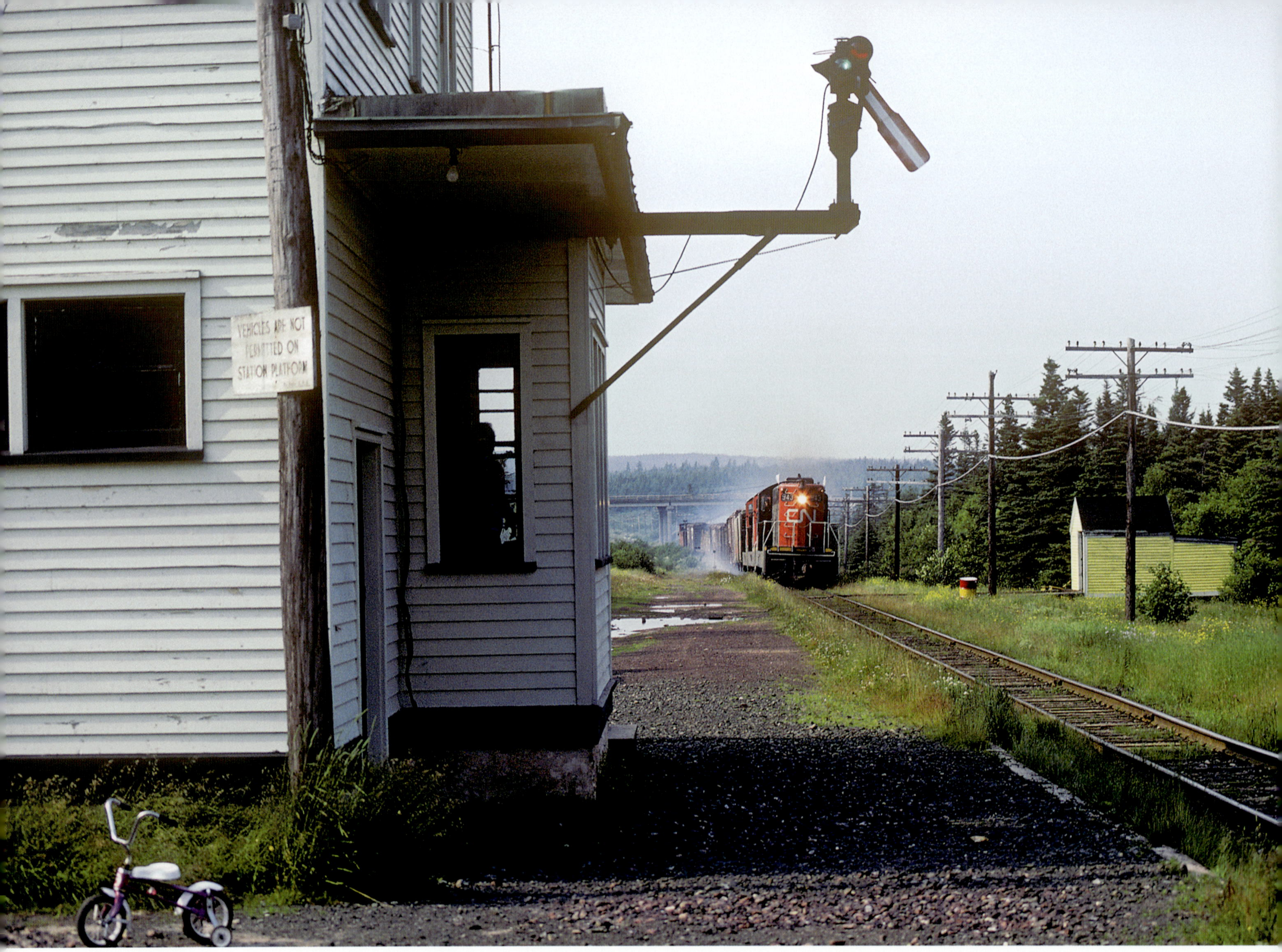

GOOBIES 1980
With the signal board in the proceed position, the agent watches carefully as Extra 943 East approaches the station at Goobies, having just passed under the overpass with the same name on July 29, 1980. This station, as well as most along the route from Port aux Basques to St. John's, would close its doors for good by September of 1984. *Joe McMillan photo*

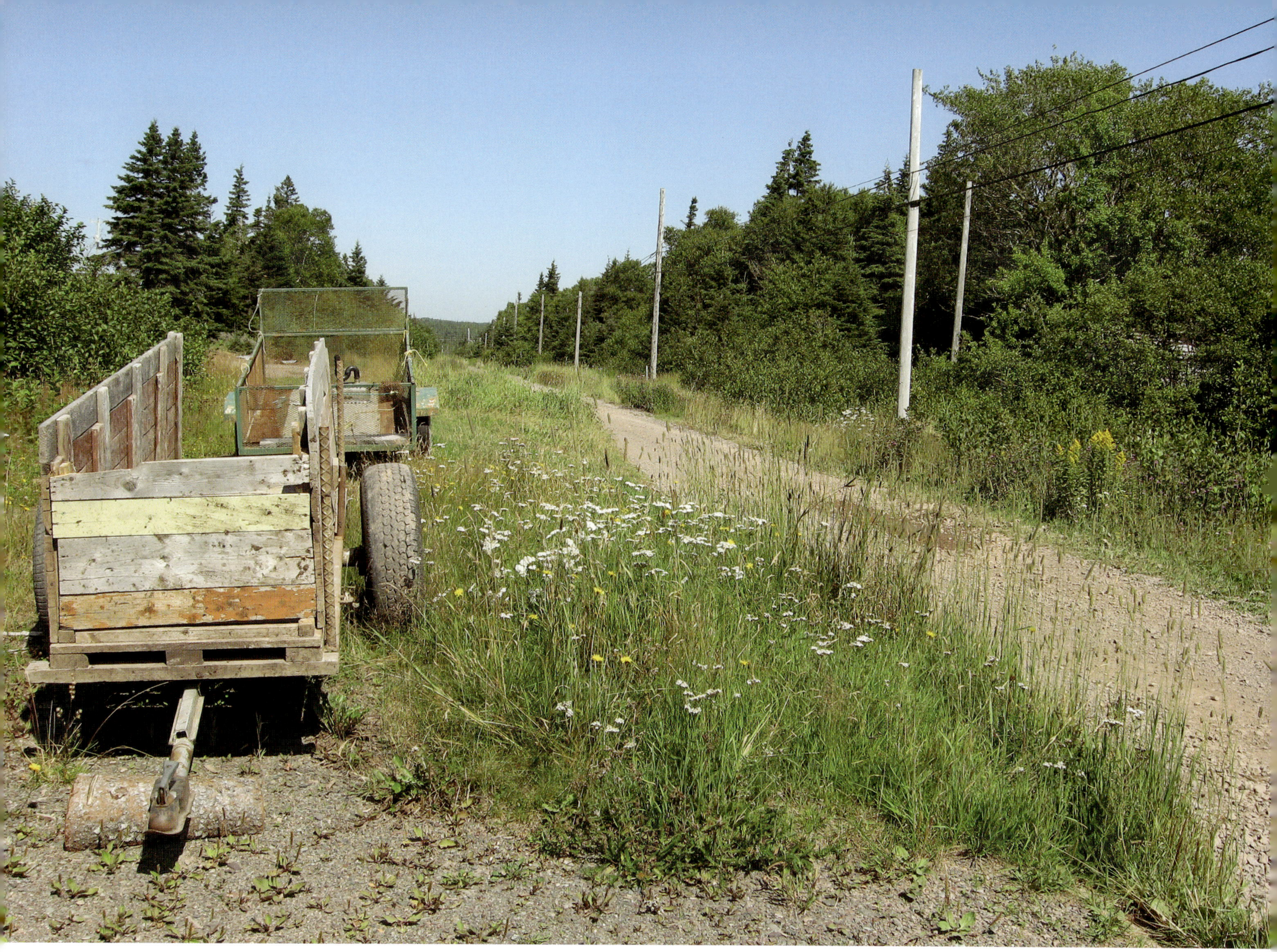

GOOBIES TODAY
Two handmade trailers await the call to duty at Goobies, once the junction for the proposed 102 mile Fortune Bay Branch. With 43 miles of rail laid to Terrenceville, it was never operated and abandoned early in the 20th century. The concrete overpass for the Burin Peninsula Highway has been replaced by a steel culvert but 943 survived to be sold to Nigerian railways in 1990. *Author photo*

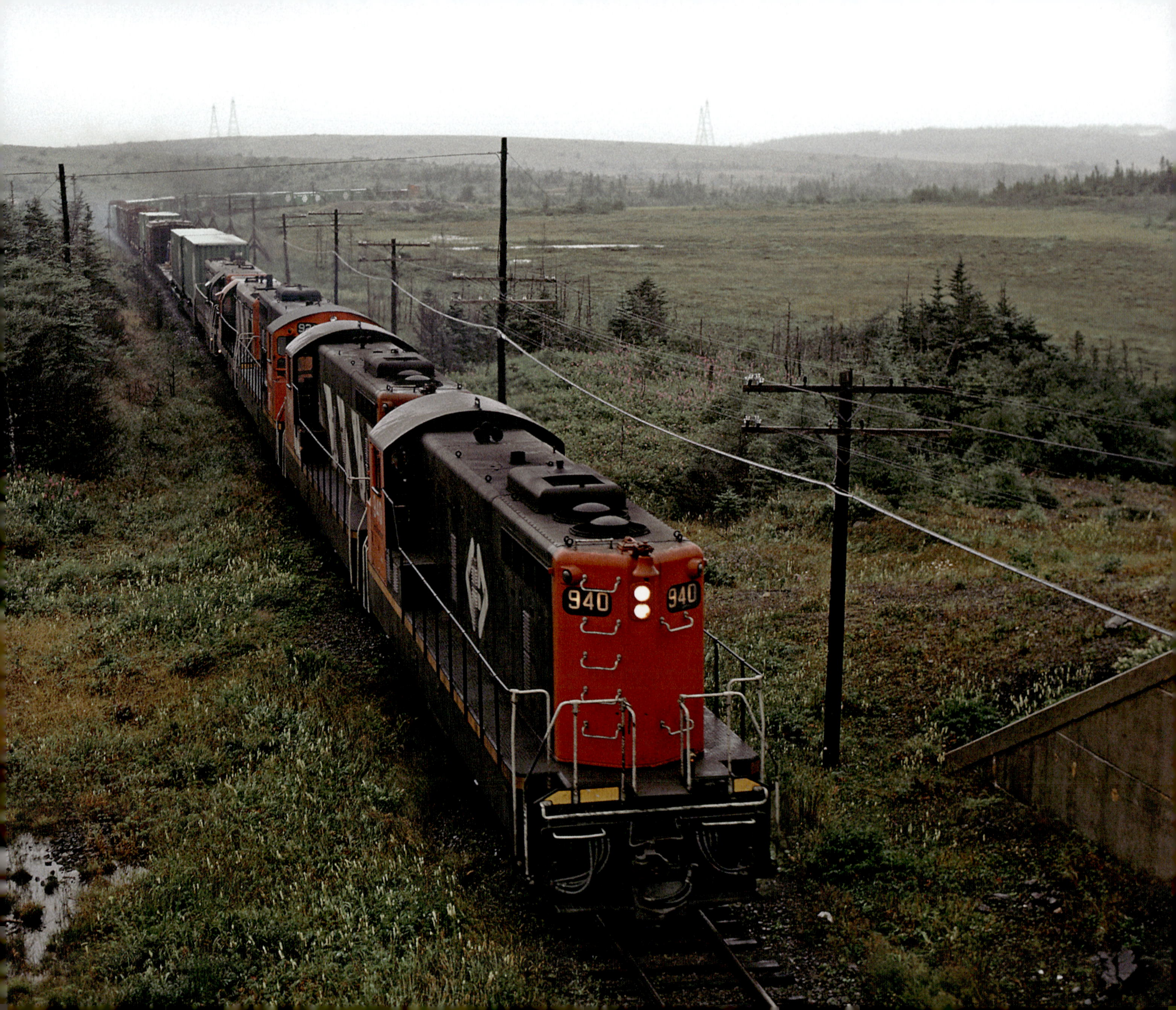
940
940

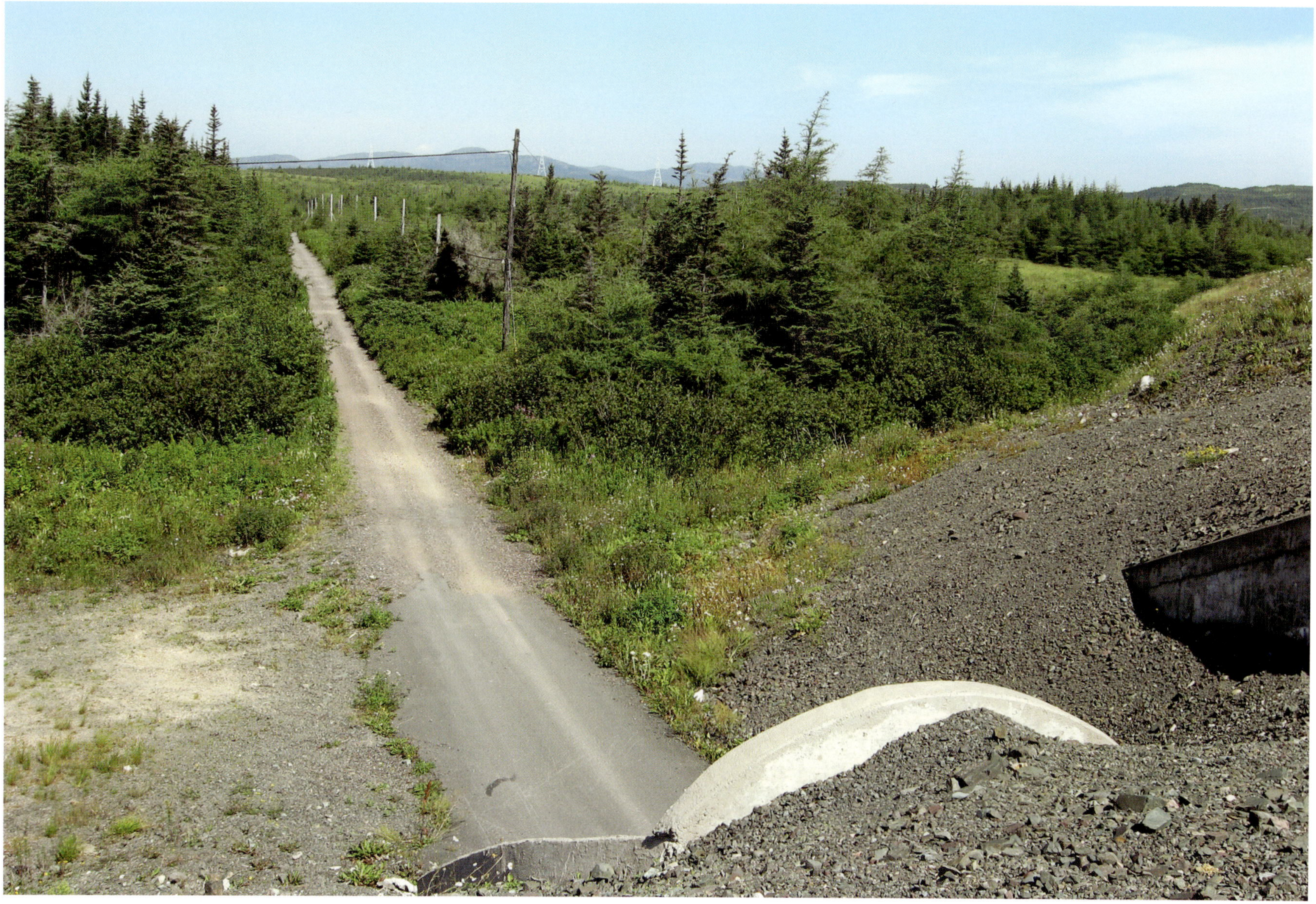

ARNOLD'S COVE OVERPASS 1982
Terra Transport eastbound freight 204 approaches the overpass near Arnold's Cove on a damp and drizzly August 26, 1982. Headed by NF210 940 and sisters 941 and 920, the 204 also has G8s 802 and 800 just behind them, probably headed to the St. John's shops for maintenance. Bill Liney had chased and photographed both those units on mixed trains 205 and 206 up and down the Bonavista branch the previous day. *Bill Linley photo*

ARNOLD'S COVE OVERPASS TODAY
The remains of the original overpass have since come into view, perhaps due in part to erosion caused by Hurricane Igor, September 2010, which struck this area particularly hard. The large transmission towers in the background pass directly over the east end of the former wye and provide power to the nearby North Atlantic Refinery at Come By Chance. When opened in 1973, this 115,000 barrel a day facility had a spur line to the Canadian National mainline. *Author photo*

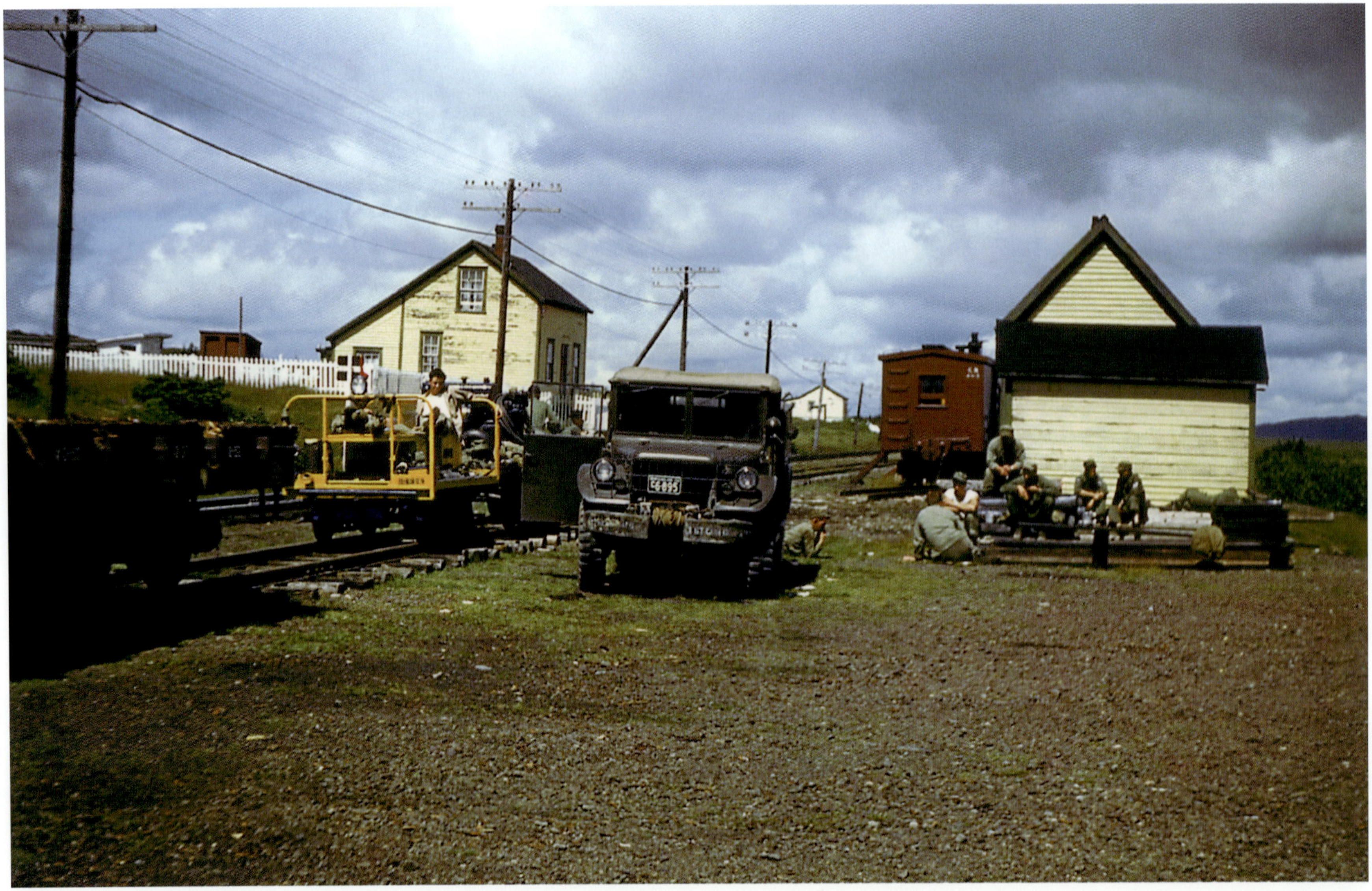

ARNOLD'S COVE STATION 1953

Airmen of the 1ST Communications Construction Squadron of the US Air Force take a break at Arnold's Cove Station during the summer of 1953. With the speeder on the siding, they are probably waiting for a CNR train to pass before resuming work. Their work of replacing the poles and anchors along the route had to be regulated with the CNR schedule.

Jerome Young photo - Merritt C. Scharnweber collection

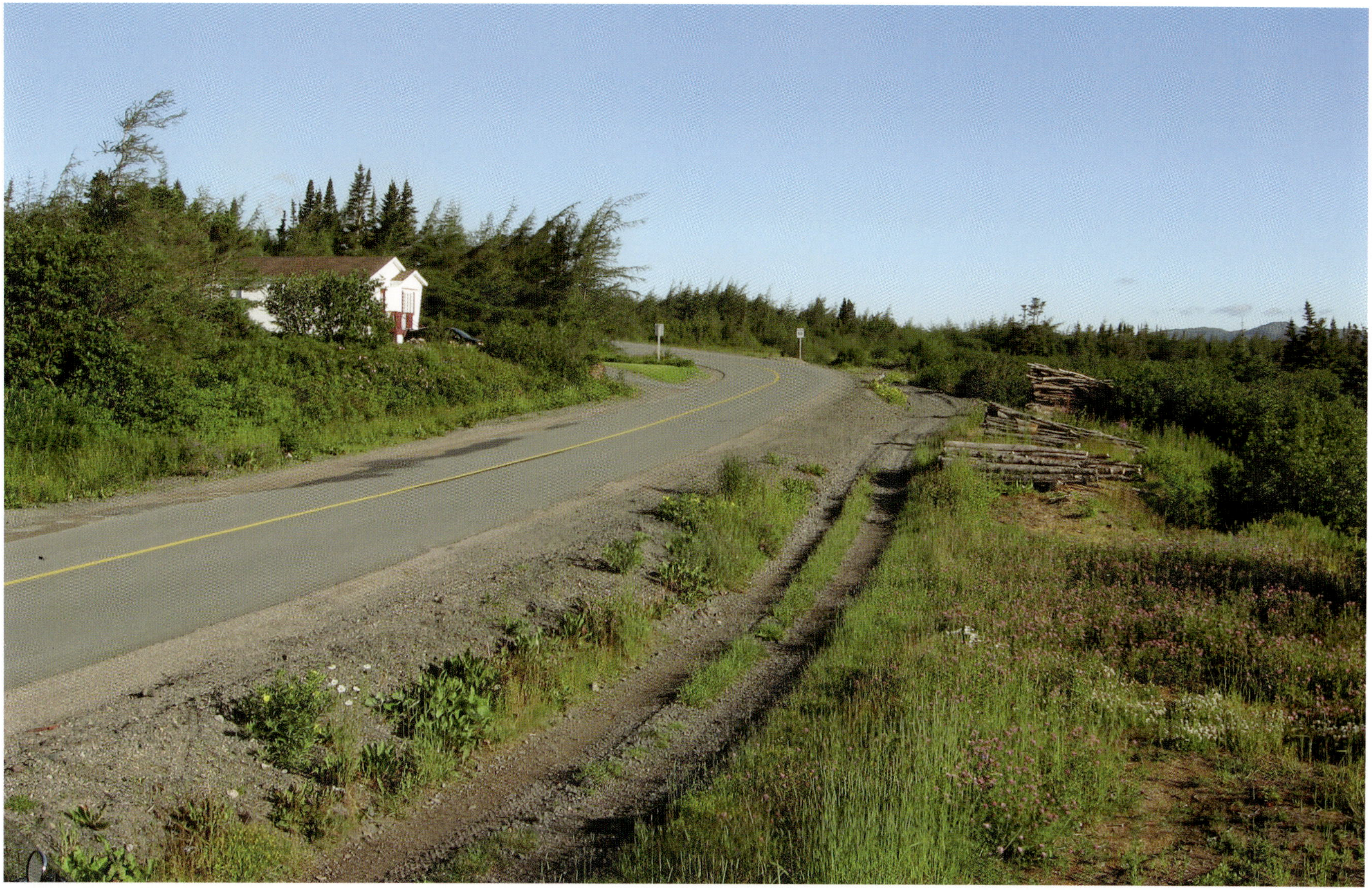

ARNOLD'S COVE STATION TODAY

A new paved highway where the tracks once ran connects this tiny community to the Trans Canada Highway. Established in the 1890s with the coming of the railway, it bypassed Arnold's Cove proper, located south of this point and on the waters of Placentia Bay. With the Resettlement Program of the 1960s, many people moved their homes across the bay to that location. *Author photo*

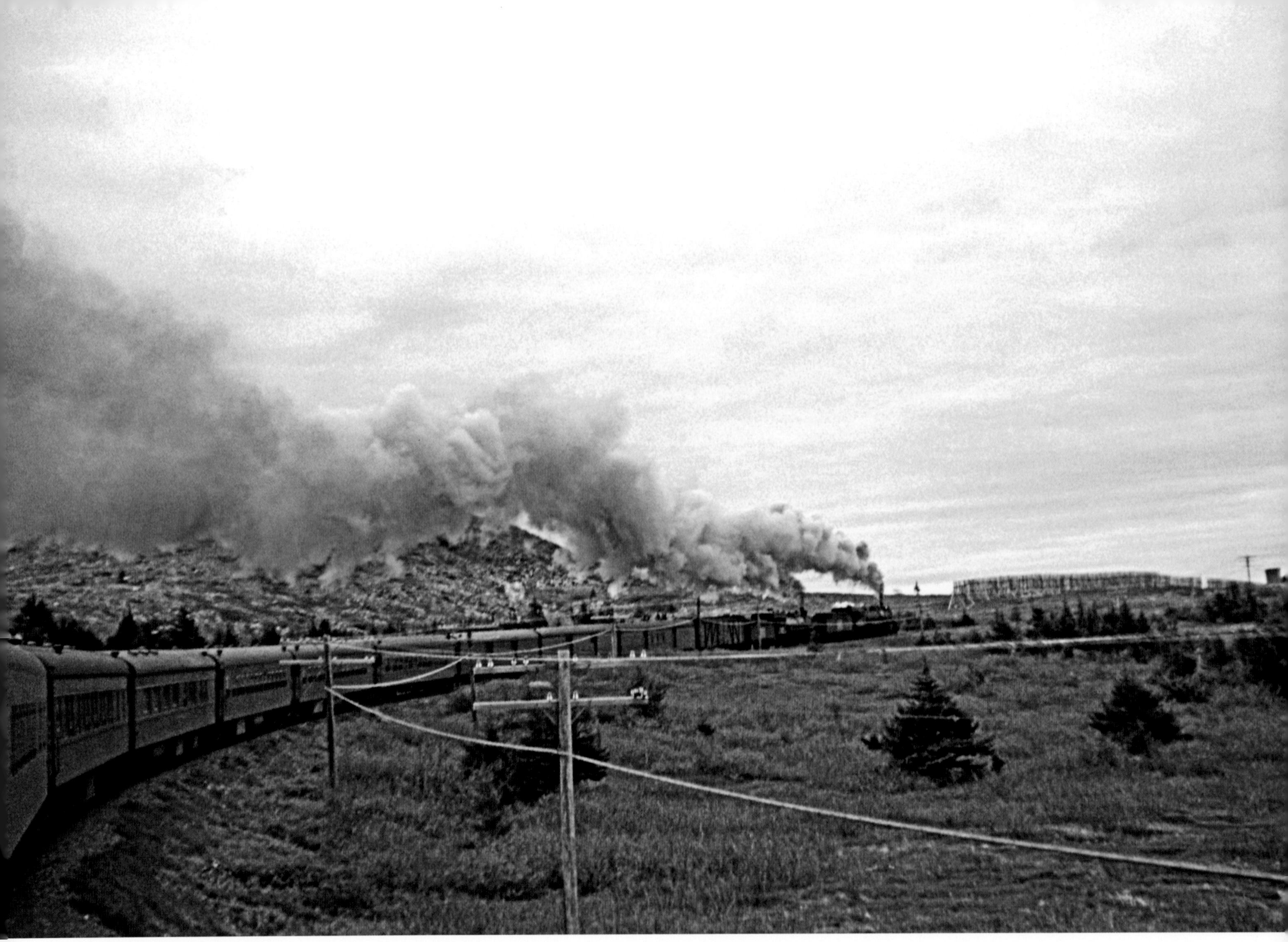

ISTHMUS OF AVALON 1956
2-8-2 Mikado #310 and 4-6-2 Pacific #598 head up CNR Train No. 2 on the Isthmus of Avalon between Rantem and Tickle Harbour on June 20, 1956. The engines were changed at Bishop's Falls and normally the run would be handled by two Mikados. They are about to crest upgrade between the wooden snow fences, thus making for a most interesting scene.
Robert J. Sandusky photo

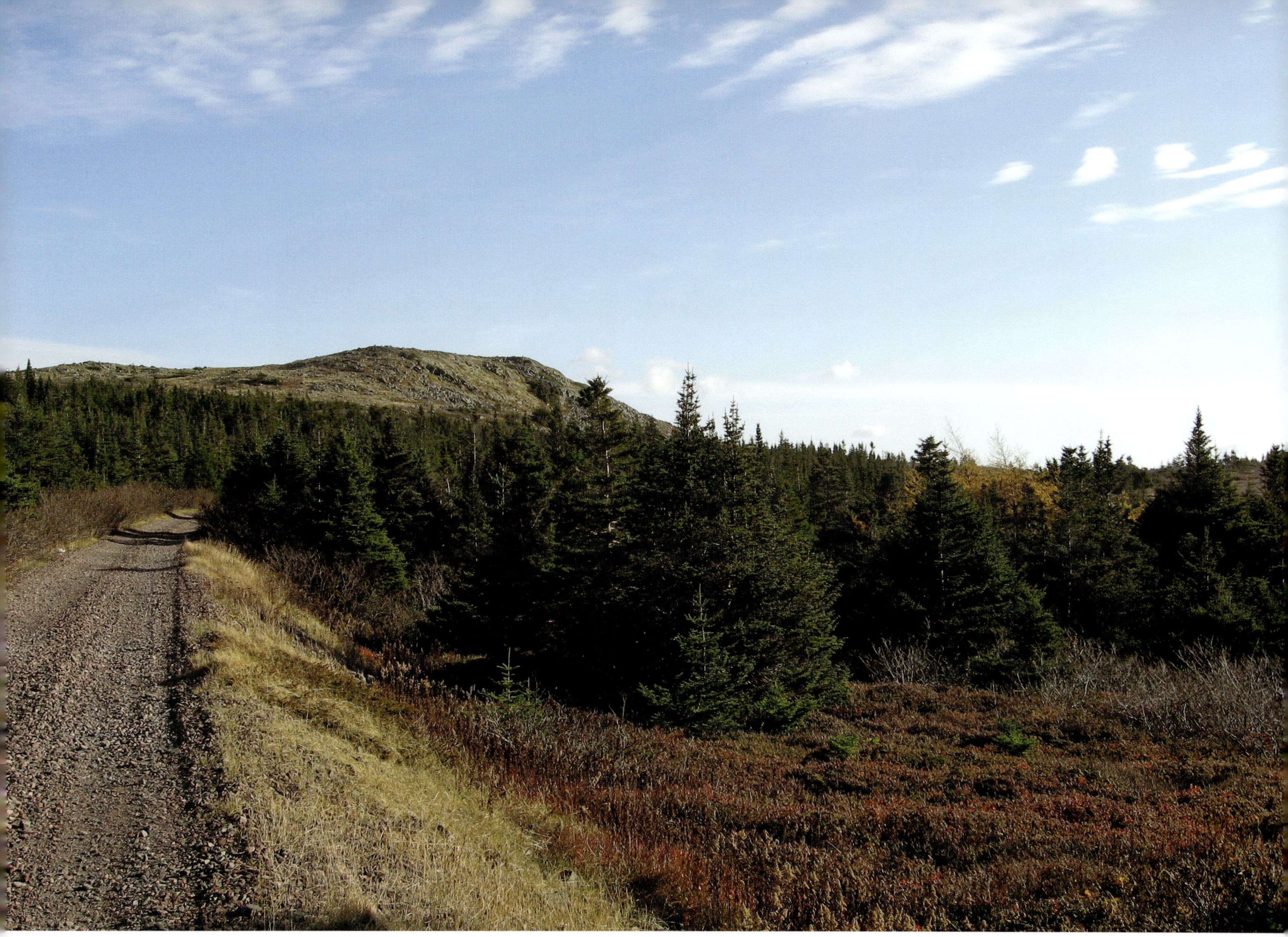

ISTHMUS OF AVALON TODAY

Not a great deal has changed since the rails were laid in the early 1890s; the area is as rugged and uninhabited as ever. At approximately 5 kilometers wide, the Precambrian rock of the Isthmus of Avalon connects the heavily populated Avalon Peninsula with the rest of Newfoundland. The challenge of building a railway through here was daunting to say the least.
Author photo

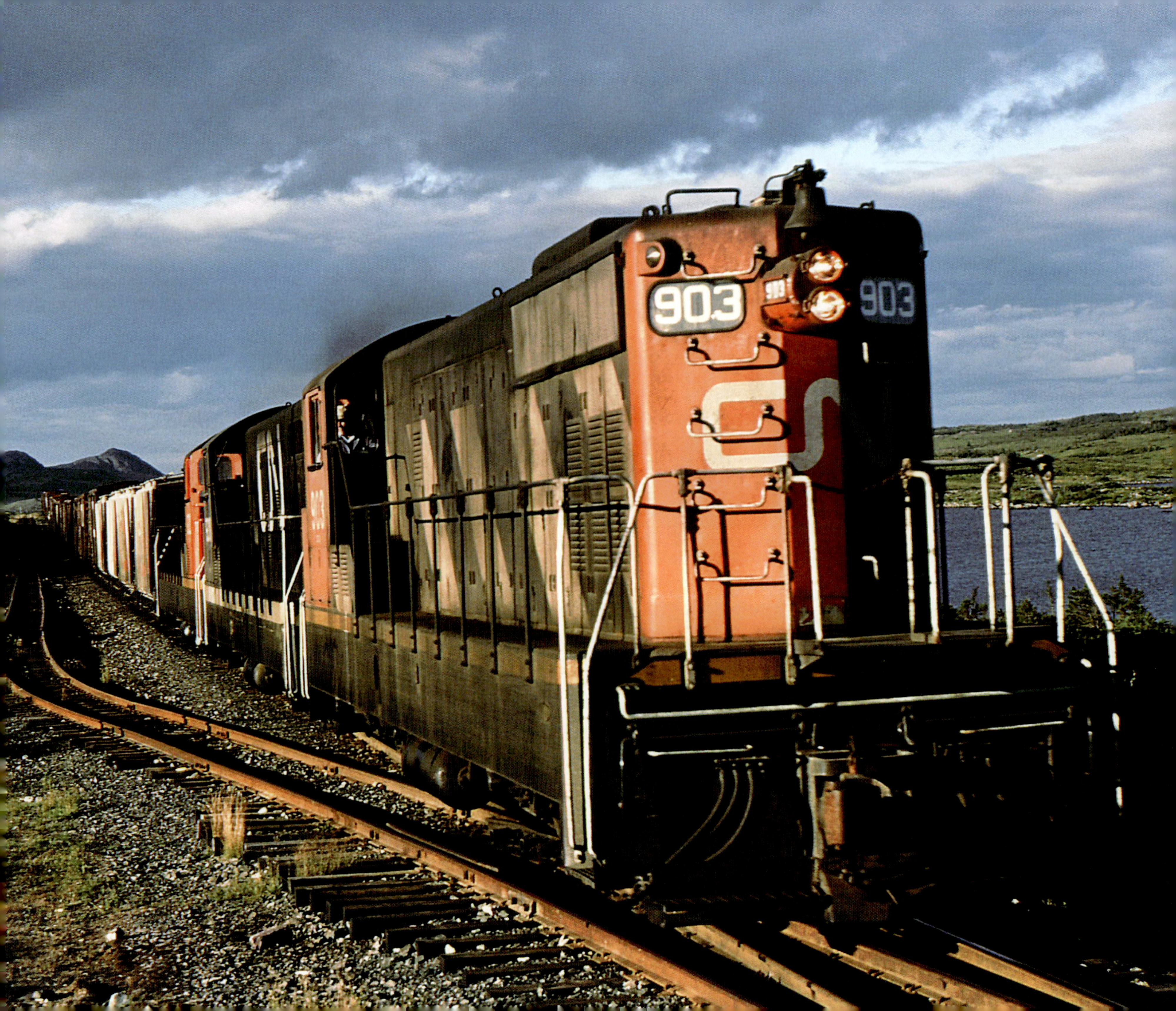
903
903

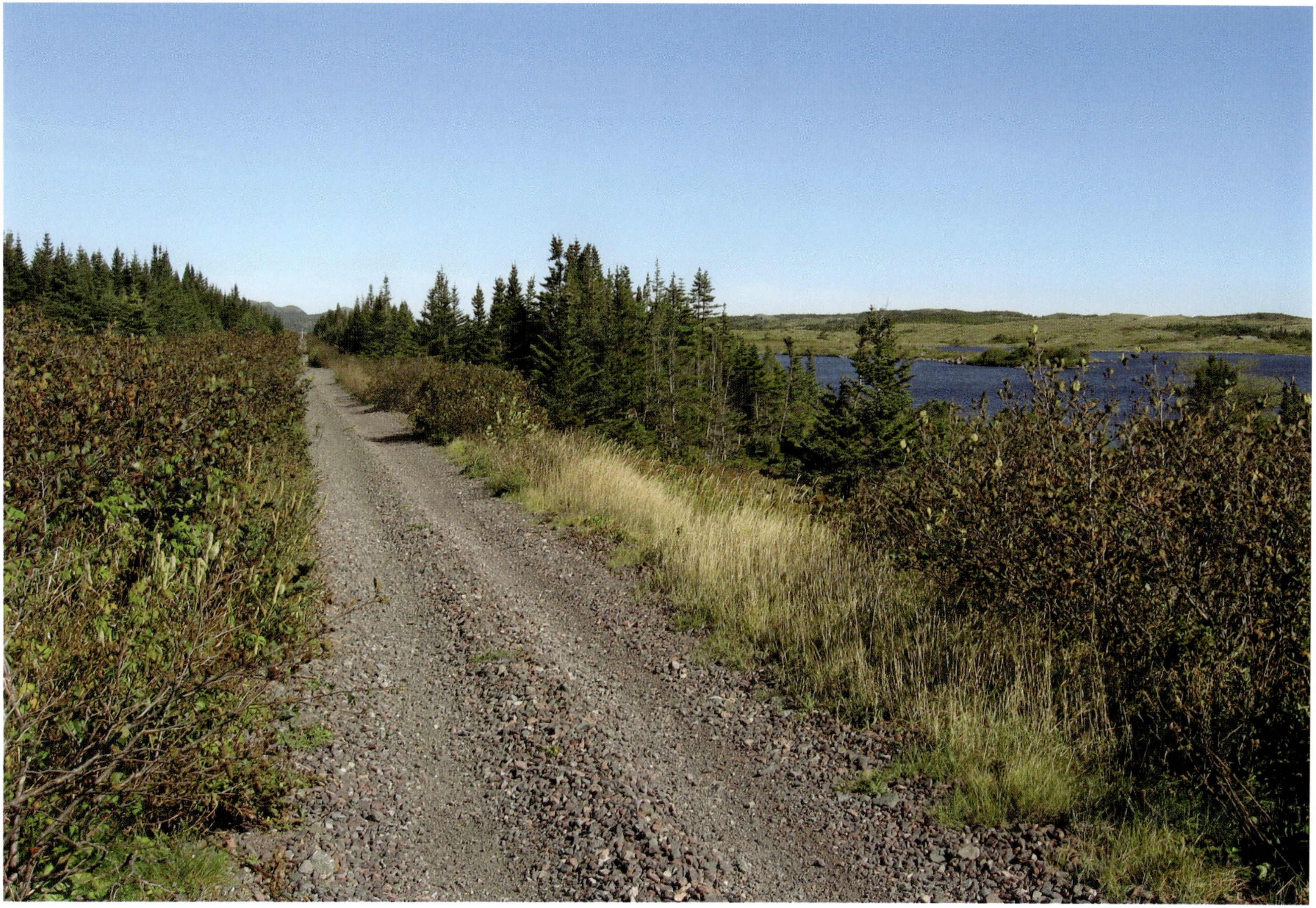

TICKLE HARBOUR 1978

With the Doe Hills as a dramatic backdrop and illuminated with the last rays of the setting sun, Canadian National Train 204 with NF110 903 and two additional engines cruises through Tickle Harbour late in the evening of August 25, 1978. Delivered to Newfoundland by GMD in 1953, 903 was in the second batch of NF110s ordered and was soon accompanied by a further five units. *Rich Taylor photo*

TICKLE HARBOUR TODAY

Tickle Harbour was a flag stop on the Isthmus of Avalon to serve communities such as Fair Haven in Placentia Bay and Bellevue in Trinity Bay until passenger service ended July 3, 1969. At exactly 80 miles from St. John's, freights 203 and 204 continued to pass by the tiny station. Today only cabins overlook the adjacent Station Pond, accessible by the somewhat ironically named highway, Route 203. *Author photo*

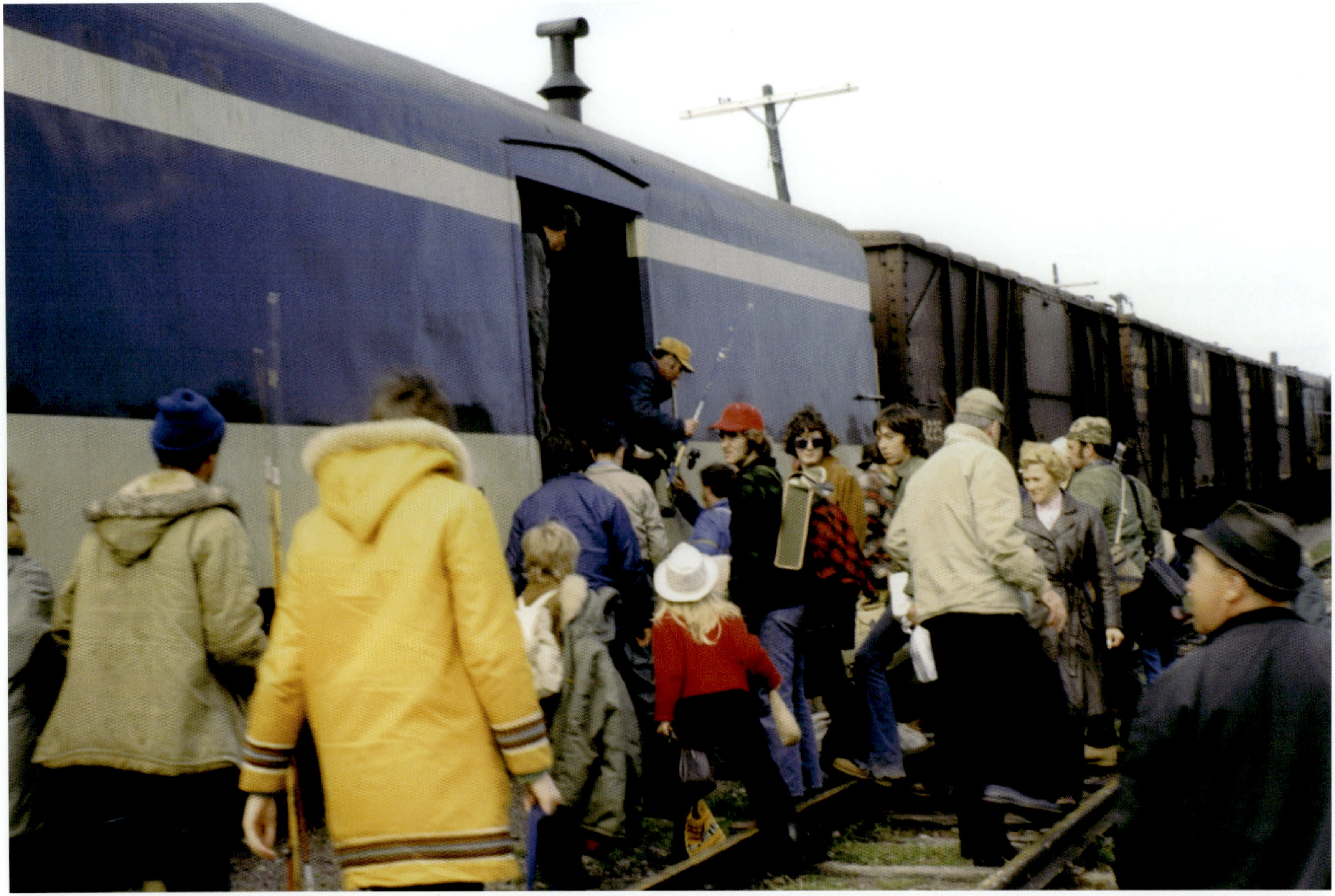

PLACENTIA JUNCTION 1972
Riders on the *Trouters Special* gather their equipment from the baggage car at Placentia Junction on Victoria Day, May 1972. Earl Roberts and fellow members of the newly formed Terra Nova Model Railway Club rode this train as one of its organized events. A yearly tradition, the train, usually with a trio of G8s, would travel from St. John's to Argentia return, dropping and picking up anglers along the route. *Earl Roberts photo*

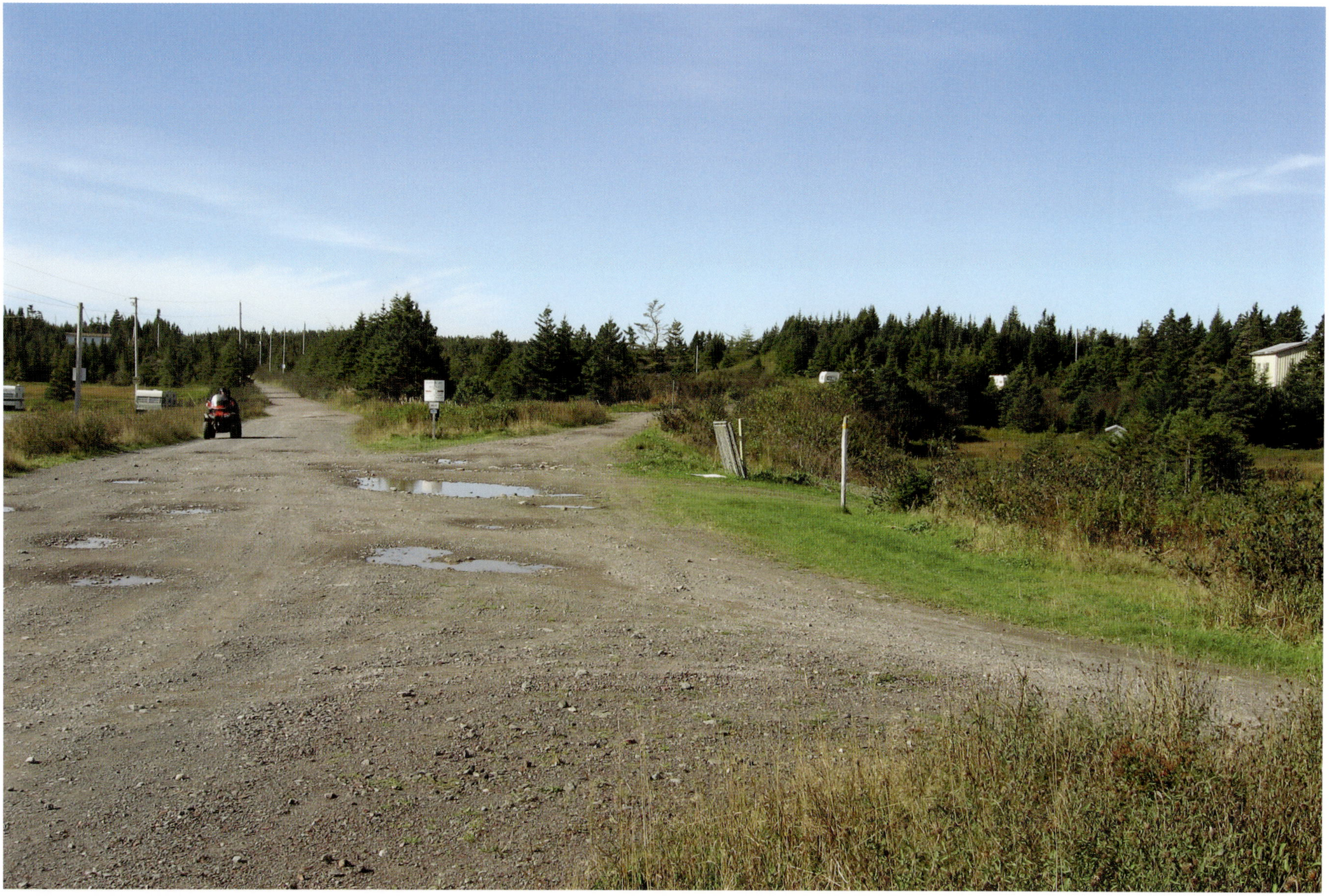

PLACENTIA JUNCTION TODAY
An ATV rider approaches the mainline from the former Argentia Branch at Placentia Junction. First settled in 1893 with the building of the railway, this little community and the nearby Station Pond and Junction Pond has become prime cabin country. Thanks to the well marked sign in the middle, riders and other trail users are advised that Argentia is 20 miles to the left while Port aux Basques is 486 miles to the right. *Author photo*

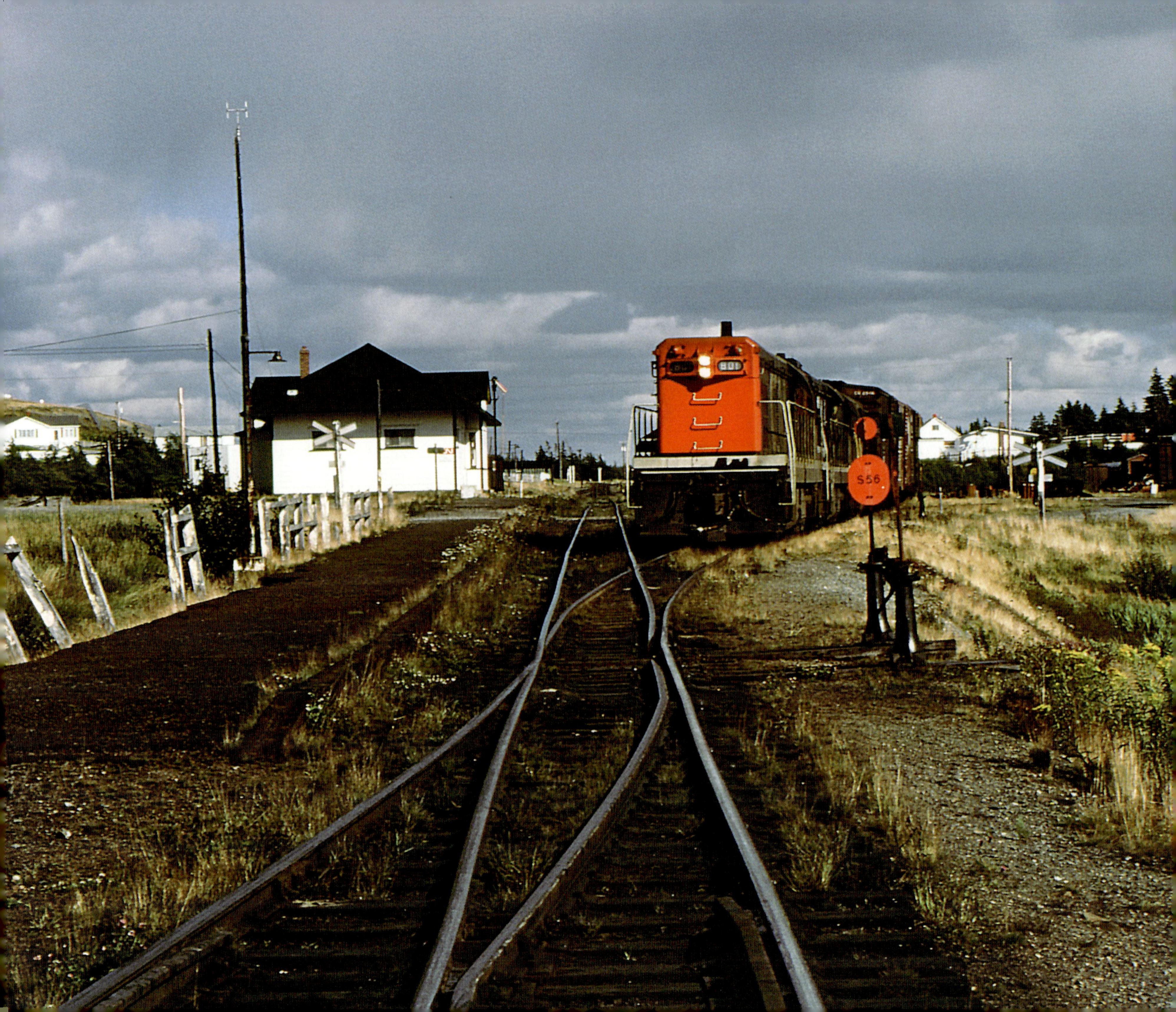
S56

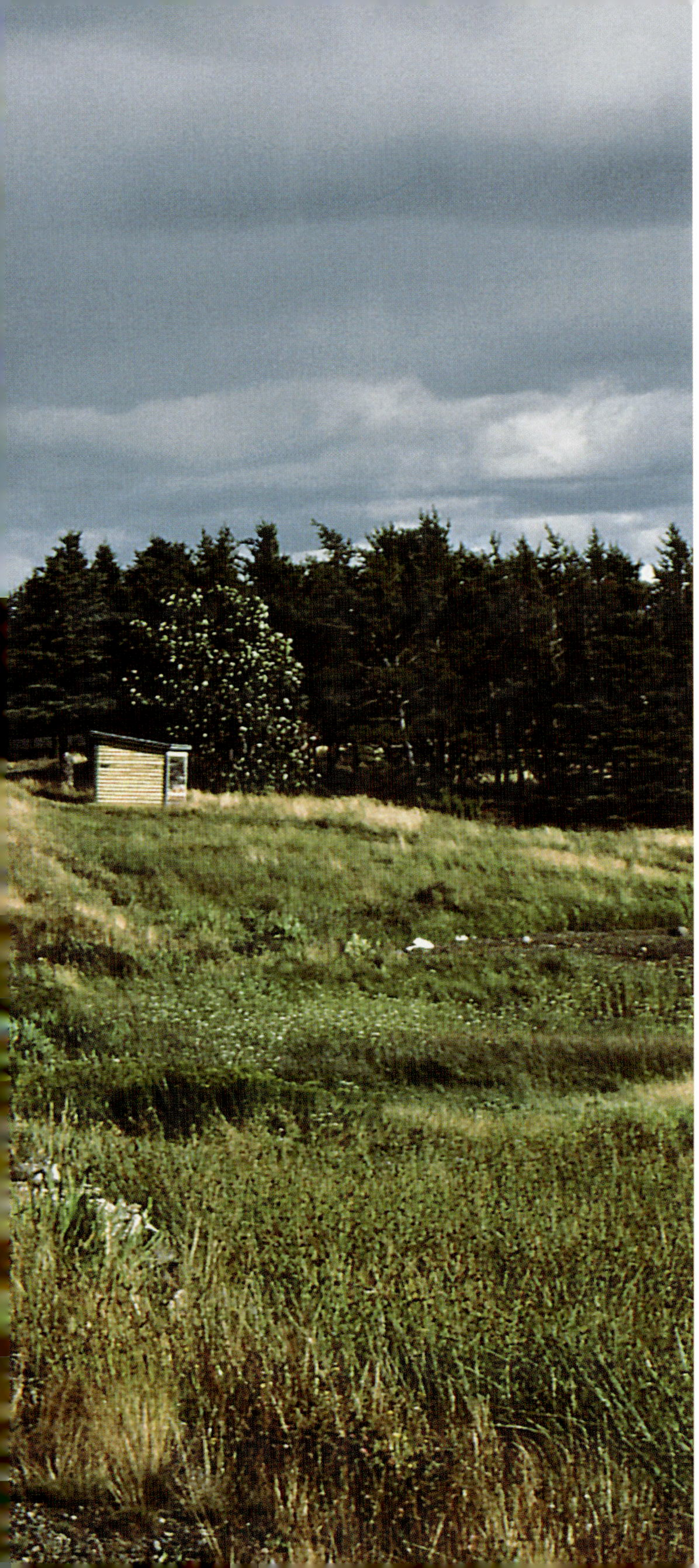

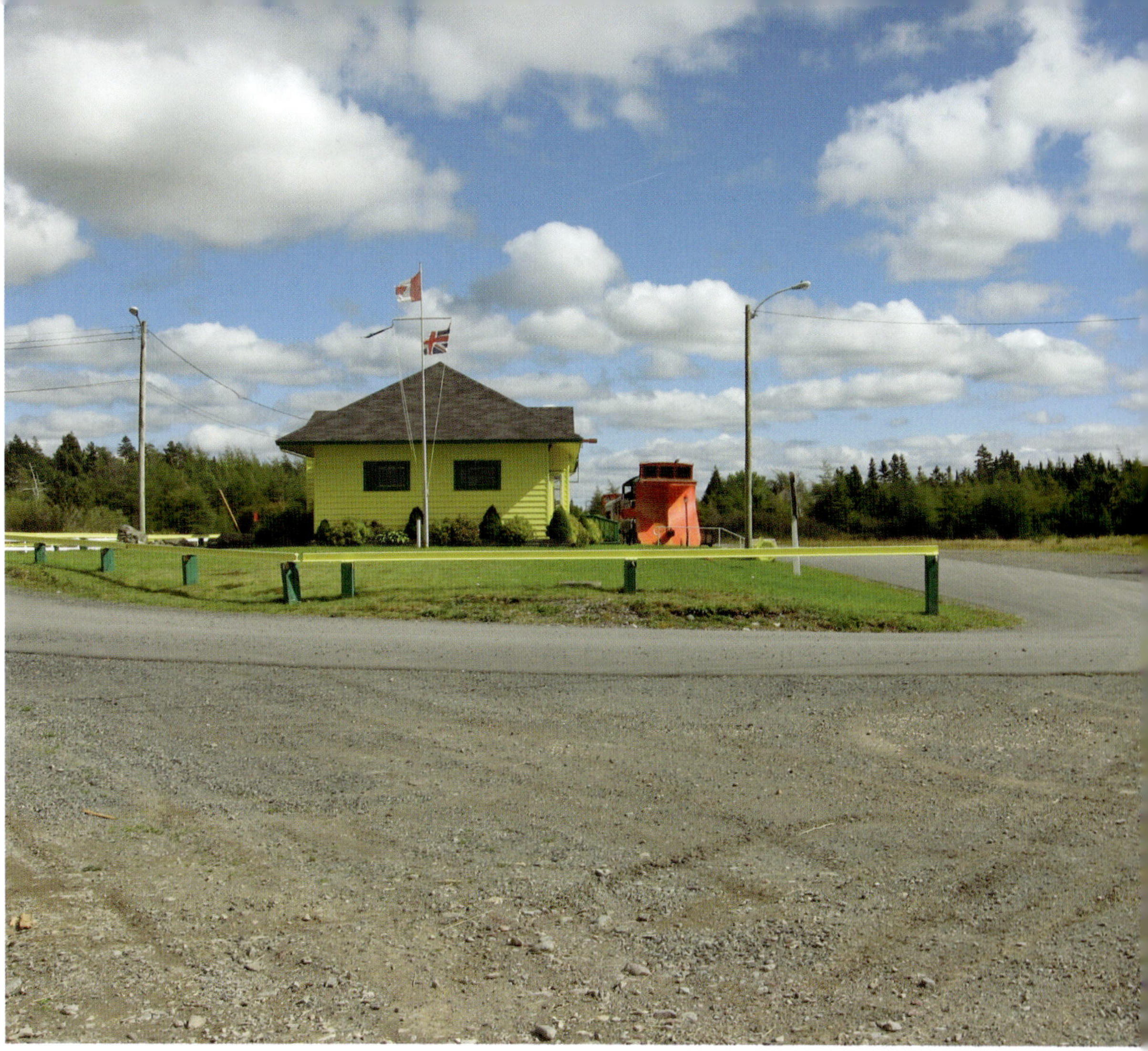

WHITBOURNE 1978

G8 #801, one of six export model 875 HP roadswitchers built for the CNR's Newfoundland branch-line duty in 1956, leads mixed train No. 207 on to the mainline at Whitbourne before continuing to Argentia on August 25, 1978. Upon arrival at Argentia, this small train with three units, three boxcars and three pieces of passenger equipment will return that same day as No. 208 and overnight at Whitbourne. *Rich Taylor photo*

WHITBOURNE TODAY

Credited with being 'Newfoundland's First Inland Town', Whitbourne was developed with the coming of the railway in 1880. Railway shops here completed the final assembly of passenger cars for the newly formed Newfoundland Northern and Western Railway. The former station has been beautifully restored and today is home to the municipal council, local museum and a static train display with NF210 940. *Author photo*

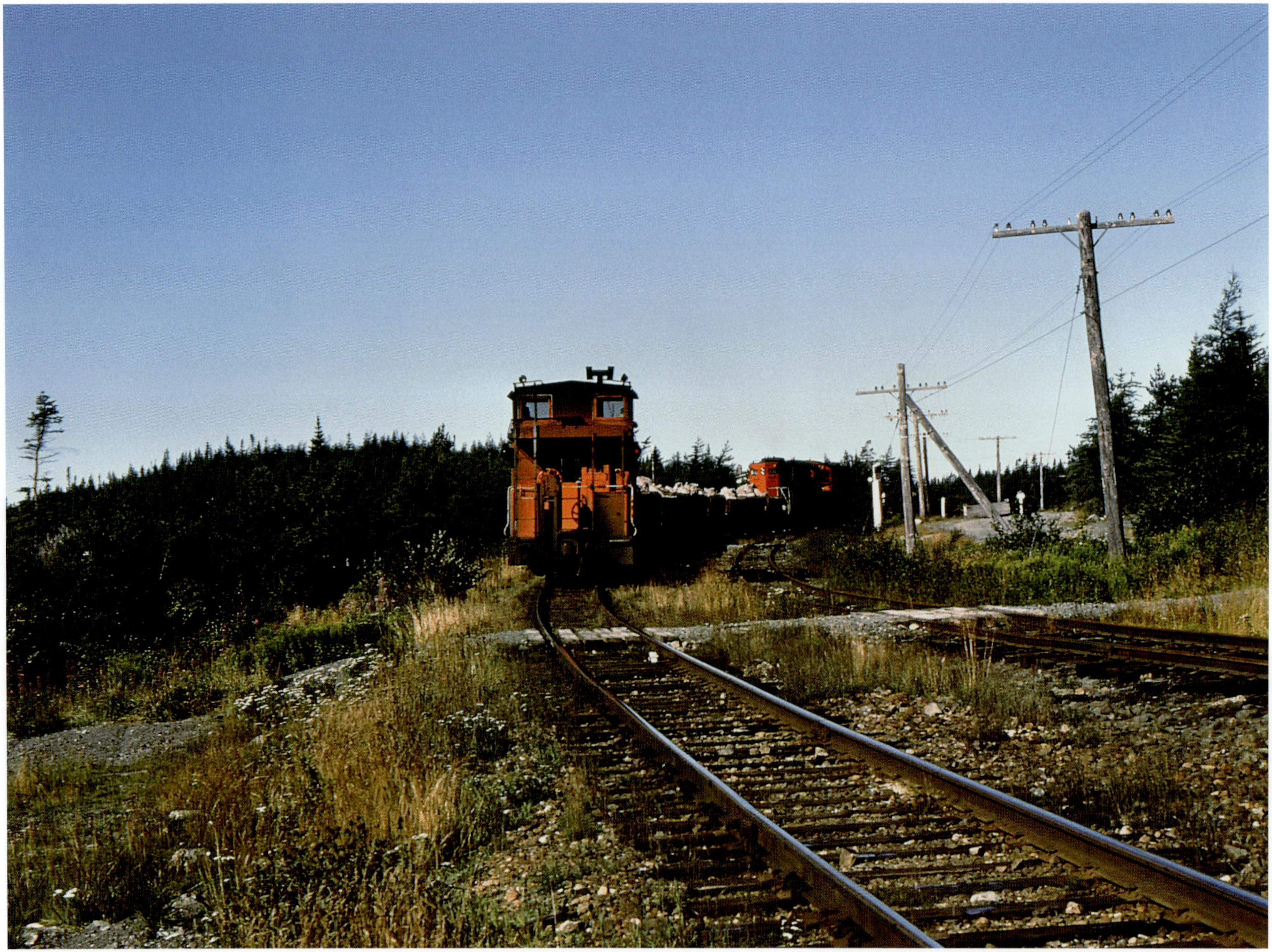

OCEAN POND 1978
Canadian National Extra 932 West passes through the mainline at Ocean Pond with sister engine 930, ten side dumps filled with rock and a steel caboose on cloudless August 25, 1978. NF210s 932 and 930 were among twenty-six diesels delivered from Montreal to St. John's by the *M.V. Christian Smith* in December 1956 to forever banish steam engines from the Island. *Rich Taylor photo*

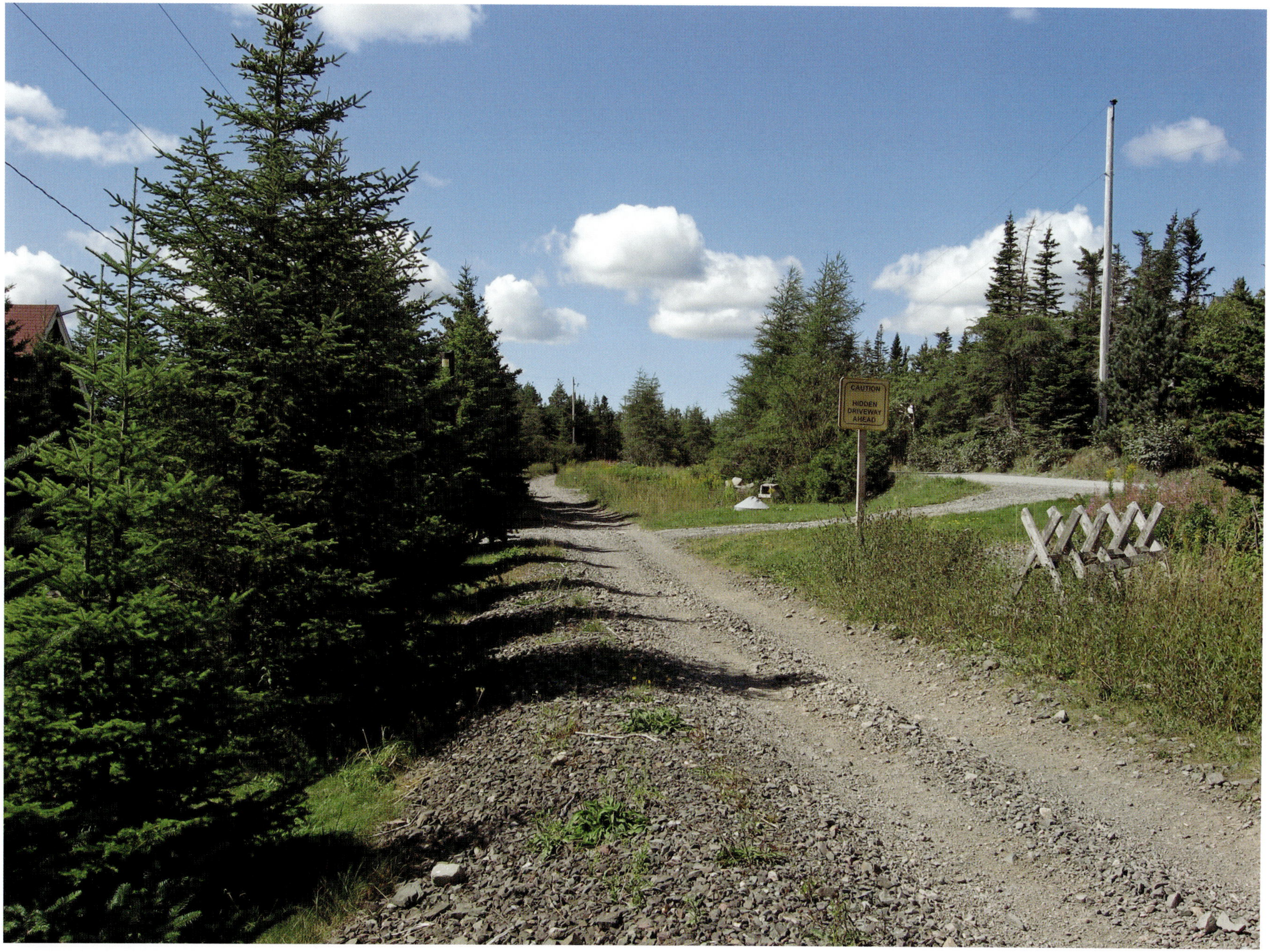

OCEAN POND TODAY
The old wood horse has well served its owner by supplying heat on many a cold winter's night and 932 has survived into the 21st century on static display in Bonavista. In the 1970s, when the atmospheric conditions were just right, the train whistle at Ocean Pond would travel down the valley and could sometimes be heard in the author's hometown of Colinet, 18 miles away. *Author photo*

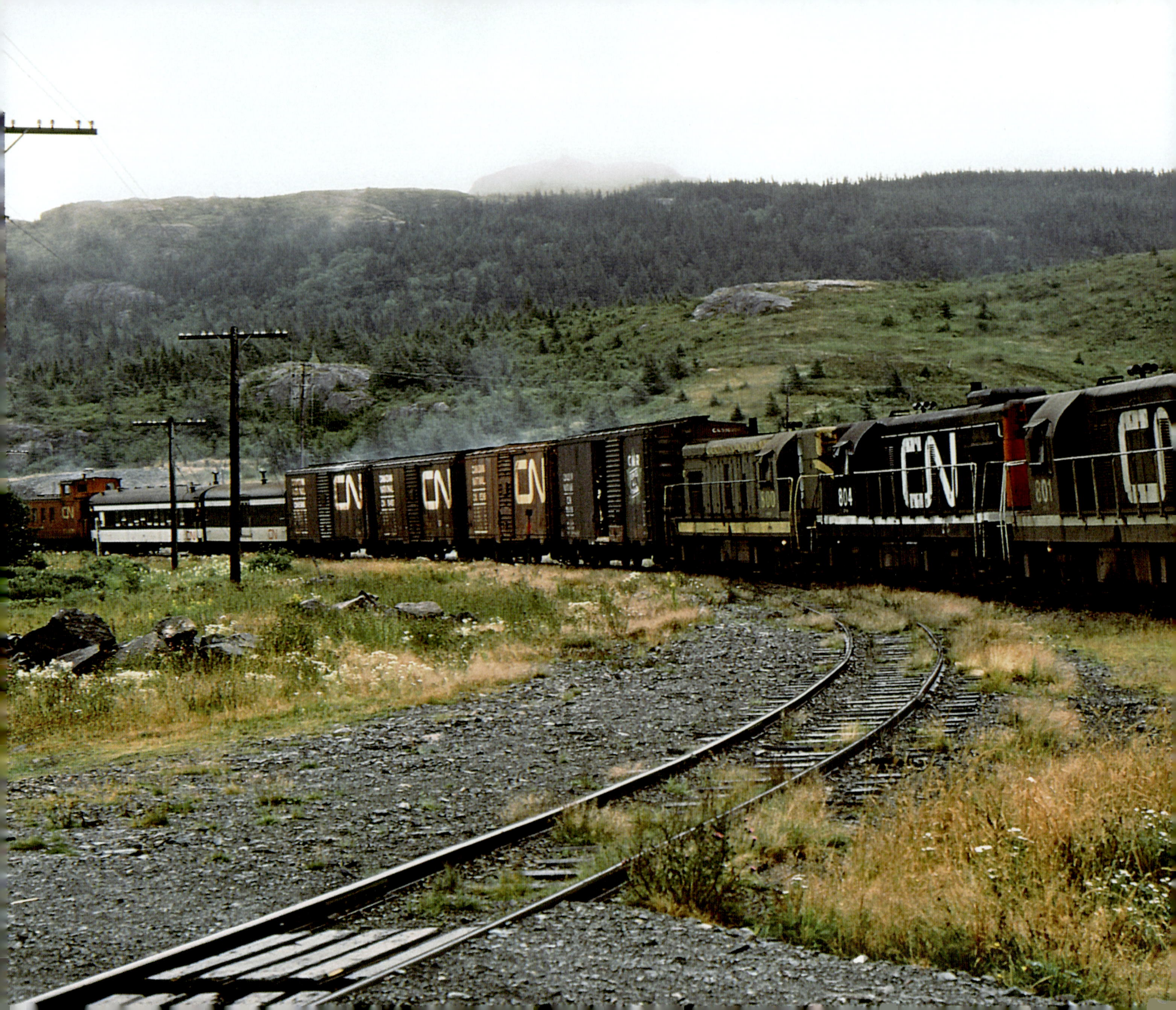
CN
804
801

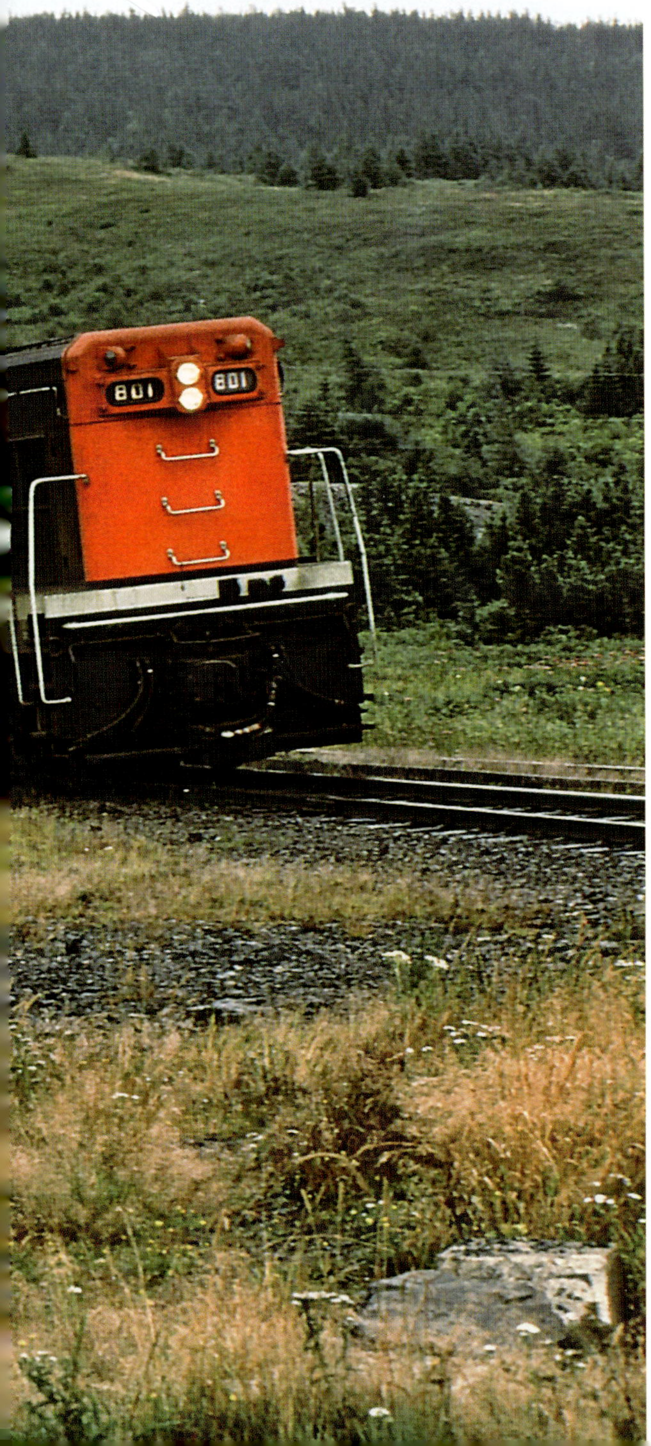

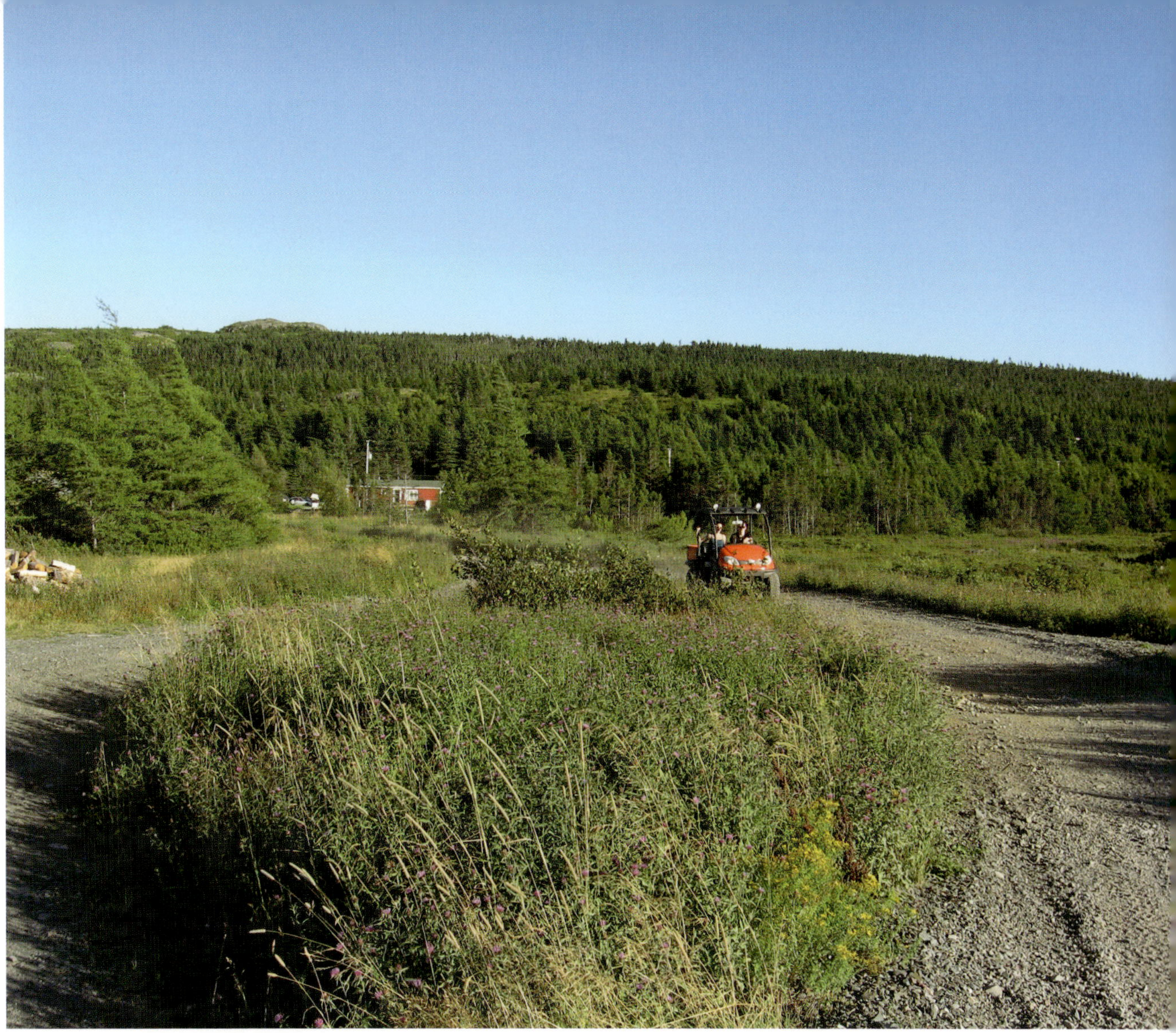

BRIGUS JUNCTION 1978
Canadian National mixed train No. 207 with G8s 801, 804 and 800 stops at Brigus Junction to entrain passengers heading to Argentia on a rainy August 23, 1978. Returning from Whitbourne the next day as 208, the train would make the 38.5 mile trip north to Carbonear as No. 211, back to Brigus Junction as 212 and from there to St. John's as No. 232. *Rich Taylor photo*

BRIGUS JUNCTION TODAY
A young couple enjoy riding their side by side ATV into the setting sun at Brigus Junction. A former water stop for steam locomotives, it has become one of the most sought after cottage and cabin areas on the Avalon Peninsula. The last mixed train through here to Argentia was on September 19, 1984 with two G8s, a baggage car and three coaches. No freight cars were carried on that last run, thus making it pure passenger. *Author photo*

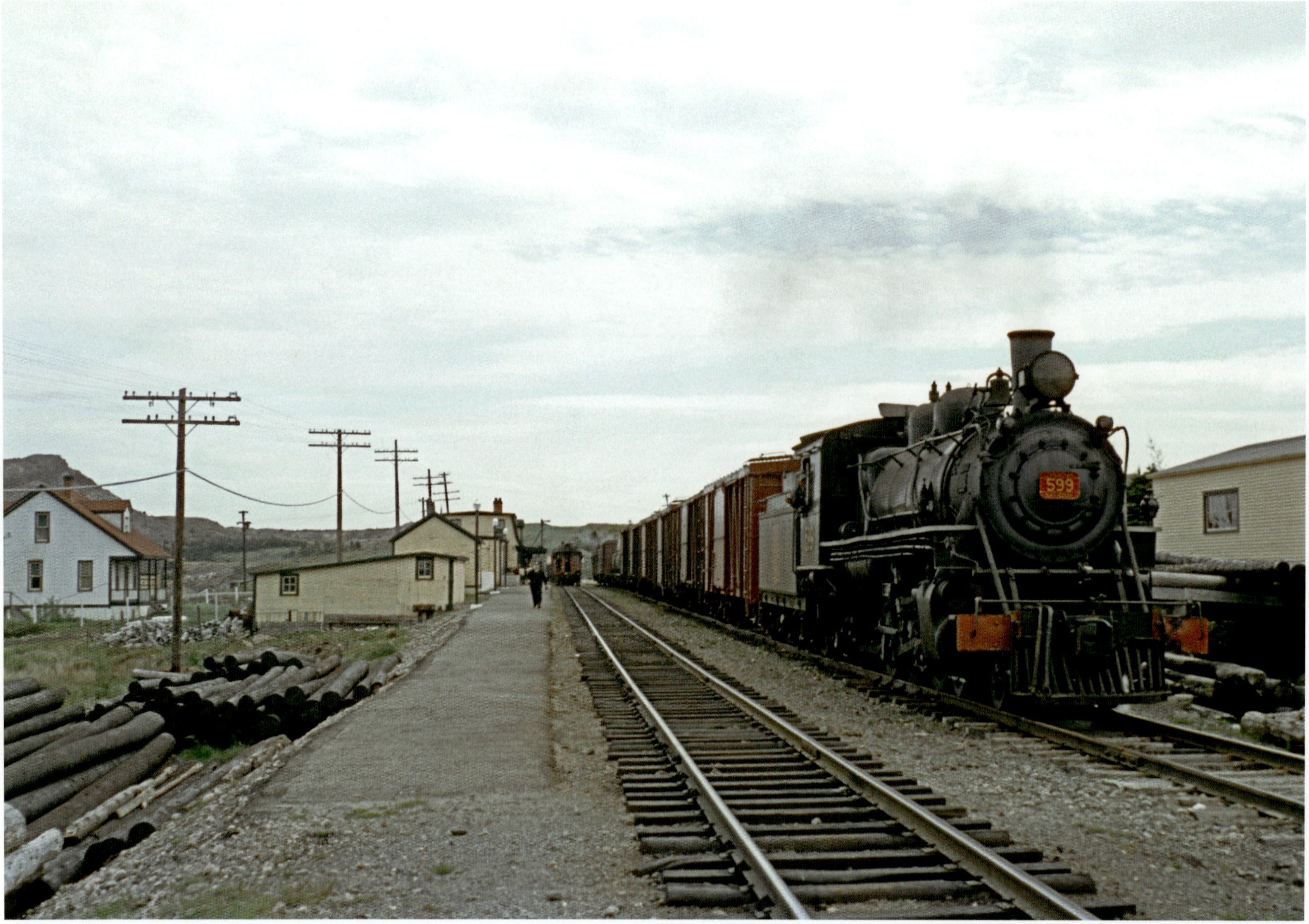

AVONDALE 1956

CNR 4-6-2 Pacific 599, built by American Locomotive Works of Schenectady, New York in 1929 as 199 for the Newfoundland Railway, was the last of ten of the series. This sleek engine holds the Carbonear mixed on the siding at Avondale while an eastbound freight clears on the mainline on June 21, 1956. Originally built to haul mainline passenger trains, the 190 class was relegated to switching and branchline duties after the arrival of the bigger and more powerful Mikados. *Robert J. Sandusky photo*

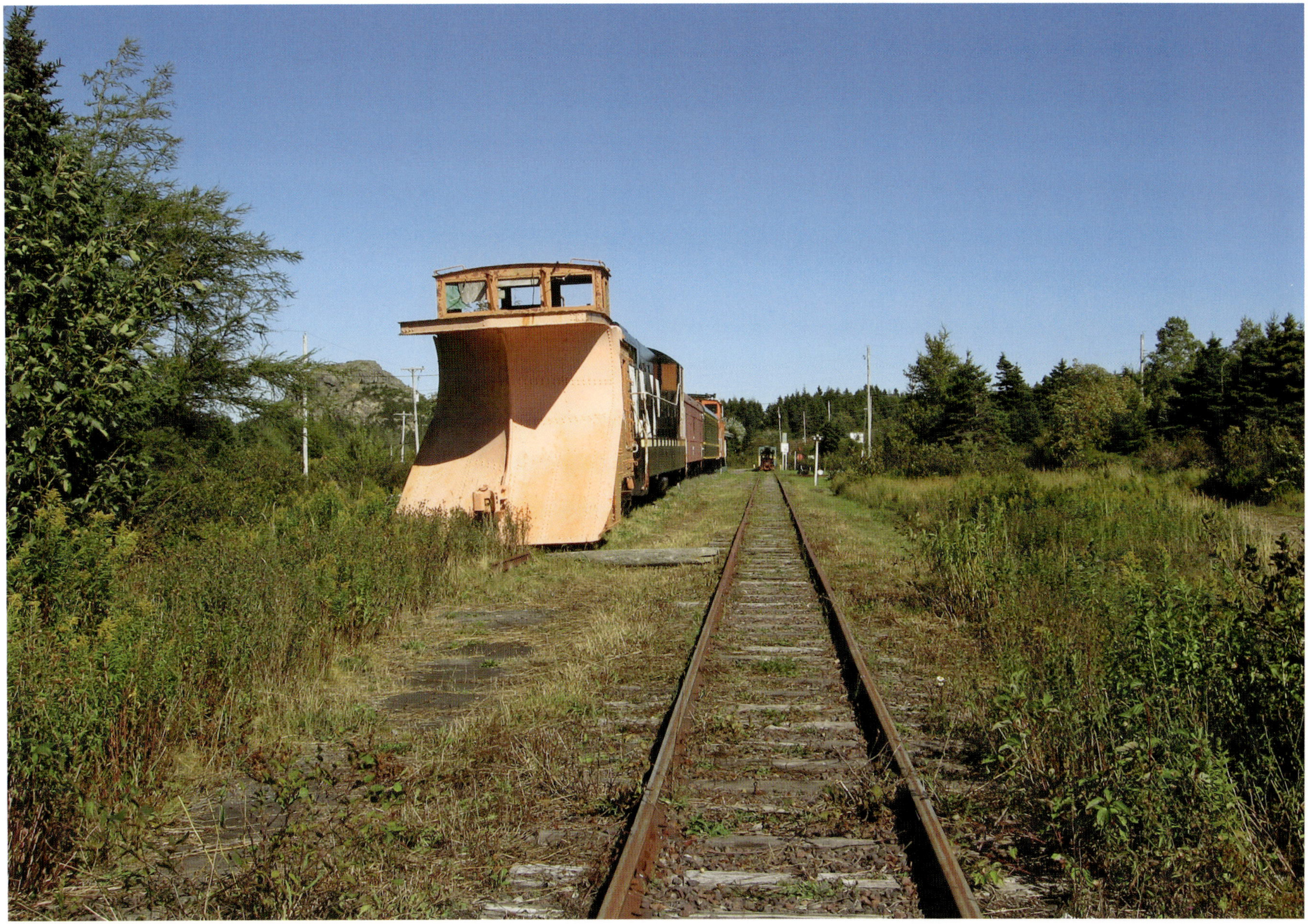

AVONDALE TODAY
The town of Avondale can proudly boast of having the oldest surviving wooden station as well as an excellent static display of former equipment. Included with NF210 925 is former RPO 1803, coach 769, caboose 6069 and snowplow 3465 on the front. At 1.8 miles, it also has the longest section of original mainline track remaining in Newfoundland. *Author photo*

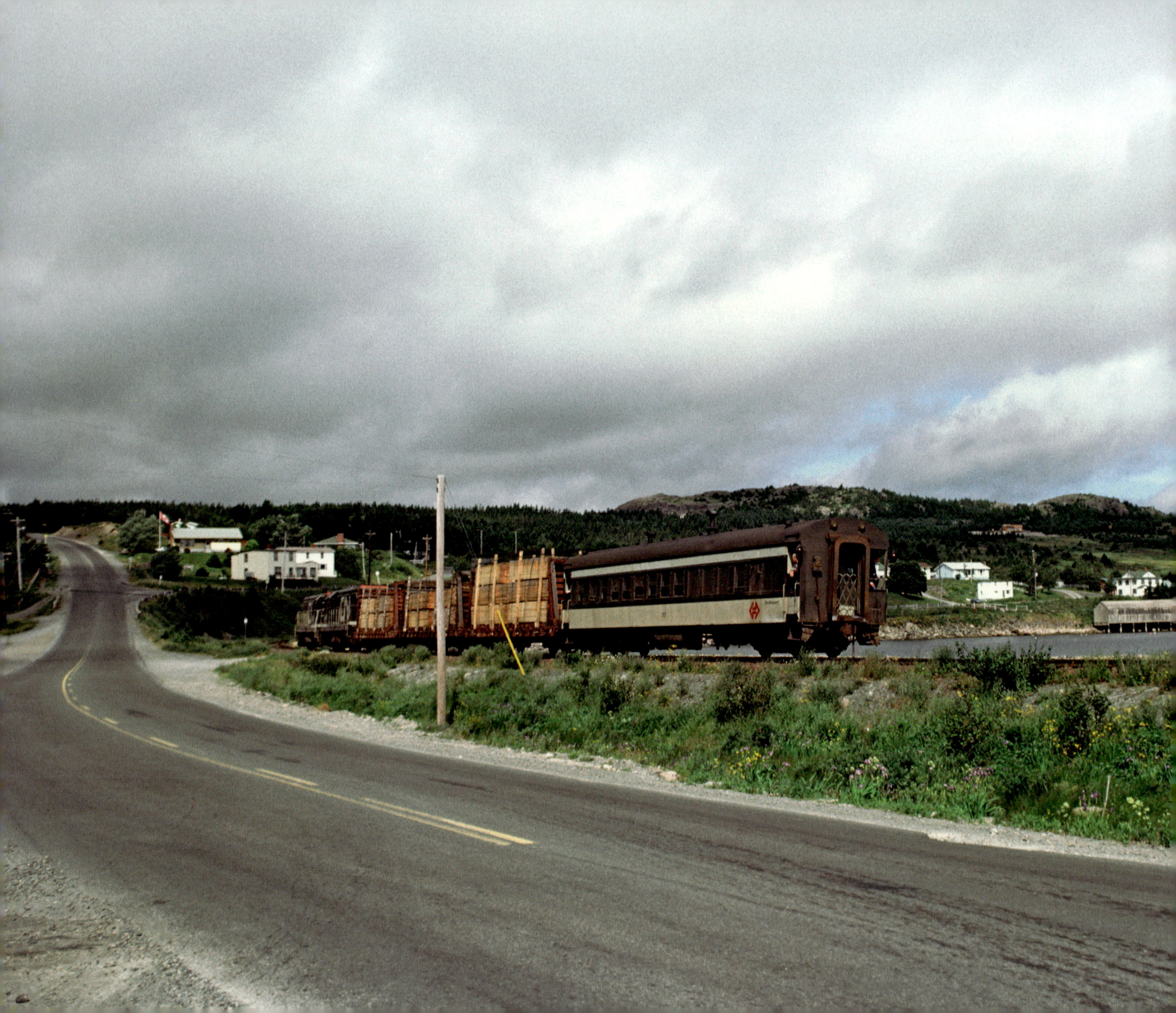

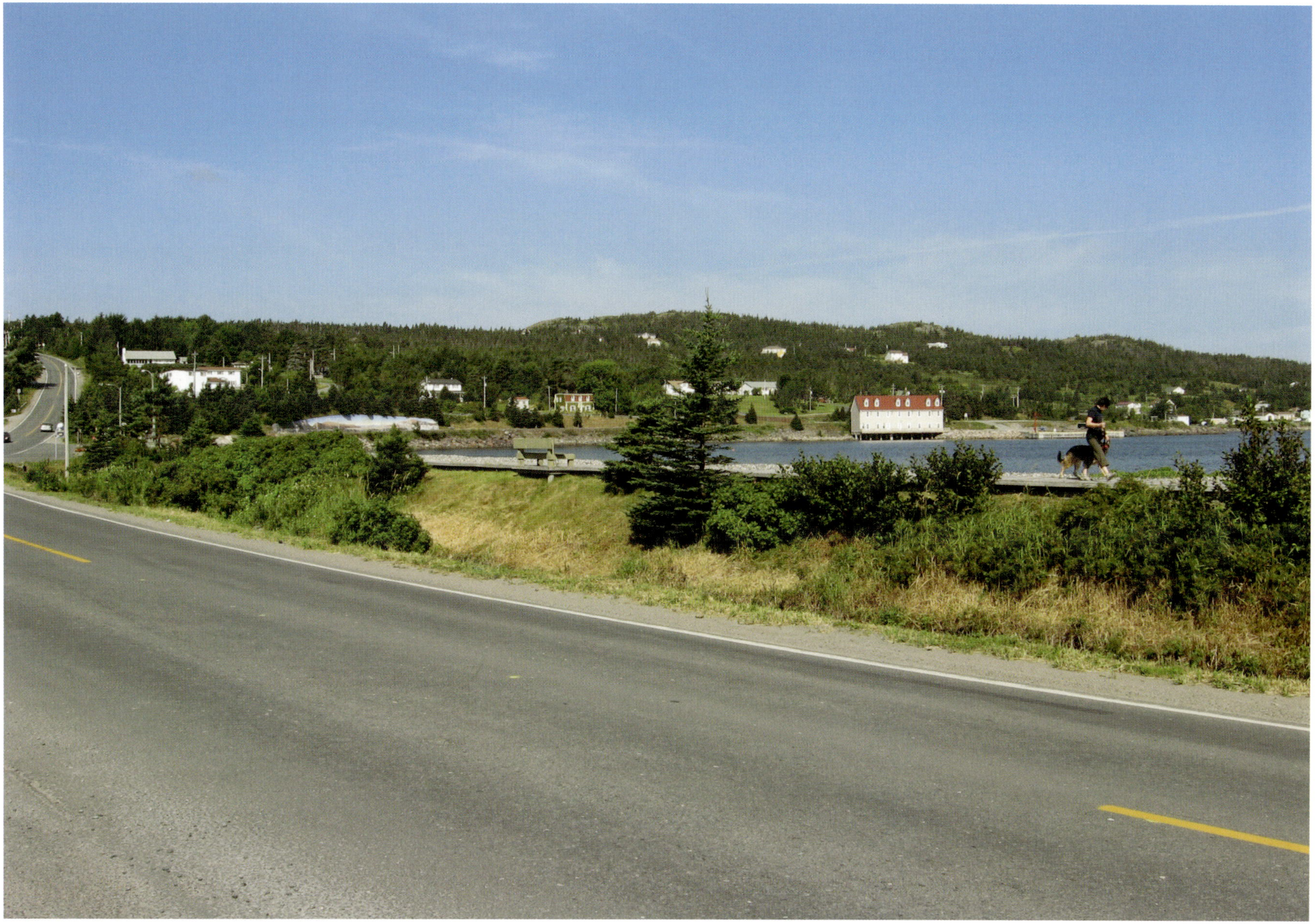

HOLYROOD 1984

A very short Terra Transport Mixed Extra 805 West, the Carbonear mixed, with G8s 805 and 804 leading three cars of lumber and coach 757, crosses the beach at Holyrood on July 12, 1984 in its last few months of operation. Unlike operations in the 1970s, No. 207 would now make a same day return trip to Carbonear from St. John's rather than overnight at Whitbourne. *Robert J. Sandusky photo*

HOLYROOD TODAY

A woman and her dog stroll along the wooden boardwalk that follows the old railway line across the beach at Holyrood. The railway still lives on at the nearby Holyrood Marina where caboose 6065 has been totally restored to its former glory, complete with Terra Transport markings. G8 805 is now part of a Newfoundland display at Exporail in Delson, QC, the largest railway museum in Canada. *Author photo*

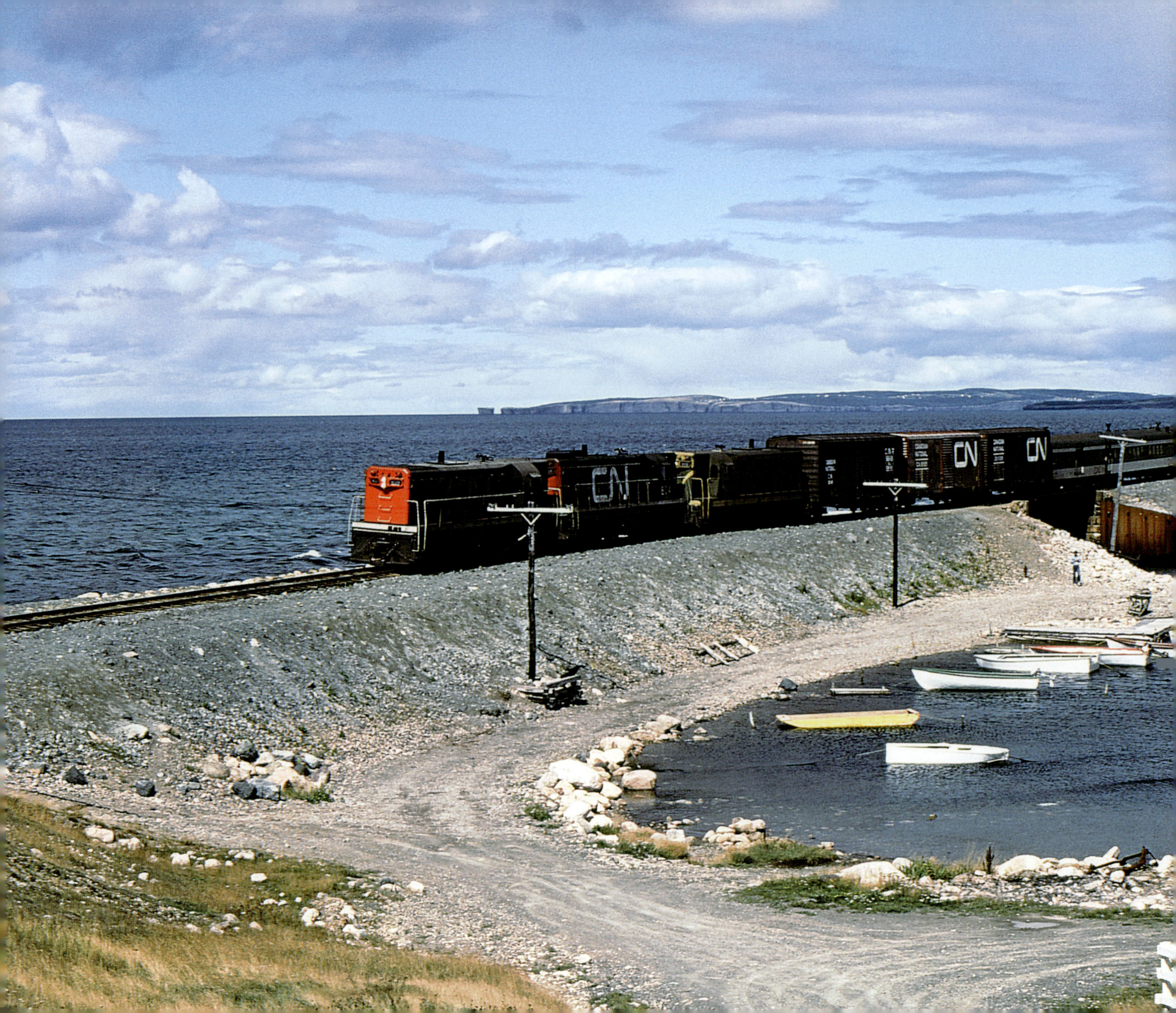
CN
CN
CN

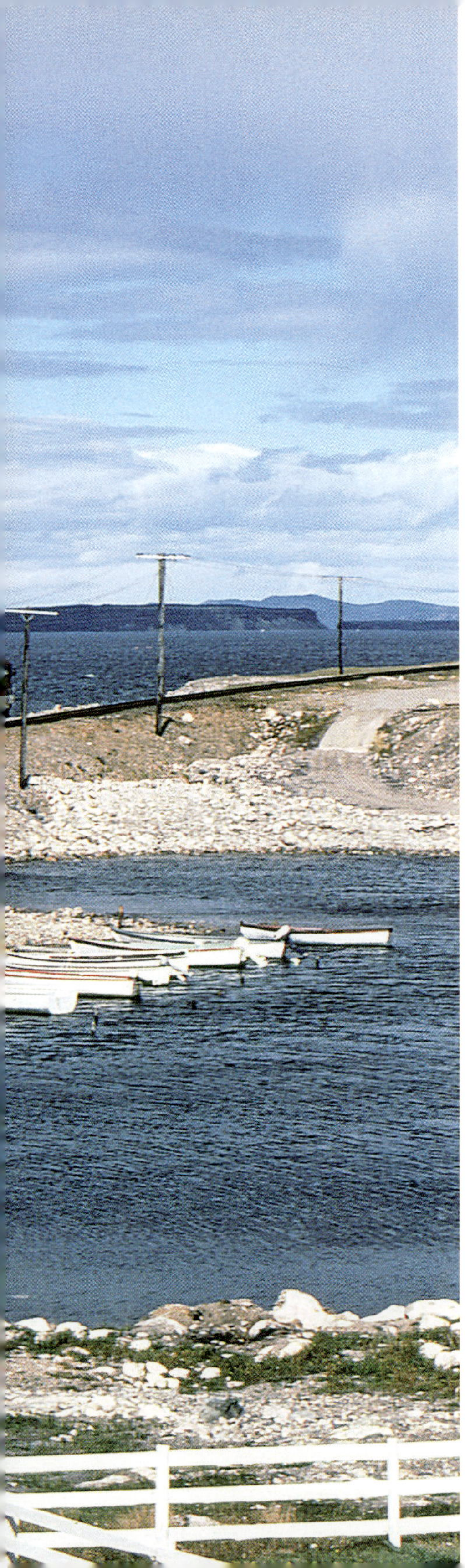

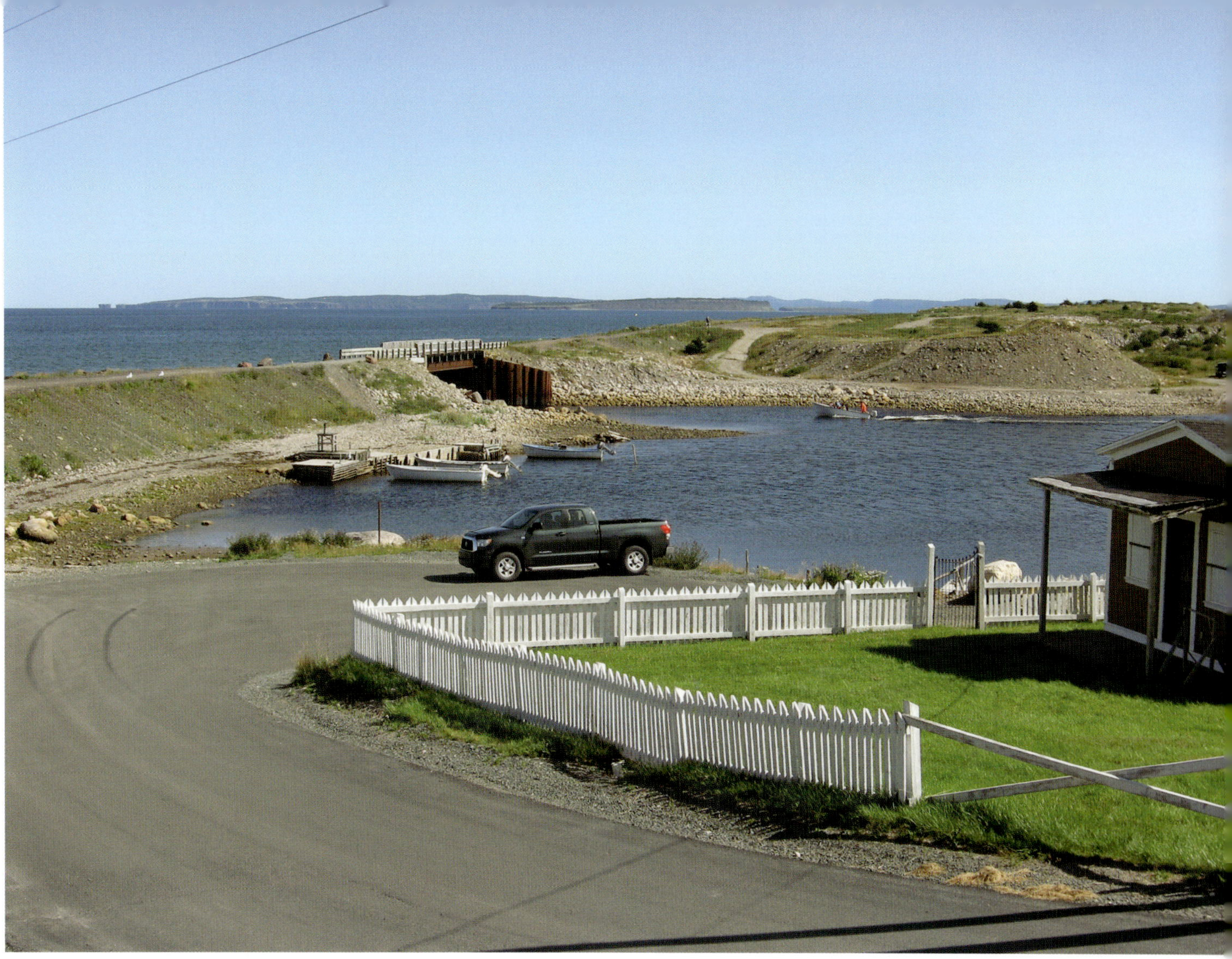

SEAL COVE 1978

Having left St. John's at 10:30 a.m. for Argentia, Canadian National mixed train 207 with G8s 801, 804 and 800 skirts the shore of Conception Bay at Seal Cove by late morning on August 25, 1978. The all steel passenger equipment that was previously part of the *Caribou's* consist continues to provide revenue service. This train will return the next day from Carbonear as 232. *Rich Taylor photo*

SEAL COVE TODAY

An eager fisherman steams out under the bridge in Seal Cove to partake in the twice yearly recreational food fishery. With the collapse of the cod fishery and the moratorium declared by Ottawa in 1992 to rebuild the stocks, a 500-year way of life disappeared along with the railway. *Author photo*

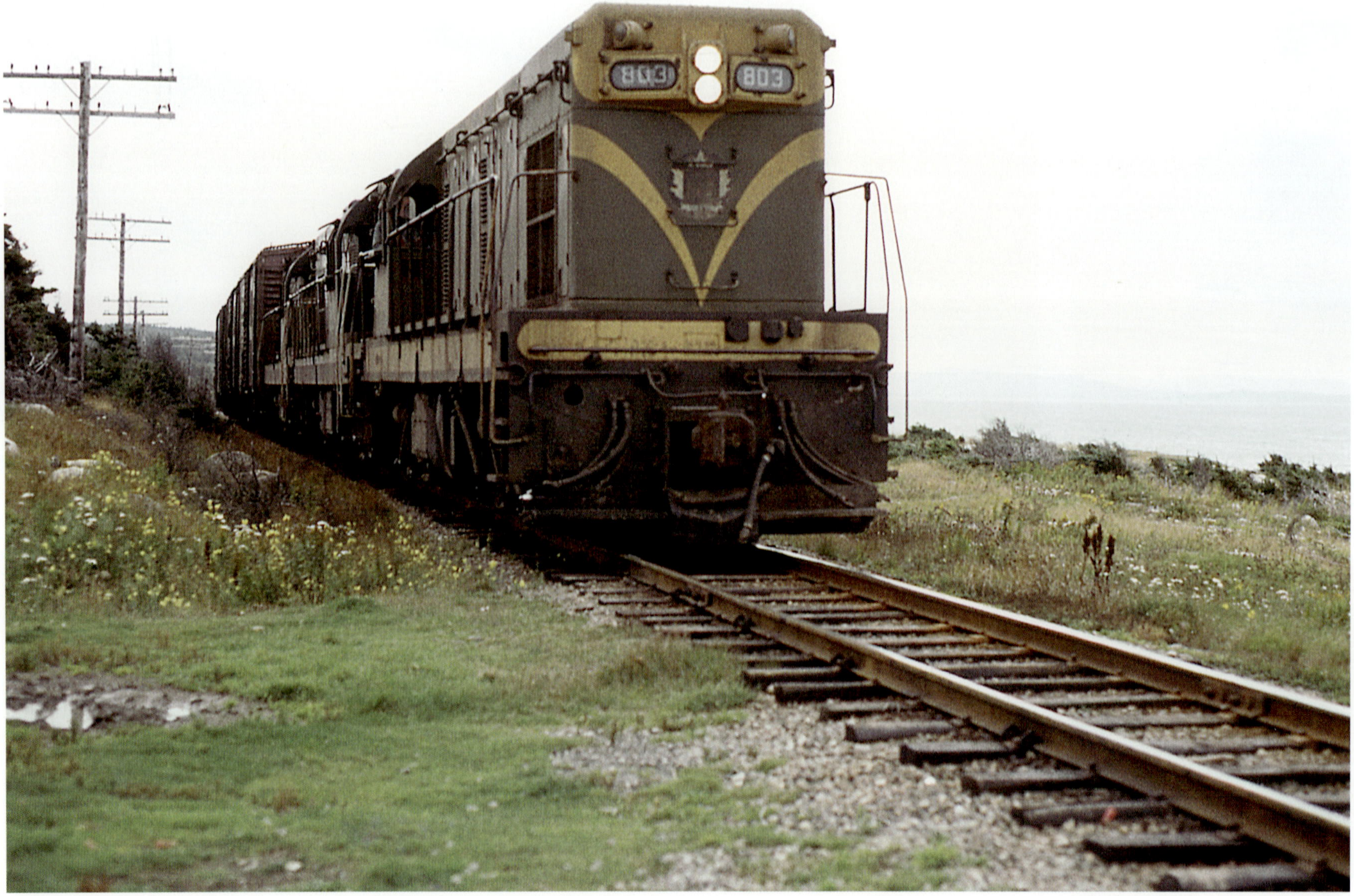

UPPER GULLIES 1976

Historian and volunteer David Othen travelled from Nova Scotia for a week of Newfoundland rail photography in the fall of 1976. He shot G8 803 on the head end of Canadian National mixed train No. 232 at Upper Gullies on September 23, 1976. Returning to St. John's from Carbonear, the consist included 804 and 802 as well as four boxcars, baggage and coach 757 on the rear. The next day, he and his wife would take this train to Holyrood and experience the ride for themselves. *David Othen photo*

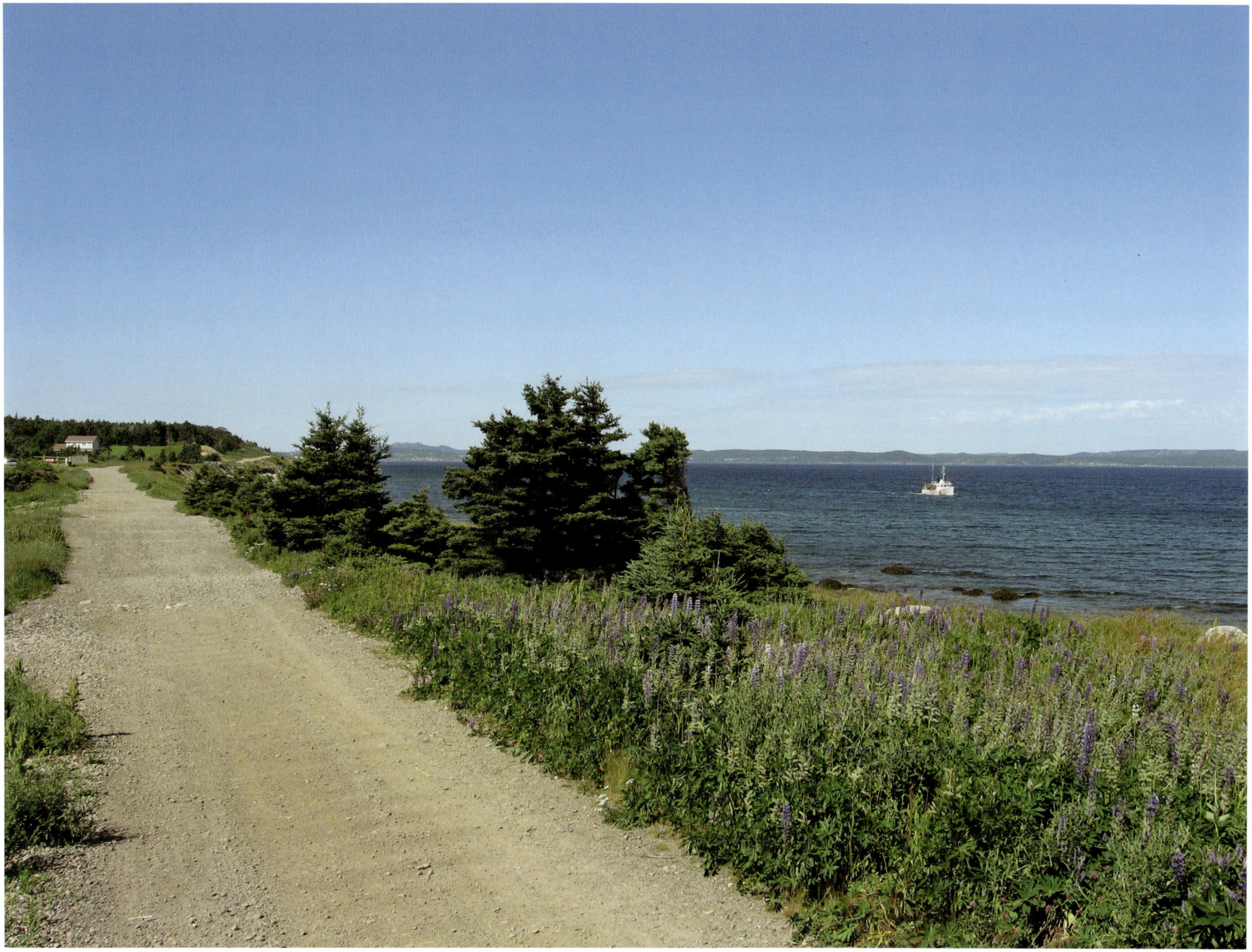

UPPER GULLIES TODAY
The creosote from the railway ties still leaves an imprint at Upper Gullies decades after their removal. When settled in 1832 as an agricultural area, it was named after the two gullies, the other being lower, that were formed from the rivers nearby. Built in 1956 by GMD of London, the 803 is on display near the also preserved Carbonear railway station. *Author photo*

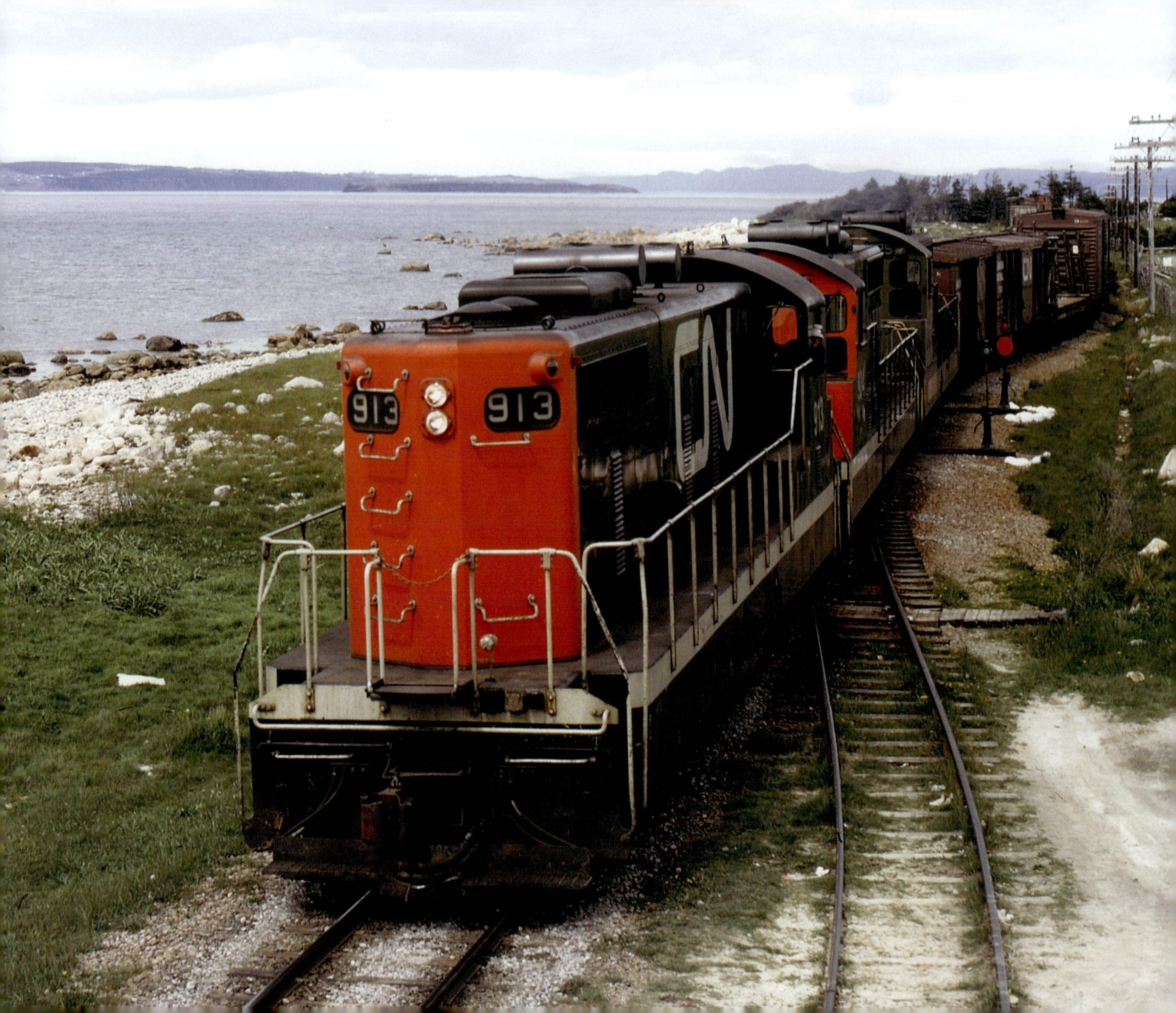
913
913
CN

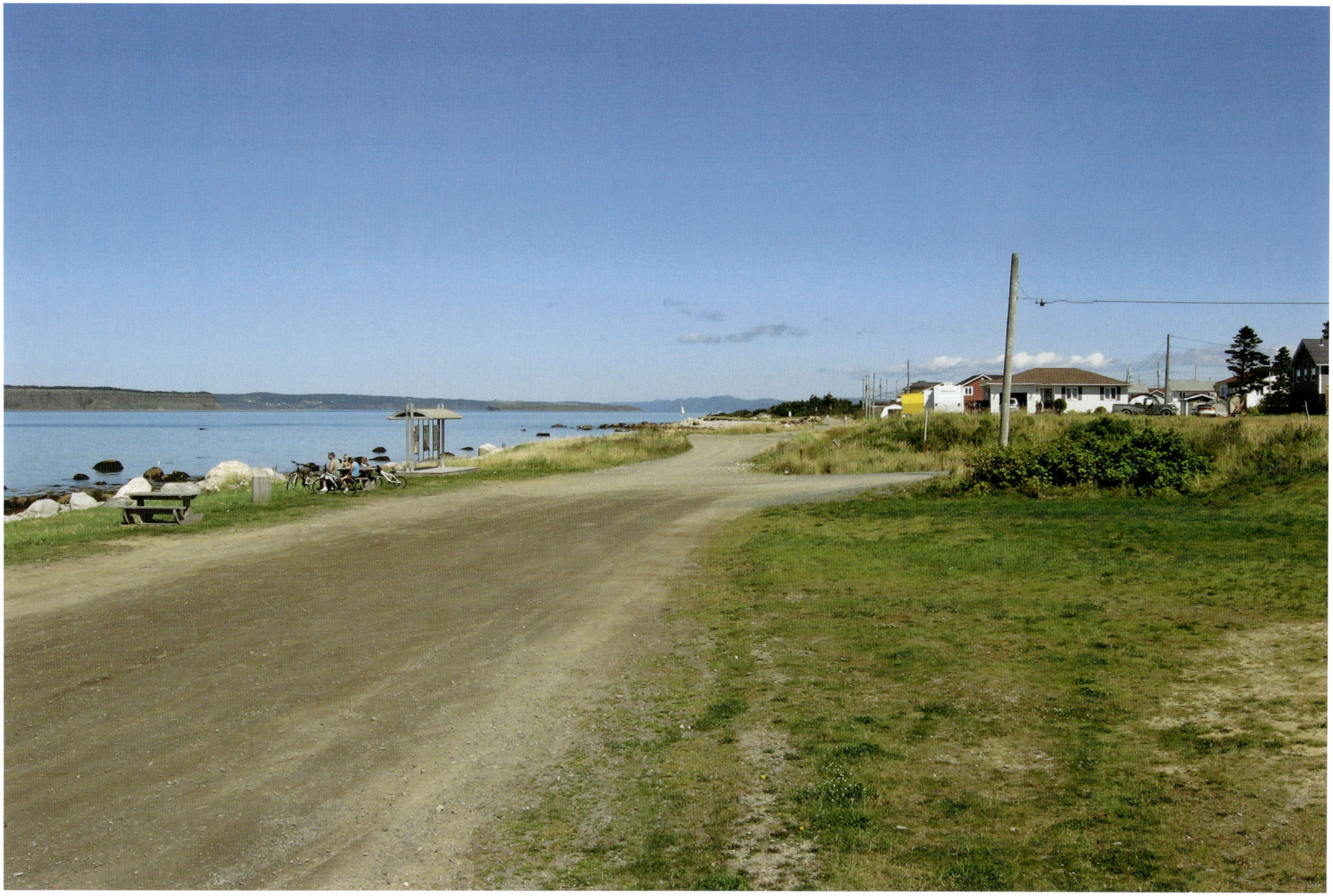

KELLIGREWS 1967

With the backdrop of Kelly's Island, Bell Island and Little Bell Island, NF210 913, built in 1956 by GMD along with NF110 904 and NF210 925 heads westbound freight 401 alongside the waters of Conception Bay at Kelligrews on June 22, 1967. Freights 401 and the eastbound 400 augmented 203 and 204 at this time but had disappeared from the timetable by 1971. *James A. Brown photo*

KELLIGREWS TODAY

A young family takes a break from bicycling the Trailway at Kelligrews, made famous by the folk song "Kelligrews Soiree", while there is barely enough breeze to push the sailboats in the background. This site is now home to the Kelligrews Railway Folk Festival, featuring music, food and fun and a display of railway memorabilia. *Author photo*

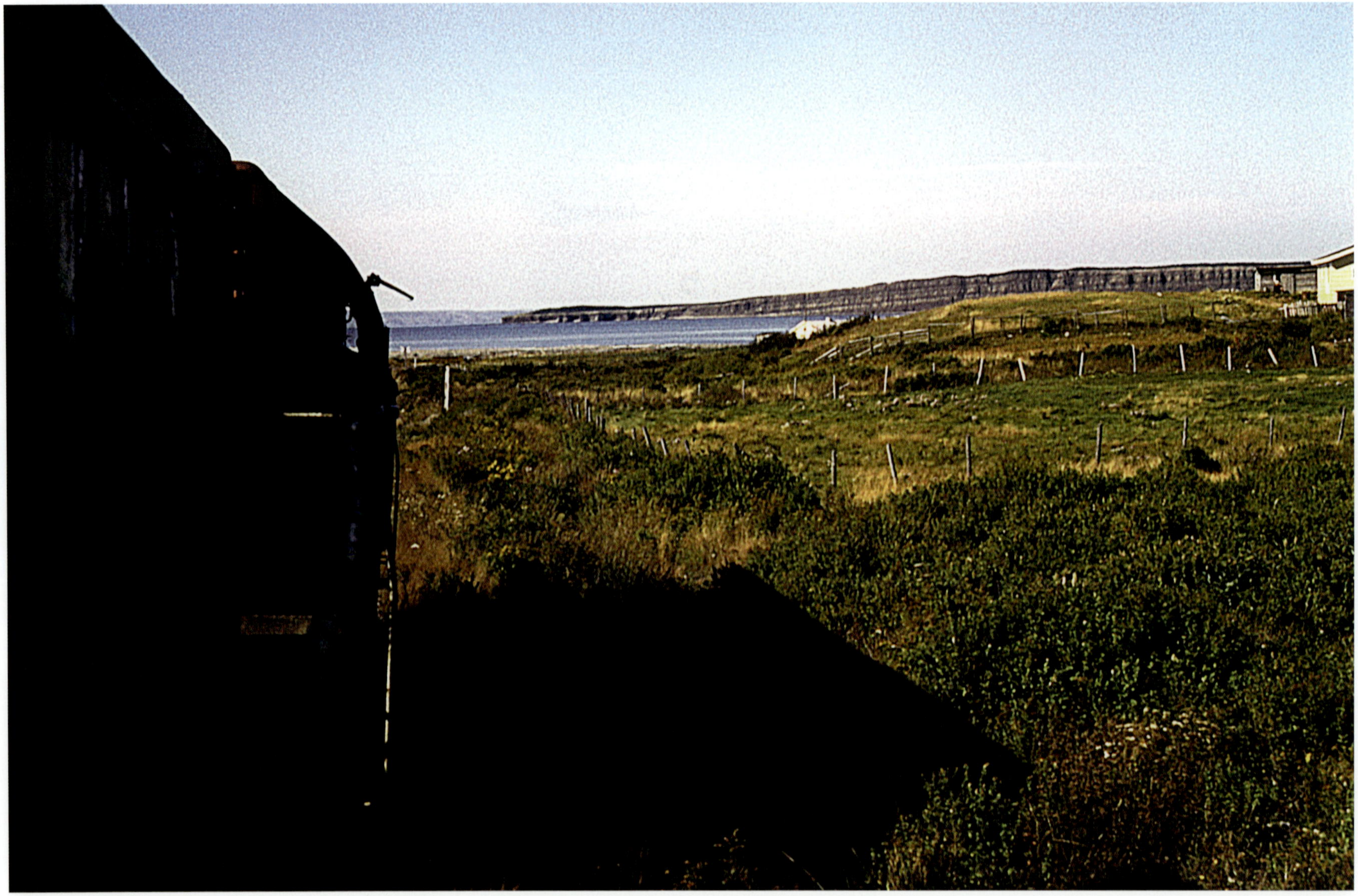

FOXTRAP 1976
Canadian National mixed train 207 approaches the waters of Conception Bay at Foxtrap on September 24, 1976. For the next 16 miles the rails will hug the shore before turning inland at Woodfords Station, thus giving this train the name *Shoreline*. In the 1906 Reid Newfoundland Timetable No. 6, this area was designated as Fox-Trap "Y". *David Othen photo*

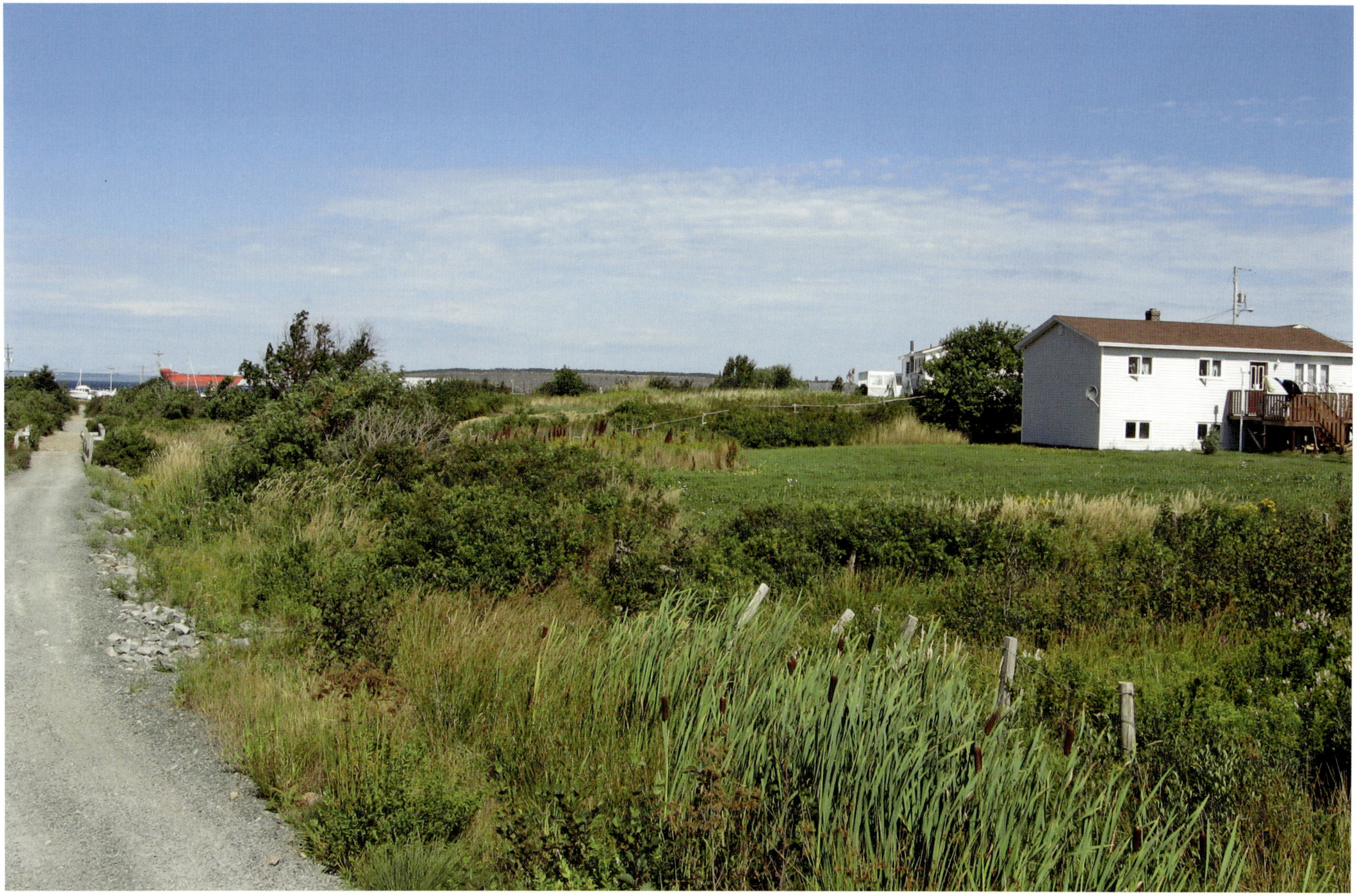

FOXTRAP TODAY
Looking northwest towards the Foxtrap Marina, this community now forms part of the Town of Conception Bay South. Urban expansion and economic development is evidenced by not only new homes and businesses but also the Canship Ugland shuttle oil tanker offshore. It is not uncommon to see up to three of these 1 million barrel crude oil capacity ships moored near Foxtrap, awaiting duty at the Hibernia, Terra Nova or Whiterose oil fields. *Author photo*

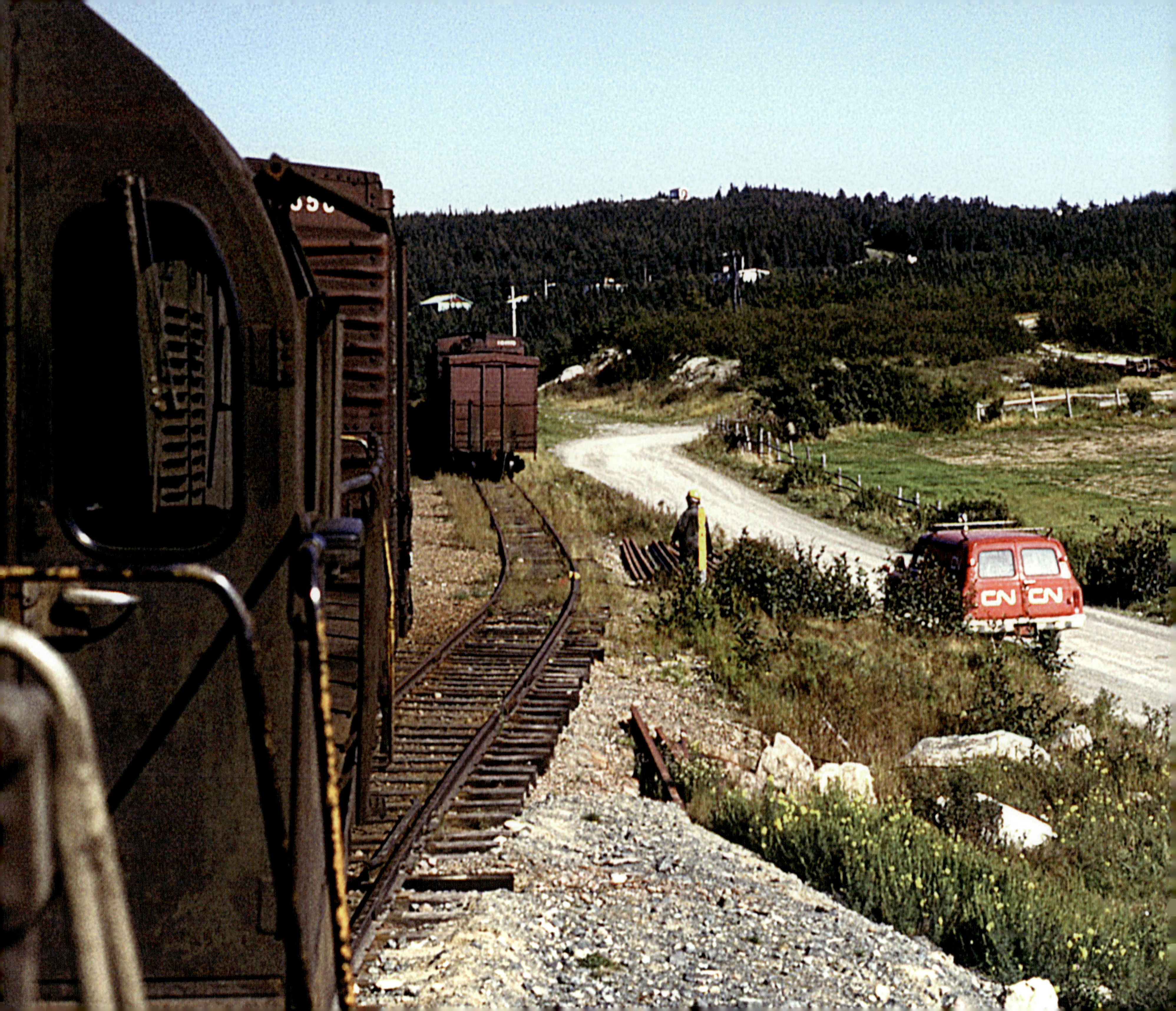
CN CN

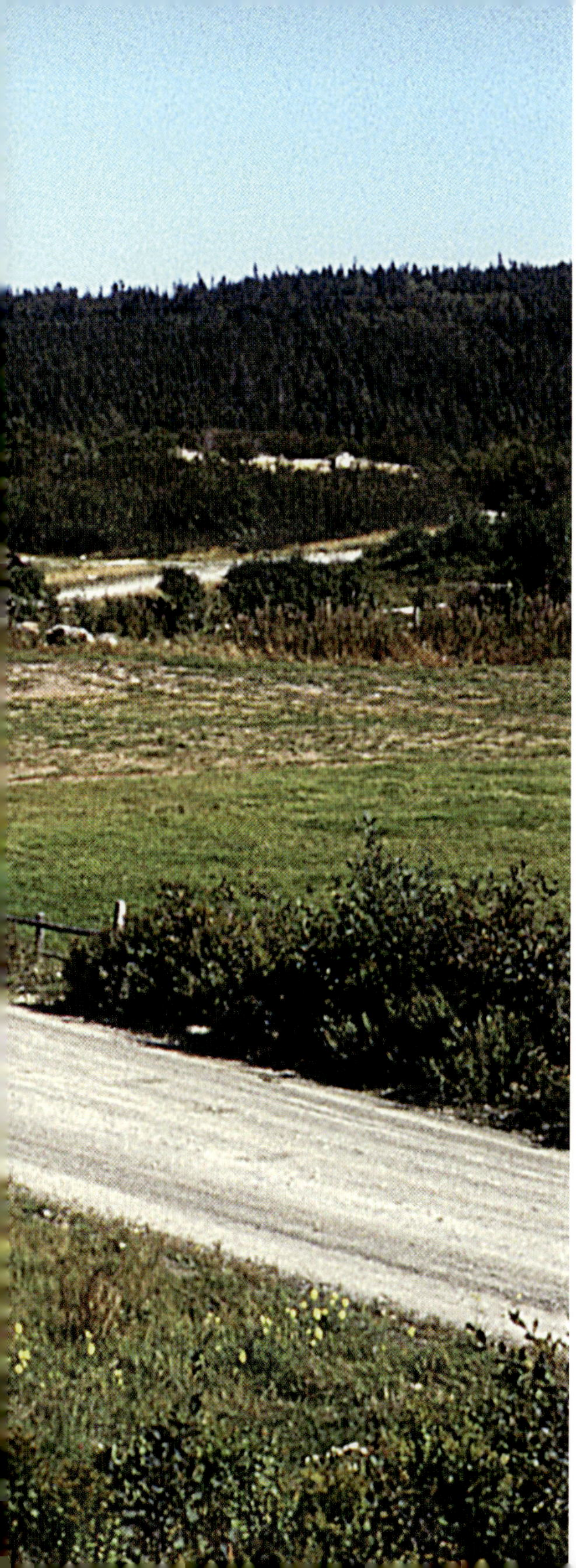

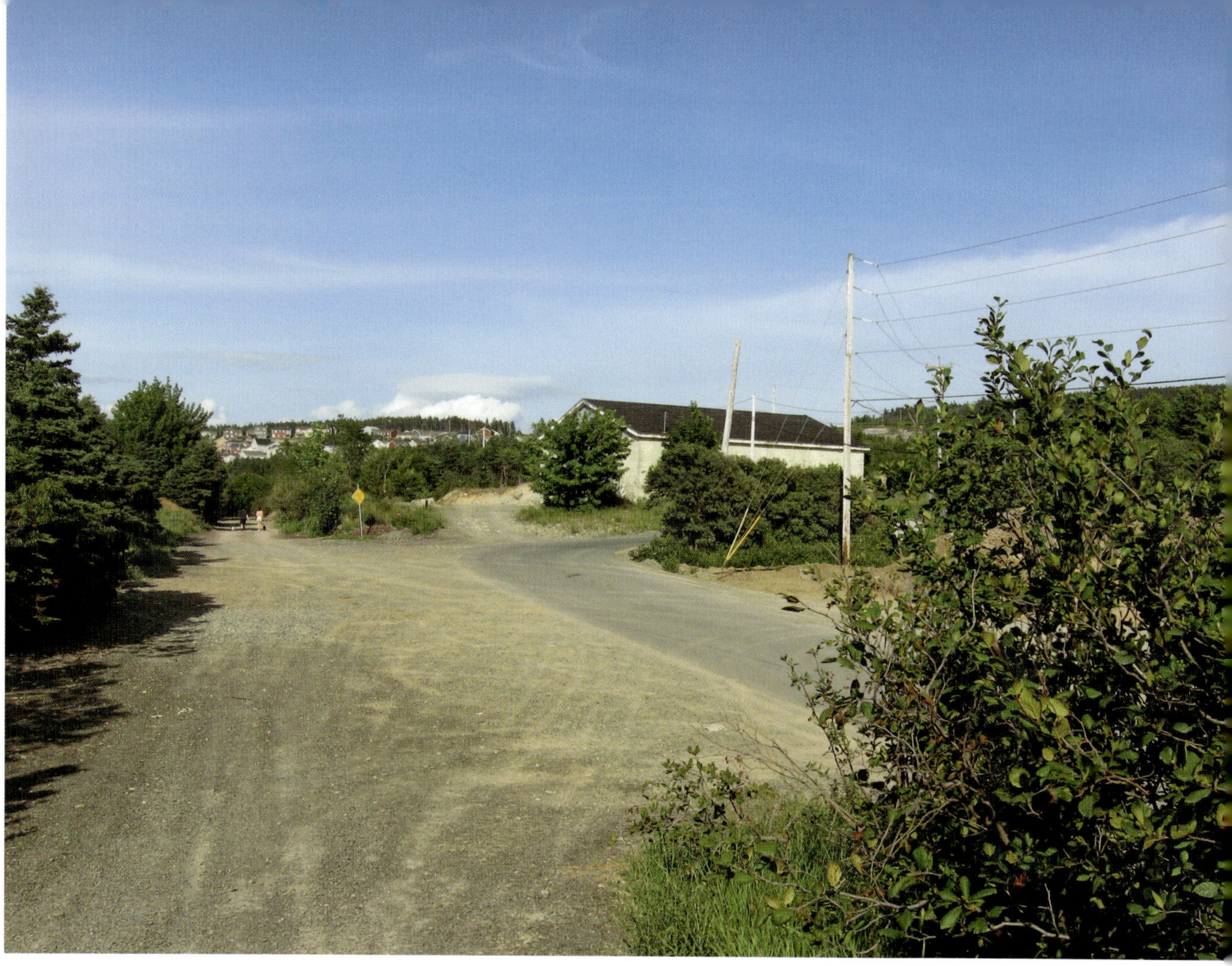

LONG POND 1976
CN Train # 207 passes through the siding at Talcville in the community of Long Pond on the clear afternoon of September 24, 1976. The track foreman is inspecting the passing train for any defects such as sticking brakes, hot bearings or dragging equipment. The small siding with a capacity for seventeen cars has a standard forty-foot steel boxcar coupled to a smaller outside braced former Newfoundland Railway one. *David Othen photo*

LONG POND TODAY
Long Pond is now the site of the Royal Newfoundland Yacht Club and was one of nine communities that joined to form the town of Conception Bay South in 1973. The name Talcville was given to the claim area where large deposits of pyrophyllite or talc were found. In 1904 an overhead aerial tramway was built to bring the mineral to the Newfoundland railway. *Author photo*

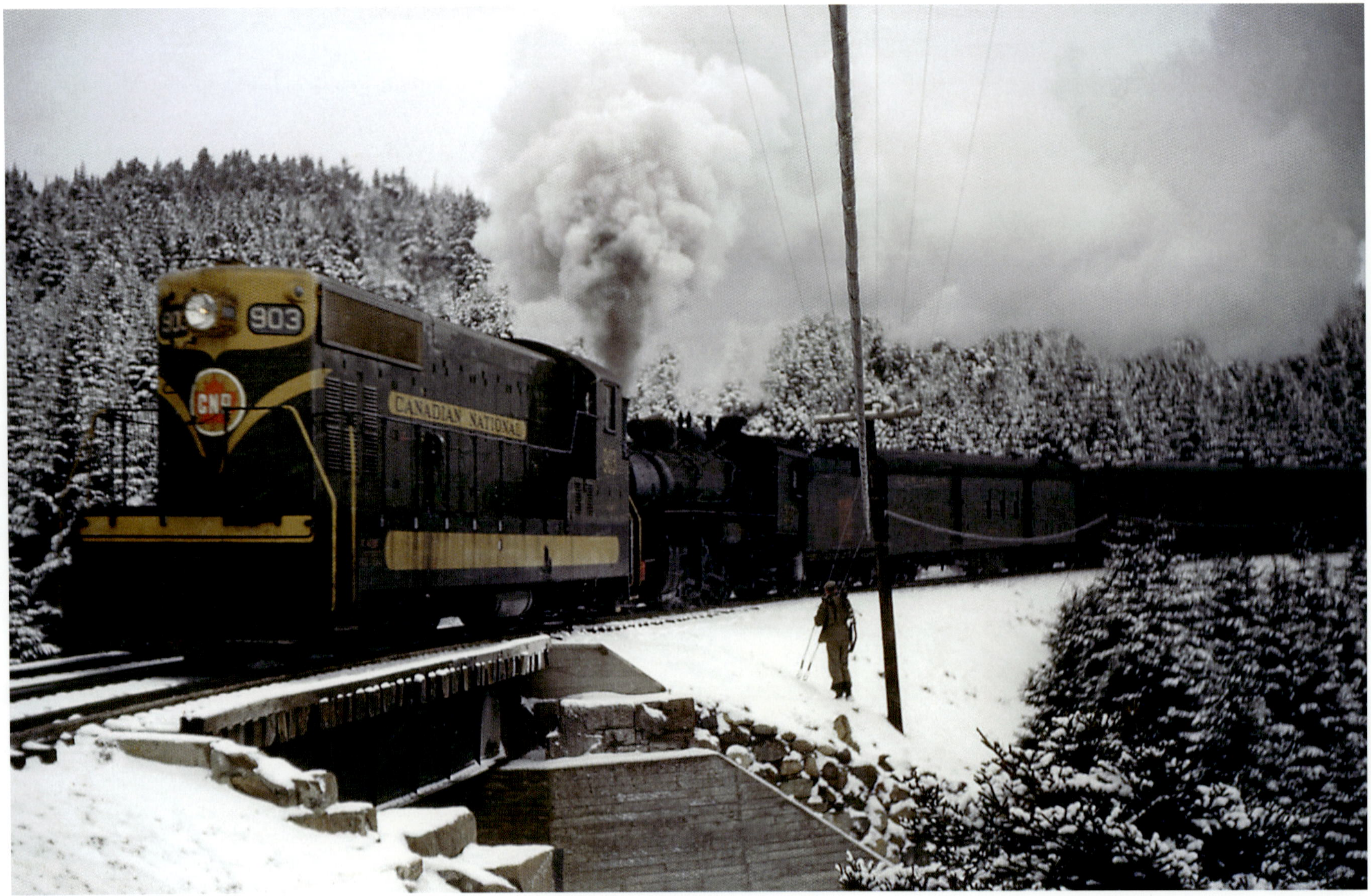

MANUELS 1954
CNR NF110 903 double heads the *Caribou* with one of the Mikado steam engines while crossing the Manuels River Bridge during the early winter of 1954. Members of the 1ST Communications Construction Squadron continue installing new lines and over the winter months are housed at Fort Pepperall, the US Army Base in St. John's. Full dieselization of the *Caribou* would not occur until the arrival of five steam generator cars in 1956. *Jerome Young photo - Merritt C. Scharnweber collection.*

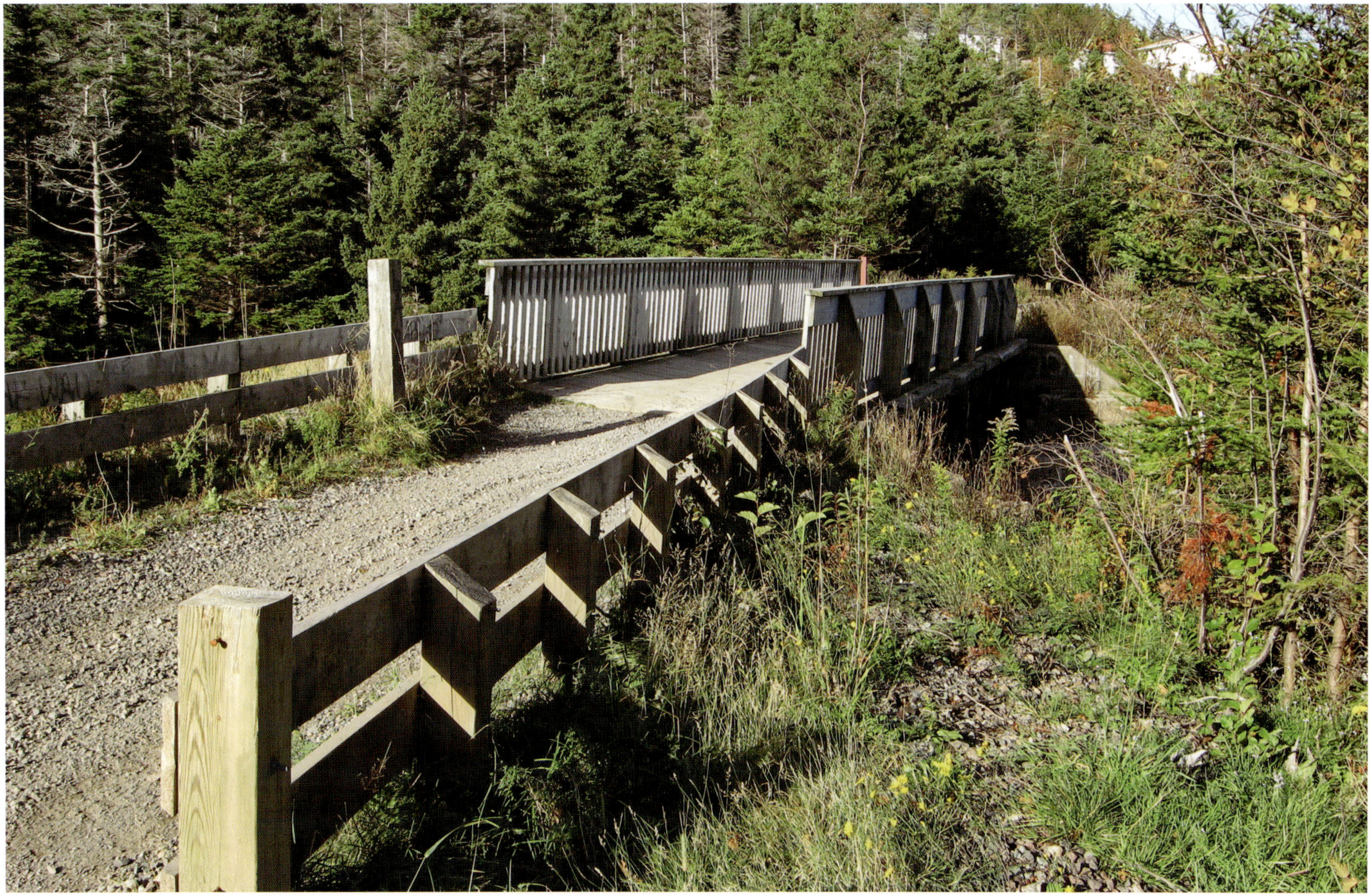

MANUELS TODAY
500 million year old rocks lie under the railway bridge and are remnants of an ancient African plate that collided with North America about 400 million years ago. The valley that the bridge runs over was formed 10,000 years ago by a glacier draining the Avalon ice cap. This area is famous the world over for its fossilized trilobites and the Manuels River Hibernia interpretation Center is adjacent to the old railbed. *Author photo*

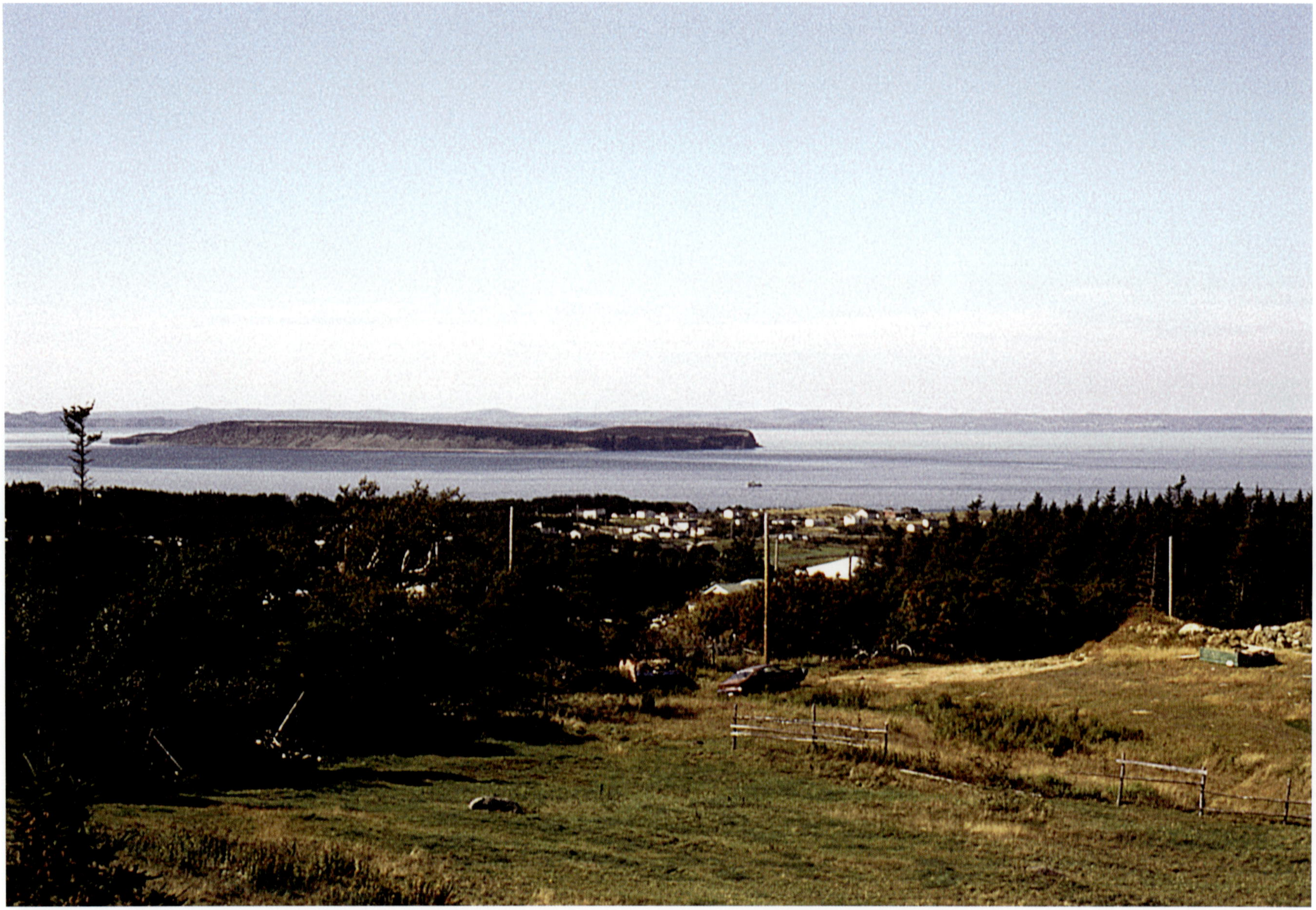

CHAMBERLAINS 1976
The view of Conception Bay and Kelly's Island from the cab of G8 802 is nothing short of breathtaking as CN Train 207 approaches the Fowlers Road grade crossing in Chamberlains on September 24, 1976. Vistas such as this were commonplace anywhere the tracks followed the contours of the many bays and coves. This light train would continue its descent and reach the water's edge at Foxtrap approximately 4 miles away. *David Othen photo*

CHAMBERLAINS TODAY
Boasting some of the best weather on the Avalon Peninsula, spectacular sunsets over Conception Bay are the norm when walking the Trailway in the Chamberlains area. Originally known as Chamberlain, an English family name of Gloucester, the railway here was 65 metres above sea level. The former right of way is being developed as a 22 mile linear park. *Author photo*

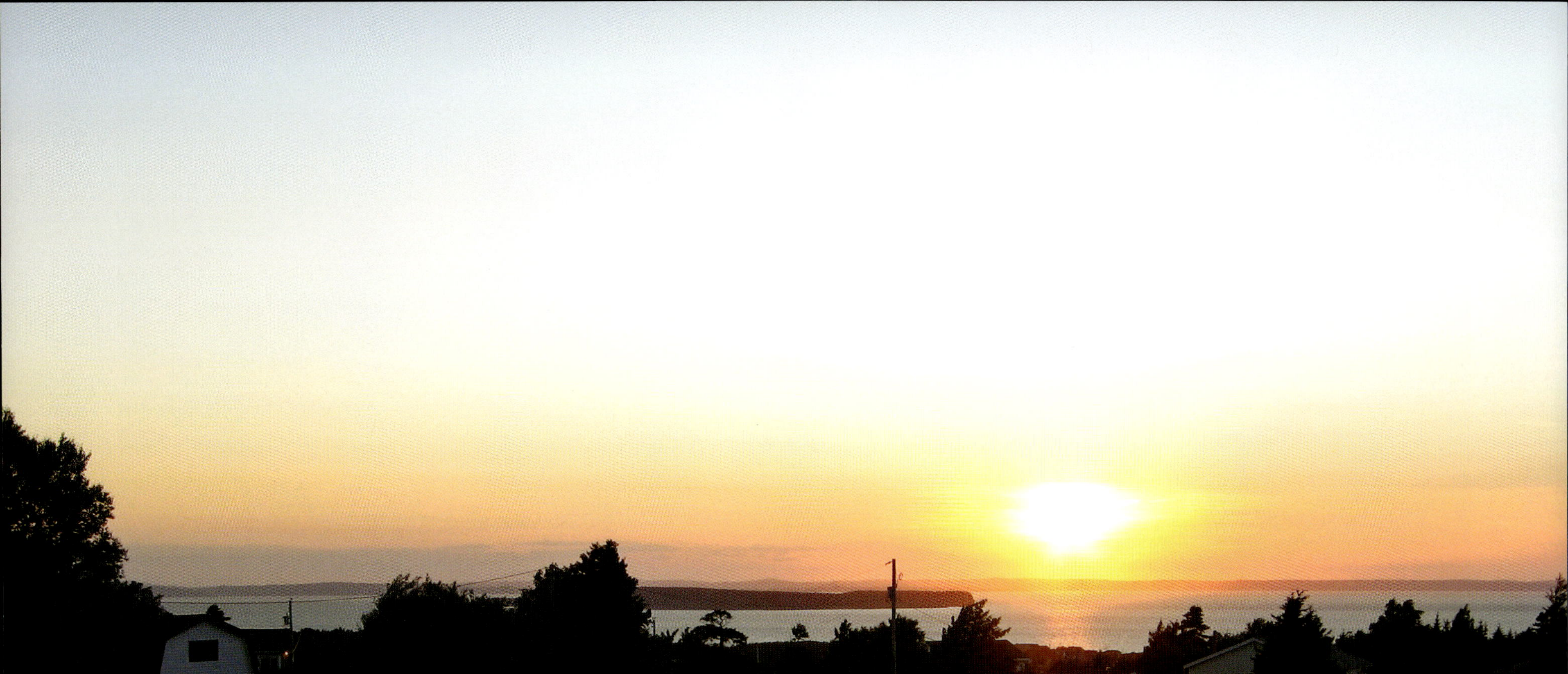

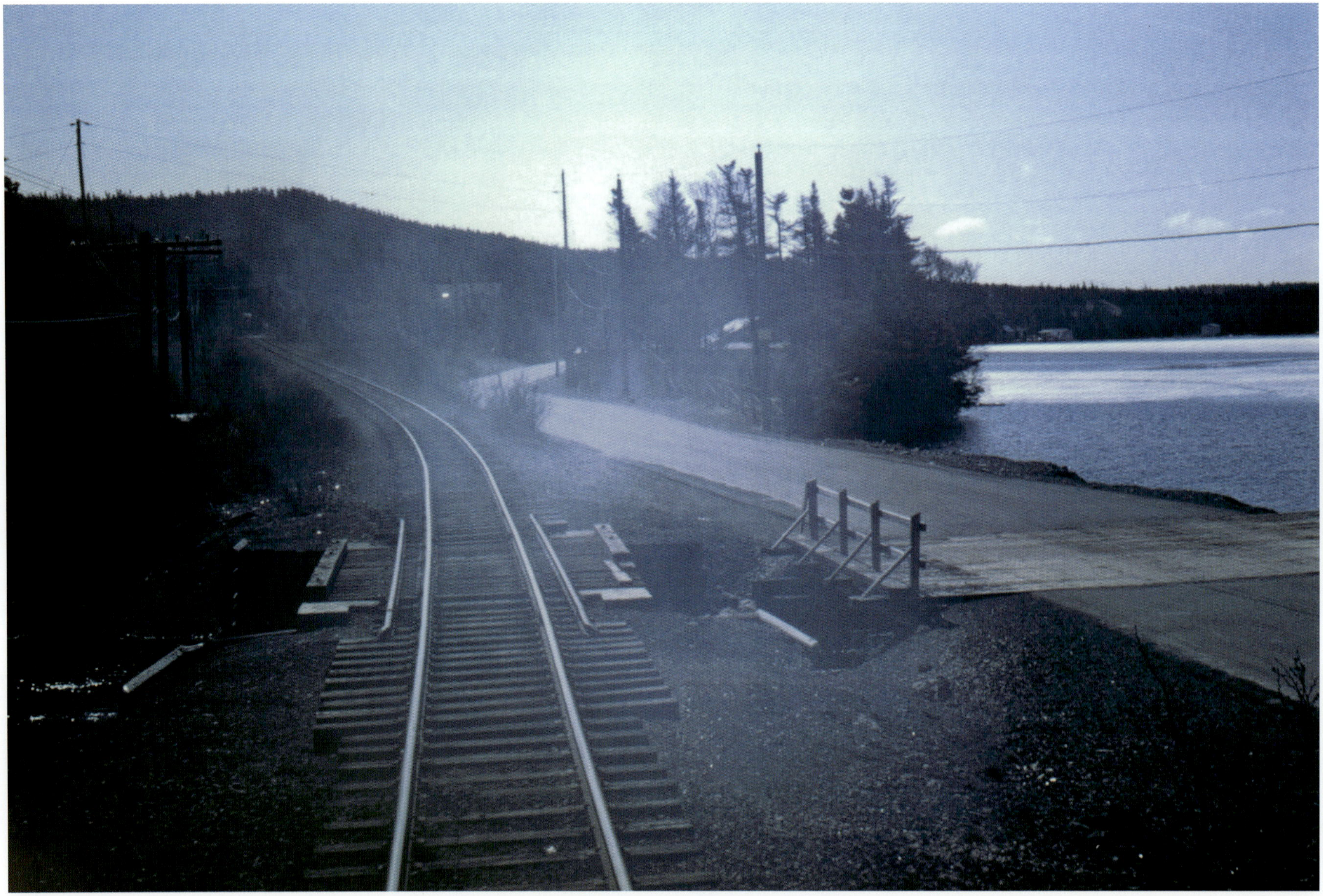

TOPSAIL 1982

Railfan David Woodhead's 1982 trip to Newfoundland resulted in hundreds of fascinating images. Here he captures the brake shoe smoke from CN Train 207 as it envelops the rearward view from coach 757. On the downgrade, the engineer has skillfully applied all brakes as it crosses over the small bridge at Topsail Pond on April 24, 1982. The parallel road was once the original right of way until relocation early in the 20th century. *David Woodhead photo*

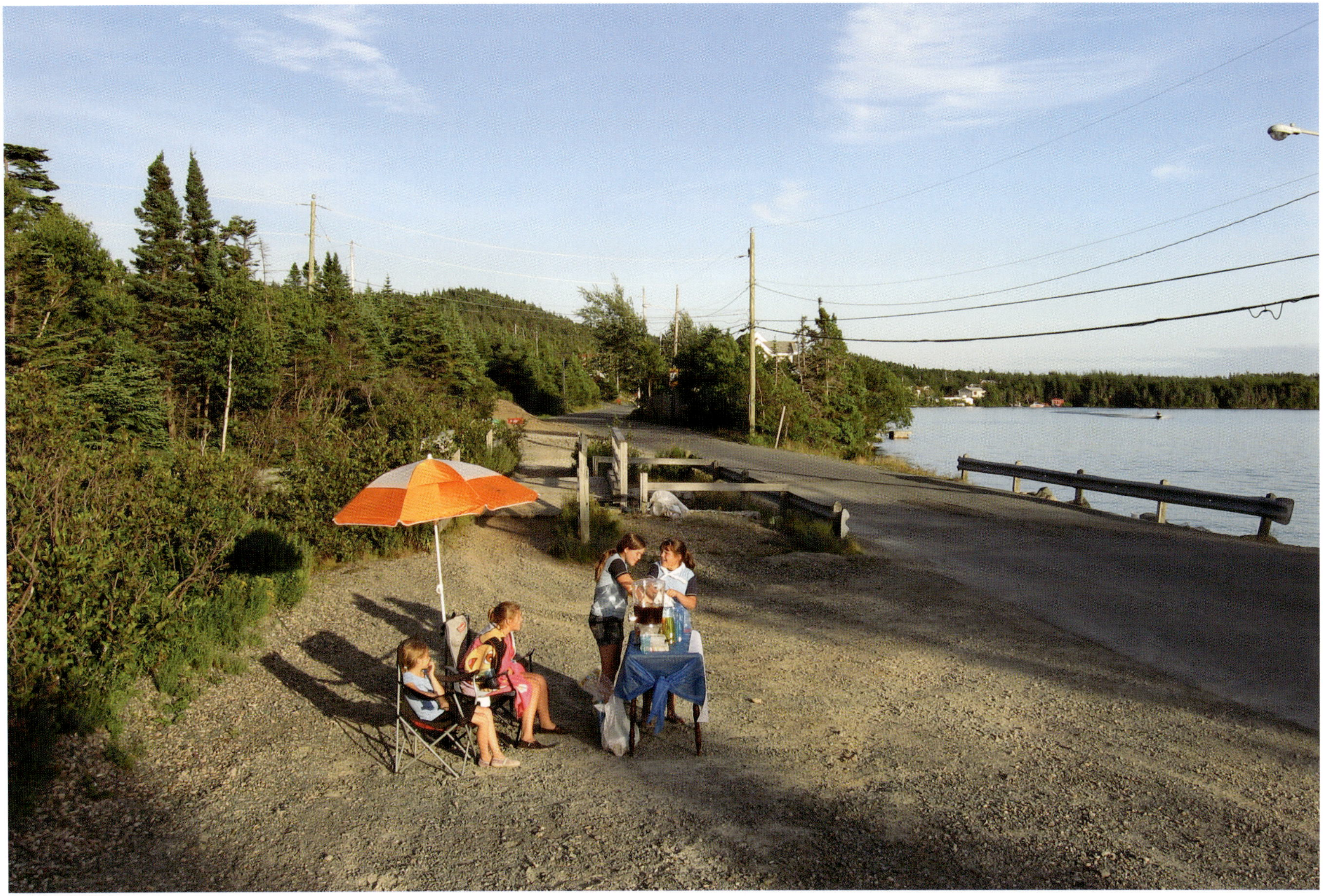

TOPSAIL TODAY
The young Brownies have set up a lemonade stand to raise funds on the site of the 207's route. Topsail is the easternmost former community that is now part of Conception Bay South and one of the most desired places for a home on the Avalon Peninsula. In the early days of the railway, special excursion trains were operated from St. John's. The 1893 timetable lists a departure time of 10:00 a.m. and arrival at Topsail 45 minutes later, for the first class fare of sixty cents one way. *Author photo*

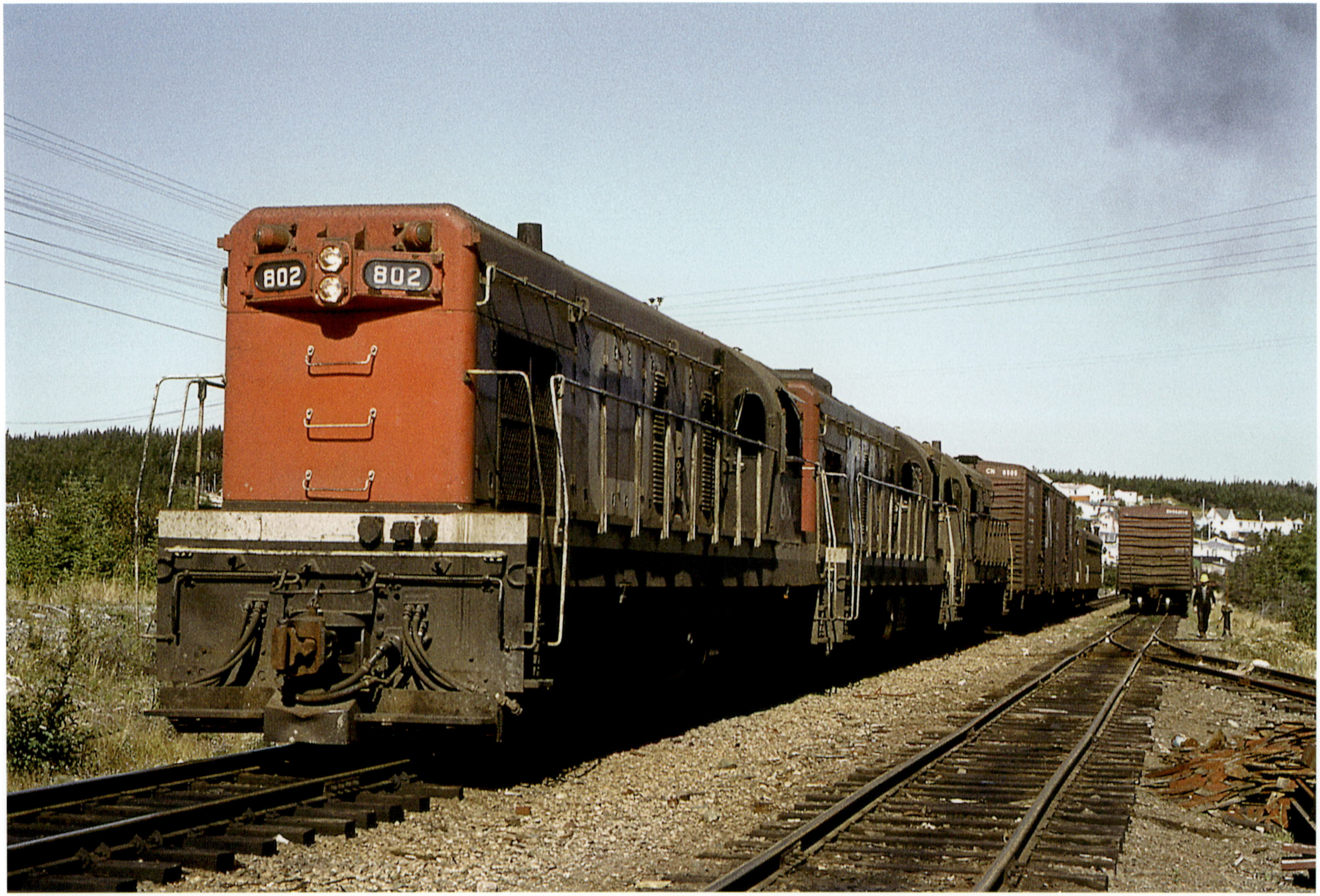

OCTOGON 1976
The three G8s, 802,804, and 803 of Canadian National mixed train 207 are uncoupled from the rest of the train at Octogon to switch at the nearby steel mill on September 24, 1976. In addition to the switching, they will re-rail a freight car while the remainder of the consist lies parked on the mainline. Within an hour, they will return to couple and resume the trip to Argentia. *David Othen photo*

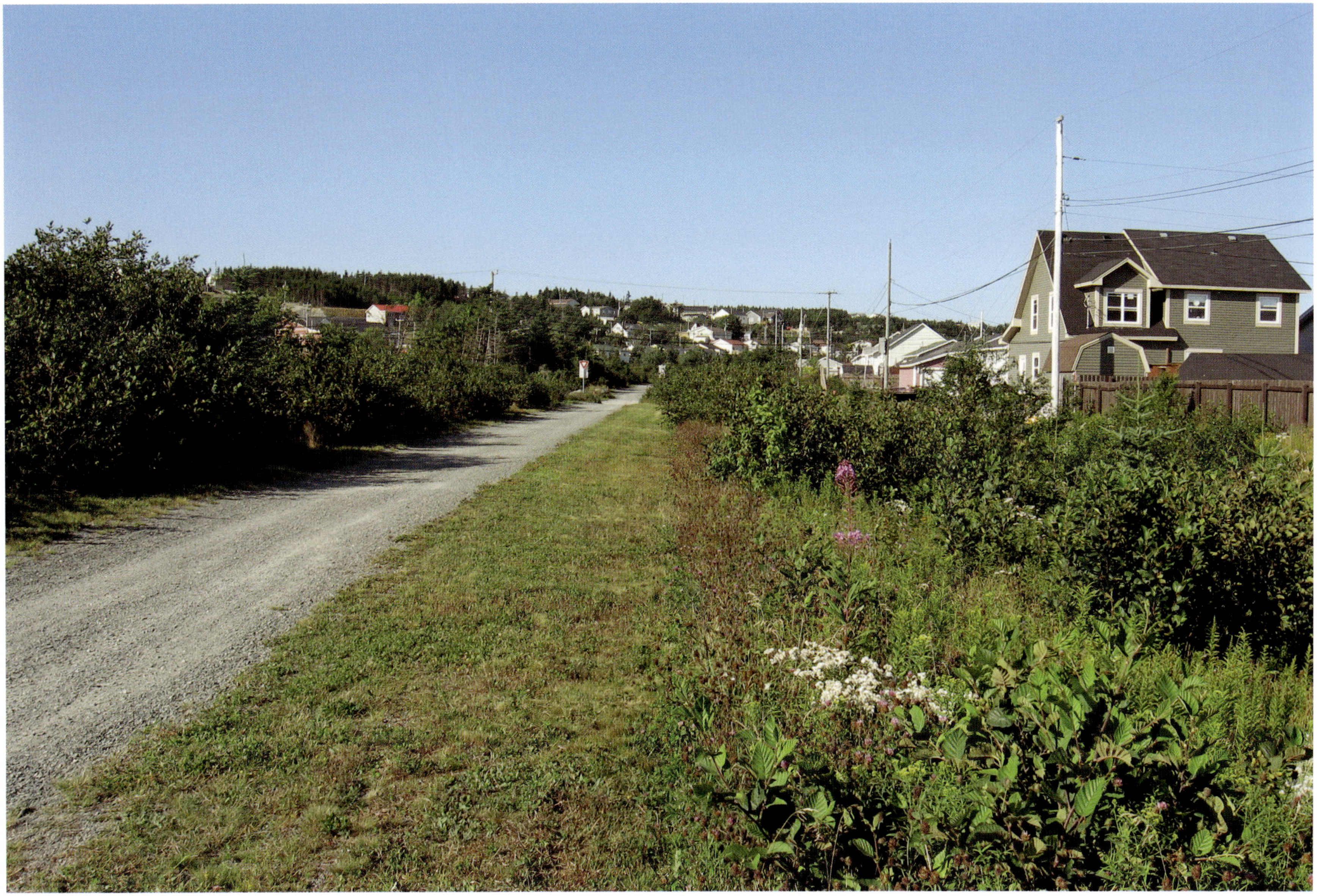

OCTOGON TODAY
The former rail bed now makes up a portion of the remarkable Grand Concourse through the town of Paradise. This is an award-winning network of trails that link this community with the cities of Mount Pearl and St. John's. With grades no steeper than that of the railway, it is ideal for the hundreds of walkers, hikers, joggers and bicycle enthusiasts that use it daily. *Author photo*

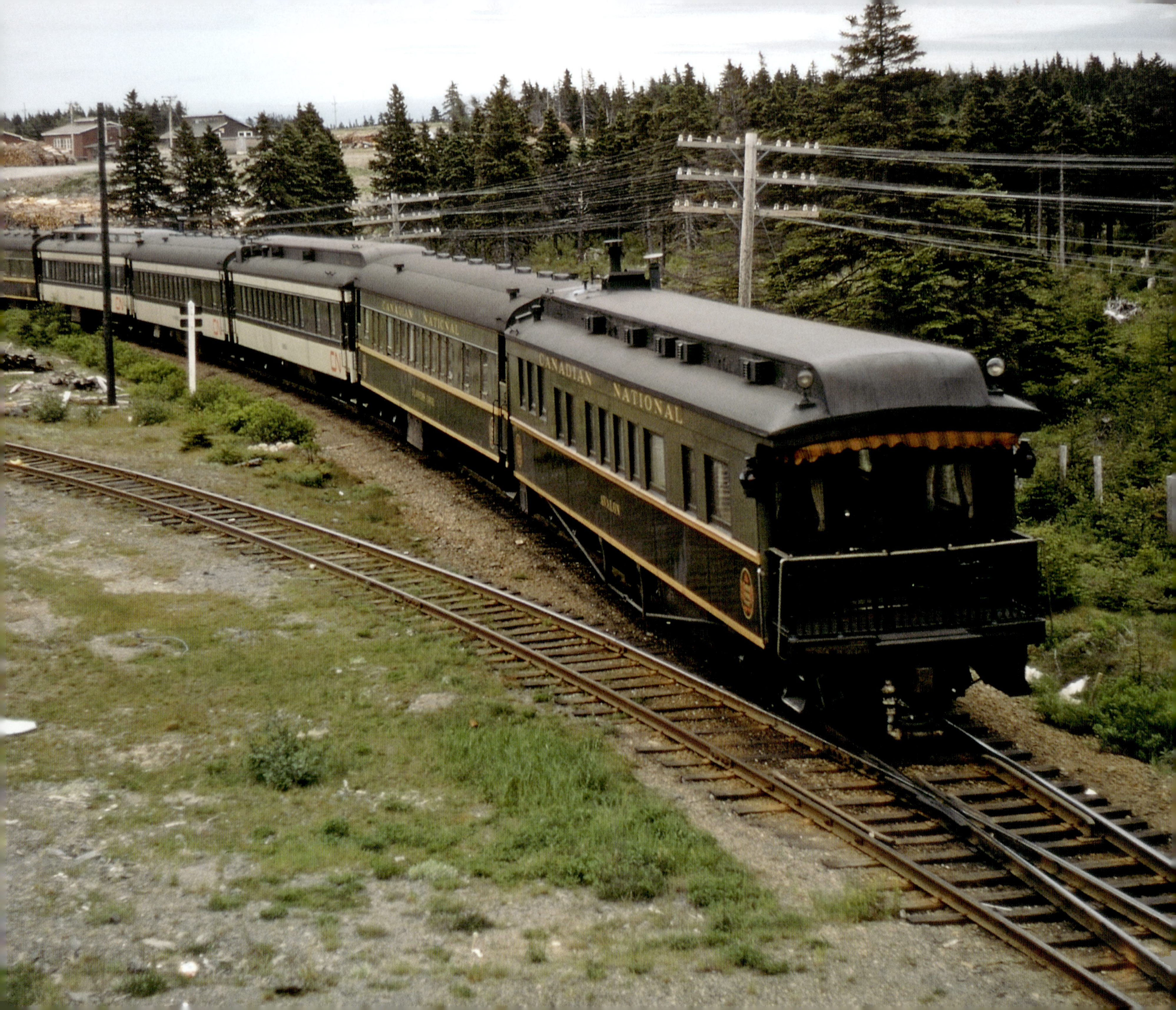
CANADIAN NATIONAL
CANADIAN NATIONAL
CN

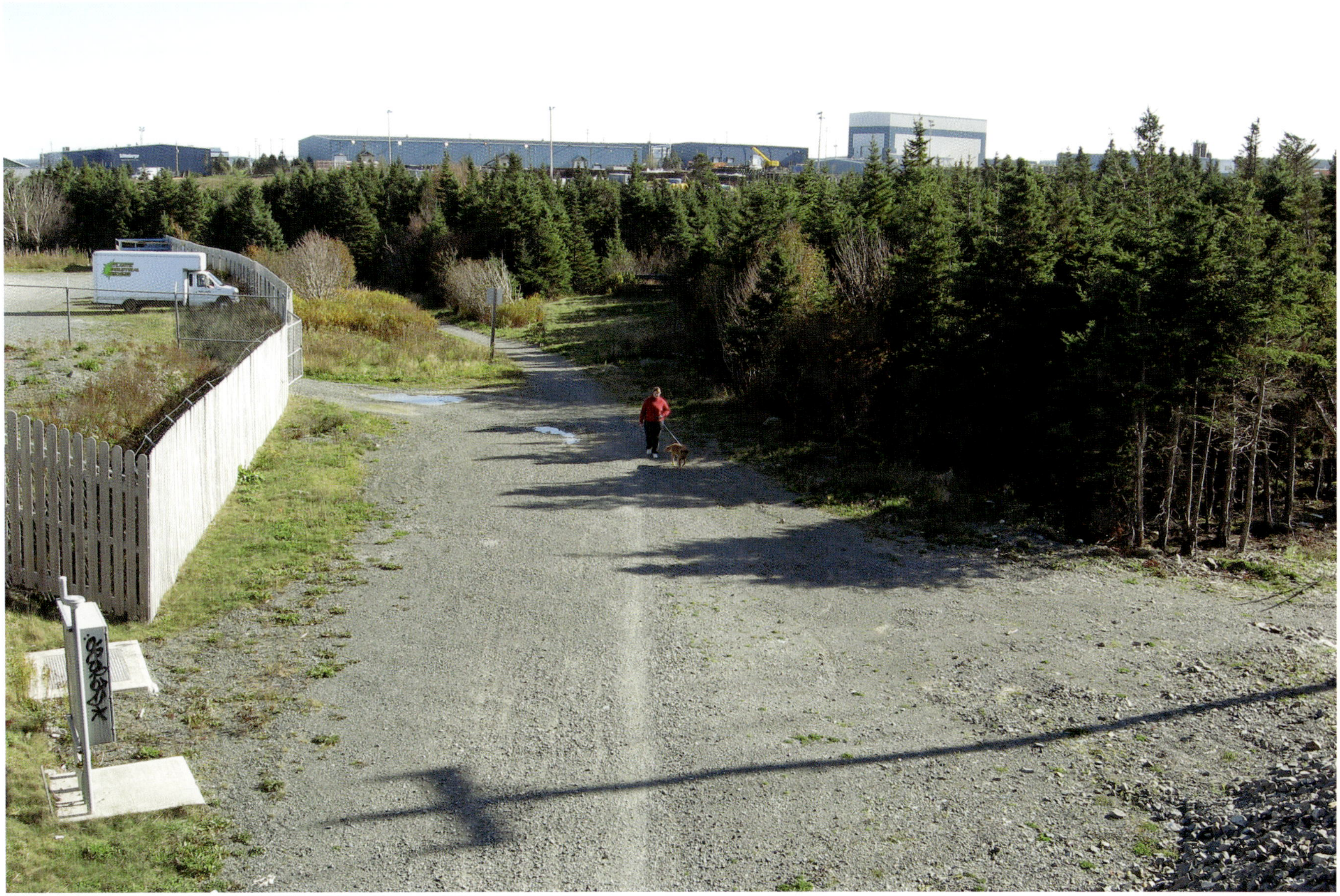

DONOVANS 1967

Business Car 2, the 'Avalon', brings up the rear of CN train No. 102, the eastbound *Caribou*, passing through Donovans on the early morning of June 22, 1967. Led by NF210 925 and 915 on the head end as well as a steam generator unit, this eleven car consist wearing two different paint schemes is only about 7 miles from its final stop at the St. John's station. *James A. Brown photo*

DONOVANS TODAY

The author's wife Michelle takes a beautiful autumn walk with their golden retriever Molly along the former railbed. The industrial growth is quite evident in this view taken near the old overpass at Kenmount and Topsail Road, once the unofficial dividing line between the City of St. John's and the rest of the Island. Built in 1918 by the C.C. & F., 'Avalon' was originally called 'Quidi Vidi', the private car of Sir William Reid and spent several years at Bowring Park after the closure until it deteriorated beyond saving. *Author photo*

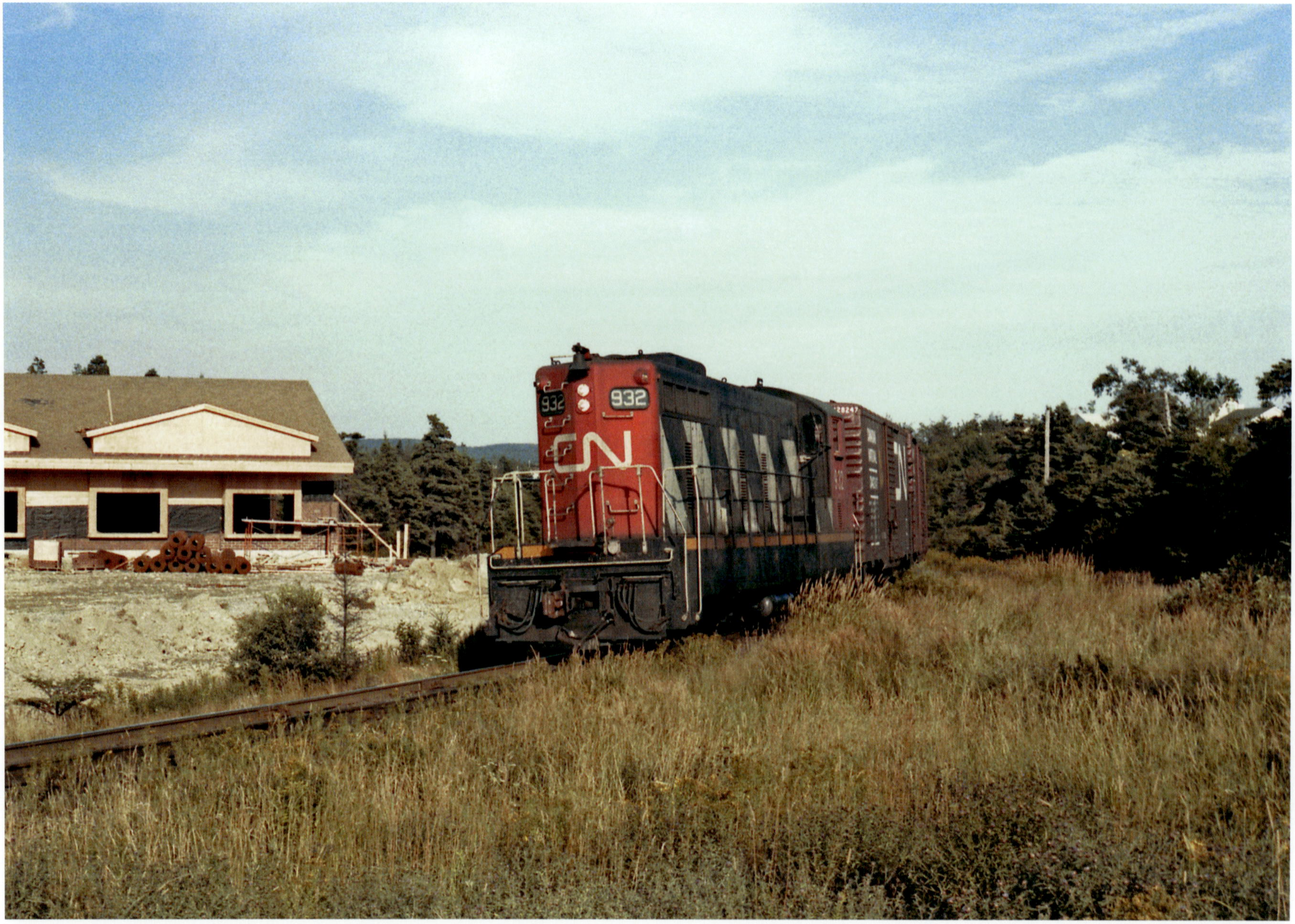

MOUNT PEARL 1984
Terra Transport westbound train 203 lead by single unit NF210 932 in the zebra scheme approaches the grade crossing at Commonwealth Avenue late in the evening of August 14, 1984. By this time in the Terra Transport timetable, the daily 203 and the eastbound 204 were the only trains remaining that operated across the entire Island. *Dan Rowsell photo*

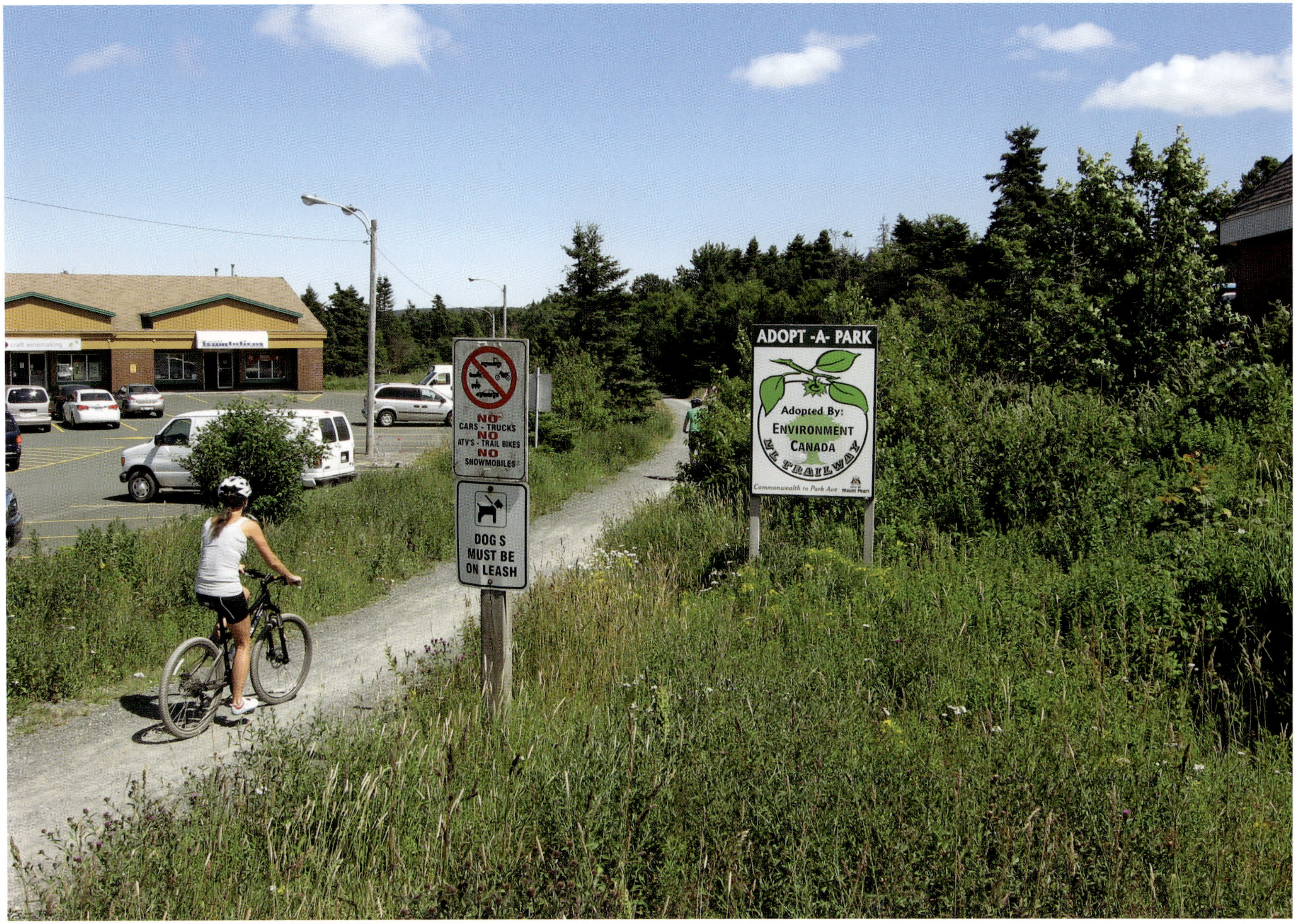

MOUNT PEARL TODAY
No other street is as synomonus with Mount Pearl, Newfoundland's third city, as Commonwealth Avenue. Where 203 once rounded the turn, bikers and hikers ride and run the well-worn trail. The adjacent and well patronized Mount Pearl Plaza has sprung up, offering plenty of specialty stores to the delight of the many shoppers. *Author photo*

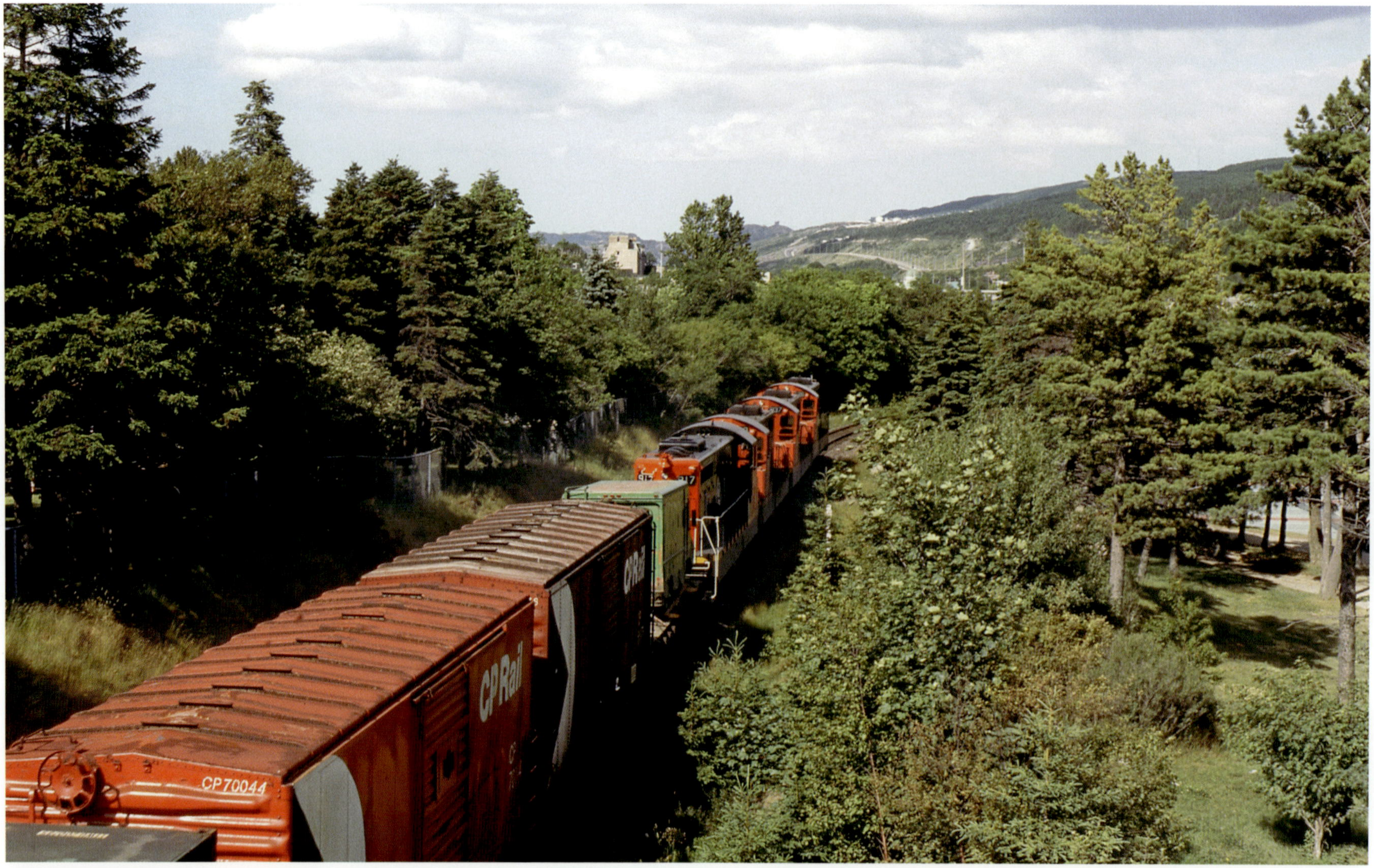

BOWRING PARK 1987

Terra Transport Train 204 runs downgrade through Bowring Park in St. John's on a hot Sunday afternoon in July 1987. The author was crossing the bridge at just the right time to witness this unique train. With rarely seen CP Rail boxcars and the green TT containers, both coasts of Canada were well represented in this particular consist. *Author photo*

BOWRING PARK TODAY

A trio of walkers traverse the Grand Concourse while the trees obscure the view of Signal Hill. The land for this park was donated by Sir Edgar Bowring in 1911 to commemorate the 100th anniversary of his family doing business in Newfoundland. For a great many decades, an afternoon stroll in this beautiful park almost guaranteed an encounter with a train. *Author photo*

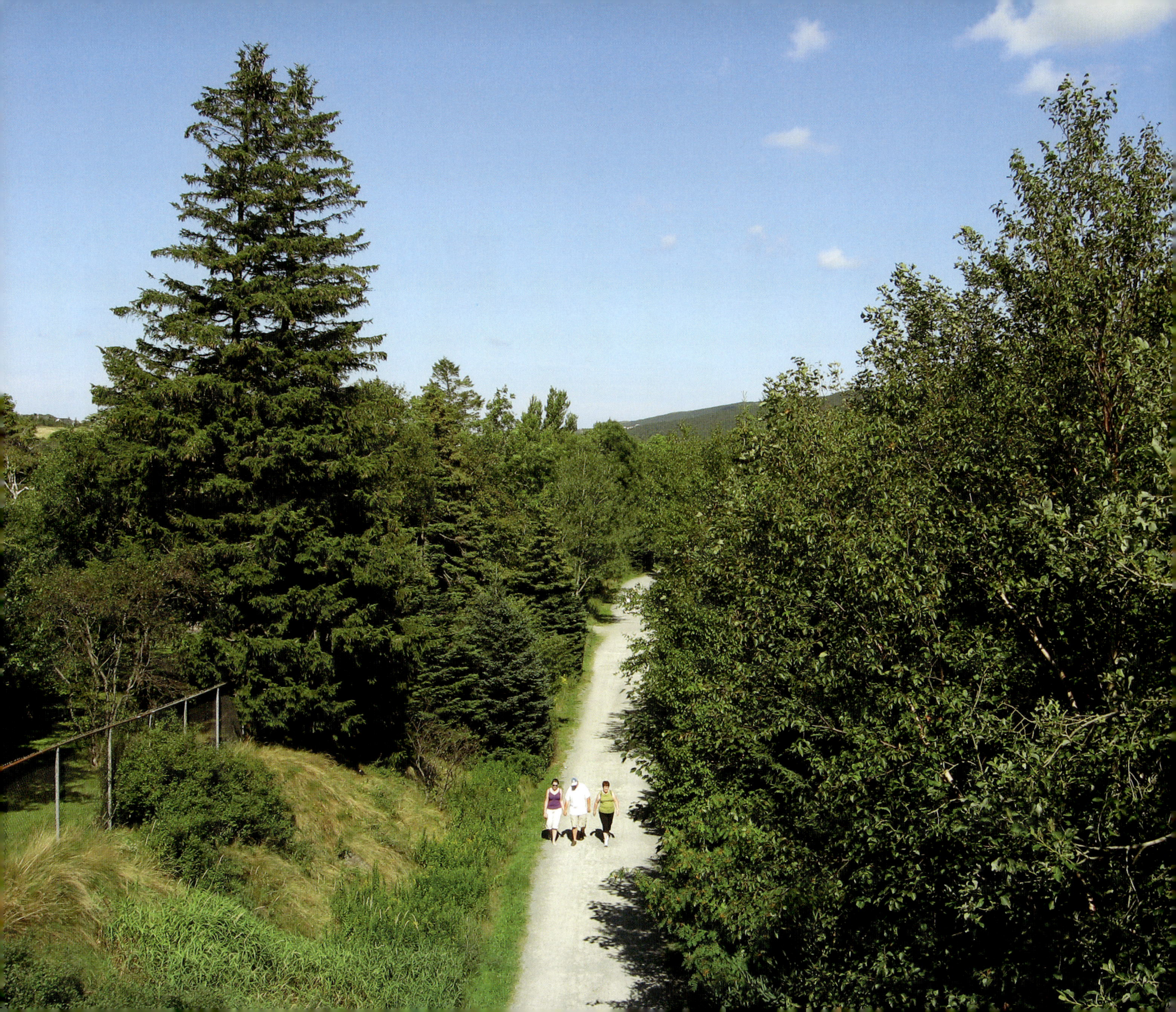

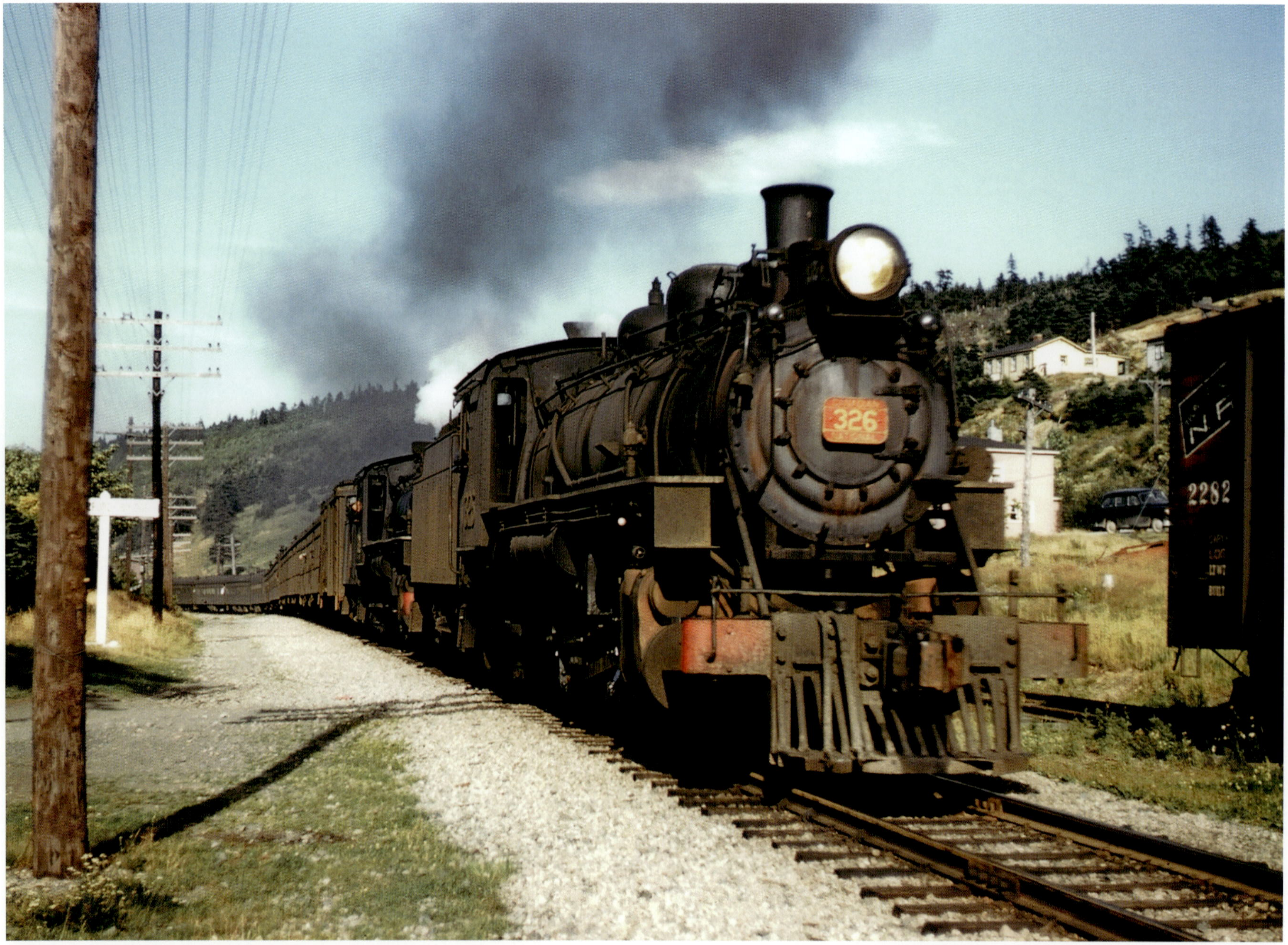

WATERFORD BRIDGE 1955

During his only visit to Newfoundland, Sandy Goodrick photographed 2-8-2 Mikado 326, built in 1949 by Montreal Locomotive Works on CNR Train No. 15 at Waterford Bridge on August 26, 1955. Train No. 15 as well as eastbound No. 16 were the three days a week St. John's-Corner Brook express train. Boxcar 2282, still wearing the former NR logo, is on what was once the junction for the 104 mile branchline to Trepassey. *Sandy Goodrick photo*

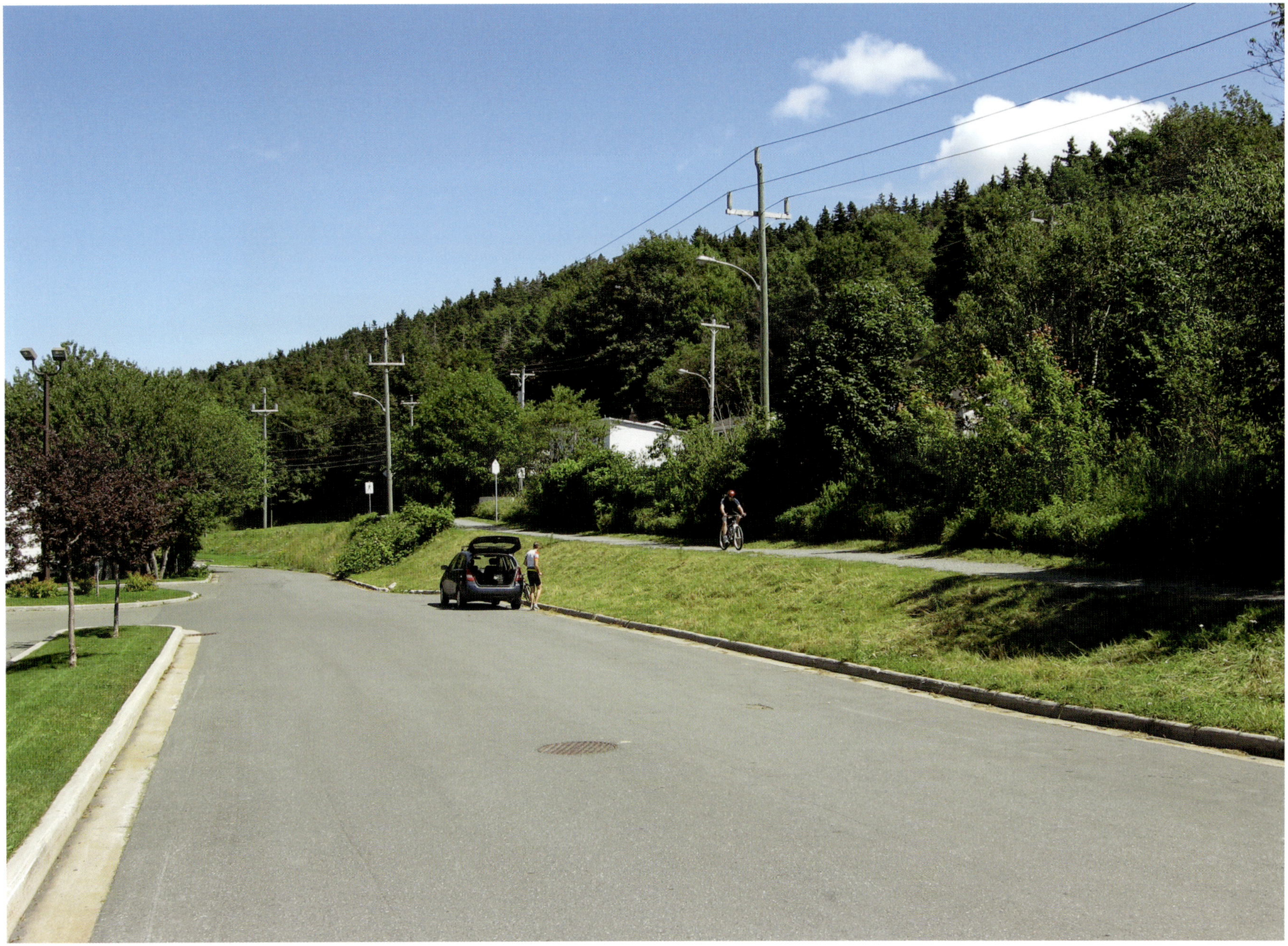

WATERFORD BRIDGE TODAY

The former Waterford Bridge station stop has become Mackey Place in the City of St. John's. Pavement replaces the tracks in this very popular start and finish spot for cyclists and hikers accessing the Grand Concourse. The well-marked signs and the adjacent Waterford River make the portion of the trail in this affluent area a most enjoyable excursion.
Author photo

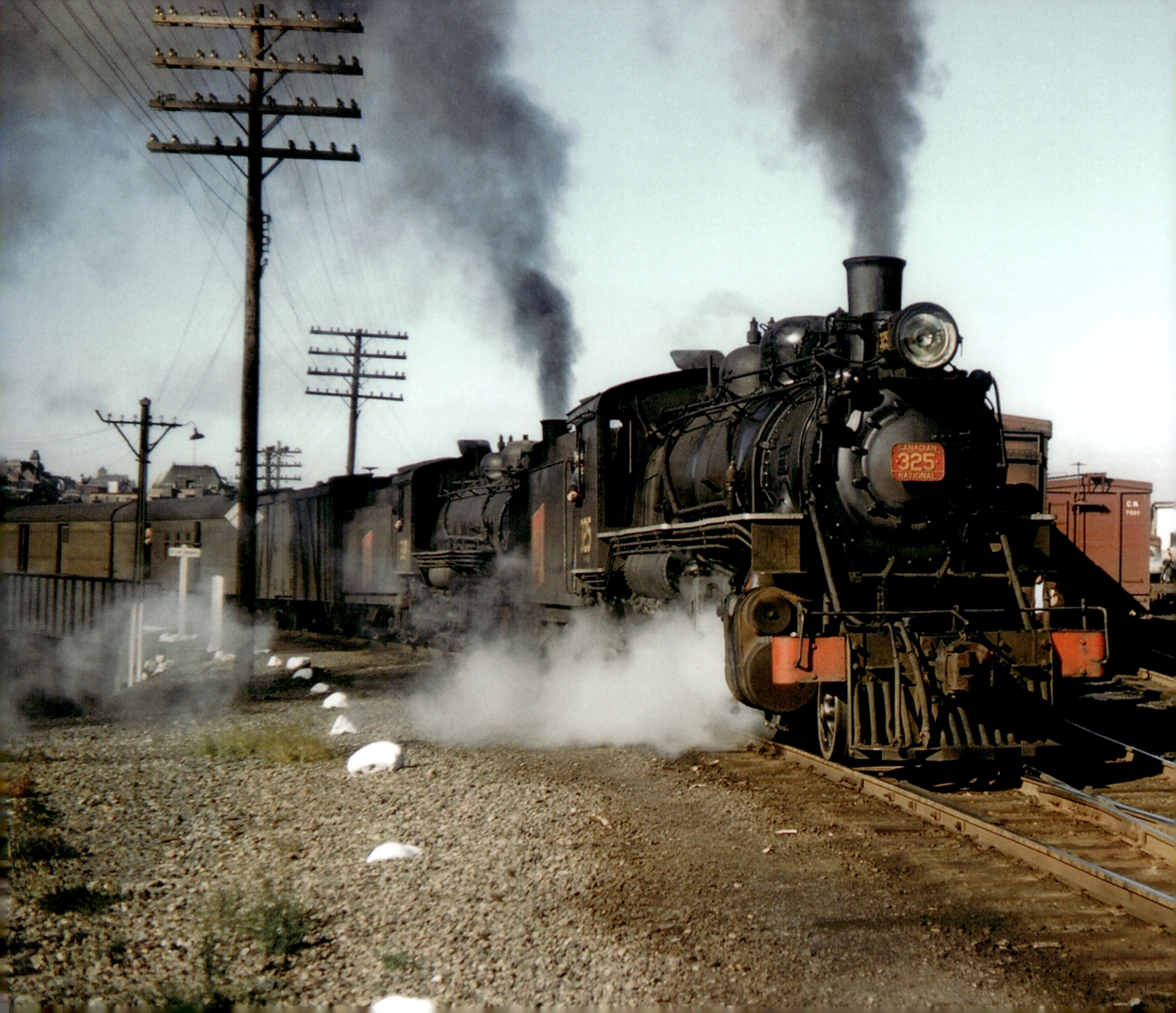
CANADIAN
325
NATIONAL

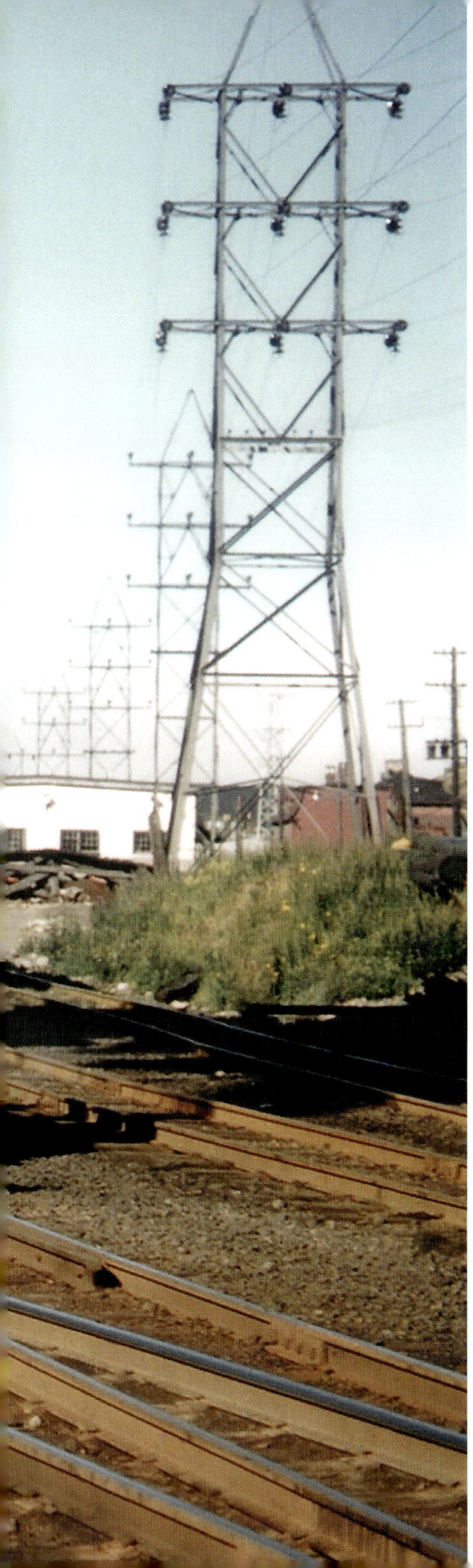

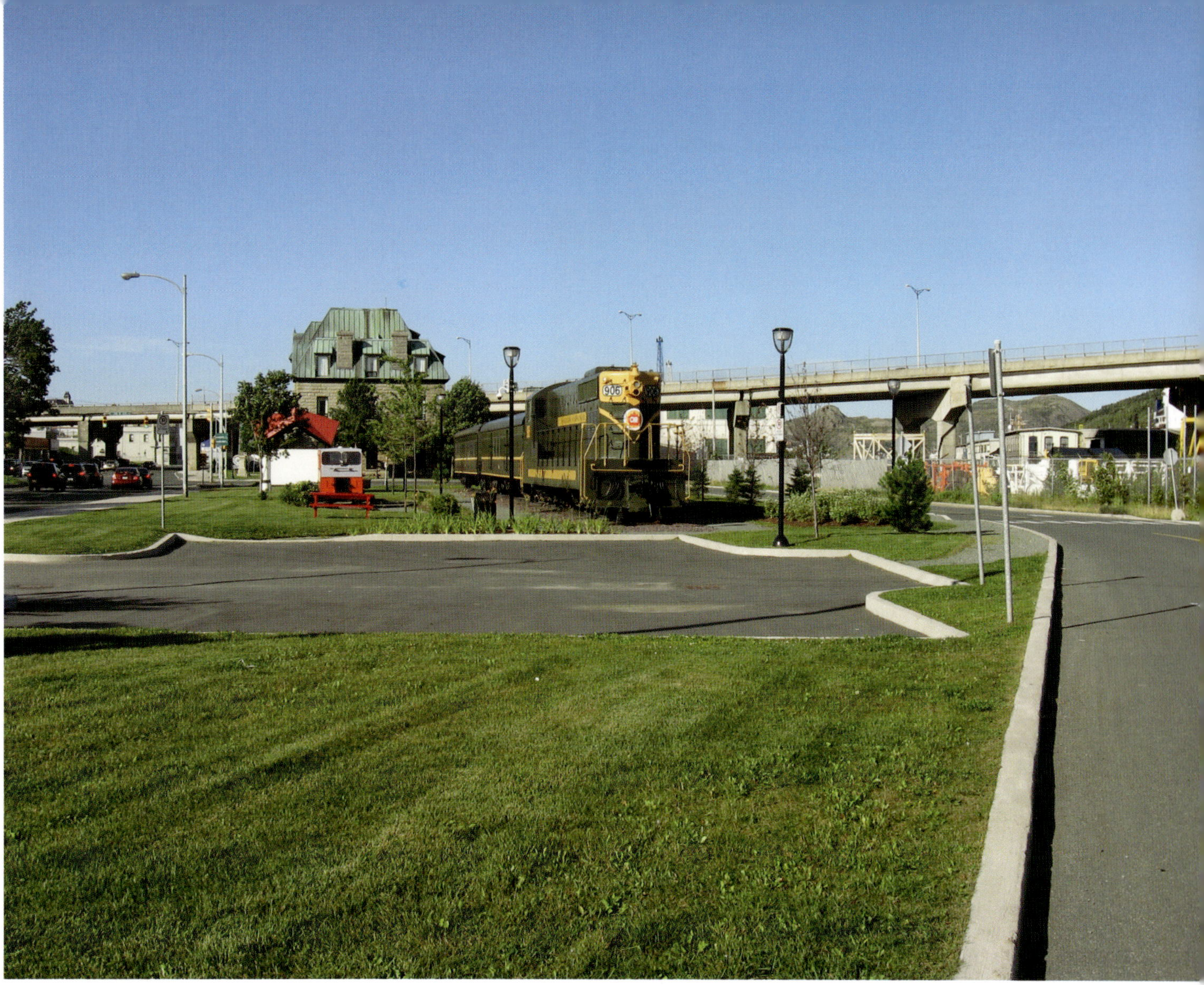

ST. JOHN'S 1955

CNR Train No. 1 with double headed Mikados 325 and 317 has just departed from the Victorian-era Newfoundland Railway Station in the capital city of St. John's on the sunny evening of August 27, 1955. The two oil burning engines are spewing clouds of black smoke as it gets the passenger consist moving. Its final destination of Port Aux Basques and mainland steamship connections lie 547 miles and almost 27 hours to the west. *Sandy Goodrick photo*

ST. JOHN'S TODAY

The Victorian-era Newfoundland Railway Station is home to the Railway Coastal Museum and the static display of NF110 906 beautifully restored to its original green and gold colours. Once on display in Bowring Park for many years, 906 had the honour of being one of three diesels that pulled the last east bound *Caribou* into St. John's on July 3, 1969. The 'Oldest City in North America' has prospered in recent years with the booming oil industry. *Author photo*

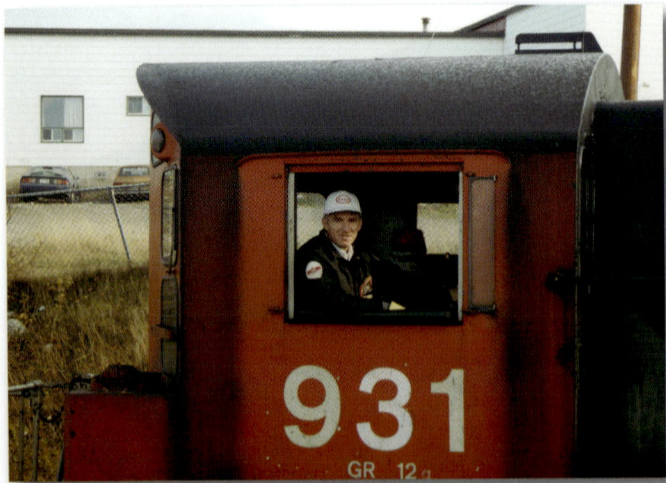

A Railroader Remembers

BRENDAN DAVID DICKS

Born: December 12, 1941
Entered service with the Canadian National Railway in Newfoundland on July 29, 1961, at 19 years of age.
Retired on December 12, 1996, with 34.5 years of service.

WHY AND HOW DID YOU BEGIN YOUR CAREER AS A RAILROADER?

I was born into a railway family of three generations. On my father's side of the family, the Dicks' have 334 years of railway service, and on my mother's side, the Hannon's have 1192 years of railway service.

Growing up in Humbermouth, Newfoundland, and only approximately 30 feet from the railway stand, train station, roundhouse and rail yard, with numerous other railway families strung out around us, automatically, it seems, piqued their children's interest in railroading. They lived it each and every day of their lives at home; frequenting the shunting yard they called their 'playground'. There they would test various components of the stationary locomotives, rail cars and air brake hoses that were pressurized with air and made it a regular daily routine. So it came as no surprise that a great number of those children looked to the railway for employment and acquired jobs in different departments.

This interest remained with me throughout my initial work-years while working at six different jobs that were not associated with railway work in any way. My employment with the Canadian National Railway here in Newfoundland began with a ten day probation period that commenced on Wednesday, July 19th and ended on Saturday, July 29, 1961. This was the day my name was placed on the Trainmen's Spare Board List and the same day I worked my first shift as a Yard Helper at the Corner Brook rail yard. It was the beginning of what I had set my sight on for so many years---to work with my dad, uncles, brothers, cousins, other relatives and friends. I very swiftly realized that the void in my life had now been filled.

Railroading became a job I really looked forward to each day---loved every moment--- switching in the rail yard and on the road, working the passenger trains, through-freight, mixed-freight, way-freight, road switchers, work, extra, snow plow, wood and ore trains, and the list goes on. This passionate career had now become my great love.

WHAT WERE THE DIFFERENT POSITIONS YOU HELD?

Throughout my career, I filled the positions of Trainman, Conductor, Express Messenger on the passenger trains, Yard Helper, Yard Foreman, Pilot for management's private Rail Car 600, Lone Locomotives and Snow-blower Cranes, Yardmaster, Engine Service Employee and Locomotive Engineer.

WHICH ONE WAS YOUR FAVOURITE AND WHY?

My favourite was Locomotive Engineer. Grandfather, Samuel J. Dicks, drove the steam locomotives fueled by coal; his sons, David, Charles, John Samuel (my father) and Gerald drove the steam locomotives fueled by coal and those fueled by oil, the 1200 horsepower diesel locomotives (900 class); the 380 hp diesels electrics (700 class) and the 875 hp diesel locomotives (800 class). John Samuel's three sons, Brendan, Michael and John drove the 1200 hp diesel locomotives (900 class).

There were eight Locomotive Engineers in my family, twenty-five railway workers from a single family. I was so fortunate, on Thursday, February 12, 1976, to have driven (along with Locomotive Engineers Edward W. (Ned) Peddle and Adolphus A. (Dolph) Robertson) the longest train that operated on our narrow gauge line (137 railcars and 6 locomotives as motive power with the last one in the consist 'isolate'). Three records for us as a family on the Newfoundland railway.

My brothers were also railway workers. Bartholomew was a Conductor/Trainman; Francis worked as a labourer in the roundhouse, on the section and on Extra Gangs; while Thomas worked on Extra Gangs and, at times, at section work. I was so privileged to have worked with my Dad, Uncle David and my brothers, unfortunately, my Uncle Charles and Gerald were not on the job when I was hired. I also got to work with the Hannon members of our family – my uncles, William F. Hannon, Locomotive Engineer; P. Leonard Hannon, Conductor; Ronald G. Hannon, Conductor/Trainman; Peter Hannon, Section Foreman; D. James Hannon, Conductor/Trainman and other relatives; George Hannon, Conductor; L. Gordon Hannon, Reginald Hannon and Thomas P. Penney, Locomotive Engineers.

My railroading career was further enhanced when, on Saturday, October 11, 1975, I attended the railway's Locomotive Engineer's Training School in Gimli, Manitoba, to become a Locomotive Engineer. The knowledge I acquired in the two months I spent there was extremely rewarding, driving trains on simulators, learning all about the brake valves, flow of air and pressure, brake system, rules and regulations, train orders and manual block system bulletins and clearances. Upon completion, I returned home and began my trial trips on the road under supervision of each train's regularly assigned Locomotive Engineer.

The joy of a lifetime came on Sunday, July 9, 1978, when I throttled my first locomotive as Locomotive Engineer in the rail yard at Corner Brook. Another memorable experience was on Wednesday, June 20, 1979, when as Locomotive Engineer, I drove my first train-on-the-road (No. 203, a regular timetable mixed-freight). Being at the throttle of five locomotives of 6000 horsepower operating as a single unit with 60 carloads of freight in tow, driving a train over the narrow gauge line from Corner Brook to Port aux Basques with nature's beauty at its best; hearing the powerful roars of the locomotives with the advancement of the throttle to higher positions, the hissing of air from the air-brake valve, the clickity-clack of the wheels over the rail-joints, the rocking and rolling of the locomotives and trailing cars as they round the numerous curves in the line.

My career resulted in main line travel of 394, 738 miles and yard shifts that amounted to 2221 miles that occurred during all four seasons. Especially during the picturesque, carpet-coloured season of fall; over hill and dale, through communities and towns, over rivers, ponds, brooks and streams; where the true natural aesthetics encompassed our narrow gauge line; where wild game roamed the barrens – the caribou, moose, bears, foxes, rabbits, geese, ducks and grouse.

What were the challenges of working on the railway in Newfoundland?

To apply the knowledge of the road I had gained on how to drive a train from A to Z and to do it in a safe manner as to ensure that no injuries occurred to fellow workers and no damage occurred to the freight, motive power and other rolling stock and equipment.

Throttling my train at track speed to its destination safely and on time, stopping at all timetable and flag stops en route regardless of weather conditions.

Climbing the high percent grades in our line with tonnage-trains and to brake the trains down the grades safely and at track speed.

What are some of your fondest memories of those years?

My first tour of duty under pay (Saturday, July 29, 1961).
My first shift as a yard helper in the rail yard at Corner Brook (Saturday, July 29, 1961).
My first road trip as Brakeman on a Way Freight train (Monday, July 31, 1961).
My first trip with my Dad (Wednesday, November 8, 1961).
Receiving my Conductors Certificate (Tuesday, December 1, 1970).
My first tour of duty as Conductor (Tuesday, December 29, 1970).
My first tour of duty as Yardmaster (Saturday, June 3, 1971).
Receiving my Locomotive Engineers Certificate (Friday, October 15, 1976).
Driving the longest train on the Newfoundland Railway while under training (Thursday, February 12, 1976).
My first trip on the road as Locomotive Engineer (Wednesday, June 20, 1979).
My first shift in Yard Service as Locomotive Engineer (Saturday, June 23, 1979).
As Locomotive Engineer on what the train dispatcher referred to as the 'Dicks' train from Corner Brook to Stephenville and return (Monday, August 10, 1981).
As Locomotive Engineer removing loaded rail cars from and loading the railway ship *Frederick Carter* with empty railcars at Port aux Basques (Tuesday, June 11, 1985).
The recording of each workday during my railway life's employment (Saturday, July 15, 1961 to Thursday, November 22, 1990).
My family's 'three records' in our railway's history.
Working with fellow workers of all crafts who were second to none.
Working with my Dad, uncles, brothers, relatives and friends/buddies.

Do you have any negative memories of those years?

The serious injuries I received in a railway accident at the rail yard in Corner Brook on July 18, 1972.

Witnessing the permanent abolishment of main line trains and yard switchers, way freights, passenger, through-freight and mixed-freight, pulpwood, paper, gypsum and ore trains.

The enormous reduction in employees.

On Wednesday, October 12, 1988, Mr. Reginald (Reg) Roach and Mr. Robert (Bob) Bailey removed the bolts that held the main line rails in place at mileage 339.8 on the Bishop's Falls Subdivision to began the Rail Removal Program. Also, on that same day, Mr. Augustus (Gus) O'Quinn, via Burrow Crane # 3358, lifted the first rail from the ties and roadbed to break the main line tracks.

The permanent closure of our Newfoundland Railway line of 547.8 miles.

What involvement did you have with the Rail Removal Program, family service history or anything else?

My two brothers, John and Michael, and I were the Locomotives Engineers who operated the locomotives that were engaged in taking up the rails of our Newfoundland Railway. My Grandfather was a Locomotive Engineer who most likely played a role in laying the first rails of the Newfoundland railway. His grandsons were Locomotive Engineers who throttled the 900 class, 1200 hp diesel locomotives used in the removal of the Newfoundland line.

Would you do it all over again?

The railroading life was a wonderful life, a real treasure, the best anyone could ask for. I actually got paid for working on the railway. It was for me, a labour of love. I wouldn't have changed a thing---I would definitely do it all over again.

Sincerely,
Brendan D. Dicks

ACKNOWLEDGEMENTS

There are many who have helped me on this wonderful journey of discovery of not only the glorious images of our unique narrow gauge railway's past, but also of the pristine beauty of this wonderful place we affectionately call 'The Rock'. I must thank all who have contributed the photos; Jon Archibald, Andrew Baird, Randy Blackwood, Steve Bradley, James A. Brown, Peter J. Byrne, Clayton D. Cook, Robert Coolidge, Bren Dicks, Don Driscoll, Charlie Falk, Sanford Goodrick, Vida Greening, Gary Hadfield, Sherry Harris, Peter Hawksford, Fred Headon, George Jarvis, Omer Lavallee, Wendell Lemon, Bill Linley, Phil Mason, Joe McMillan, Brenda Mulrooney, Gerard Murphy, David Othen, Karl Purchase, Ronald S. Ritchie, Earl Roberts, Dan Rowsell, Robert J. Sandusky, Merritt B. Scharnweber, Jim Scribbins, Mike Shufelt, Conrad Steeves, Rich Taylor, David Whitnall, Ted Wickson, David Woodhead, Jerome Young and Gary Zuters. Without them, this project could never be and my only regret is that it was physically impossible to use all images. Halfway through this project, our family suffered a terrible personal tragedy in the sudden loss of our eldest son and I poured myself into finishing the book. Although they did not know it at the time, the kindness and generosity shown to me by them went a long ways in the healing process. With each new image, each piece of railway information and each encouraging email, I saw that there still remains so much goodness in this world.

Others who have helped in so many ways both big and small, from supplying vehicles and scanning photos to giving me accommodations, include Dion Broderick, Dave & Georgette Clairmont, Brendan Dicks, Robin Dicks, Robert & Joanne Flynn, Bill & Marie Gregory, John & Elsie Kelly, Mont Lingard, Michelle Pieroway, Thomas Pieroway, Mike Shufelt, Rick & Deanne Solo and Ann Marie Whelan.

I would also like to thank Donna Francis, Pam Dooley, Todd Manning, Joanne Snook-Hann and the entire staff of Creative Book Publishing for believing in me and bringing my dream of celebrating the Newfoundland railway to fruition.

Finally, my thanks go out to my family. To my late parents, George and Anne Pieroway who in their decision to adopt a baby boy, surrounded me with an amazing extended family and set me on a course in life that has brought me to this point. I am so very grateful to my Dad for introducing me to trains all those years ago and giving me a lifelong passion and for Mom's extraordinary command of the English language and the power of the written word. To Michelle, my wife of nearly 25 years and soul mate for even longer, who has accompanied me on many local, national and international train journeys as well as numerous retake missions, for her unwavering support and standing by me. You complete me and there is no one I'd rather have by my side as we journey through life. To Thomas, my youngest son who has also accompanied me on many rail journeys and retake photo sessions miles from the middle of nowhere, you inspire me with your positive outlook on life and I am so proud of the man you are becoming. To William, who is looking down from Heaven with that special grin and always watching and guiding us, you are never far from my thoughts and I am so grateful for the time we had together. I love you son.

WORKS CITED AND CONSULTED

Cook, Clayton D., *Tales of the Rails, Volume IV.* St. John's : Flanker Press, 2005

Dicks, Brendan D., *The Railway Ties...That Bind.* Corner Brook: Brendan D. Dicks, 1999

Dicks, Brendan D., *The Railway Ties... That Bind...The Sequel.* Corner Brook: Brendan D. Dicks, 2010

Lavallee, Omer, *Narrow Gauge Railways of Canada.* Markham: Fitzhenry & Whiteside, 2005

Lingard, Mont, *Next Stop: Gaff Topsail.* Grand Falls-Windsor: Mont Lingard, 1996

Lingard, Mont, *Next Stop: Wreckhouse.* Grand Falls-Windsor: Mont Lingard, 1997

Lingard, Mont, *Next Stop: Trinity Loop.* Grand Falls-Windsor: Mont Lingard, 1998

Lingard, Mont, *Next Stop: St. John's.* Grand Falls-Windsor: Mont Lingard, 1999

Lingard, Mont, *The Newfie Bullet.* Badger: Mont Lingard, 2000

Murray, Tom, *Canadian National Railway.* St. Paul: MBI, 2004

Othen, David, *Newfoundland Railway.* Blurb.com, 2010

www.heritage.nf.ca

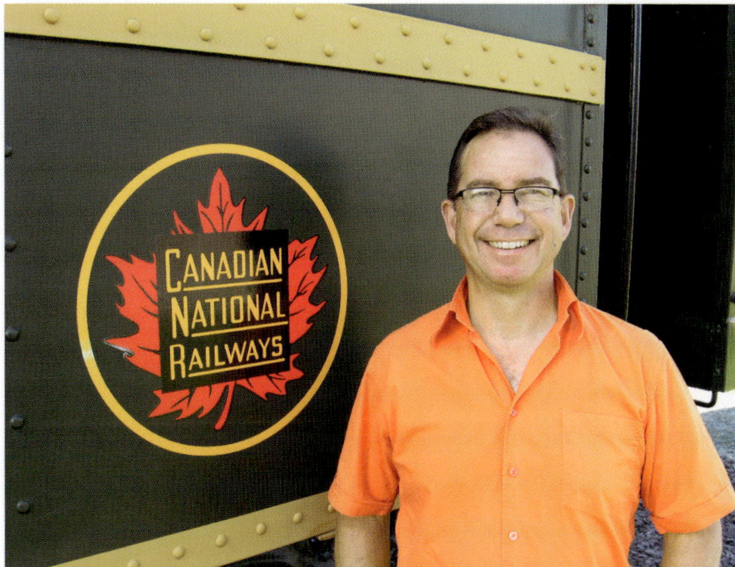

KENNETH G. PIEROWAY was born in Corner Brook but grew up in Colinet. He obtained his BSW from Memorial University and is a Registered Social Worker. His passion for trains was introduced by his father at a very young age and he still rides and photographs them at every opportunity. Kenneth resides in CBS with his wife Michelle and son Thomas.